International Business Transactions

Kendall Hunt
publishing company

Douglas H. Peterson

Cover image © Shutterstock.com

Kendall Hunt
publishing company

www.kendallhunt.com
Send all inquiries to:
4050 Westmark Drive
Dubuque, IA 52004-1840

Copyright © 2017 by Douglas H. Peterson

ISBN 978-1-4652-9359-6

Published in the United States of America

This text is dedicated to the parents of Douglas Peterson.

Contents

Chapter 6 *Incoterms*   147

Chapter 7 *Intellectual Property*   171

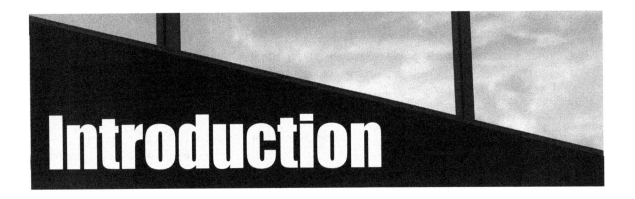

Introduction

International Business Transactions explores the importance of legal knowledge when conducting international business transactions. Possessing an understanding of the risks, limitations, and opportunities of international business dealings is an asset for both individuals and organizations in a globalized economy. Every day the world is engaged in a huge transfer of goods and services between entities from various countries leading to various legal issues. Such issues include the sales or services agreement itself, the delivery and payment of the goods, governing laws, enforcement aspects of the agreement, taxation on the goods and services, enforcement of judgments, and other jurisdictional matters.

This text explains the basic legal principles in a way that is applicable to real-world business situations. It emphasizes the importance of the legal approach to doing business, and more particularly the importance of a proactive approach to the planning of an international business transaction.

This text examines various legal aspects of business, and with an understanding of these concepts, it can assist in making effective business decisions by managing risks and capitalizing on opportunities. *International Business Transactions* was written with the intent of creating a text that utilizes the author's knowledge obtained from over 20 years of practical experience in working in international business transactions. While written by a Canadian author, the focus of this text has an international scope and the content is applicable to be taught in schools outside of Canada as well.

The topics covered in this text are organized as follows:

- **Chapter 1** explores the different types of business structures and the various liabilities and tax implications associated with each.
- **Chapter 2** focuses on the principles of contract law and what is involved in international contract negotiations, in particular the unique international aspects of cross border contracts. Contracts are a vital part of conducting business and are important in dispute resolution when parties in various jurisdictions are involved.
- **Chapter 3** looks at the methods of dispute resolution alternatives and the importance of jurisdiction when dealing with international business transactions.
- **Chapter 4** focuses on the financial aspects of conducting international business; various ways international transactions can be financed, what a letter of credit is, and the risks associated with different forms of acceptance.
- **Chapter 5** is an overview of the international rules and conventions governing carriers of goods and passengers by land, air, and sea.
- **Chapter 6** provides an understanding of the objectives and proper use of the International Commercial Terms included in the Incoterms® 2010 publication.

- **Chapter 7** provides an understanding of the legal aspects of intellectual property: how to create intellectual property rights, protect them and enforce them in different jurisdictions.
- **Chapter 8** addresses the issues of taxation in different jurisdictions and how it varies on different streams of income. The importance of tax treaties in international business is addressed and strategies of how taxes can be avoided or reduced.

With organizations following a trend of corporate social responsibility this text also looks at ethical considerations throughout the chapters. The intent of these are to provide practical examples to review and apply the material learned in the chapters while raising awareness of ethical issues faced by individuals and businesses in international transactions. Additionally, the case studies throughout the text assist to illustrate principles and concepts of the material covered. To gain an international perspective, these case studies are examples from various jurisdictions to highlight the differences in the legal process in other jurisdictions.

Acknowledgments

The compilation of this text required the effort of a group of individuals and acknowledge the following:

- Victoria Jankowski
- Talisa Pon
- Yasmine Al-Hussein
- Alexander Crisp
- Michael Moore
- Edward Ilnicki
- Jordan Rowley
- Brett Walsh
- Riley Kendrick
- Artem Barsukov

CHAPTER 1

Business Structures

Learning Objectives

After reading this chapter, you will have an understanding of:

1. Structure of different types of business organizations

2. Tax and liability implications of these business organizations

3. Benefits of choosing one structure over another

4. Entering foreign jurisdictions

Introduction

Choosing a business structure that is right for your company is crucial as it will act as the foundation upon which your company is built. Whether in international or domestic settings, the main focus is risk management, in particular, reducing liability and taxes. Throughout this chapter we will determine who bears the risk, enjoys the profits, and/or is responsible for the losses. Governments greatly influence the types of business entities within their jurisdiction by limiting the types of structures, or imposing various legal requirements, such as tax and ownership. These policies may target specific business types, sizes, and industries. Challenges may be further complicated when businesses expand beyond their **home state** jurisdiction, to foreign (**host state**), and have to conform to foreign business policies.

This chapter will explore various business structures, focusing on which ones are most suitable for entering foreign markets, and analyzing the advantages and disadvantages of each. One must balance tax and liability. Some structures provide reduced liability, others greater tax reduction. Businesses need to analyze which is more important—tax reduction or limiting liability. This depends on the nature of the business. An oil company building a pipeline or a pharmaceutical company selling drugs is at a greater risk than a company that produces and sells clothing. There is no perfect structure that optimizes both tax and liability. One will prevail over the other. Further, the use of a certain structure may be limited by the host state. Certain markets may set restrictions or special rules for foreign businesses, which may limit the use of various structures in the **host state**. This increases the importance of understanding these per country barriers, and more importantly, how to legally work within these restrictions with the business structure you require. Finally, often it is not required to enter into the host state, but rather simply export the product through a resale model or agency model. A company will need to decide when they enter a foreign jurisdiction, which form of business to use.

Ethical Considerations 1.1

Foreign Corrupt Practices Act

United States of America v. Vadim Mikerin 8:14-CR-00529-TDC (2015),

http://www.justice.gov/criminal-fraud/file/782186/download

International business transcends both borders and individuals. Once a business enters into the international market, a new set of guidelines and ethical standards are set into place. Take for instance the case of Vadim Mikerin.

Vadim Mikerin was a Russian national and general director of TENAM USA, a Russian subsidiary of TENEX that operates in Bethesda, Maryland, which specializes in the trading of uranium fuel between Russia and the United States. Mikerin was arrested and charged with extortion and conspiracy for causing financial harm to the parent company. Mikerin, along with two conspirators, accepted millions of dollars in kickback payments for providing over $33 million worth of contracts for the carriage of radioactive material from Russia to the USA.

Were these kickbacks ethical? US Attorney Rod J. Rosenstein states that "Kickbacks deprive honest competitors of the opportunity to compete for business, and they cheat a company of its right to faithful decisions by its employee." Rosenstein's viewpoint reflects the common view on the concept of bribery and corruption agreed upon by the Foreign Corrupt Policies Act (FCPA). Nevertheless, can we assume that a Russian national believed in the same definition of bribery? In some nations giving customary gifts to officials helps expedite the process of business. Were Mikerin's actions ethical?

Liability

A business may face two types of liability:

1. Contractual liability; and
2. Tort liability

1. Contractual Liability

Contractual liability is narrow compared to tort liability, which is broad. Contractual liability can be limited through the concept of privity and different types of exclusion clauses. Contracts are a voluntary activity; a business chooses whether or not they enter into a contract, and can decide which of their entities enters into that contract. Further, damages under contracts are usually limited to the actual loss that one suffers.

Privity is a simple rule that only parties to a contract have rights and duties under a contract. A business can decide which entity (usually a corporation) they contract through. Only that particular entity can be sued for breach of contract.

Exclusion clauses play a crucial role in commercial law. They allow a business to limit or reduce liability or damages. Such clauses come in different forms.

An **indemnity clause** shifts potential costs from one party to another. To indemnify is to absorb the losses caused by another party, rather than seeking compensation from that party, or compensate that party if something you do (or fail to do) causes them to experience loss, damages, or a lawsuit from a third party. An indemnity is only as good as guaranteeing a party's ability to pay. A party may be entitled to an indemnity under a contract, however, that indemnity will have little effect where the other party does not have adequate funds with which to indemnify the benefiting party. Indemnity clauses are often tied directly to representation clauses. In a technology license agreement, the licensor would represent they have the rights to the intellectual property they are licensing to you. If the licensee is sued by a third party for intellectual property infringement, the licensor will indemnify the licensee.

Exclusion Clauses. Exclusion clauses seek to completely remove a party's liability for certain types of conduct or events. Exclusion clauses can vary widely in the range of their effect. Some clauses may seek to avoid liability for any happening, while others may be narrowly drafted so as to remove liability for only specific events. The advantage of exclusion clauses rests in their ability to completely remove liability, which would otherwise rest with the benefiting party. As such, they are not subject to the same weakness as indemnity clauses given their effectiveness is not dependent upon the financial position of the indemnifying party.

Limitation clauses differ from exclusion clauses as they seek to limit, rather than completely remove, a party's potential liability. Limitation clauses may limit damages payable upon the happening of a certain event, the time period for which a party may be liable, or a combination of the two. Limitation clauses allow the party relying on them to calculate their potential liability to a certain amount, or to rule off their books once the liability time period has been reached. Commercially this allows a business to better assess the cost of insurance.

Tort Liability

Tort liability in law is broader than contractual liability. No privity is required in tort to bring an action. A tort is simply a wrong against a person, their property, or their reputation where the injured party is physically harmed, financially harmed, or both. Where an action in contract requires privity, a tort action may be brought when a party had a duty of care and breaches that duty. Businesses may not even have a relationship or know a party who brings a tort action against them. Damages in tort are almost always higher than in contract because the damages are for not only the loss but a wrong that has been committed.

Table 1.1: Comparing Tort and Contract Liability				
	Obligation	Privity	Damages	Risk
Tort	Imposed by law	No privity	Potentially unlimited (place party in position if tort had not occurred)	Broad Based on duty in law Unpredictable
Contract	Voluntarily imposed	Privity	Limited (place party in position if contract had been honored)	Narrow Predictable Limit damages through exclusion clauses

Various Business Structures

There are various forms of doing business:

1. Sole Proprietorship — tax deductions, unlimited liability
2. Branch — taxed in host State, not separate entity for liability
3. Partnerships
4. Limited Liability Company
5. Joint Venture
6. Corporation
7. Subsidiary

1. Sole Proprietorship

What is a Sole Proprietorship?

A sole proprietorship is the most basic and simplest form of business organization. **Sole proprietorships** exist when an individual carries on business, without adopting any other form of business organization, such as a corporation.[1] Generally no formal registration process is required. Examples of these can range from an individual agreeing to clean his friend's house each week, to a cleaning company with hundreds of employees. Sole proprietors can exist in any type of business (a plumber, a baker, a lawyer, etc.) A sole proprietorship is easily established with the acquisition of a business license, which is needed for most types of business organizations. Also, dissolving the business is as simple as discontinuing business activities, both being attractive characteristics of sole proprietorships.

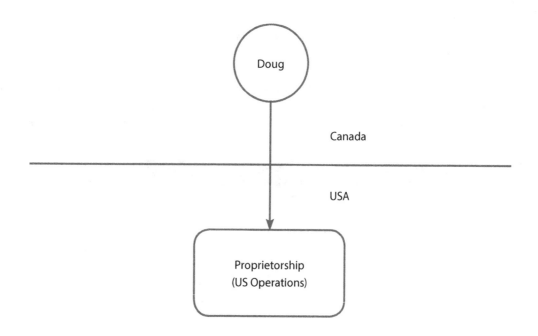

Figure 1.1: Sole Proprietorship

---

[1] Mitchell McInnes, Ian Kerr, and J. Anthony VanDuzer. *Managing the Law.* (Toronto, ON: Pearson, 2006).

Tax & Liability

In this form of business, the owner (proprietor) and the business (proprietorship) have no legal separation. Because of this, the owner will enjoy all of the benefits that the proprietorship receives such as all the earned income. However, the owner is then held personally liable on proprietorship's income earned, or losses suffered in terms of tax liabilities. The proprietor will also most likely be able to take advantages of certain tax deductions but will be personally liable for all other obligations of the proprietorship. These obligations could include the performance of all contracts entered into and personal liability for torts committed in connection with the proprietorship.

Due to the lack of separation between the owner and the proprietorship, the owner is known to have **unlimited personal liability**. This includes the ability for third parties to access the owner's personal assets in order to fulfill business obligations. This presents the greatest risk for the owners of sole proprietorships, especially as the company grows. As the number of contracts increases, so does the need for employees, as well as the associated risk of increased amounts of contracts. Sole proprietorships may be suitable for small business, but as a business grows it is wise to adopt another form of business organization, such as a corporation.

2. Branch

What is a Branch?

Using branches is a cheap and easy method of entering foreign markets. Branching methods are most often seen in the banking industry. A **branch** is known to exist in another location, other than the main office, where business is conducted. Branches are often separated into different specialties of the main company, such as marketing, accounting, or HR departments. In banking however, branches are often used to expand business operations in a mass scale. Often only several commercial banks control the majority of a banking industry throughout one or more jurisdictions. They do so by establishing branches across these areas they wish to cover. Branch operations remain fully controlled by their parent companies, which gives the parent company the ability to ensure certain management and operational goals are met.

Tax & Liability

Due to the tight relationship between a parent company and their branches, they are not considered separate legal entities from one another. Certain liability issues may arise may arise; the parent may be liable for the obligations of a branch in certain instances.

Though they are not considered separate legal entities from the parent, branch locations will still establish tax liabilities in the host state (where they conduct business). For example, a branch tax is [also] levied on the after-tax income of the entity, reduced by an investment allowance reflecting the retention of business assets and retained earnings in Canada.[2] This means that a foreign company may be taxed differently, depending on whether they keep the money invested in Canada, or if it is withdrawn.

They will also be held to the host state's laws and regulations. The parent and host state's legal differences may cause some conflicts, or allow the parent company to use certain host state laws to their advantage. An example of this is banks opening branches in a host state. The home state may request the bank to provide customer information but the host state laws confidentiality rules prevent the disclosure of such information. There is a conflict between the host state and home state laws. By default, the host state laws should prevail over the home state laws as the bank is located in the host state.

---

[2] Crystal Taylor. 2016. "Branch vs. Subsidiary, Which Is Right for You?" Blog. *Carrying On Business in Canada For Non-Residents.* http://www.millerthomson.com/en/blog/carrying-on-business-in-canada-for-non/branch-vs-subsidiary-which-is-right-for-you.

3. Partnership

A. General Partnership

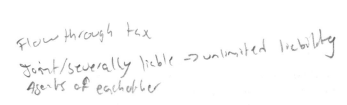

What is a General Partnership?

Partnerships are established when two or more parties carry on combined business activities, with a goal to profit. A **general partnership** is a partnership in which partners share equally in both responsibility and liability.[3] Partners become jointly and severably liable and have unlimited liability. Partners will merge their individual knowledge, skills, and assets into the partnership. Also, a partnership may be deemed to exist in a court hearing, regardless of the intention of the partner, if the court views the business dealing to satisfy the makings of a partnership; two legal persons carrying on business in common with a view of profit.[4] In Canada, the statutory regulation of partnerships falls under provincial jurisdiction. Partnerships are generally created when the partners start operating as a partnership and a formal registration process is not usually required.

Tax & Liability

Like a sole proprietorship, the partnership and the individual partners are not separate legal entities. Each individual partner will have unlimited legal liability towards the partnership's obligations, therefore, their personal assets may be used to fulfill partnership obligations. It also means that a partner may be jointly and severably liable for the misconduct and negligence of another partner. Partners in a partnership are viewed as agents of each other, and will be able to perform duties as such. You can [however], establish the terms of your business with your partner and protect yourself in case of a disagreement or dissolution by drawing up a specific business agreement.[5] These agreements should be agreed upon before formation of the partnership to protect each individual's personal interests, and to establish all major terms of the partnership.

Along with combining resources, partners also share in the profits in which the partnership is entitled.

One major advantage to a partnership is the *flow-through tax* benefits. Partnerships are seen as a flow-through entity (FTE), meaning that the profits earned by the entity are passed directly to the investors and owners (partners). These profits are then taxed as revenues of the investors and owners, rather than taxing partnership revenues first, then taxing the partner revenues subsequently. FTEs represent a good way for people to avoid double taxations on the business revenues they earn or to reduce overall tax paid. In jurisdictions that do not recognize a partnership as an FTE, using other common FTEs such as income trusts, S corporations or limited liability companies, may be a more financially attractive option.

B. Limited Partnership (LP)

What is a Limited Partnership?

Limited partnerships (LPs) include at least one partner that has unlimited legal liability (general partner), AND at least one partner who has only limited liability (limited partner). In the partnership the limited partners are viewed as passive, an investor, and the general partner is viewed as active. A limited partner then, would not be held personally liable for the partnership's obligations, nor would he or she be liable for misconduct or negligence of other partners in the arrangement. In order to maintain this limited liability position however, these partners are limited to the amount

---

[3] Arthur Sullivan, and Steven M. Sheffrin *(2003). Economics: Principles in action. (*Upper Saddle River, New Jersey 07458: Pearson Prentice Hall, 2003), 190.

[4] Partnership Act, RSBC 1996, c 348, <http://canlii.ca/t/520vw> retrieved on 2016-02-03

[5] Canadabusiness.ca,. 2016. "Corporation, Partnership, or Sole Proprietorship? — Canada Business Network". http://www.canadabusiness.ca/eng/page/2853/#toc-_partnerships.

of involvement they have in daily business activities of the partnership such as management duties. Failing to do so, or presenting themselves as a general partner, may be sufficient enough to override the "limited liability" status. Other than the limited partner stipulations, all other aspects of general partnerships and limited partnerships are equivalent. The advantage of a limited partnership is retaining the flow-through benefits of a partnership but having limited liability as a limited partner. The disadvantage is the inability to be involved in the day-to-day decisional affairs of the partnership. This does not preclude a limited partner from providing management services through a separate company, if the limited partner is an individual, or through an individual if the limited partner is a corporation.

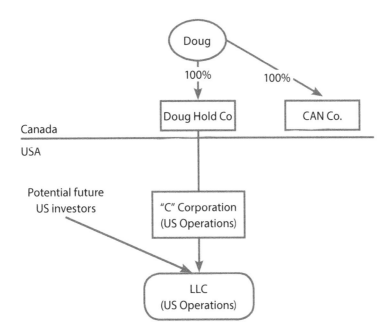

Figure 1.2: Limited Partnership

C. Limited Liability Partnership (LLP)

What is a Limited Liability Partnership?

Limited Liability Partnerships (LLPs) are partnership arrangements in which ALL partners have some degree of limited liability. One major difference of the LLP from general and limited partnerships is that one partner is not liable for the misconduct or negligence of another partner. Further, some partners may actually hold limited liability similar to that of a shareholder of a corporation, which can make this type of partnership an excellent investment tool. Some countries limit the use of LLPs by requiring at least one or several partners to absorb unlimited liability, which actually reflects a Limited Partnership (LP) structure. LLPs are governed by statute and are restricted to particular types of industries like accounting and law.

4. Limited Liability Company (LLC)

What is a Limited Liability Company?

A **Limited Liability Company (LLC)** is a United States-specific form of what is otherwise known as a private limited company. These business organizations take various different forms, which depend on the statutes that govern them in their respective US state. An LLC is not a corporation, but a hybrid company that holds taxation similar to a partnership, and liability of a corporation.

Table 1.2: Liability & Taxation of Partnerships

	General Partnership	Limited Partnership	Limited Liability Partnership
Structure & Liability	- Partners share equally in full absorption of responsibility and liability - Joint and severally liable for misconduct or negligence of another partner	- At least one partner has unlimited legal liability (general partner), AND at least one partner has only limited liability (limited partner) - Limited partner loses limited liability if they take an active role in the management of the partnership	- ALL partners have some degree of limited liability - Partners are not liable for misconduct or negligence of another partner
Taxation	Flow-through taxation	Flow-through taxation	Flow-through taxation

Tax & Liability

The members of an LLC company cannot be held personally liable for the debts or responsibilities of the company. The greatest advantage of an LLC is that it combines benefits like the flow-through taxation of a partnership, with the limited liability of a corporation. A major disadvantage to an LLC is that they are NOT governed with any sort of protective provisions for members. Instead, members must draft strong operating agreements, and use these agreements to ensure their best interests are being taken care of. Thus, an LLC is often best suitable for single-owner companies.

5. Joint Venture

What is a Joint Venture?

A **Joint Venture** is formed when a relationship is formed, whose main purpose is to perform some type of business operation. Companies typically pursue joint ventures for one of five reasons:

- To gain faster entry into a new market,
- To acquire expertise,
- To increase production scale,
- Efficiencies or coverage, or
- To expand business development by gaining access to distributor networks.[6]

There are two main types of joint ventures: **equitable** and **contractual**. Some jurisdictions prohibit the use of wholly owned foreign subsidiaries, which may influence the use of an equity or contractual joint venture instead. These restrictions are often established with the objective of protecting local businesses.

---

[6] Alexander Roos. 2016. "Getting More Value From Joint Ventures | Transaction Advisors". *Transactionadvisors.Com.* https://www.transactionadvisors.com/insights/getting-more-value-joint-ventures.

A. Equitable Joint Venture

Equitable joint ventures (EJVs) can be described as a long-term arrangement between two partners. EJV partners will establish a new entity in the host state, such as a corporation or a limited liability company (LLC). New entities are established in order to limit the liability that parties of the EJV will assume. The contracting parties in the EJV will each own equity in this new entity. Through the EJV, the new entity (corporation or LLC) will always be taxed in the host state, however further taxation (such as withholding taxes) may be applicable, depending on the tax laws of the jurisdictions involved. The main disadvantage of an EJV arrangement is that it may be difficult to unwind, because of the establishment of a separate entity, instead of a contractual agreement.

B. Contractual Joint Venture

A **Contractual Joint Venture (CJV)** is a contractual agreement between two or more parties to run a business venture together. The relationship is contractual and the contract outlines the terms under which the parties to the contract will work together. This contract may outline everything from the duration of the venture, to its specific purpose and much more. CJVs do not establish a new entity, but rather allow for a contract to outline the roles and responsibilities that the parties will assume. The ability to control the CJV through a contract provides flexibility in the relationship between the parties. It can also aid in a relatively easy winding-up process, as terms in the agreement can trigger such processes. Certain factors such as taxation (where will the taxes be levied?), liability (who will bear liability?) and the laws of host countries will largely influence the type of contract that is chosen in the CJV. The contract will set out the objectives of the joint venture, the contributions of the parties, whether financial or in the form of management services or technology, decision making process, the termination of the project, and/or ownership of assets. Many jurisdictions will recognize CJVs as partnerships, for tax purposes. This would result in a flow-through arrangement of taxation for the CJV and instead of taxing the parties directly for profits or losses incurred throughout the contractual agreement.

Table 1.3: Common Joint Venture Clauses

The Purpose Clause—maps the scope and goals of the business enterprise. (These include things such as *geography, products and services, or duration*) * Includes both parties' intentions for the joint venture, as well as possible future of the venture

Exception Clause—provides exceptions to the purpose clause. Will allow for adjustments against any overly specific statement by the purpose clause

Extraordinary vs. Ordinary Decisions—listing of what an ordinary or extraordinary decision would include. This clause will explain how the decisions will be made. i.e., shareholder or board of director's vote

Capitalization—outlines the procedures that will be used to raise capital. i.e., debt or equity? When? How much?

Transfer of Ownership—often refers to the possible transfer of Intellectual Property i.e., details for selling or leasing requirements. Can restrict transfer all together

Noncompetition Clause—prohibits a party from entering or starting a similar profession or trade, in competition with the other party

Confidentiality/Non-Disclosure Agreement—outlines confidential material, knowledge, or information that the parties share with one another, yet should not be shared to any third party

---

The advantages of a CJV is the ability of the parties to retain ownership of their own assets, business, and employees, rather than transferring them to a joint venture vehicle. It avoids the initial and ongoing administrative costs of an EJV and avoids the relative formality and permanence of a corporate structure. A CJV is easier to terminate and unwind than an EJV. A CJV has no effect on the direct taxation of the joint venture parties and there is usually no transfer of their respective businesses to a separate legal entity. A CJV may often be used for the following type of ventures:

- Construction or property development projects
- Resource sharing arrangements
- Strategic alliances
- Joint tenders for a particular project under a consortium arrangement
- Research and development or technology collaborations

Comparing Joint Ventures

Equitable and contractual joint ventures differ in how they are organized and managed, thus they each offer certain benefits to the parties utilizing them. Unless restricted to using one form or the other (from host state laws or regulations), parties will weigh the advantages and disadvantages, to decide what form of venture agreement is right for them. Table 1.4 compares the common advantages and disadvantages to these different forms of joint ventures. Table 1.5 compares an EJV and CJV in China as an example. Please note such regulations are as of the date of publication of this text.

Table 1.4: Equitable Joint Venture vs. Contractual Joint Venture	
Equitable Joint Venture	**Contractual Joint Venture**
Structure	Structure
- Creates new entity	- Created by contractual agreement
Advantages	Advantages
- Used in long term business arrangements	- Used in short-term or project based arrangements
- Easily transfer parties' interests; ex. Transfer of shares	- Flexible relationship outlined by contract; ex. Duration, CJV purpose
- Limited liability to parties similar to Corporation liability principle	- Not regulated by corporation law of the host country
- Profit distribution ratio = Shareholder distribution ratio	- Easy to unwind; the CJV will terminate according to contractual terms
Disadvantages	- Percentage of the CJV owned by parties can change throughout the life of a CJV
- Difficult to unwind in certain cases, corporation existence must be explicitly; ex. Vote by directors, notification of stakeholders, settle with creditors	Disadvantages
	- Establishment of CJV can be time consuming and expensive due to negotiation of contractual terms
- Subject to overriding Corporation Laws in host country	- Parties to the CJV are joint and severally liable to venture obligations
- Taxation is at the level of the new entity created by the EJV; this can "trap" losses incurred by the EJV, which could otherwise be used by parties to net against other income	- Profit sharing outlined by contract; can be a drawback as future shareholdings and changes in registered capital can change

Table 1.5: Equity vs. Contractual Joint Ventures

	Equity Joint Venture	Contractual Joint Venture
Legal Entity Status	Must operate as an LLC - Liability of the partners is limited to contributions made to the Registered Capital of JV	May operate as either an LLC or without "legal person" status - Avoidance of taxes & fees related to land contribution (i.e. transfer &/or purchase of land title) - Contributions remain property of the partners, income becomes joint property - Jointly & severally liable
Distribution of Power "Mind & Management"	Board of Directors - 3 members min; appointed - Representation must be in proportion to ownership interest - Either party may elect Chairman - Some decisions require unanimous approval, can mandate for all General Manager - Appointed - Deputy GM = appointed by opposite partner	More flexibility regarding division of power - Decision making & otherwise - Contracted rights, obligations, sharing of risk / liabilities, management, ownership of property @ termination Board of Directors can be disproportionate - Joint Management Committee instead if not an LLC No Deputy General Manager
Profit Distribution	Proportionate - Profit Distribution Ratio = Shareholder Ratio	Negotiated (Contractual Agreement) - Chinese partner can receive fixed payments only (i.e. "Renting" their business license) - Attractive to investors who desire a fast ROI, but whose partners are reluctant to handover control
Registered Capital	Must be paid in the proportion agreed to & set out in EJV contract - Foreign Partner min contribution = 25% (to achieve FIE status & related tax benefits) - Max contribution = 99% (<50% in "Restricted Industries") - Capital contribution of Chinese Partner limited to 50% of its own net asset value Capital contributions to EJV must be made in: - Cash - Capital Goods / Assets - Patented & Unpatented Tech - Materials & Equipment - Other Property Rights (Land, Clearance Fees) and approved by the relevant Chinese Authorities	May be recovered and repatriated prior to JV termination
Unilateral Termination	Not Possible	Possible upon breach of contract

6. Corporation

What is a Corporation?

Corporations are the most common form of business organization. A **corporation** is authorized to act as a single and separate legal entity, recognized as such in law. A corporation is a creature of statute, a legal fiction, which enjoys many of the rights and responsibilities that an individual possesses; that is, a corporation has the right to:

- enter into contracts,
- loan and borrow money,
- sue and be sued,
- hire employees,
- own assets and
- pay taxes.[7]

A corporation is created only when certain documents are filed with the appropriate government office under either the federal *Canada Business Corporations Act* (CBCA) or similar legislation in each province or territory.[8] The articles of incorporation must include the fundamental characteristics of the corporation such as its name, the class and number of shares authorized to be issued, the rights and privileges attributable to each class of shares, the number of directors, any restriction on transferring shares, and any restriction on the business that the corporation may conduct.[9]

Corporations can be run very differently in foreign markets due to difference in corporation laws in these jurisdictions. These things could include structure, tax and liability implications, sometimes varying between provinces within the same country. For example, the table below depicts differing corporate director residency requirements between the provinces in Canada, which could potentially influence which province a foreign investor may choose to invest in.

As it is in Canada, United States corporate law is governed separately by individual states, with minimum standards being set by federal laws. One major difference however, is that companies are allowed to incorporate in the state of their choice regardless of which state their headquarters are located in. This has influenced many of the major public American companies to incorporate in the state of Delaware, to benefit from the favorable Delaware General Corporation Law advantages. These include such things as lower corporate tax rates, and limited shareholder rights against corporate directors. In fact, more than 50% of all publicly-traded companies in the United States including 64% of the Fortune 500 have chosen Delaware as their legal home.[10] Delaware is also popular with e-commerce because of its advanced internet laws. Other corporations, more notably private corporations, incorporate in Nevada to take advantage of disclosure requirements for shareholders and no informational sharing agreement with the IRS.

In the United Kingdom, Company Law regulates corporations formed under the Companies Act (2006). UK law offers shareholders, excluding employees, sole voting rights during the general meetings that the corporation holds. In these meetings, shareholder voting rights may act to alter the company's constitution, change board members, or determine resolutions to issues.[11]

---

[7] Investopedia, 2003. "Corporation Definition | Investopedia". http://www.investopedia.com/terms/c/corporation.asp.

[8] *Canada Business Corporations Act,* RSC 1985, c C-44 (CAN.)

[9] The equivalent of articles under the NSCA is the memorandum of association; under the BCBCA, it is an incorporation agreement that contains a notice of articles, combined with some elements of articles under the CBCA; under the PEICA, it is the letters patent.

[10] "About Agency". Delaware Division of Corporations. Statistic as of February, 2016.

[11] United Kingdom. The Companies Act. (2006)

Table 1.6: Corporate Director Residency Requirements (Canada)

Each jurisdiction has its own requirements concerning the residency of a corporation's directors. Residency requirements by jurisdiction are as follows:

Jurisdiction	Director Residency Requirement
Federal (Canada)	25% resident Canadian Directors Required
Alberta	25% resident Canadian Directors Required
British Columbia	No Canadian Directors Required
Manitoba	25% resident Canadian Directors Required
New Brunswick	No Canadian Directors Required
Newfoundland	25% resident Canadian Directors Required
Nova Scotia	No Canadian Directors Required
Ontario	25% resident Canadian Directors Required
Prince Edward Island	No Canadian Directors Required
Quebec	No Canadian Directors Required
Saskatchewan	25% resident Canadian Directors Required

Please note that it is only directors which are specified, not officers or shareholders. Officers and shareholders do not need to be Canadian residents. Note also that Canadian residents are specified, not Canadian citizens.

Table 1.7: Corporation Advantages and Disadvantages

Advantages	Disadvantages
Liability—Considered a separate legal entity, thus shareholders cannot be liable for further amounts than the amount invested; ex. Shares owned	**Creation/Dissolution**—High costs to create and wind-up a corporation (filing fees, legal costs). Largely due to "separate entity" status
Tax—Depending on jurisdiction and legal rules, corporate tax rates should be low enough to entice investors	**Tax**—Corporations may be subject to higher taxation in certain instances, usually when conducting business in a foreign jurisdiction
Financing—Easier to obtain financing compared to Sole proprietorship, as in this instance personal financial issues can interfere	**Regulation**—Corporate law and statues will govern how corporation must act; ex. Record keeping, annual general meetings
Transfer of Ownership—Easily done through transfer of shares	**Disclosure Rules**—Share offerings and financial statements must be shared with public
Existence—The lifespan of a corporation is continuous, until dissolved	**Loss of Control**—Voting rights of a corporation are held with owners of voting shares, causing a loss of control

Tax & Liability

Corporations act as a great tool for investment in business. Tax rates on corporations are very attractive in comparison to personal income tax rates, which would be used in taxation of sole proprietorships and partnerships. These rates will vary by province/state, and size of the corporation (small business, tax deductions), but act as an attractive feature in incorporating your business. Corporations also act as a separate legal entity from the owners of the corporation themselves. The owners are recognized as shareholders of the corporation, and the shareholder's risk is limited to their investment in the corporation. For example, as a shareholder in a corporation that goes bankrupt, you would only be liable to lose the amount you invested in the shares of the corporation. Similar to limited partners, a shareholder's liability is limited because they are a passive investor. They do not take an active role in the day-to-day management of the corporation. Shareholders' normal right is to vote in directors and approve certain actions of the directors. The directors in turn are the mind and management of a corporation and make the major decisions. With such power comes liability. The directors in turn appoint officers to run the day-to-day affairs of the corporation.

7. Subsidiary

What is a Subsidiary?

A **Subsidiary** is a company that is wholly or partially owned by another company, with the controlling interest (>50% voting stock) in the subsidiary. Subsidiaries can be a company, corporation, or a limited liability company (LLC). It is common practice to use a subsidiary to enter foreign markets; however it can be one of the more expensive options of doing so. In these cases, the laws in the jurisdiction that they operate, not necessarily the same laws of the parent company, govern the subsidiaries. This can be an attractive feature for using subsidiaries to enter foreign markets, as certain jurisdictions may offer more favorable taxation policies than those in place in the parent company jurisdiction. In contrast, foreign laws may be restricting and act as a barrier in opening a subsidiary in this location. Balancing the positive and negatives in these policies will determine whether or not to choose a subsidiary option when entering a foreign jurisdiction.

Tax & Liability

For the purposes of liability, taxation, and regulation, subsidiaries are distinct legal entities.[12] Thus, the parent company of the subsidiary does not bear responsibility for the liabilities incurred by its subsidiary. Also, a subsidiary will be subject to the taxation and legal liabilities of the host state, in where it is carrying on its business. However, under limited circumstances, a parent company may be found liable for the obligations of a subsidiary. A court may use the doctrine of "piercing the corporate veil" to seek redress from the shareholders.

A. Affiliate & Associate Companies

An **Affiliate** or associate company is similar to that of a subsidiary as it refers to being partially owned by what is known as a parent company. The difference between an affiliate and a subsidiary is the degree of ownership. An affiliate only has a minority share of its stock owned by the parent. In most cases, the terms affiliate and associate are used synonymously to describe a company whose parent possesses only a minority stake in the ownership of the company.[13] The affiliation exists because one company owns less than a majority of the voting shares of the other, usually less than 50%, or when both are subsidiaries of a third corporation.

---

[12] Investopedia, 2003. "Subsidiary Definition | Investopedia". http://www.investopedia.com/terms/s/subsidiary.asp.
[13] Ibid.

B. Sister Company

Sister companies are subsidiary companies owned by the same parent company. Each sister company is independent of the other sister companies, and the only relationship between them may be their common relationship to the parent company. Sister companies may produce a range of products that are quite different from each other or from those of the parent company. For example, Berkshire Hathaway is the parent of many subsidiary companies; these subsidiaries are then sister companies to one another. Sister companies may even be competitors, in some instances. However, there are sometimes arrangements between sister companies for information sharing or special pricing. In instances where sister companies have a common target market, the companies can reap the benefits of reduced costs from sharing marketing and advertising materials. From a tax perspective, a sister company offers the parents jurisdictional tax advantages, especially in the case of individual shareholders who are the parents. Sister companies are usually narrowly held private companies. It is difficult for a public company with hundreds or thousands of shareholders to be a sister company, instead public companies almost always operate as subsidiaries.

C. Wholly Owned Subsidiary

Another common form of subsidiary relationship is that of the **Wholly Owned Subsidiary**. These are formed in situations where the parent company owns 100% of the subsidiary company. This form of business structure is commonly known as a Wholly Foreign Owned Entity (WFOE), when used to enter into foreign (host) markets.

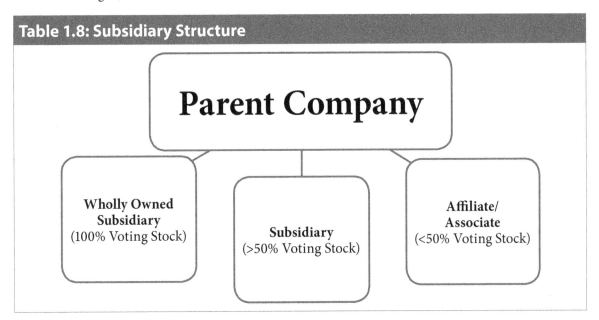

Table 1.8: Subsidiary Structure

Piercing the Corporate Veil

A corporation is a legally distinct entity separate from its shareholders. The limited liability status that shareholders, and to a lesser degree directors and officers, have to a corporation is essential to encourage the investment, and continuous growth of that corporation, and the overall economy. Without this limited liability, investment in corporations would be severely limited, as risks of personal liability would outweigh the potential benefits to investing. It is possible however, to challenge this limited liability protection that a corporation offers to shareholders, and this is known as "**Piercing the Corporate Veil**." Generally courts have a strong presumption against piercing the corporate veil, and will only do so if there has been serious misconduct.[14] However, "lifting the veil" in some instances, to protect against fraudulent and improper use of corporation protection is necessary. As a general rule of thumb, corporations are first separate and independent entities from those that own them and manage them, and second from other corporations. For example, individuals in law are either minors or adults. As a minor you are a dependent because someone in law, usually the parent, has the legal authority to make decisions for and on behalf of the child. The child is dependent upon the parent. When a minor reaches the age of majority, which varies by state, he or she becomes an adult and is classified as an independent. Although they may be independent in law, they may still rely on the parent for support, and the parent may still make decisions for them. Think of the parent as parent companies and the child as subsidiaries. When a company lacks independence, the courts may disregard the corporate structure and attach liability to the person who is really making the decisions. The corporation cannot be the mere agent or puppet of a shareholder or a parent company.

Several Actions That May Justify the "Piercing of the Corporate Veil"

1. *The Company is totally dominated:* Financing and management are so closely connected to the parent that it lacks independence (ex: Shared personal and business bank accounts).

2. *The Alter-Ego Company:* Co-mingling corporate and personal assets, using company assets for personal benefit use, or failure to hold proper records or meetings (ex: Exploiting free trips with company funds, not for company benefit or use).

3. *Undercapitalization (Thin Capitalization):* A situation when a business has insufficient funding, assets, or capital to support its operations (shielding the liability of shareholders or another company from debts, with an undercapitalized corporation).

4. *Personal Assumption:* In certain situations, persons may accept personal liability "by reason of [his or her] own acts or conduct."[15] The most common form is a personal guarantee or corporate guarantee.

5. *Fraud:* In situations where the company is incorporated for an illegal, fraudulent or improper purpose OR when its mind management are found to have committed or directed illegal or fraudulent act(s) of the company. An example of using a corporation for an improper purpose is illustrated in the case of *Chan v. City Commercial Realty Group Ltd.*

Chan v. City Commercial Realty Group Ltd. (2011)

Facts:

In the case of *Chan v. City Commercial Realty Group Ltd.,*[16] the court "pierced the corporate veil" to hold the principals (two brothers) of a real estate brokerage firm personally liable for the debts of their corporation. In this case, **City Commercial Realty Services Ltd.** (City 1) acts as the corporate defendant. They had a previous judgment against them, and lost the subsequent appeal, which ordered Services to pay costs to Chan. However, these costs went unsatisfied. Before the second appeal was heard, one of the brothers resigned from City 1, and established a new real estate brokerage—City Commercial Realty Group Ltd. (City 2). In doing so they attempted to carry on business in essentially the same manner as City 1 did prior, but to avoid the obligations that had been ordered against them to the plaintiff.

---

[14] LII / Legal Information Institute, 2016. "Piercing the Corporate Veil." https://www.law.cornell.edu/wex/piercing_the_corporate_veil.

[15] Model Business Corp. Act § 6.22(b) (1985).

[16] *Chan v City Commercial Realty Group Ltd*, 2011 ONSC 2854 (CanLII), 90 CCEL (3d) 235 [*Chan*].

Issue:

Was the formation of the new entity (City 2) done in a legally acceptable fashion? Chan claimed that City 2 was incorporated for illegal, fraudulent and/or improper purpose, namely, to prevent the plaintiffs from collecting their lawful debts.

The defendants however claimed the reasons for establishing City 2 were for legitimate business purposes, which would disallow the "piercing of the corporate veil."

Decision:

The Ontario Superior Court of Justice "lifted the veil" on City Commercial Realty Group. In doing so, it found "Martin and Samuel are jointly and severally liable to pay to Combi and Mr. Chan the aggregate principal sum of $70,000 and to Messrs."[17,18]

Reasons:

The trial judge, Justice A.D. Grace of the Ontario Superior Court of Justice, found that "City 2 engages in the same business, occupies the same premises, and uses the same furniture, phone number, business name, signage and some of the same personnel."[19] The judge found, "the plaintiffs' inability to recover any amount on account of costs is attributable to the improper conduct of Samuel and Martin."[20] This case exemplifies how piercing the corporate veil can be used to limit the ability of illegal, fraudulent, and/or improper use of corporation dealings.

Since directors are the mind and management of a corporation, it is advisable that parent and subsidiaries do not have the exact same board of directors.

Franchise

Franchising offers a cheap and easy way to expand and grow a business into foreign markets. **Franchise** arrangements involve the franchisor providing a license to the franchisee:

- The right to use or offer specific products or services,
- In a certain jurisdiction,
- For a certain period of time,
- For certain business purposes.

Franchises are controlled through the use of franchise agreements, which can involve many different schemes and clauses that may limit, or allow the actions of the franchisee. This can be a positive or a negative feature depending on the strength and simplicity of the franchise agreements, which in some cases can be a hindering factor to set up the franchise efficiently. In the franchise agreement, the

---

[17] *Ibid* at para 58.

[18] The plaintiffs filed a calculation of interest to the date of trial showing accrued interest of $31,135.59 using the rates of 4% per annum in the case of the trial judgment and 5% per annum in respect of the decision on appeal.

[19] *Chan, supra* note 16 at para 8.

[20] *Ibid* at para 57.

franchisor provides the business plan, expertise, and may license necessary intellectual property. The franchisee pays fees, follows the plan, and conforms to certain standards and rules that are established in the franchise agreement. Many clauses are included in the franchise agreement; however some of the most common clauses that are included are portrayed in Table 1.9.

Table 1.9: Common Clauses of Franchise Agreements
Duration—States the length of time or "duration" of the agreement
Operational Standard—The franchisor's expectations, outlining how a franchisee must run their business
Territorial—Exclusivity rights prohibit other franchisees under the same company to open in your assigned territory.
Renewal—These clauses outline how a franchise may be renewed or terminated.
Resale—Franchisors may put in resale clauses that limit the ability of a franchisee to resell the franchise. These include *buy back* and right of *first refusal clauses*, which allow the franchise the right of the first option to buy back the business at a fair price.
Non-Competition—Limits the ability of a franchisee to open similar operations in the future that will be in competition with the franchise the agreement is drawn for.

Tax & Liability

One major advantage to franchising a business is that each franchise that opens under a franchisor name, (ex.: chain restaurants) are seen as separate entities from one another. With this, tax and liability problems are also transferred to the franchisee, and franchisee obligations cannot be transferred to the franchisor. It extremely common for a franchise agreement to disclaim any agency status, as unfavorable liability to the franchisor may arise if an unwanted agency relationship is found. The general rule is where a franchise agreement gives the franchisor the right of complete or substantial control over the franchisee, an agency relationship exists.[21]

Judgment to determine if an agency relationship exists is further explained in the table below.

Table 1.10: When can a Franchisor be found liable?
A franchisor may be held vicariously liable for the torts of its franchisee under agency liability when it exercises a significant degree of control over the franchisee and its operations or when the complainant believes that they were dealing with the franchisor, relying on the fact that the franchisee was an agent of the franchisor. This liability can be found regardless of an anti-agency clause in the franchise agreement.
A court will not find the franchisor to be vicariously liable for its franchisee's acts where the franchisor does not exercise substantial or significant control over the day-to-day operations of the franchisee. The franchisor-franchisee relationship has led courts to narrow the defining terms of what day-to-day control of a franchisee would include. A franchisor attempting to protect a trademark does not create an agency relationship, nor do quality and uniformity procedures of products or experiences.

---

[21] *Cislaw v Southland Corp*, 6 Cal Rptr (2d) 386, 4 Cal (4th) 1284 at 1288 (App Ct 1992).

Below is an example of a court upholding the separate existence of a franchise.

Patterson v. Domino's Pizza LLC (2014)[22]

Facts:

In the case of *Patterson v. Domino's Pizza LLC (2014)*, the California Supreme Court was tasked with ruling whom held the liability in a sexual harassment lawsuit that was initiated by a Domino's employee. The parties in the case include Sui Juris, LLC (franchisee), and Domino's Pizza Franchising, LLC (franchisor). Under the franchise agreement Domino's imposed and enforced standards for marketing and operating the franchise to ensure customers received a consistent experience upon patronizing any of their franchised stores. Through the agreement however, the franchisee retained the autonomy to implement the operational standards or "day-to-day" operations, including hiring and firing, controlling and regulating workplace behaviors, and so forth. Taylor Patterson was hired by the franchisee in 2008, and shortly thereafter Patterson alleged that she was sexually harassed by Renee Miranda, the assistant manager. A lawsuit by Patterson was initiated against Miranda, the franchisee, and Domino's Pizza LLC. *Issue:*

Patterson claimed that Domino's should be held vicariously liable under traditional agency principles for the acts of its franchisee. Further, Patterson's argument included the fact that franchisors such as Dominos control their franchisee's general operations, and liability for personal harm sustained in a course of business should be absorbed by the franchisor.

Decision:

The Supreme Court of California found that Domino's Pizza LLC could not be held vicariously liable for the acts of or against their franchisee's employees.

Reasons:

The decision by the Supreme Court of California found that Domino's Pizza LLC "lacked the general control of an 'employer' or 'principal' over relevant day-to-day aspects of the employment and workplace behavior of [the franchisee's] employees."

After *Patterson*, franchisors doing business in California can protect themselves from lawsuits brought by their franchisees' employees by ensuring that franchisees retain the right to hire, fire, discipline, and manage their own employees.[23]

Sale of Products Through Resale Models

Sometimes the easiest and cheapest method to enter a foreign market is by not actually entering the jurisdiction themselves, but through one of the simple resale models. Such resale methods are an effective way to enter a foreign jurisdiction, there is no need to set up a "brick and mortar" location, as the distributor, dealer, or agent will sell or provide services through an already established sales chain or service structure. As mentioned above, incorporation has administrative costs. In addition, potential tax issues surround the sale of goods and services such as both the home state and host state claiming taxes and transfer pricing. In particular, one has to deal with not only the home state's revenue department but also the host state's revenue department. There are several ways that a company can do so and that is through the use of a distributor, a dealer, or an agent all being active in the

---

[22] *Patterson v Domino's Pizza* LLC, 333 P(3d) 723, 60 Cal (4th) 474 (Sup Ct 2014).

[23] Hamilton, Kevin, and Leonard MacPhee. 2016. "Patterson v. Domino's Pizza, LLC: Franchisors Are Not Vicariously Liable As "Employers" Or "Principals" For Their Franchisees' Employees' Workplace Conduct, California High Court Rules | JD Supra". *JD Supra*. http://www.jdsupra.com/legalnews/patterson-v-dominos-pizza-llc-franch-20383/.

foreign jurisdiction. Each of these options present different advantages and disadvantages, and vary slightly in structure. Each one could be considered an agency relationship or treated as an independent contractor. It is important that written contracts are used to govern such relationships. The terms distributor and dealer are close but have some differences.

A. Distributor

A **Distributor** is an entity that will purchase products or entire product lines directly from the supplier, to then resell to other retailers or directly to dealers or in some instances, the end customers who wish to buy the product. Along with reselling the product, the distributor may offer independent warranty services for revenue generation, but is not required to by law. A distributor can begin operations in any jurisdiction they are legally able to in order to sell their product. Home states often require both a license to sell products and a license to import the product. The distributor will take on the risk of the goods they purchase, with no risk remaining for the supplier. In most cases, suppliers use distributorship arrangements to avoid the liability that comes with agency, thus normal distributorship agreements disclaim agency. However, if a distributor looks like an agent and acts like an agent, an agency may exist. One disadvantage is that the supplier will retain very little control over the distributor; ex: Where they choose to resell? Price they resell for? Who do they resell to?

B. Dealer

A **Dealer** is an entity that will most often buy goods from a distributor or in some instances from the supplier. Dealers usually sell to, and deal with the end customer by selling the products that they either own (resale), or merely hold. Legally and contractually, dealers and distributors are the same, except that dealers are based at the **retail** level and distributors are at the **wholesale** level. In some instances, dealers may not be able to afford the goods that they resell outright. For example, an RV dealership may house hundreds of RVs at any one time, worth hundreds of thousands of dollars each. In these instances, dealership agreements may allow the dealer to sell on credit, without needing the capital to buy the expensive products upfront.

C. Agent

Agency relationships occur when one party acts for and on behalf of another party, for some specific purpose. This relationship includes a principal, agent, and a third party, where the principal appoints an agent to act on his or her behalf, to perform a specific duty. The agent may be able to bind the principal to contracts, or may be restricted to merely assist a principal. Using an agency relationship is an effective way to enter a foreign jurisdiction, as it is the simplest and cheapest way to do so. In these instances, there is no need to set up a brick and mortar location, as the agent will perform their duties to the principal through their already established location. Agency relationships are risky as the agent can bind the principal to a contract, and that principal may be bound, even if the agent exceeded their authority. Bribery is one example of where an agent in the host state can cause great harm to the home state. Most bribery laws attach liability to the principal for bribery committed by the agent. A further disadvantage of agency is the loss of control that comes with this type of relationship. In most instances, suppliers will retain the risk of physical loss, and non-payment by the customer until the goods are delivered, and paid for. Agents are able to act on behalf of the principal, but can be controlled through express agreements, upon creation of the agency relationship. These agreements are crucial to risk management of agency relationships abroad. Also, host state laws may be able to restrict who can be the agent and what acts an agent in their jurisdiction can perform.[24] For example, these restrictions may limit agents to citizens of the host state, or register with a government office. Agents provide the role of an intermediary and they offer legitimate advantages such as assisting with unfamiliar environments, including cultural, legal, accounting, and logistical complexities and obligations of the host state. Agents can provide a wide range of services, such as legal advice, market research, sales and after-sales services, logistical services, and identify possible business projects or execute various other business related activities.

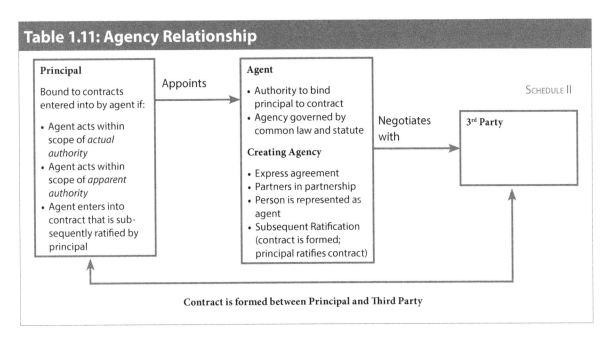

Table 1.11: Agency Relationship

Principal

Bound to contracts entered into by agent if:

- Agent acts within scope of *actual authority*
- Agent acts within scope of *apparent authority*
- Agent enters into contract that is subsequently ratified by principal

Appoints →

Agent

- Authority to bind principal to contract
- Agency governed by common law and statute

Creating Agency

- Express agreement
- Partners in partnership
- Person is represented as agent
- Subsequent Ratification (contract is formed; principal ratifies contract)

Negotiates with →

SCHEDULE II

3rd Party

Contract is formed between Principal and Third Party

Operating Company (OpCo)/Holding Company (HoldCo)

One common method of creating tax and liability efficiencies is through proper corporate structuring. Liability is reduced by limiting the assets that exist in the OpCo and holding the assets elsewhere known as a holding company (HoldCo). Separating your business interests between an OpCo and HoldCo entails having the entity which carries on an active business, the OpCo, and one that holds the assets, including the shares of the OpCo through a HoldCo. If someone sues, they have to sue the OpCo and only the assets in the OpCo will be at risk.

Creditor Protection

The OpCo holds little assets, including cash, as a means of minimizing the seizure of assets from a potential liability claim. In a an overly litigious business world, it is necessary to protect assets from a potential unfavorable ruling, especially in the United States, where juries often award damages in excess of the true nature of the loss.

Tax Free Dividends

The OpCo can also pay monies to the HoldCo from the OpCo by means of a dividend (often tax free in most jurisdictions) and shelter excess business earnings. The HoldCo is able to invest the money received from the OpCo and avoid or defer taxes.

---

[24] European Union; duties of the agent to the principal and of the principal to the agent; default remuneration provisions; notice requirements for termination; and compensation for the agent after termination. Council Directive 86/643, OJ (L 382), 17-21 (Dec. 31, 1986)

Entering a Foreign Jurisdiction—US Case Study

Let's review some of the structures that CanCo or the beneficial shareholder, [Douglas Peterson ("Doug")] of CanCo may consider in carrying out business activities in the United States.

Facts and Assumptions

1. All parties involved are residents of Canada and currently not taxable under any other foreign jurisdiction (i.e., not a US Citizen or green card holder).
2. All parties involved are related persons.
3. CanCo is a Canadian-controlled Private Corporation, incorporated under the laws of Alberta. All of CanCo's shares are held by Doug.
4. Business activities will be carried out in the United States and these activities would be carried out through a permanent establishment.
5. All business activities to be carried on in the United States would be active in nature and not passive (i.e., generating interest, dividends, rents, royalties etc.).

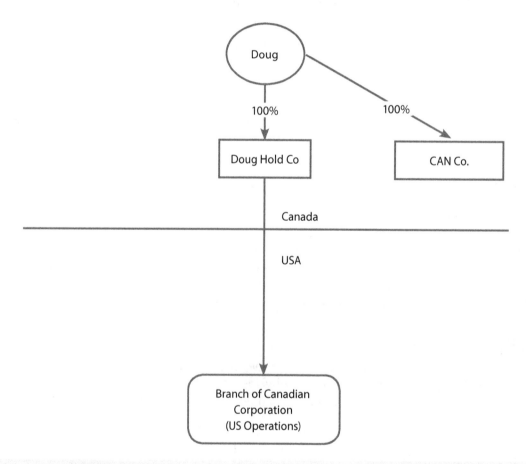

Figure 1.3: Tax Free Dividends

6. The Internal Revenue Service ("IRS") and the Canada Revenue Agency ("CRA") would both assess tax.

7. There would be $100,000 of US source business income and that all income would be subject to tax at the highest marginal rates of tax which are currently or expected to be as follows:

	Canadian	US
Corporate Federal	15%	35%
Corporate—Provincial/State	10%	[25]
Individual—Federal (ordinary income)	29%	35%
Individual—Provincial/State (ordinary income)	10%	[26]
Individual—Federal/Alberta (ineligible dividends)	27.71%	n/a
Individual—Federal/Alberta (eligible dividends)	19.29%	n/a
Withholding taxes (dividends to corporation)	n/a	5%
Withholding taxes (dividends to individual)	n/a	15%

Potential Structures

1. **Sole Proprietorship**

Under this scenario Doug would carry out the US business activity personally.

Taxes. The taxes that will ultimate be payable by Doug. Since income is earned from a permanent establishment in the United States, the income is subject to tax in the United States. As a resident of Canada for tax purposes Doug is taxed on his worldwide income. Doug would get a credit to reduce taxes otherwise payable for the taxes paid in the United States. Doug would in essence pay the tax rate had the income been earned in Canada.

US Tax	
Taxable Income	$100,000
US tax (35%)	$35,000
Canadian Tax	
Taxable Income	$100,000
Canadian Tax (39%)	$39,000
Foreign Tax Credit	($35,000)
Net Canadian Tax	$4,000
Total Tax	$39,000
Effective Tax Rate	39%

Liability. Doug would be personally liable as a sole proprietor, both for contracts and torts. His personal assets would be at risk.

---

[25] State taxes are not integrated into the analysis. The highest rate of state tax is Iowa and is currently at 12%.
[26] State taxes are not integrated into the analysis.

2. Use of a US Limited Partnership

A US corporation as the general partner and CanCo or Doug HoldCo hold the shares of this company. Doug would be the initial limited partner. The General Partner would have the control of the partnership.

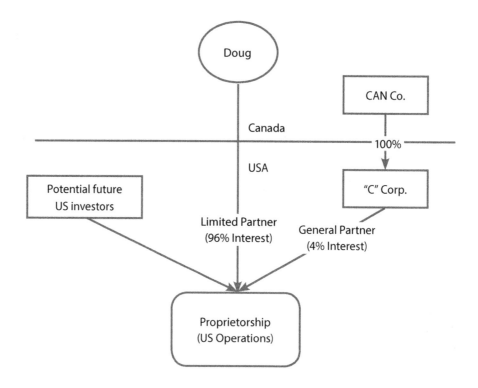

Figure 1.4: Sole Proprietorship

Taxes. A partnership agreement would give control of the Partnership to the General Partner.

- The limited partners would give power of attorney to the General Partner. This allows new limited partners to invest in the future.
- The Limited Partnership would have to prepare and file both US federal and State Partnership. The limited partners (initially Doug) would have to file US federal and state personal income tax returns, which would report his US source income from the Partnership.
- In addition to the personal taxes identified, the General Partner would be allocated 4% of the income and will be subject to tax on this. The General Partner would have to file US and state corporate tax returns.
- The limited partners (initially Doug) would have to report the US Partnership income that is allocated to him in the United States on his Canadian Income Tax Returns. To the extent there are Canadian taxes associated with the Partnership income, a foreign tax credit can be claimed for the US personal income tax paid.
- Under this structure the US Limited Partnership is not required to file Canadian Partnership returns and the General Partner does not file Canadian corporate returns.
- Under this scenario there will be obligations to withhold income tax on the non-residents' partnership income allocations on an annual basis. The withholdings are at the highest tax rate and would be reported annually.

US Tax	
Taxable Income	$96,000
US tax (35%)	$33,600
Canadian Tax	
Taxable Income	$96,000
Canadian Tax (39%)	$37,440
Foreign Tax Credit	($33,600)
Net Canadian Tax	$3,840
Total Tax	$37,440
Effective Tax Rate	39%

Liability. The limited partner would have limited liability but the general partner would have unlimited liability.

3. **US Corporation owned by an Individual**

Doug would personally hold the shares of the company.

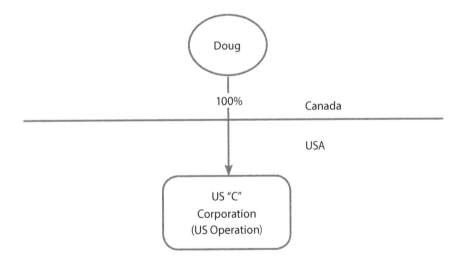

Figure 1.5: Wholly Owned C Corp

Taxes. The US Corporation (US Corp) would be subject to tax in the United States. Dividends paid to non-resident individuals are subject to a 15% withholding tax that the US Corp is obliged to withhold and remit to the IRS. There would be tax filing obligations with both the IRS and CRA. The US Corp would file US federal and state corporate income tax, and would be required to withhold tax on the dividend paid to Doug (a non-resident individual). The withholdings are reduced by the Canada/US tax treaty to 15% on dividends paid to individual shareholders. Doug would report the dividend received and would get a foreign tax credit for the US withholding tax paid.

The taxes ultimately payable by Doug would be as follows:

US Tax	
Taxable Income	$100,000
US tax (35%)	$35,000
Available for Distribution	$65,000
Withholding tax (15%)	$9,750
Canadian Tax	
Taxable Income	$65,000
Canadian Tax (39%)	$25,350
Foreign Tax Credit	($9,750)
Net Canadian Tax	$15,600
Total Tax	$60,350
Effective Tax Rate	60.3%

Liability. As a shareholder Doug would have limited liability.

4. **US Corporation owned by Canadian Corporation**

Doug HoldCo would own the shares of the US Corp. In addition an LLC would be put in place to carry on the active business in the United States. This allows for future investors to be brought into the business.

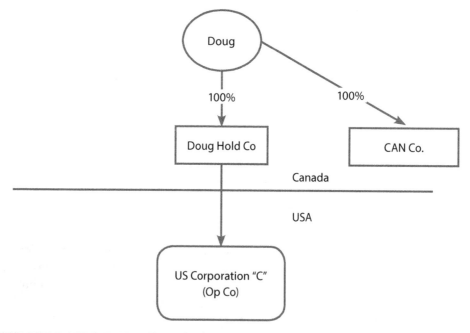

Figure 1.6: Hold Co & Branch

Taxes. Since the LLC is "disregarded" in the United States for tax purposes, its income would be allocated to the "single member," in this case the US Corp. If US partners are brought into ownership in the future this would occur at the LLC level and the income will be allocated and taxable by the members/owners, similar to a partnership.

- There will be tax filings with both the IRS and CRA.
- The LLC would have to prepare and file US federal and state partnership returns similar to what a partnership would file as previously discussed.
- The US Corp would have to file a US and state corporate tax returns to report any income allocations, which it may have received and reported related to the LLC.
- The US Corp would be required to withhold tax on the dividend paid to the non- resident. The withholdings are reduced by the Canada/US tax treaty to 5% on dividends paid to a parent corporation. The withholding taxes would be reported annually.
- Doug HoldCo would file its Canadian income tax return, which would report the dividend received from the US Corp. Since the earnings that are being distributed to Doug HoldCo were from an active business being carried on in the United States, the dividend received would not be taxable in Canada.
- Doug would have to report the dividend received from Doug HoldCo on his Canadian Income Tax Return. Since this dividend is being received from a Canadian corporation, it will be subject to the gross up and dividend tax credit.

US Tax—US Corp	
Taxable Income	$100,000
US tax (35%)	$35,000
Available for Distribution	$65,000
Withholding tax (5%)	$3,250
Canadian Tax—Doug HoldCo	
Dividend Income	$65,000
Deductible Dividend	($65,000)[27]
Taxable Income	$0
Canadian Tax (25%)	$0
Foreign Tax Credit	($0)[28]
Available for Distribution	$61,750
Canadian Tax—Doug	
Taxable Income (Dividend)	$61,750
Canadian Tax (19.29%)	$11,912
Foreign Tax Credit	($0)
Net Canadian Tax	$11,912
Total Tax	$50,162
Effective Tax Rate	50.1%

Liability. The US Corp is a separate entity from CanCo and Doug HoldCo and therefore shareholder limited liability applies.

---

[27] Dividends received from a US Subsidiary that are from after-tax earnings related to an active business are deductible to determine taxable income in Canada.

[28] Since there is no foreign source income taxable in Canada there is no ability to claim the foreign tax credit for the US withholding tax that was withheld on the payment of the dividend to Doug HoldCo.

5. **Branch Operation**

Using CanCo (a Canadian corporation) to carry on US operations as a "branch."

Taxes. Using Doug HoldCo to carry on the US operations as a "branch" has similar tax implications as where a US Corp is used that is held by a Canadian corporation. Doug HoldCo would still be subject to tax in the United States on the US business income and with the Branch tax there is effectively a 5% withholding tax on "distributions" to Doug HoldCo.

Doug HoldCo is used instead of CanCo because if CanCo were used it could impact the status of the shares of CanCo so they no longer qualify for a capital gains exemption.

Liability. Doug HoldCo would have liability for the actions of the US Branch.

Ethical Considerations 1.2

Foreign Corrupt Practices Act

United States of America v. James McClung, 15-CR-00357-MLC (D.N.J. 2015)

http://fcpa.shearman.com/?s=matter&mode=form&id=b5cf14a4601e960e4893c214bf416729

http://www.justice.gov/criminal-fraud/file/642081/download

There will always be a grey area of the law, which is partly due to the ethical considerations one must take into account before operating internationally. What seems ethical to one person may be deemed unethical to the next. The key to having a stake in the international community is to abide by international treaties, conventions, and customary international law.

Louis Berger International, Inc., a private consulting firm based in New Jersey, came under scrutiny by the American Federal Bureau of Investigation for bribery schemes committed in Indonesia, Vietnam, India, and Kuwait. Louis Berger International, under its Senior Vice President James McClung, concocted a $3.9 million scheme to bribe government officials to secure government contracts. James McClung and his co-conspirator, Richard Hirsch, disguised these direct Foreign Corrupt Practices Act violations through "commitment fees" and "shell foundations." James McClung approved of these corrupt bribes and on June 2015, McClung plead guilty to one count of conspiracy to violate the FCPA and one substantive count of violating the FCPA's anti-bribery provisions.

James McClung and his co-conspirator cannot claim ignorance of the FCPA guidelines due to the fact that they consciously concealed the fact of their briberies, but what if they were faced with the dilemma of either providing these "gifts to government officials" or the nations would refuse to do business with the company? What would you do in this situation?

Summary

Which structure is the best for Doug and CanCo to operate? The answer depends upon what is more important—liability or tax.

Tax. From a pure tax perspective the best alternative would be carry out the business activities as a sole proprietor or through a US limited partnership.

Liability. A sole proprietorship and a branch provide little liability protection; they both will have any liability in the US attributable to Doug and CanCo respectively. A limited partnership provides protection for the limited partner but not the general partner. Using a subsidiary wholly owned by Doug provides him with limited liability. Similarly, a wholly owned subsidiary of Doug HoldCo also provides shareholder limited liability.

Entering a Foreign Jurisdiction—China Case Study

When a company chooses to expand its operations beyond that of its home state jurisdiction, there are many things to consider. Entering China for instance, may cause distinct challenges to foreign firms due to the differences between Chinese and other jurisdiction policies. In particular, let's examine some of the options that are available to CanCo, as it looks to enter the Chinese market. Let's assume the purpose of entering China is to manufacture. What is paramount—the reduction of taxes or the protection of intellectual property? What jurisdiction should be used depends on the answer to the above question? If the primary focus is to reduce taxes, then a joint venture should be used. If the primary purpose is to protect intellectual property, then a wholly foreign-owned subsidiary may be best. If CanCo wants to reduce taxes and also protect intellectual property then a joint venture would be best. In addition, setting up in a special economic zone with a local government has additional benefits.

The Wholly Foreign-Owned Enterprise (WFOE)

In recent years the WFOE has become the most popular business model to enter into China. A WFOE creates a new, independent legal entity in China. Unlike a JV, a WFOE allows a foreign owned corporation to enter into China without a Chinese partner.

Advantages. The most significant benefit to using a WFOE is that it allows the foreign corporation to retain full control of their business. This is why the WFOE offers the best protection for a foreign company's IP. Full control is also important when a foreign corporation considers their long term strategy in China. In the case of a WFOE, a foreign corporation has the option to stay long term in China simply by reinvesting in the WFOE. Alternatively, if the corporation is not successful in China, they can liquidate their assets and operations. This flexibility is not afforded in a JV when a Chinese partner may:

A. not be able to reinvest their equal share in the WFOE, or

B. veto the liquidation.

Another important advantage is the fact that a WFOE is a limited liability company, which can further shelter CanCo's assets.

Disadvantages. The biggest risk in setting up a WFOE in China is entering a new jurisdiction with a substantially different set of regulations, institutions and cultural norms. Therefore, establishing a WFOE in China can be quite cumbersome and will often require a substantial initial investment of time, money, and resources. Unlike a JV, there is no local partner that will assist with the administrative processes. From an administrative standpoint, only certain business activities are permitted under a WFOE and a WFOE cannot be incorporated to conduct general business activities. Without a Chinese partner a WFOE may be treated less favorably by Chinese officials. In addition, there are several restrictions concerning shareholders and directors in a WFOE. There must be at least one director, but a WFOE is prohibited from having corporate directors.

Joint Ventures

A JV is a form of foreign invested enterprise created through a partnership between foreign and Chinese investors, who together share the profits, losses, and management of the JV.[29] The defining feature of a JV is the contractual arrangement with the Chinese partner, which can be a company, an enterprise, or another commercial entity. A JV is an attractive option if CanCo wishes to rely on a close relationship with its partner. There are two main types of JV's: Equity Joint Ventures (EJV) and Contractual Joint Ventures (CJV). Depending on CanCo's needs, one type can be more suitable than the other.

Advantages. Given the close relationship with a local party, CanCo can benefit from making use of the Chinese partner's existing workforce and facilities. Moreover, if CanCo wishes to also distribute their products on the Chinese market in addition to manufacturing them in China, the partner's existing channels for sales and distribution, along with their local market expertise, can be of significant value.

Disadvantages. Typically, it takes between four to six months to set up a JV, which is considerably longer and implicitly more costly than setting up a WFOE. In addition, the relationship with the local partner could also be detrimental to CanCo if the two parties have conflicting interests or different management styles. Finally, in a JV, CanCo would have to divide profits with the Chinese partner. Some of these disadvantages however, can be overcome by choosing the right type of JV.

Variations of a JV

In an EJV the parties will share the profits, risks, and losses in proportion to their respective contribution to the registered capital. An advantage of an EJV however, is that it is not subject to Article 27 of the *Company Law*.[30] This Article requires that all non-monetary asset contributions, such as building, factories, IP, or proprietary technologies are subject to a valuation by a government qualified appraisal firm.[22] Therefore, the exemption from Article 27 allows the parties to negotiate the price or the pricing method of such non-monetary assets. In the event that the Chinese partner would supply the factory for the manufacturing of CanCo's products, this feature of the EJV can provide flexibility in negotiating with the price of such non-monetary asset contributions. Notwithstanding this exemption, the EJV remains a rather rigid option. EJVs are generally more regulated than CVJs.

A CJV can be established with an independent legal personality, which would provide CanCo with a shield from liability. Although subject to Article 27 of *Company Law*, a CJV allows for a more flexible business arrangement, as it does not require profit sharing to be proportional to the parties' equity contribution.[31] Consequently, the CJV option can be very beneficial if CanCo wishes to rely on their Chinese partner to provide non-equity contributions, such as undertakings to supply certain services, in exchange for a profit sharing arrangement. Finally, subject to certain conditions, the CJV would allow CanCo to recover capital investment before the termination of the CJV. This peculiar feature of the can be valuable if CanCo wishes to have a more efficient exit strategy from the CJV.[32]

---

[29] The Government of Canada, "Establishing a Joint Venture in China," The Canadian Trade Commissioner Service (14 October 2014) online.

[30] Chengwei Liu, Chinese Company and Securities Law (Netherlands: Kluwer Law International, 2012), 19.

[31] Ibid, 20.

[32] Ibid, 21.

Hong Kong Holding Company

Many investors establish their presence in China through a Hong Kong based Holdco. While Hong Kong is in China, it is, under the "one country two systems" principle, a separate legal jurisdiction. Hong Kong's legal system is based on English common law and is generally regarded as more investor-friendly and convenient than the civil law of China.[33] Setting up a holding company in Hong Kong offers many potential benefits and very little downside.

Table 1.12 below is an example of the differences between a joint venture and a WFOE in China.

Table 1.12: Joint Ventures vs. Wholly-Owned Foreign Enterprises		
	Joint Venture	**WOFE / WFOE**
Risk of Partnership	Foreign Partners - Are generally willing to forego profits to build market share or reinvest profits into the venture Chinese Partners - Usually looking for quick cash to finance [their own] expansion / pay off debts or dump excess workers Poor Corporate Governance Standards	No pressure to find the "Perfect Match" - Unless partners are perfectly compatible, the balance between advantages & disadvantages is dependent on the level of control No due diligence / investigation of Chinese Partner required - Often poor transparency & inadequate documentation - Problems often include: under reporting of tax, complicated debt & security arrangements (not arm's length), under-funding of employee social welfare obligations, incomplete title evidence, reputation
Restrictions	Fewer restrictions on project approval: - Therefore business in "Restricted" industries is possible	Business in a "Restricted Industry" is impossible More "Red Tape" to obtaining approval
Investment & Risk	Upfront investment ($$$) likely lower - For the foreign investor Potential for less [upfront] investment risk: - Transfer of existing customers & sales contracts	No risk of "inheriting baggage" - Excess workers, poor reputation with suppliers, customers, etc.

---

[33] Maarten Roos, *Chinese Commercial law: A Practical Guide* (Netherlands: Kluwer Law International, 2010), 118.

Table 1.12: Joint Ventures vs. Wholly-Owned Foreign Enterprises (*continued*)		
Level of Control & Assistance	Assistance in obtaining: - Government Approvals - Labor Recruitment - Sourcing Raw Materials - Acquiring Land & Production Facilities - Market Access - Distribution Channels Possibility of disappointment when Partner does not perform to expectations / exaggerates promises Can structure JV so that it is converted into a wholly owned sub of an offshore vehicle - Both partners hold shares offshore - Foreign investor has full control - Uncommon—Chinese investors face multiple difficulties w/ setup	No unilateral control of operations: - Significant risk of partner disputes &/or losing control - Foreign partner has power of veto over major decisions (require unanimous approval) ***EJV Only*** No risk of "Invisible" Control - Staff—transferred from Chinese Partner—retain original objectives, practices, & loyalties Likely more difficult to gain a "toehold" in the market
Labor	Workers from abroad can be employed only with special permission from the local labor authorizes, obtaining employment certification & proof of residence.	Chinese citizens cannot be hired directly by foreign companies - Requires use of Local Labor Intermediaries
Timing	Potential to "hit the ground running" sooner	More "Red Tape," Less contacts (supplier, etc.)
IP Protection	Well-developed legislature Multiple treaty ratification **VERY POOR IP ENFORCEMENT**	Less risk of infringement - No exposure of IP to a foreign company
Other Factors	Potential to acquire JV Partner in the future	

Chapter Summary

This chapter focused on how companies utilize various forms of business structures in order to take advantage of certain taxation and liability benefits they offer. These situations were explored for both home and host countries, where laws and regulations could possibly influence the formation of one structure over the other. This analysis included various business structures such as Sole Proprietorships, Partnerships, Limited Liability Companies (LLCs), Corporations, Joint Ventures, Franchises, as well as Subsidiary and Branching arrangements. Sole proprietorships are the simplest form of business organization to establish, yet offer no tax and liability benefits to the owners. Partnerships offer flow-through taxation benefits to the parties involved, which can be a major benefit to forming one of the many partnership arrangements. However, liability protection in partnerships will vary depending on General Partnership, Limited Partnership (LP), or Limited Liability Partnerships (LLP) status. A Limited Liability Company (LLC) is not a corporation, but a hybrid company that holds taxation similar to a partnership, with the liability of a corporation. A host state's corporation laws govern the specific rules and regulations that Corporations in their jurisdiction must follow, and thus will differ depending on where a company is incorporated. Equitable Joint Venture agreements are better suited for long-term strategic business arrangements while Contractual Joint Ventures are for single-project or duration-based arrangements, due to their structural differences in forming an entirely new entity versus a mere contractual agreement. Alternatives to the formation of these entities are also identified, such as the establishment of a simple resale model. One must compare the implications of the different resale models (Distributors, Dealers, and Agents), and how they may vary drastically from the laws and regulations of one host state to the next.

Identifying the proper business structure to use can be a difficult task, given the different advantages and disadvantages to each, as well as the certain barriers of home and host state laws. This chapter should be used to increase your understanding of these different business structures, and how to legally work within the rules and regulations that may act as an obstacle to establishing the business structure that is right for you.

Glossary

Affiliate: A subsidiary relationship where a company is owned by another (parent) company, with a non-controlling interest in the other (<50% voting stock).

Agency: One party (agent) acts on behalf of another party, for some specific purpose; Agent may be able to bind the principal to contracts, or restricted to merely assist a principal.

Branch: Often used in the banking industry, branches are used to expand businesses to many different locations, sometimes offering specialized services per location.

Contractual Joint Venture: Contractual agreement between two or more parties to run a business together.

Corporation: A company or group of people authorized to act as a single and separate legal entity, recognized as such in law.

Dealer: An entity that will most often buy goods from a distributor or in some instances from the supplier themselves.

Distributorship: An entity that will purchase products or entire product lines directly from the supplier, to then resell to other retailers or directly to dealers or in some instances, the end customers who wish to buy the product.

Equitable Joint Venture: A long-term arrangement between two partners. EJV partners establish a new entity, such as a corporation or a limited liability company (LLC).

Franchise: The franchisor provides a license to the franchisee, the right to use or offer specific products or services, in a certain jurisdiction, for a certain period of time; done through a contractual agreement.

General Partnership: Partnership in which partners share equally in both responsibility and liability.

Home State: A country where a company that is based in, partakes in business activities.

Host State: A country where a company that is based in another country, partakes in business activities.

Joint Venture: When a partnership is formed by contract, whose main purpose is to perform some type of business operation; Equitable or Contractual.

Limited Partnership (LP): Includes at least one partner that has unlimited legal liability (general partner), AND at least one partner whom has only limited liability (limited partner).

Limited Liability Partnership (LLP): Partnership arrangements in which ALL partners have some degree of limited liability.

Limited Liability Company (LLC): Is not a corporation, but a hybrid company that holds taxation similar to a partnership, and liability of a corporation.

Partnership: When two or more parties carry on combined business activities, with a goal to profit.

Piercing the Corporate Veil: Challenging the limited liability protection that a corporation offers to shareholders; deeming these shareholders or mind management of a corporation liable for obligations of the corporation.

Sole Proprietorship: When an individual carries on business, without adopting any other form of business organization, such as a corporation.

Subsidiary: A company that is partially owned by another company, with the controlling interest by the other (>50% voting stock).

Transfer Pricing: The prices at which services, tangible property, and intangible property are sold between related parties.

Unlimited Personal Liability: The ability for third parties to access the owner's personal assets in order to fulfill business obligations.

Wholly Owned Entity: A subsidiary relationship where a company is wholly owned by another (parent) company (100% owned).

Bibliography

Canadabusiness.ca, 2016. "Corporation, Partnership, Or Sole Proprietorship? — Canada Business Network. http://www.canadabusiness.ca/eng/page/2853/#toc-_partnerships.

Canadian Trade Commissioner Service, The. (2015, February 9). Business Taxes in China. Retrieved From: <http://www.tradecommissioner.gc.ca/eng/document.jsp?did=132269>

Cra-arc.gc.ca,. 2016. "International Transfer Pricing". http://www.cra-arc.gc.ca/E/pub/tp/ic87-2r/ic87-2r-e.html#P154_12171.

Gosselin, G. (2006, September). The Barbados-China tax treaty: its business application. Retrieved from http://www.cidel.com/pdfs/News/gosselin.pdf

Hamilton, Kevin, and Leonard MacPhee. 2016. "Patterson v. Domino's Pizza, LLC: Franchisors Are Not Vicariously Liable As "Employers" Or "Principals" For Their Franchisees' Employees' Workplace Conduct, California High Court Rules | JD Supra". *JD Supra.* http://www.jdsupra.com/legalnews/patterson-v-dominos-pizza-llc-franch-20383/.

Investopedia,. 2003. "Corporation Definition | Investopedia. Retrieved From: http://www.investopedia.com/terms/c/corporation.asp.

Investopedia,. 2003. "Subsidiary Definition | Investopedia. Retrieved From: http://www.investopedia.com/terms/s/subsidiary.asp.

LII / Legal Information Institute,. 2016. "Piercing The Corporate Veil". https://www.law.cornell.edu/wex/piercing_the_corporate_veil.

McInnes, Mitchell, Ian Kerr, and J. Anthony VanDuzer. 2011. *Managing The Law*. Toronto, ON: Pearson Canada.

Partnership Act, RSBC 1996, c 348, <http://canlii.ca/t/520vw> retrieved on 2016-02-03

Roos, Alexander. 2016. "Getting More Value From Joint Ventures | Transaction Advisors". *Transactionadvisors.Com*. https://www.transactionadvisors.com/insights/getting-more-value-joint-ventures.

SCOCAL, Patterson v. Domino's Pizza, 60 Cal.4th 474, 333 P.3d 723, 177 Cal.Rptr.3d 539, 2014 WL 4236175 (Cal.), 124 Fair Empl.Prac.Cas. (BNA) 994, 79 Cal. Comp. Cases 1111, 14 Cal. Daily Op. Serv. 10,174, 2014 Daily Journal D.A.R. 12,005 available at: (http://scocal.stanford.edu/opinion/patterson-v-dominos-pizza-34358) (last visited Thursday February 18, 2016).

Sullivan, Arthur Steven M. Sheffrin *(2003). Economics: Principles in action*. Upper Saddle River, New Jersey 07458: Pearson Prentice Hall, 2003).

Taylor, Crystal. 2016. "Branch Vs. Subsidiary, Which Is Right For You?" Blog. *Carrying On Business In Canada For Non-Residents*. http://www.millerthomson.com/en/blog/carrying-on-business-in-canada-for-non/branch-vs-subsidiary-which-is-right-for-you.

Contracts

CHAPTER **2**

Learning Objectives

After reading this chapter, you will have an understanding of:

1. What is involved in international contract negotiations
2. The principles of contract law
3. What legal doctrines can be used pre-contractually as guarantees
4. Outcomes and remedies from contractual non-performance
5. The standard clauses that are included and how they decrease liability on behalf of the parties

International Contract Law

The Role of Contracts in Private International Law

Commercial contracts are an everyday part of commerce, but an international element adds significance. The creation of an international contract is more complex and riskier than a contract between two parties residing in the same country with the same culture. In cross-border transactions there are different legal systems, societal values, cultural differences, and governments that create different challenges for businesses. The role of a contract in an international commercial transaction is of particular importance with respect to the matters described below.

Cultural Differences

Cultural differences have an impact on business dealings and the resulting contract. Different cultures view contracts and their significance differently. North American culture tends to take a more legalistic view of contracts and views the contract as a final and binding agreement under which the parties' rights and duties are firm and should be adhered to. Asian cultures tend to view the contract as a living, breathing document that reflects the relationship and leans towards working matters out. A part of the learning process should be dedicated to mutually agreeing on how the parties will handle a disagreement or situation especially since in many Asian countries, a signed contract is regarded as the beginning point where the contract can be renegotiated if certain conditions change. The idea of a constantly re-worked and changing contract is unimaginable to American companies that expect full and complete performance of the honored document.

Culture also relates to nations' different perspectives on litigation proceedings. In North America there is a common view that going to court is among the first steps of a dispute, whereas a contracting party in the Middle East may prefer to keep the matter private through mediation, arbitration, or a settlement among the two sides.

Provisions in an international contract need to be drafted to reflect different cultural norms and legal systems. The difficulty is simultaneously retaining the cultural and legal matters of importance to both parties when often these are in conflict. Legalese is problematic when the contract needs to be translated into a different language. A contract which reflects the cultural expectations of both parties is more likely to be honored and performed to the satisfaction of both parties.

Balance of Power

The general rule of contract law is "freedom to contract." In other words, no one is forced into a contract. A presumption in law is that parties have equal bargaining power. In reality this is far from the truth; one party usually has a stronger position than the other. This author has dealt with some of the largest multi-national companies in the world, and the scenario is usually a standard form take-it-or-leave-it agreement. Several provisions in the contract highly favor the stronger, larger company while restricting the rights of the other company through exclusion, indemnity, and similar clauses.

Who Serves First? There is significance as to which party drafts the contract. The balance of power may shift towards the party who drafts the contract first. Even if the terms were negotiated, the drafting party often inserts clauses they find favorable. On the other hand, the party who drafts the contract first usually has higher legal costs.

Enforcement: The enforcement of one-sided contracts varies by country. Certain courts and arbitration bodies may refuse to enforce unreasonable terms that are unusual, onerous, or unconscionable. The common law concept of *contra proferentum* uses a strict interpretation against the party who drafted the terms, since that party had the chance to draft a clear and unambiguous contract.

Enforcement and Remedies

International contracts are more difficult to enforce. Most countries require agreements to be in writing, or at least certain types, and will not recognize verbal contracts. Some secular law countries do not enforce certain interest provisions of agreements. The laws that apply to the interpretation and validity of the contract and the place where disputes will be heard are most important. Such matters need to be decided at the time of the contract's formation to alleviate and reduce uncertainty and enforceability issues. The parties need to select a mutually agreeable remedy so it is clear what to expect if performance fails.

Principles of International Contract Law

International commercial contract law is utilized in daily business transactions all over the world, and all follow similar guidelines even though there is no singular body that regulates contractual rules or protocols included within a contract for the sale of goods or services. Although there are a number of differences among the cultures around the world, certain principles of contract law are shared and grown alongside customary international business standards. The similarities and universal customs are what make transactions between a civil and common law state possible, because the largest difference is usually found in the style of the contract rather than what it includes. However, over time the international community has developed a system of laws and rules to be applied in preference of local laws in transactions between parties located in different countries. (See below). The purpose of adopting uniform, international laws is to ensure the parties of a cross border transaction are subject to the same set of rules even though their own local laws may differ. It is, however, unwise to rely on international law to interpret a contract as it leads to unexpected and possibly unfavorable results. Business is about risk management and predictability. Even though international treaties and organizations exist, in practice it is more common for the parties to a contract to choose the rules between themselves.

History of International Law

Lex mercatoria means "Law of Merchants" and speaks to business customs or trade practices created by business people from around the world that help stimulate international transactions. Law of Merchants was a body of commercial law used by merchants throughout Europe during the medieval period. In today's world, there is a minor existence of the *lex mercatoria*, which includes certain transnational trade usages and commercial customs recognized internationally by the mercantile community. It extends to certain international conventions and even national laws relating to international economic relations.[1]

Prior to drafting a proper contract the parties should be familiar with international contract law and able to decide their source of law between three possible choices—international contract law, and need to choose the source of law. The parties must choose between international contract law, the national laws of each party, or the **lex mercatoria**, or a possible combination of the three.

International Organizations and Treaties

International Chamber of Commerce

While there is no current body that regulates international business law, the International Chamber of Commerce (ICC) is adopted almost universally, which demonstrates the movement towards more unified customary international business law. The original group was comprised of five countries, and the ICC's main focus in the 1920s was to settle war debts and reparations. Today, the organization has gained thousands of companies as members in more than 120 countries and covers a wide variety of specializations within international business transactions. In 1933, in the midst of the Great Depression, the ICC issued the *Uniform Customs and Practice for Documentary Credits* (a first version) that is still seen in our banks to finance trade all over the world. **Incoterms**, standard trade definitions, also made an appearance through the ICC and they have been responsible for updating the terms as necessary throughout the years. Eventually, the United Nations recognized the ICC with an award of the highest level consultative status allowing the organization to bring together private sector representatives and UN special agencies to continually advocate for open multilateral trading systems[2]. The International Chamber of Commerce most importantly has aided in the development of international treaties and various conventions to merge international business law. An example of this is demonstrated in the *Convention on Contracts for the International Sale of Goods* (CISG), ratified by the United Nations.

---

[1] Ole Lando, "The *Lex Mercatoria* in International Commercial Arbitration," 34 *International & Comparative Law Quarterly 747* (1985).

[2] The International Chamber of Commerce, "The merchants of peace," (2014) http://www.iccwbo.org/about-icc/history/

Convention on Contracts for the International Sale of Goods

The Convention on Contracts for the International Sale of Goods (CISG) is highly regarded as the best effort to unite commercial law in the large international scope. The ultimate goal of CISG is to abolish barriers to international trade, especially ones concerning choice of law, through the creation of current and practical rules that outline the obligations and rights of parties entering international sales contracts. CISG came from two other international agreements regarding the formation of contracts and international sale of goods, and these conventions supported the creation of UNIDROIT Principles of International Commercial Contracts. All of these resolutions were stepping stones to ensure that countries would follow uniform rules for international sales—and once the CISG was finalized and approved, contracting countries became accountable to the set standards.

The CISG prevails over global sales contracts if the circumstances satisfy two elements: both parties are within contracting countries and that private international law leads to the application of the law of a Contracting State[3]. The convention will regulate sales between parties that are not from the same country and it also deals with exchanging offers and acceptance of a final contract. The CISG contains the rules governing the formation of contracts and outlines the the various obligations of each party such as delivery, price, proper documentations, and transferring rights of the goods. This section also has attainable remedies in the case of a contract breach[4]. A pivotal theme of the convention is the autonomy of the parties to enter into contracts with each other for the sale of international goods, meaning that either party may eliminate any CISG rule or entirely remove the applicability of the CISG to instead be governed by another law. It must be noted, however, that the CISG does not apply to every situation between the contracting parties—such as the validity of a contract—and the appropriate law must take up those issues.

VLT. Middle East LLC v. Trenzas y Cables de Acero PSC SL[5]

Facts:

A case seen by the Cantabria Provincial High Court (Spain) in 2013 included a buyer from Dubai and seller from Spain providing steel cable. In January of 2008, the buyer placed two new orders that were accepted by the other party and signed accordingly to the CISG agreement. Payment was to be accepted by either open credit telegraphic transfer or by letter of credit 90 days from the bill of lading date. The seller immediately sent two *pro forma invoices* (stating their commitment to deliver the products to the buyer at a set price). However, the court of first instance, prior to the appeal, noted that these invoices held no contractual effectiveness since the original agreement would be established by the purchase orders.

Issue:

The appellate court disagreed with the previous statement since the wording of the seller's statement recognizes that a change in the documentary credits has been implied and should be held. The seller's representative sent a document to inform the buyer that they have a credit of US$ 600,000, which will not cover the entire cost of US$ 1,860,000, but a complementary "letter of credit or letter of agreement from [the buyer] may do." Article 29 of CISG states that "a party may be precluded by his conduct from asserting such a provision to the extent that the other party has relied on that conduct," which the provincial court held was applicable to the case at hand. The buyer being granted an irrevocable and unconditional guarantee from their Swiss bank for an amount of only US$ 930,000 (half the contracted amount)—and this is the event that led the court to point towards article 29.

---

[3] LawTeacher, "Cases of International Sale Contracts Contract Law Essay," *United Kingdom* (2013).

[4] United Nations Commission on International Trade Law, "United Nations Convention on Contracts for the International Sale of Goods" (Vienna, 1980) (CISG), (2016) http://www.uncitral.org/uncitral/en/uncitral_texts/sale_goods/1980CISG.html

[5] VSL Middle East LLC v. Trenzas y Cables de Acero PSC SL http://cisgw3.law.pace.edu/cases/130709s4.html

The buyer had not completed its obligation by paying half of the agreed upon price, a breach against the contract itself and the CISG convention (articles 53 and 54). The company was to guarantee US$ 1,860,000 through the agreed options, and their failure to do this action became a fundamental breach of the contract meaning they could not invoke any breach to the obligations of the seller. This concept aligns with article 80 within the CISG stating that "a party may not rely on a failure of the other party to perform when the failure was cause by the first party's act or omission".

Decision:

The court dismissed the appeal from VSL Middle East LLC.

Reasons:

VSL Middle East LLC did not ensure the full amount of the transaction successfully which frustrated the purpose of the contract. The agreement clearly stipulated that although the buyer had a credit amount available, they were still required to pay the remainder through a letter of credit or letter of agreement. Those documents are a guarantee to the seller that payment will come through for the goods and must be respected.

Ethical Considerations 2.1

Walmart and the Bangladesh Factory Disaster

S. Prakash Sethi, "The World of Wal-Mart," *Carnegie Council: for Ethics in International Affairs,*

May 8, 2013, http://www.carnegiecouncil.org/publications/ethics_online/0081

Multinational corporations are defined by their subsidiaries and sister companies located around the globe. The way those companies operate relates largely to the parent organization which sets corporate standards and controls for its overseas factories and labor force. Many countries have significantly lower safety standards for their workers and their workplace than there would be in a company on North American soil. However, the appeal of offshore production is the reduction in price to create the same goods or services. Should a North American company ignore unsafe and hazardous work sites for the financial gain to their business?

In 2012, a clothing factory for US and European brands located in Dhaka, Bangladesh was engulfed by a fire that killed 111 and injured another 150 due to inadequate fire safety measures and exit systems. This factory was producing clothing for large retailers such as Wal-Mart and Sears who then denied any connection between themselves and the Bangladesh factory. In fact, the 2012 fire was not the first garment factory disaster in the country's history—fires and building collapses had been prevalent since 2000. Major retailers operating in Bangladesh have not pulled through on their promise to increase building safety and eliminate fire hazards, which means that working conditions are unlikely to change.

The minimum wage for clothing industry workers in Bangladesh is $37 a month (one of the lowest amounts in the world). Is it unethical for multinational corporations to move production into a country that pays their employees less than the minimum wage of the home country? What if the $37/month can supplement an employee's standard of living quite well in the host country—should the parent company discontinue business relations with them?

Pre-Contractual Liability

1. Promissory Estoppel

A common theme among Western nations, especially North American contracting parties, is to conduct a transaction under good faith principles. There is no legal duty to perform in good faith; however, under certain systems (such as US common law) negotiations may be terminated from bad faith bargaining and thus not be liable for the other party's legal expenses. One major exception exists, which is *reliance theory*—also known as **promissory estoppel**. Claiming promissory estoppel can be used when one party's promise during negotiations is relied upon and the wrong can only be prevented if a court enforces the promise that was originally made.

In the case of *McIntosh v. Murphy*, 496 P. 2d 177—Haw: Supreme Court 1970[6], George Murphy verbally offered a job in Honolulu to Dick McIntosh who resided in Los Angeles at the time. The agreement was to begin 30 days from their initial phone call and Murphy offered a one-year contract that McIntosh accepted. The new employee moved his belongings to Hawaii and turned down other employment opportunities for this job. After only two and a half months, the employer discharged McIntosh for not being able to close deals. The employee sued for damages since the contract was for one year, but the defendant (employer) claimed that the contract went against the Statute of Frauds and should be void. The court decided that since the employee relied on the promise of a job for an entire year the employer should be estopped from enacting the Statute of Frauds.

The doctrine of promissory estoppel has been used as both a sword and a shield in different nations. England maintains the traditional use of estoppel, which is to protect an individual's reliance on promises made during negotiations—used in defense as a shield. On the other hand, the United States transformed an estoppel claim to wield it as a sword and be able to push through an independent claim for relief rather than just protection from the damaging act. Although the American Law Institute did not pull back the reigns of promissory estoppel in 1981, each state may develop the doctrine independently as they would with their common law of contracts[7]. The sword vs. shield dichotomy does not require a nation to pick which side it will take because even England and the United States have had cases where their opinions have changed depending on the case at hand, but it is useful to have the knowledge that if you are a contracting party with foreign nation X, they (for the most part) will handle estoppel claims in either a sword or shield manner.

2. Culpa in Contrahendo (Fault in Conclusion of a Contract)

Rudolf von Jhering, German jurist and founder of a modern sociological and historical school of law, wrote an article in 1861 that addressed the need to have recoverable damages against a party that conducts themselves with bad faith during the negotiations period. The impacts of the article have reached further than German law concepts and have spread throughout the world for nations to debate this issue. Within Jhering's statements the doctrine of *culpa in contrahendo* (fault in conclusion of a contract) made its first appearance and it was brought upon by his discussion on Germany's flawed common law system in the late 19th century. At the time, the validity of the contract was seriously questioned at the onset of any small matter. There was no restitution for parties that relied on complete performance of a contract and did not receive it—there was even a concern that the offeror of the transaction would die and the other party still had no system of aid for the uncompleted tasks. Jhering noted that the "blameworthy"

---

[6] McIntosh v. Murphy, 496 P. 2d 177 – Haw: Supreme Court 1970 http://scholar.google.ca/scholar_case?case=30188576914
83243719&q=mcintosh+v.+murphy+1970&hl=en&as_sdt=2006&as_vis=1

[7] Charles Calleros, "Cause, Consideration, Promissory Estoppel, and Promises Under Deed: What Our Students Should Know about Enforcement of Promises in a Historical and International Context," *2 Chi.-Kent J. International & Comp. L. Vol XIII* (n.d.)

party does not need to be held liable to the innocent party, but he proposed that the courts could restore their *status quo* by approving reliance damages—this defines *culpa in contrahendo*[8].

The doctrine quickly became associated with fair dealings and good faith bargaining principles and is believed to infiltrate all phases of contract law and controls all legal transactions. Two parties that come together in the hopes of forming a business relationship place a large amount of trust in each other to perform according to the contract, no matter the outcome. Therefore, to ensure that parties feel secure in entering contracts, *culpa in contrahendo* exists to keep partners liable for carelessly forming expectations of a contract that in reality they know cannot be realized. A clear example is one where a guest walks into a restaurant and is injured due to unsafe conditions of the location—the owner assumes responsibility for not fulfilling their duty of maintaining a safe space for the restaurant guests.

It is common for international literature to group many European countries together when explaining their legal views; however, every country operates differently and should be explored separately. The chart below outlines seven European countries and their view on pre-contractual liability as it pertains to one general case.

Table 2.1: Pre-Contractual Liability Case[9]	
Joel and Marina conduct negotiations on the sale of a piece of land that Marina owns and Joel would like to build a house on. Marina believes she is the sole owner of the property. The two agree to sign the sales contract on March 2. However, on March 1 Marina finds that the land property is an inheritance from her father and is also jointly owned by her and her two other sisters who do not agree to the sale. Marina thus does not sign the contract. Joel has already incurred negotiation expenses such as real estate agent fees, travel tickets and agreements with a professional architect. Does Marina have any liability to Joel?	
Austria	Marina has no contractual liability. The risk falls entirely on the buyer and the contract was not conducted in bad faith.
Finland	Land sales are held to a high standard; thus the liability falls on Marina under the basis of *culpa in contrahendo*. Marina will cover Joel's costs.
France	No contract had been concluded so compensation may only be through tort. Fault, harm and causation must be proved to have Marina cover expenses.
Germany	Marina is not liable; 1) Negotiations were terminated for a good reason, 2) And the contract must be presented in a specific land property form to be valid. Only exceptional circumstances will grant reliance damages of *culpa in contrahendo*.
Greece	Marina's behavior is at fault and subject to pre-contractual liability. Joel was right to assume that Marina solely owned the property and begin expenses.
Portugal	Marina is liable to Joel and should pay all incurred fees, even though the fault was unintentional. Pre-contractual liability can also give way to negligence claims.
Scotland	Marina's actions were not intentional; thus the act is misrepresentation leading to negligence. In Scotland, a proximally close relationship between parties would more likely find liability applied.

---

[8] Friedrich Kessler and Edith Fine, "Culpa in Contrahendo, Bargaining in Good Faith, and Freedom of Contract: A Comparative Study," 77Harv.L.Rev. (1963/64).

[9] John Cartwright and Martijn Hesselink, *Precontractual Liability in European Private Law* (Cambridge University Press, 2008), 93-112.

Culpa in contrahendo is much like promissory estoppel on the line of good faith dealings; however, promissory estoppel may be enacted prior to the formation (or lack thereof) of a contract and protects the parties who rely on the communicated expectations. The former compensates those that have been injured by the other party and returns the innocent individual back to the position they were in prior to the wrongdoing. Dutch law attempts to avoid the possibility of an offense with bad faith deals by making it mandatory for parties to disclose pertinent information, ...as well as conducting necessary diligence, seeking investigations, and refraining from negotiating with third parties. In American law, these ideas are mainly seen in pre-contractual negotiations in the form of misrepresentation, firm offers, negligence, and estoppel cases. The famous case of Texaco v. Pennzoil illustrates the danger of not clearly stating if a contract exists or not. Texaco and Pennzoil entered into "agreements in principle." Customs dictated that "agreements in principle" are not a contract, but a jury disagreed and found a "meeting of the minds" and held Texaco liable for the tort of contractual interference. A jury awarded compensatory damages of $7.53 billion and $3 billion in punitive damages. The result was the bankruptcy of Texaco.

Texaco Inc. v. Pennzoil Co. 729 S.W.2d 768 (Tex. App. 1987)[10]

Facts:

As background to *Texaco Inc. v. Pennzoil Co. (1987)*, Getty Oil and Pennzoil entered a merger agreement to have Pennzoil acquire Getty. The two companies signed a **Memorandum of Agreement** for each respective board to approve and then issued a press release on the matter. Texaco then made its own offer to Getty Oil to which Getty retracted the agreement with Pennzoil and accepted Texaco's terms. Pennzoil sued Texaco for tortious interference of contract, but Texaco rebutted with the fact that a Memorandum of Agreement was not a binding document as it was still in the process of being approved by Getty's board of directors. The memorandum would have expired if it were not approved. Pennzoil then noted that the contract was in fact binding because the memorandum was executed by a group of parties that controlled the majority of outstanding Getty shares. The jury stated their verdict, which was then appealed by Texaco.

Issue:

The first statement questions whether the party's intent to be bound by the contract is one of fact for the fact finder or a question of law for the judge. The question alludes to asking whether such a document is to be treated as a legal contract both within and outside of the court. Also, it must be determined to what extent should the terms of the contract be conclusive to create enforceability of the contract.

Decision:

The court decided that determining whether parties intended to be bound by the contract was not a question of the law, but rather one for the fact finder and the terms of that contract must be determinable to a reasonable degree for it to be enforceable. There was a clear breach of the contract and damages were to be awarded to Pennzoil for the interference of their contract.

Reasons:

The intent behind Pennzoil and Getty's deal had substantial evidence that they were to be bound upon approval of their board members. The Memorandum of Agreement and press release are two ways in which the intent was proved. There is in fact a difference between a transaction being subject to certain requirements and contracts being formed on condition of the completion of those requirements. Nonetheless, even though there was clear language of reservation, Getty and Pennzoil's intent to be contractually bound is to be evaluated as a question of fact determined by the situation of the case—as in the wording of agreements change case by case and should be treated individually.

---

[10] *Texaco Inc. v. Pennzoil Co., 729 S.W.2d 768 (Tex. App. 1987)*. https://supreme.justia.com/cases/federal/us/481/1/case.html and http://www.lawnix.com/cases/texaco-pennzoil.html

3. Pre-Contractual Instruments

Prior to a formal agreement, companies will often provide documents that are not contracts, often referred to as **comfort instruments**. Letters of intent ("LOI"), memorandums of understanding ("MOUs"), letters of assurance or the most common types of pre-contractual instruments. Their purpose is to encourage contractual obligations or to be used as a way to include a third party into business transactions. The issue is the enforceability of such pre-contractual instruments and whether or not they are enforceable agreements. If they have no binding and legal effect what is the purpose in signing them? They serve a business purpose and convey parties' intentions. Further, signing them and then failing to enter into a more formal binding agreement could have detrimental harm to one's reputation. Whether or not they are binding contracts depends not so much on what they are called but what they say. Such comfort instruments can carry some moral weight and cultural importance. Failing to honor a comfort letter could cause word to spread that the organization is unreliable and should not be trusted to conduct proper business with another party. Also, while the letters are currently not legally bound to their obligation it is possible that if the wording indicated promissory intent in the future tense, then a court will treat the letter as a legal obligation.

An interesting example comes from *Banque Brussels Lambert SA v. Australian National Industries Ltd.* A bank in Brussels gave a line of credit to Spedley Security Ltd. (SSL) but asked for a guarantee from their parent company (Australian National Industries Ltd.) and when they could not secure one, they sent a comfort letter to the bank with two relevant terms[11]:

1. "We acknowledge that the terms and conditions of the arrangements have been accepted with our knowledge and consent and state that it would not be our intention to reduce our shareholding in Spedley Holdings Limited from the current level of 45% during the currency of this facility. We would, however, provide your bank with ninety (90) days notice of any subsequent decisions taken by us to dispose of this shareholding, and furthermore we acknowledge that, should any such notice be served on your bank, you reserve the right to call for the repayment of all outstanding loans within thirty (30) days.

2. We take this opportunity to confirm that it is our practice to ensure that our affiliate, Spedley Securities Limited, will at all times be in a position to meet its financial obligations as they fall due. These financial obligations include repayment of all loans made by your bank under the arrangements mentioned in this letter."

Years following the line of credit extension, the Australian parent firm sold its existing shares in SSL without notifying the Brussels Bank, which meant that the bank could not collect its debt so they brought on a lawsuit for breaching a contract. The Australian company tried to claim that they were free from liability due to the comfort letter's unenforceability; however, the Supreme Court of New South Wales struck this down and held that such letters must be interpreted through the language used and the surrounding circumstances. In this case the bank sought strong language from the Australian firm and rejected a draft that expressed the letter was not a guarantee. Furthermore, the organization was made aware that the bank considered comfort letters as binding obligations. In the end the court stated that there was in fact clear intention and language present making the Australian parent company liable for their subsidiary's debts.

Obviously the clearest and simplest method to avoid confusion as to whether a comfort instrument is binding or not, a contract or not, is to specifically state that it is not a binding contractual agreement, and specifically state no binding obligations are created. The recent trend is to have a comfort

---

[11] *Banque Brussels Lambert SA v. Australian National Industries Ltd. (1989),* 21 N.S.W.L.R. 502 (S.C.).

instrument that has binding provisions and non-binding provisions. The titles, techniques and language are where binding versus nonbinding contracts differ the most and a nonbinding instrument can carry quite a bit of moral or political weight. The first note is to ensure that both sides of the agreement confirm that they are aware of the status of contract—be it binding or not. Next, the terminology of the contract could provide guidance as to whether parties intended a nonbinding contract, thus ambiguity should be avoided. Examples of terms that are identified as binding versus their nonbinding counterparts are outlined in the chart below.

Table 2.2: Binding vs. Nonbinding Agreement Terms[12]	
Binding Terms	**Nonbinding Terms**
"Treaty" / "Agreement"	"Memorandum of Understanding"
"Parties"	"Participants"
"Shall" / "Agree" / "Undertake"	"Should" / "Intend" / "Expect"
"Entry into force"	"Is to come into operation" / "activities are to commence"
"Done at" / "Concluded at"	*Avoid jurat (a sworn in statement) clauses
Reference to "equal authenticity"	Can include different languages of the document
Provides disclaimer that the document is binding	Provides disclaimer that the document is nonbinding

As with many other aspects of international law, countries treat nonbinding contracts in differing ways from one another. An example can be provided through the United States where their practice is to not automatically consider a Memorandum of Understanding to be a nonbinding document as it is commonly associated. Also in the United States, the use of the term "will" does not always mean that the obligation is not legally binding when looked at on the international level.

4. Non-Performance Excuses

There could come a time when a contracting party notices that they are in a situation where a portion of the contract becomes difficult or even impossible to fulfill and the party decides that it is necessary to breach the contract. Courts do not easily allow parties to evade their contractual obligation even if their inability was not their fault; nonetheless, the claim may be made to address overriding events that were out of their control, made the obligations impossible or financially unreasonable. The reason for strict compliance to the contract is that entering into such an agreement should prompt the parties to discuss risks and mitigate foreseeable hardships. The ideal is not always reflected in reality and roadblocks occur unexpectedly, thus the courts have a system in place to determine whether non-performance may be permitted or not.

Frustration in History

The doctrine of frustration—as it is known to modern society—developed from English contract law around the 1860s. Even earlier in 1647, cases such as *Paradine v. Jane* EWHC KB J5 (1647)[13] demonstrated the courts' approach to frustration that generally was not in favor of the individual especially when the Crown had involvement. In this historic case the defendant (Jane) was ordered to continue paying rent to the landowner (plaintiff), even though the land had been invaded by Royalist forces—a situation that would warrant frustration easily in the modern era. Frustration had not truly

---

[12] U.S. Department of State, "Guidance on Non-Binding Documents," (2009), http://www.state.gov/s/l/treaty/guidance/
[13] *Paradine v. Jane* EWHC KB J5 (1647) http://www.bailii.org/ew/cases/EWHC/KB/1647/J5.html

formulated until 1863 with the case of *Taylor v. Caldwell*[14] where two parties agreed to utilize a music hall for concert performances. After the contract was signed, but before the performances began, the hall burned down and Judge Blackburn held that the contract was frustrated as obligations were impossible to perform. Such historic cases shine a light on how the current doctrine was formed and has been shaped over time with new situations always challenging the courts to make a legally fair decision.

Frustration

Frustration has different forms:

1. Frustration of Purpose
2. Impossibility
   a. Destruction of the Subject Matter
   b. Supervening Illegality
3. Commercial Impracticability

1. Frustration of Purpose

Frustration of purpose occurs when the principal purpose of the contract has been compromised or no longer exists; there has been a radical alteration, subsequent to the making of the contract, in the fundamental conditions under which the contract was to have been performed so that its continued performance becomes physically or commercially impossible or utterly impractical.[15] A contract is frustrated when its basic object is no longer capable of attainment.

The leading case is the famous 1903 case of Krell vs Henry[16] which arose around the coronation of King Edward VII. The defendant entered into a contract to rent a flat for the purpose of watching the coronation procession of King Edward VII. The coronation was cancelled. The court ruled specifically that the contract was not frustrated for impossibility, as the flat could have been leased, but that the cancellation of the coronation frustrated the purpose for which both parties had originally contracted. An issue that could arise is whether to allow changes or adjustments of the contract or to only include a strict rule of choosing full performance or termination on the basis of frustration. Many elements are considered including reasonableness, good faith and practicality.

2. Impossibility

There are a few categories of frustration due to impossibility. Impossibility means the contract cannot be performed under any reasonable circumstances. Impossibility is not hardship or difficulty. The most common example of impossibility is an act of God/nature. The general test of impossibility is that no party could perform what is required under the contract.

a. Destruction of the Subject Matter

The subject matter of the contract is destroyed due to circumstances beyond the control of the parties and such destruction was not foreseeable. Foreseeability does not mean possibility and is often

---

[14] *Taylor v. Caldwell* EWHC QB J1 (1863) http://www.bailii.org/ew/cases/EWHC/QB/1863/J1.html

[15] *Dryden Construction Co. v. Ontario (Hydro-Electric Power Commission)* (1958), 14 D.L.R. (2d) 702 (Ont. C.A.); affirmed (1960), 1960 CarswellOnt 64 (S.C.C.).

[16] *Krell v. Henry* [1903] 2 KB 740

weighed against the industry and subject matter of the contract. It is foreseeable that a mine may collapse. Most often this is referred to as acts of God or acts of nature.

It is important to draft contracts to be specific, especially with supply contracts. A contract that states that Farmer Brown will provide 2000 bushels of apples will have difficulty arguing frustration if his crop is destroyed by fire. Farmer Brown will have to buy the apples elsewhere and supply them. However, if the contract specifies that Farmer Brown will provide 2000 bushels of apples from his northern fields, then circumstances beyond his control made delivery impossible.

b. Supervening Illegality

This is when a subsequent event arising after the formation of a contract or a change in law renders it illegal to perform the contract. The change of law must be one that parties did not foresee and for which no express or implied provision is made in the contract. In addition, the illegality must not be temporary or minor in nature when the contract is viewed as a whole. Subsequent laws, domestic or foreign, or subsequent judicial or administrative action such as expropriation which prevents performance of the contract will be considered frustration. Governments will often declare that doing business with certain countries is illegal. Examples are South Africa when they held the policy of apartheid or Iraq after their invasion of Kuwait.

3. Commercial Impracticability

Impracticability excuses a party from a specific duty outlined in a contract when that duty has become unreasonably difficult, excessively burdensome, unbearably difficult, or extremely expensive for the party to perform. This doctrine is not recognized in all countries but is in the United States. In Canada, economic loss less than frustration is an insufficient basis for invoking the doctrine of frustration if the contract has simply become more onerous, expensive, or less remunerative or beneficial. This contractual excuse is narrow and has been codified in the Uniform Commercial Code and in the CISG. As a general rule a contract cannot be frustrated merely because it creates a hardship. However, the courts have had difficulty determining what is unfeasibly difficult or expensive, an unreasonable expense, or an extreme hardship. Compared to impossibility, which is an objective test, impracticability is a subjective test. Courts look for the following:

1. An occurrence of an unforeseen circumstance or condition.
2. The unforeseen condition must render the duty unreasonably difficult or expensive to perform.
3. The extreme expense or difficulty could not have been anticipated by either party to the contract.

In applying the subjective test, the courts will ask if the cost of performing the contract is so expensive that performance is rendered unrealistic and senseless and threatens the viability of the business itself. An example would be if performance would render a company bankrupt. The subjectivity allows the court flexibility in the assessment.

Additional characteristics of commercial impracticability that courts look to are unforeseen events and market fluctuations. If a party is claiming non-performance but could foresee the potential detrimental event, they will not be awarded a release from their obligations. Occurrences that could be anticipated should be mitigated from the onset of the contract and prepared for prior to beginning the transaction. An event that has the potential to truly disrupt a party's work should be noted in the contract, explicitly stating their excusal in case such an activity occurs. Market fluctuations such as inflation, shortages, or sharp price changes can in fact be estimated, mostly, by the contracting parties and thus should be taken into consideration during the negotiations of contractual obligations. Past cases that have attempted to claim commercial impracticability due to price drops of resources have been unsuccessful in court, especially considering market changes are generally due to a number of positive or negative economic stimuli and catalysts over a period of time before the fluctuation becomes noticeable in everyday business transactions.

Table 2.3: Common Frustrating Events	
Destruction of the Subject Matter	• An item or necessary building has been destroyed. Neither party is at fault. • The event renders performance impossible. • Within the Sale of Goods Act 1979; goods that parish (at no one's fault) before the risk transfers to the buyer renders the agreement void. • However, if the contract does not *specify* goods, the act cannot apply.
Supervening Illegality	• A contract is frustrated if a passed law directly renders fundamental contracting principles illegal. • i.e. War could make certain trading acts illegal; changes in the law such as making certain materials in a building illegal.
Incapacity or Death	• Generally for personal service performance; frustration occurs if a person/group is unavailable (death, illness…etc.). • Does not apply to services that may be accomplished by other individuals.

Frustration Around the World

Nations around the world decide if their law will adopt a claim to frustration in its broadest scope, or with tight restrictions so as to retain the sanctity of a contract. Prior to the 19th century, Roman law did not recognize frustration unless there was absolute and objective impossibility—a condition not easily met. German courts moved to a "social" interpretation of contracts in the 19th century, which most notably includes the ability to adjust contract duties if frustration is found to render the tasks impossible. In the United States, the doctrine of frustration continues to be a vague theory and courts are found to be reluctant in granting relief to parties unable to perform. The concept went through a number of revisions and definitions throughout the 19th century and it is currently no clearer. In the United States, most courts stand by the black and white rules regarding termination of a contract, but scholars hope that they will review their viewpoints in the Uniform Commercial Code and Second Restatement of Contracts to include contractual obligation adjustments.

Glidden Co. v. Hellenic Lines, Ltd., 275 F. 2d 253—Court of Appeals, 2nd Circuit (1960)[17]

Facts:

Glidden, an American manufacturing company conducted a contract between four charter parties to transport ilmenite from India to America by waterway. All agreements included a **force majeure** clause and section 4 of the **Carriage of Goods Act** that would excuse their obligations if an "act of war" were to occur or any causes that are without fault on the parties. The charter parties also included the route by which the goods may travel: "via Suez Canal or Cape of Good Hope, or Panama Canal," and would arrive at a safe US port that the charterer declares before passing Gibraltar. Once the Canal closed, the charterer declined to perform the obligations.

---

[17] *Glidden Co. v. Hellenic Lines, Ltd.*, 275 F. 2d 253 – Court of Appeals, 2nd Circuit (1960), http://www.cisg.law.pace.edu/cisg/biblio/rapsomanikas.html#131

Issue:

The contract was seen as frustrated from the charter parties' points of view as their route of choice was closed. If the closure took place while the goods were on route, would it be reasonable that the charterer changes course and adds additional travel time on to their schedule? Additionally, the clause that included disclosing what route they were taking and which port they would enter was typed in later on printed contracts making the court question whether the carrier originally assumed the risk of route closures or if they were attempting to avoid future litigation and disputes.

Decision:

The trial court held that the charter parties frustrated their contracts; however, the United States Court of Appeals noted that the parties were obligated to continue by any one of the alternate routes established by the negotiations. Therefore, neither Section 4 of the Carriage of Goods Act nor the force majeure clause was applicable to the case at hand.

Reasons:

The contract clearly covered that the goods could take a number of routes to the option of the individual charterer and more so, they could decide on their route while traveling to the US port—a reasonable request by the American company. Additionally, the court regarded the late addition to the contract as ambiguous, thus turning to their intended negotiations. This led to the conclusion that the carrier was reasonably attempting to mitigate their risk.

Force Majeure (Unforeseen Circumstance)

A **force majeure** stems from non-performance, as it is a legal instrument that parties should include in their contracts—domestic and international—to excuse their obligations if an extraordinary event were to take place. Force majeure clauses will be covered in more detail later in the chapter, but it is important to note all of the options that a company has under extreme circumstances when performance is rendered impossible.

Material Adverse Change

Typically, merger and acquisition contracts will include a **material adverse change (MAC)** clause that allows the buyer to leave the deal or renegotiate terms of the agreement if an "unforeseen material adverse business or economic change affecting the target company occurs between executing the acquisition agreement and closing the transaction."[18] Such provisions are seriously negotiated as it also provides the seller with a way to qualify warranties so immaterial disturbances are ignored. Buyers seek to have the most flexible MAC clause to exit a deal with ease, while sellers take the opposite view pushing for narrow terms to have the transaction close at agreed-upon prices. To be successful in the international stage, an understanding of different courts and their understanding of MAC clauses needs to be developed prior to negotiations among companies or nations. Belgian law, for example, has recently introduced MAC clauses and their trend seems to align slightly with the United States as parties will use the claim to renegotiate a contract, instead of termination—however if the goal is to be protected from a specific event, then a separate clause should be utilized rather than solely a MAC clause.

---

[18] Jeffrey Rothschild et al., "Drafting Material Adverse Change Clauses," *Financier Worldwide's 2008 International M&A*, (2008)

In a downturned economy (a recession), it is observed that fewer mergers and acquisitions take place and credit markets become stricter to businesses and individuals. Thus, MAC clauses tend to shift in favor of buyers, as they now possess the power to be granted higher flexibility with transaction terminations. As well, if the buyer has certain pending concerns those must be addressed in a specific and unique MAC clause or in a closing condition. No matter the economy of the day or either party's bargaining power, material adverse change instruments to terminate transactions are important and should be crafted with precision.

Contractual Clauses

Most contracts have what are commonly referred to as general clauses or boilerplate clauses. These are clauses that are standard in most contracts. Some clauses create an understanding between partners that in the event of a disagreement they will proceed in a certain manner, while others are meant to limit liability if the parties need to go through litigation. There are also important factors to consider such as the difference in currency between countries and deciding which party is responsible for applicable taxes such as tariffs and duties. The following section will outline a number of boilerplate clauses that should be considered while negotiating an international contract.

Governing Law

There are two types of of governing law:

1. Choice of Law
2. Choice of Forum

1. Choice of Law

The first items that should be discussed in a legal contract are the laws of each nation and which jurisdiction will handle disputes. The governing body will use its laws to oversee the contract and the relationship between the two parties; by choosing a governing law, they can save time and money during a dispute by not having to fight over which should be the governing law. What makes this clause so vital on the international stage is that many large multinational corporations that are doing business around the world have connections to a number of locations and including all of those laws is unrealistic[19]. This is discussed in greater detail in the chapter on dispute resolution.

2. Choice of Forum (Jurisdiction)

Deciding on a jurisdiction sets up how a dispute will be handled, as it is almost inevitable that issues will emerge through the contract. If the parties would rather resolve their issue through arbitration, then an alternate dispute resolution clause should be drafted into the agreement. Otherwise, the parties can rely on the courts and have a named country take jurisdiction over any disagreements that transpire.

---

[19] Herbert Smith Freehills LLP, *"Governing Law" and "Jurisdiction" Clauses* (2008).

Other Clauses

A. Language

Contracting with different foreign countries may mean contracting in a different language or carefully creating multiple versions of the agreement to satisfy all parties. A language clause in an international contract sets the governing language of the transaction. If two languages must be incorporated into the contract because it is required by one of the country's laws, or it is to create security in the rights and obligations outlined therein, then the agreed upon governing language prevails over other versions—especially in the event of a discrepancy in interpretation of the terms. If this is not established, then international regulations such as UNIDROIT Principles will apply to handle the situation. Article 7.7 provides that "where a contract is drawn up in two or more language versions…in the case of discrepancies between versions, a preference for the interpretation according to a version in which the contract was originally drawn up" (UNIDROIT Principles, 2012).

If there are no restrictions set out by a nation's laws regarding contract language, the parties could look to what is used in the actual operations or any other factors they deem applicable. The main aspect to note is that the chosen language should fall parallel to the language of the governing law, which can control future problems such as an English court asked to decide on a Russian contract. It would save time and money if the contract was in the court's language or two contracts were created—one for each language.

B. Currency

A currency clause within an international agreement runs along the same logic as a language clause, in that there needs to be no confusion as to what currency will be used. Deciding a currency should aim to be in the benefit of both parties, however exchange rates fluctuate constantly and could change the situation if they are floating rather than pegged to another currency like the USD. Once the currency is agreed upon the transaction price needs to be clearly indicated by writing it in both figures and words so there is no question on amounts. If by chance the parties do not agree on a set price during the negotiations, there must be a clause explaining the method by which they will determine the cost to avoid discrepancies later. Negotiating these terms allows the parties to perform their obligations without fear of not getting paid in the way that was agreed upon by the two sides.

C. Forum or Venue

Jurisdiction often gets confused with **forum clauses** and **venue clauses**. A forum selection clause chooses which court the trial will occur in, whereas a venue selection clause decides the geographic location of the trial[20]. A venue selection clause can be used to limit the possibility of receiving a lawsuit in certain countries or specific geographic area within the country. Equally, a party may wish to narrow lawsuits to a particular federal court so as to avoid multiple litigations with different local laws.

D. Taxes

The most common form of taxes that will need to be discussed between parties is import charges—customs obligations. These responsibilities include value added taxes, excise taxes, duties, tariffs, penalties, third party brokerage fees and government assessed costs for the imported good. A good being imported or exported must also go through charges for its classification, compliance screening and

---

[20] Robert Mongole, "Defining Forum and Venue in the American Court System," *The Seasteading Institute,* June 13, 2012, http://www.seasteading.org/2012/06/defining-forum-and-venue-in-the-american-court-system/

verification to manage differences between quoted import charges and the actual costs[21]. The contract should outline which party is responsible for the various taxes and import charges especially since certain countries will tag on post-delivery costs, which may not be specified in the original contract (fines, penalties, etc.). A decision for the contracting parties would be to decide who holds the obligation to pay any charges imposed on the goods by tax and customs officials once they enter the country, which will save the parties an unnecessary dispute at the time of the event.

E. Finance

A finance clause will take care of a few items such as title finance transactions, security interests and publicity of the transaction (the means by which information must be disclosed to the appropriate authorities). Title finance such as finance repossessions and leases could possess potential issues with the title finance creditor's rights when terminating the agreement (e.g. license) and attempting to recover the equipment. A contract can clearly govern retention of title in the case of insolvency, even if assets are situated across nations. Security interests on the other hand could pose a conflict as nations have different laws to govern the interests—an issue for large organizations that hold assets in many locations. The contracting parties need to decide on a jurisdiction that will best control their interests. It is suggested that security interests, title finance, and other property transfers are governed by the contract's governing law and that property assets are governed by the law of their location. If the parties did not discuss and agree upon a choice of law, security agreements should be under the law of the habitual residence of the lender[22].

Lastly, parties to a contract will have to look into the publicity of title finance transactions and decide the filing statutes they are subject to. The location of the asset will most likely serve as the governing law and if they are under English or American-based filing statutes, the parties will be required to file in the place of incorporation as well as where the asset is located. The American system treats title finance transactions as security interests and thus requires those to be publicized as well, unlike in English law.

F. Transportation

In a constantly globalizing world, companies are required to keep up faster than ever with the competition, and they should be ready to enter new markets in foreign nations to realize the economies of scale before other companies within the industry do so themselves. Remaining competitive in the global landscape requires strategic import, export and transportation programs. The transportation clause of an international sale of goods contract should set up base rates and trade routes that will move the goods efficiently therefore benefitting all parties. An important aspect to consider in the transportation program is to create a limited number of key carriers (those that directly handle the delivery) so that the goods are secure through their movement. A number of items should be included within the transportation clause, a few of which are outlined below[23]:

- Risk transfer: at what point will the carrier/forwarder have discharged its responsibilities, and is that clearly stipulated with an **incoterm**?
- Sub-contracting: define the entitlement for sub-contracting/sub-carriers and ask for references for any sub-carriers to be used.
- Methods and routes of transportation: define all possible routes and alternatives available.

---

[21] Maxime Mekki-Kaddache & Wanissa Nemsi, Customs Provisions in International Business Agreements (2015).

[22] Philip R. Wood, *Conflict of Laws and International Finance*, (2007).

[23] CME Transportation Best Practices- Logistics Consultants PF Collins International Trade Services 11

- Description of goods and packing: provide carrier with detailed product descriptions including any special instructions for packaging, perishable goods, etc. and define responsibilities for crating, packaging, materials handling, etc.
- Dangerous goods: if applicable, identify any respective responsibilities for handling dangerous goods. Ensure that carriers are certified/trained in handling dangerous goods.
- Inspection of goods: reserve the right to inspect goods and correct insufficient packaging.
- Trade regulations: identify responsibilities for duties, taxes, possible fines, expenses or losses resulting from illegal or incorrect carrier operations.
- Freight forwarder and carrier liability: define and identify maximum liability.
- Delay and consequential losses: identify maximum liability timeframes.
- Notice of loss or damage: identify an acceptable procedure.
- Failure to notify: establish a clearly defined notification process.

G. Force Majeure

The force majeure clause should be drafted with time sensitivity to ensure that reasonable measures were taken to limit or even prevent the effects of the accident. A strike, for example, could delay the arrival of goods but should not slow the payment between parties. Another added aspect is a contingency plan or a contractual backup plan if performance is impossible so that benefit of a particular business relationship does not need to be sacrificed entirely. All of the non-performance clauses serve a way to limit liabilities—a concept that is paramount in law and the reason for most clauses within a contract.

A force majeure clause should specify the events that will allow this clause to be put into effect alongside a more general statement to cover anything that is not listed specifically. If obligations are interrupted, a force majeure clause can extend the contract by a period of time equal to how long the interruption lasted. Nonetheless, if the event lasts for 180 days[24], then the court may grant a notice of termination.

Parties should also agree on how they will proceed with their transaction if such activity were to happen, as well as remedies available to them. Force majeure events cover a large range such as acts of nature (such as extreme weather conditions—tornados, floods…etc), war or riots, industrial strikes, embargoes or the unavailability of goods. Usually the clause will group together omitted events by providing *"any other event or circumstance beyond the parties' control"*[25] to have their rights and obligations clear for both parties.

H. Counterparts

A counterpart clause is most often utilized when the contracting parties are implementing separate copies of the contract. This is most pertinent in large-scale business transactions that involve multiple parties that may not all be present at the time of signing the contract, creating no single agreement with all signatures. Such a contract clause is also common in property sales where the only page exchanged is the signature portion and it is kept by each party or any transaction where one copy of the contract cannot be signed by all parties on the signing date. Parties may also ask for a counterpart clause to ensure that each copy of the agreement is recognized as the original one for regulatory, tax or administrative purposes.

---

[24] World Bank, "Sample Force Majeure Clauses," *Public-Private Partnership in Infrastructure Resource Center* (March 10, 2015), http://ppp.worldbank.org/public-private-partnership/ppp-overview/practical-tools/checklists-and-risk-matrices/force-majeure-checklist/sample-clauses

[25] Ince & Co. International LLP, *International Trade, Force Majeure Clauses: Their Role in Sales Contracts*, (2011).

I. CISG Application

Clearly indicate that a contract is to follow the rules and regulations of the Convention on Contracts for the International Sale of Goods so that this will be held by the court in the event of a dispute or contract disagreement. If the contract is not subject to CISG rules, then a judge or arbitrator must rely on the agreement itself and determine what is reasonable under the circumstances. The benefit of allowing the transaction to fall under CISG rules is that if a clause was missed during negotiations, the regulations set up by the convention generally have a provision to govern the missing aspect, thereby again saving the parties time and money by not having to go through formal litigation.

Limitations Period

Any international agreement should include a statute of limitation for any claims that either of the parties will want to bring in the future. One issue is what defines a reasonable period of time and when should that period begin. All of these questions are answered in the *Convention on the Limitation Period in the International Sale of Goods ("Limitation Convention")* sponsored by the United Nations, which provides clear standard rules regarding the amount of time by which a party must bring forward a claim under an international deal. The convention outlines the following provisions within its articles[26]:

- *Application of the Convention*: what parties will be considered under the convention and which sales it does not apply to.
- *Duration and Commencement of the Limitation Period*: beginning with the standard period as four years, then outlining other situations where the limitation period may not be so clear-cut.
- *Cessation and Extension of the Limitation Period*: stating that the timeframe may be terminated by agreement of both parties, or once legal or arbitral action officially begins.
- *Modification of the Limitation Period by the Parties*: the debtor may extend the existing limitation period through written declaration.
- *General Limit of the Limitation Period*: no matter the type of sale, a period should not exceed ten years.
- *Consequences of the Expiration of the Limitation Period:* parties may rely on the expiration of the clause so that any claim brought afterwards is not entitled to restitution.
- *Calculation of the Period:* the expiration date should match the commencement date unless that falls on a holiday, in which case the period will expire on the day following that official holiday.
- *International Effect:* outlines the ways in which these provisions may be implemented in international transactions, declarations to apply the convention (or not) and most importantly, the fact that the convention does not override pre-existing international agreements concerned with the same matters.

The convention was signed in 1974, but later amended in 1980 to align with the international sales contract convention of the same year. As of early 2016, there are 30 member countries that have ratified the *Convention on the Limitation Period in the International Sale of Goods* including the United States, but not Canada as it has yet to accede the agreement[27]. Canada's reluctance has been linked to their decision to also not accede to the *Convention on Contracts for the International Sale of Goods* prior to December 2015[28]. Now that Canada is a part of this convention the international limitations period agreement may also be adopted. The convention recognizes a standard four-year limitation period that applies to most claims brought before the governing court. However, it is important to understand limitation periods in countries that are not members to the

---

[26] The Convention on the Limitation Period in the International Sale of Goods, V.11-84228 (February 2012).

[27] A. Claire Cutler, *Canadian Foreign Policy and International Economic Regimes* (Vancouver: UBC Press, 2007).

[28] United Nations Commission on International Trade Law, *Status: United Nations Convention on Contracts for the International Sale of Goods (Vienna, 1980)*, 2016, http://www.uncitral.org/uncitral/en/uncitral_texts/sale_goods/1980CISG_status.html

convention so that both parties may agree on a reasonable timeframe to bring forth claims during the negotiations. Japan, for instance, has two limitation periods that provide relief from their agreement obligations. The first is a ten-year limitation period that applies to civil obligations while the other is five years for commercial obligations. Either of Japan's timeframes may be interrupted by an **intervening event**, which is an act that happens *after* the initial tort of negligence and causes injury to a victim. Such events will generally cause the original **tortfeasor** to be cleared of any liability. Contracting parties must also keep in mind that certain time limitations are meant to extinguish obligations and cannot be interrupted by those intervening events. Such knowledge demonstrates the power of being familiar with other nation's contract laws, thereby creating smoother negotiations and stronger partnerships.

Intellectual Property and Licensing

Intellectual property (IP) is a "creation of the intellect that is owned by an individual or an organization which can then choose to share it freely or to control its use in certain ways" (International Chamber of Commerce, 2012) and may range from ordinary objects like computers or creative items such as music. Different countries have varying methods to protect an individual's IP rights through copyrights, patents, trademarks, trade secrets and the like. To protect the sanctity of IP, contracting parties must come to an understanding of who owns the IP and how it will be used in various nations. The agreement serves as protection in the event that there is a breach of IP rights. For example, trade secrets are common in restaurant chains and in making the decision to take the chain global the company must ensure their contracts limit unwanted leaks. Certain jurisdictions do not have specific protective legislation and are weaker in protecting trade secrets and other forms of IP; however, Article 39 of the Trade-Related Aspects of Intellectual Property Rights sets up sanctions against procurement or use of IP and in select cases misappropriation of trade secrets can be handled as a criminal offense[29].

A contract may include an international license agreement so as to give the other party permission to use property owned by someone else. This contract includes a number of important provisions; however, initially the owner must ensure they have exclusive property rights with copyrights, patents and trademarks. Below are some important clauses to be included:

1. *Approval of Licensed Goods*: An agreement which allows you to schedule periods to inspect products that are created from a license. This allows you to be sure that the quality is consistent, maintaining the value of products created from the license.

2. *Royalties and Accounting*: Challenges for paying of royalties include currency conversion, local taxes or tariffs, and any transaction fees for methods of payment such as wire transfers.

3. *Jurisdiction*: refers to which court has the right to preside over a lawsuit, including any alleged breaches in IP rights. For business transactions in China, consider where most of the business is conducted as Chinese courts have a different legal system and do not recognize American or British laws.

4. *Choice of Law:* Parties may choose which laws they are bound by in the agreement, and the licensee will generally prefer the law of their own country or jurisdiction to interpret the contract.

5. *Arbitration:* An alternative for dispute resolution instead of a lawsuit, allows the parties to enter into discussions and hopefully negotiate but can also be bound by the decisions of the arbiter if a consensus cannot be reached.

---

[29] International Chamber of Commerce, *Intellectual Property Basics* (2012)

6. *Foreign Registrations:* While American laws may protect intellectual property, it may still be valuable to register the patent in any other countries where the patent will be used, distributed, or manufactured.

Dispute Resolution

For most contracts it is not a matter of "if" a dispute will occur, but "when" one will need to be taken care of. There are a number of options that parties may take advantage of—the two most common being litigation and arbitration. The importance of a dispute resolution clause is of the same concept as having insurance on your car—being protected in case an accident occurs. At the time of a disagreement the two parties will be fully aware of the process and which remedies are accessible. This significantly reduces internal litigation time and the cost of the proceedings[30]. As an efficient way to settle disputes, many contracting parties are turning to alternative methods of dispute resolution or ADR, such as mediation and arbitration, since it is less expensive and faster than traditional court systems. The dispute resolution clause should clearly define the governing law for the arbitration, where it will take place, the language of the arbitration and number of arbitrators involved. With these tools at hand a dispute has the potential to be handled with ease and place less pressure on the relationship between the parties.

Chapter Summary

A regulatory body for international law does not exist, but there are conventions in place that set standards and rules for contracting parties to following during negotiations and in the event of a disagreement. When creating a contract with companies from other countries, it is important to discuss in what language the agreements will be formulated, which jurisdiction will serve to resolve any disputes, and the cultural, legal and political landscapes of the opposing nation.

The International Chamber of Commerce (ICC) sets out to regulate international trade and finance—creating incoterms, which better outlined delivery methods and risk transferring in the process. The ICC also led to the creation of the Convention on Contracts for the International Sale of Goods (CISG) that further harmonized global transactions and decreased the risk of creating an international contract.

During negotiations it is important that the parties act in good faith, as the doctrine of *culpa in contrahendo* would suggest, or face the liability of their actions. Promissory estoppel can be claimed if the other party made a promise during negotiations that was not realized in the end and it caused the plaintiff hardship through expenses or lost opportunities due to their reliance on the initial information. Furthermore, in the scope of pre-contractual instruments there are documents such as letters of credit, memorandums of understanding and a bill of lading that serve to guarantee assurance of liability on a party until their obligations are filled. Some countries treat these agreements as unenforceable as they lack traditional contractual intent; however, it is important to exactly understand the commitment required from the instruments so a lawsuit is avoided.

Once the contract is set in place, the next potential issue is that of non-performance either by the fault of another or by nature itself. An event that ruins the intended purpose of a contract may cause frustration which is a way to terminate a contract legally. To ensure that the liability does not fall on

---

[30] Catherine Walsh, "Nail down these two international contract clauses to save yourself future legal headaches," Global Trade Take-Aways (September 15, 2015).

either party, a force majeure clause is added which stipulates that all extraordinary occurrences could not have been reasonably mitigated and the contract should either be halted until further notice or frustrated and terminated.

Every clause added to an international contract is meant to limit liabilities and help ease the process of dispute resolution. Laying out as much detail during the negotiations will make for a smoother business journey out on the international stage. One of the most important aspects of international contract law is to remember that every nation has different customs that should be respected; pushing one method of the law onto another party creates more tension than harmony.

[31] Eun-Joo Min, "Alternative Dispute-Resolution Procedures: International View," *Intellectual Property Management in Health and Agriculture Innovation: A Handbook of Best Practices*, eds. A Krattiger, RT Mahoney, L Nelsen, et al. (Oxford, U.K.:MIHR and Davis, U.S.A.: PIPRA, 2007).

[32] International Contracts, *Language Clause in International Contracts* (n.d.)

[33] International Contracts Staff, "Key Clauses in the International Sale Contract," *International Contracts* (2012).

[34] World Bank, "Sample Force Majeure Clauses," *Public-Private Partnership in Infrastructure Resource Center* (March 10, 2015), http://ppp.worldbank.org/public-private-partnership/ppp-overview/practical-tools/checklists-and-risk-matrices/force-majeure-checklist/sample-clauses

[35] Ince & Co. International LLP, *International Trade, Force Majeure Clauses: Their Role in Sales Contracts*, (2011).

Glossary

Comfort Instruments: Documents meant to encourage contractual obligations or used as a way to include a third party into business transactions.

Commercial Impracticability: An obligation is impossible when it is not practicable, and it is not practicable when the only way to get it done is through excessive and unreasonable cost.

Culpa in Contrahendo: Good faith bargaining; duty to negotiate fairly.

Force Majeure: An extraordinary event such as act of nature, war or riots, industrial strikes, embargoes or the unavailability of goods.

Frustration of Purpose: An unforeseen event occurs that destroys the purpose of the performance that was to be conducted.

Incoterms: Standard pre-defined trade terms used in international commercial transactions.

Intervening Event: An act that happens *after* the initial tort of negligence and causes injury to a victim.

Jurisdiction: Legal authority to administer the law and justice.

Legalese: Language based on legal terms.

Lex Mercatoria: "Law of merchants"; the business customs or trade practices created by business people from around the world that help stimulate international transactions.

Material Adverse Change: A claim under non-performance that allows a party an exit strategy when the contact has materially changed.

Memorandum of Agreement (MOA): Document describing a cooperative relationship between two parties that meet an agreed upon objective and the details of that relationship.

Non-Performance: A portion of the contract becomes difficult or even impossible to fulfill and the contract is in turn breached.

Promissory Estoppel: A legal doctrine used when a party reasonably relied upon the actions of another so much so that if the actions are not taken, the party will in turn suffer.

Tortfeasor: The party that commits the tortious event or action.

CHAPTER **3**

Dispute Resolution

Learning Objectives

After reading this chapter, you will have an understanding of:

1. The various dispute resolution alternatives
2. The difference between Mediation, Arbitration, and Litigation
3. The processes of Arbitration and Litigation
4. How to determine jurisdiction
5. How various components of litigation affect jurisdiction and procedure

International business disputes can be very complex. There is risk associated with any negotiation or business transaction, be it domestic or international. When dealing with international business transactions, however, there are proportionately more associated risks and potential problems compared to a domestic deal. There is always the risk of default, insolvency, language, and cultural differences, among other things. To mitigate these issues, some form of **dispute resolution** must be selected, whether it be **mediation, arbitration, or litigation**. As this chapter goes on, we will discuss the advantages and disadvantages of each alternative, highlighting examples of each and factors that contribute to how the dispute resolution plays out.

Consider the following situation: A Canadian company sells oil and gas equipment to a Russian buyer. The most common risks are:

1. Payment default,
2. Misdelivery of goods,
3. Damage to goods en route, or
4. Equipment malfunctions.

Many questions and ambiguities are present in a dispute of this nature. Who is held responsible if there are damaged goods? Will the dispute be settled with mediation, arbitration, or litigation? Under whose **jurisdiction** does the dispute fall? Was there a **governing form** specified? Where is the closest connection to the dispute? These questions, among many others, will be discussed and explained throughout this chapter.

Alternative Dispute Resolution (ADR)

Alternative dispute resolution is oftentimes the preferred method of resolving an international commercial business dispute, as most parties wish to **settle** these disputes outside of court. In essence, Alternative Dispute Resolution is "any method of resolving disputes other than by litigation."[1] There are many advantages to ADR. It provides added privacy to a dispute, is generally cheaper, and is much more efficient. Unlike litigation (settling a dispute in a courtroom), which can be an expensive, long, and drawn out process, Alternative Dispute Resolution can frequently present a more inexpensive and timely solution. **Negotiation** is the resolution of a dispute through discussions. Negotiation(s) serve as the foundation for ADR, as it opens the floor for conversation and settlement. However, in order to move forward with ADR, both parties must expressly agree and submit to it. While there are several forms of ADR, the two main pillars are mediation and arbitration. Occasionally, negotiation itself may also be viewed as a distinct form of ADR.

1. Mediation

Of the three main dispute resolution alternatives, mediation is the least formal, or least "extreme." It serves as a private, *non-binding* process where a **mediator** is selected to help negotiate a **settlement** between the parties. The selected mediator acts as a middleman or a go-between for the two parties. They have a duty to find a mutually acceptable solution, as opposed to ruling in favor of one side or the other. Mediation, therefore, is essentially negotiation with a neutral third party.

Resolutions arising from mediation are often amicable and mutually beneficial in nature. Mediation provides a good middle ground between traditional one-on-one negotiation and formalized dispute resolution mechanisms such as arbitration or litigation. It provides more structure and formality than negotiation, but is far more timely, cost efficient, and amicable than arbitration or litigation. If the mediation process is deemed insufficient or is simply not working, both parties involved retain the right to employ the more binding and formal processes of arbitration or litigation.

In the context of an international commercial business dispute, mediation is likely too informal and non-binding to resolve most issues. It may, however, be preferred where the parties have an ongoing relationship and wish to maintain it going forward. Conversely, mediation's non-binding nature makes it less preferred where the transaction is considered a one-off, as there is little incentive for the parties to comply with the agreed resolution. If parties can agree on moving forward with mediation, due to its amicable and informal nature, it can be beneficial for future business transactions and the overall business relationship if a solution can be reached.

Advantages	Disadvantages
1. Relatively inexpensive	1. Settlement not always reached
2. Relatively quicker than arbitration or litigation	2. Inequity of negotiating power
3. Amicable solutions; preserves business relationships	3. Non-binding decisions

---

[1] Legal Information Institute, "Alternative Dispute Resolution", Cornell University Law School, https://www.law.cornell.edu/lii/terms/documentation.

2. Arbitration

Arbitration is a significantly more formalized dispute resolution alternative than mediation. Arbitration results in binding decisions that are enforceable by **courts**. Arbitration is tied to the courts necessarily, since decisions and **injunctions** granted in arbitration proceedings can only be enforced by the courts. However, arbitration remains less formal than traditional litigation, as the parties have the flexibility to choose their own procedural rules. This, coupled with the inherent privacy of arbitration, makes it an attractive alternative. In traditional litigation, court cases and associated information is public, and thus privacy is not an option. Arbitration, in contrast, is a private process and does not require the release of information to the public.

A. Arbitration Covenants/Characteristics:

Consent:[2] Arbitration is premised *entirely* on consent, and both parties must **expressly consent** to arbitration for it to move forward. If there is a **contract** between the parties, often there will be an **arbitration clause** included in the dispute resolution provisions of the contract. The arbitration clause can address things such as choice of law, governing form, forum selection, etc.

Neutrality: Neutrality of arbitration is of the utmost importance. It allows for an even playing field, where neither party has an advantage at the outset of the dispute. Arbitrative neutrality comes in many forms. One of them is the choice of the arbitrator.

The parties can agree on one single arbitrator together, or can agree to a three-member **tribunal**. A three-member tribunal serves to avoid bias and **deadlock**. Arbitrators can be lawyers, industry experts, or other individuals knowledgeable on the subject matter.

Steps in Selecting Three-member Tribunal:

1. Each party selects one arbitrator
2. Arbitrators convene
3. Arbitrators select the third (presiding) arbitrator

In addition to neutral arbitrators, arbitration also allows the parties to select a country where the dispute will be heard. This is called "**the seat of arbitration**." Parties will often select a "neutral" country to avoid extrajudicial pressures and ensure a level playing field.

Confidentiality: Unlike litigation, where records of the proceedings are publicly available due to the long-standing principle of "open court," arbitration is a private, consent-driven process that does not require parties to publicly disclose any documents or records—or the arbitral decision itself.

Finality: With a few exceptions, discussed in the "Arbitral Enforcement" section below, arbitration results usually are a final and binding decision that cannot be **appealed**. Indeed, parties to a contract will often agree from the outset that any potential arbitration will be final and binding without a right to appeal. In some circumstances, finality of arbitration proceedings may even be legislated. For instance, under the Federal Arbitration Act, which was enacted on February 12, 1925, parties concede the right to appeal in court an arbitrator's decision.

Arbitration Bodies

1. *Ad Hoc* **arbitration** and
2. **Institutional arbitration**.

---

[2] World Intellectual Property Association, "What is Arbitration?", WIPO, http://www.wipo.int/amc/en/arbitration/what-is-arb.html

Depending on the type of arbitration, different rules will apply to the conduct of the arbitration and the appointment of an **arbitral tribunal** (made up of one or more arbitrators).

1. ***Ad Hoc:*** In *ad hoc* arbitration, parties are required to set everything up on their own, so they will "therefore have to determine all aspects of the arbitration themselves—for example, the number of arbitrators, appointing those arbitrators, the applicable law, and the procedure for conducting the arbitration."[3]

2. ***Institutional:*** In institutional arbitration, the parties conduct their arbitration "under the auspices" of an established **arbitration body**. In this case, rather than setting up the arbitration on their own, the parties take advantage of established rules, procedures, and administrative resources offered by an arbitration body. Specifically, each arbitration body will typically offer detailed **rules of procedure** that the parties can adopt for their arbitration. In addition, arbitration bodies usually maintain a roster of highly respected arbitrators in various fields of specialty (*e.g.* construction, investment, etc.) to assist the parties in selecting their tribunal. Finally, in practical terms, an award issued under the auspices of a respected arbitration body may carry more weight, which may aid in its enforcement.

   The parties involved in the arbitration have the freedom to select a neutral and convenient arbitration body to hear their dispute. Oftentimes, the arbitration body is specified at the outset in the contract between the two parties. It is not uncommon for the parties to "shop around" due to the differences in procedural rules and arbitrator rosters offered by different arbitration bodies. Similarly, the choice of an arbitration body can often be a contentious point during the negotiation of the arbitration clause in the underlying contract. Note, however, that in certain domestic arbitrations, national legislation may require the parties to conduct their arbitration under the auspices of a national arbitration body.

The table below lists some of the more prominent arbitration bodies, along with their country of origin:

Location	Arbitration Body
Australia	*Australian Center for International Arbitration (ACICA)*
Austria	*Vienna International Arbitration Center (VIAC)*
Canada	ICC Canada Arbitration
China	*Beijing Arbitration Commission (BAC)*
France	*Association Française d'Arbitrage (AFA)* ICC International Court of Arbitration
Germany	German Institute of Arbitration
Sweden	Arbitration Institute of the Stockholm Chamber of Commerce (SCC)
Switzerland	*Swiss Chambers Arbitration Institute*
United States	American Arbitration Association
United Kingdom	London Court of International Arbitration
Global	*World Intellectual Property Organization (WIPO) Arbitration and Mediation Center*

---

[3] Out-Law.com, "Institutional vs. 'ad hoc' arbitration", (last updated August, 2011), http://www.out-law.com/en/topics/projects–construction/international-arbitration/institutional-vs-ad-hoc-arbitration/

Arbitration bodies usually charge significant fees for their services and follow certain administrative rules the parties must comply with. As a result, institutional arbitration tends to be more expensive and time consuming than ad hoc arbitration.

A major advantage of arbitration, especially in international context, is that the awards are binding, final and susceptible of enforcement anywhere in the world.[1] Though it may sound paradoxical, arbitration awards are in fact more readily recognized in courts of various countries than foreign court awards. This is in large part due to the **New York Convention**, which provides for "the enforcement of arbitration agreements and for the recognition and enforcement of awards in all contracting states."[4] With over [150] countries in the world being parties to the New York Convention, and only few countries recognizing each other's court awards, arbitration often presents the only feasible dispute resolution mechanism in the international context.

Arbitration Clauses

An arbitration clause that is included at the outset of a contract will often stipulate that should a dispute arise between the parties involved in the contract, binding and compulsory arbitration is agreed upon as the sole dispute resolution mechanism.

Sample Clauses

The various arbitration bodies discussed in the previous section will often develop and publish model arbitration clauses that parties can insert in their agreements, should they choose to use them for future dispute resolution. Some of these model clauses include:

- From the *International Court of Arbitration* (part of the International Chamber of Commerce):
  - "All disputes... shall be finally settled under the Rules of Arbitration... by one or more arbitrators appointed in accordance with the said rules."[5]
- From the *Chartered Institute of Arbitrators*
  - "Any dispute... shall be determined by... a single arbitrator to be agreed [on or] failing agreement within 14 days, after [a party has given written request to concur], by an arbitrator... appointed by the President or a Vice President of the Chartered Institute of Arbitrators."[6]

Arbitration clauses serve to avoid uncertainty and ambiguity surrounding the **legal action** to be taken should a dispute occur in the future.

---

[4] International Chamber of Commerce, "Arbitration", (Recognition and Enforcement of Awards), http://www.iccwbo.org/products-and-services/arbitration-and-adr/arbitration/

[5] International Chamber of Commerce, "Standard ICC Arbitration Clauses", http://www.iccwbo.org/products-and-services/arbitration-and-adr/arbitration/standard-icc-arbitration-clauses/

[6] Chartered Institute of Arbitrators, (CIArb), "Dispute Resolution Clauses", "'Catch All' Dispute Resolution Clause", http://www.ciarb.org/docs/default-source/das/contract-clause.pdf?sfvrsn=4

DirecTV, Inc. v. Imburgia et al. (2015)[7]

Facts:

In the case of *DirecTV v. Imburgia (2015)* the Supreme Court of the United States had to make a ruling about whether or not an arbitration clause included in an agreement between DirecTV and its customers was enforceable or not. A class action lawsuit was filed by Amy Imburgia, stating that "DirecTV had improperly charged early termination fees to its customers."[8] It was originally decided in the California Court of Appeal that the arbitration agreement was not enforceable due to state law that held some arbitration clauses unenforceable.

Issue:

The California Court of Appeal and the Supreme Court of the United States had differing viewpoints on this case. The California court of appeal ruled that the arbitration clause is unenforceable due to applicable California Law, while the Supreme Court of the United States claimed that the Federal Arbitration Act takes precedence and is therefore the governing law.

Decision:

It was decided that the arbitration agreement must be upheld and enforced.

Reasons:

The Supreme Court of the United States' decision to uphold the arbitration clause is due to the fact that State Law is preempted by the Federal Arbitration Act and therefore the arbitration clause must be enforced, and the decision was reversed.

Enforcement of Arbitral Awards

A cornerstone to the enforcement of arbitration awards is the New York Convention, an international convention created in June 1959. In essence, the convention obligates contracting states to recognize and enforce arbitration awards issued in other contracting states, as if they were judgments of their own domestic courts. Without the convention, it may be prohibitively difficult, if not impossible, to enforce an arbitral award in a foreign state, as it would have no status under the domestic law of that foreign state. A very large number of countries have adopted the New York Convention in order to facilitate international trade and business.

The New York Convention thus effectively provides a blanket enforcement right for arbitral awards. Accordingly, the main issue with the convention is what it *doesn't* cover. There are only a select few conditions/**defenses** under which the enforcement of an award under the New York Convention can be successfully resisted:

1. *If one of the parties to the arbitration agreement was incapacitated in some way according to their local laws*
2. *If the arbitration agreement itself was not valid under the governing law defined in the agreement*
3. *If parties are not given proper notice for the arbitration or not able to present their arguments*

---

[7] SUPREME COURT, DirecTV, INC. v. Imburgia ET AL., CERTIORARI TO THE COURT OF APPEAL OF CALIFORNIA, SECOND APPELATE DISTRICT, DIVISION ONE., No. 14-462., Argued October 6, 2015 – Decided December 14, 2015., Available at: (http://www.supremecourt.gov/opinions/15pdf/14-462_2co3.pdf) (Last visited Thursday March 3, 2016).

[8] "DIRECTV, Inc. v. Imburgia." *Oyez.* Chicago-Kent College of Law at Illinois Tech, n.d. Mar 3, 2016. <https://www.oyez.org/cases/2015/14-462>

4. *If the ultimate award is granted on grounds not originally raised in the submission for arbitration, or if it ultimately went beyond the scope of the arbitration. This is limited somewhat as an award may be enforced on the matters that were brought for arbitration, with only the inappropriate awards not being enforced*

5. *If the tribunal for arbitration did not match the agreement of the parties, or if there was no agreement, the prevailing law of the jurisdiction where the hearing occurred*

6. *If the award has been set aside, suspended, or is not yet binding on the parties (subject to being in the country where the arbitration occurred, or according to the arbitration agreement)*

7. *If the substance of the award could not be resolved by arbitration*

8. *If it would be against public policy to enforce the award*

As can be seen from the above exceptions, the majority of defenses available under the New York Convention reflect the fundamental principle that underlies arbitration and ADR in general: consent.

Advantages	Disadvantages
1. Freedom to choose tribunal	1. More costly than one would think
2. Ability to have the dispute adjudicated by specialists in the field	2. Little opportunity for appeal
3. Relatively faster than litigation	
4. Confidentiality	
5. Enforceability (especially in international context)	

Ethical Considerations 3.1

Countermeasures Draft

Kristen Boon, "The Responsibility of International Organizations: The Controversy Over Countermeasures," *Opinio Juris*, (November 19, 2009), http://opiniojuris.org/2009/11/19/the-responsibility-of-international-organizations-the-controversy-over-countermeasures/

In 2009, a draft article for the responsibility of International Organizations stirred some controversy—especially with regards to the use of countermeasures. Countermeasures are separate from lawful sanctions and are actions taken in response to a negative stimulus (action) that would contravene international law if not for the prior wrongful act. The draft stipulated that prior to the final draft, non-performance was the only countermeasure available under international state obligations.

The controversy stems from the absence of a common enforcement body in the international playing field. Countermeasures in international law are largely self-enforced, which adds the doubt that multinationals are utilizing any type of responsible international institutions. The fear then transpires into the encouragement of retaliation measures, coercion, subjectivity and the interruption of existing international organizations.

Do countermeasures have a place in international law, or should the regulation come from member states of a reputable International Organization? If matters are taken into the company's hands is an element of fairness lacking since there is no centralized standard?

Culpa in Contrahendo

Friedrich Kessler & Edith Fine, "Culpa in Contrahendo, Bargaining in Good Faith, and Freedom of Contract: A Comparative Study," (1964), *Faculty Scholarship Series*, Paper 2724, 406

http://www.trans-lex.org/125100/#head_21

http://digitalcommons.law.yale.edu/cgi/viewcontent.cgi?article=3735&context=fss_papers

The concept of *Culpa in Contrahendo* was first noted by German article writer—Jhering—in 1861. It states that damages should be provided by the party that could be blamed for preventing the validity and perfection during negotiations of a contract. In today's civil law code, *Culpa in Contrahendo* is fixed to the doctrine of good faith dealings and fairness amongst all legal transactions.

The case of *Ultramares Corp v. Touche* demonstrates that while good faith bargaining is an important aspect of contract law, the courts continue to be reluctant when increasing the breadth of liability when the party misrepresented to made economic use of the information—furthermore when the misrepresentor should have been aware that may occur.

Should courts be stricter on parties that fraudulently misrepresent contracting partners? Are damages enough of an award to the plaintiff? Would a monetary restitution revert the loss of an economically or financially important deal for the company?

3. Litigation

Litigation is the third alternative for dispute resolution, in addition to mediation and arbitration. It refers to "the rules and practices involved in resolving disputes in the court system."[9] Litigation is the most formal, time consuming, and expensive process of the three. By definition, litigation means "to **prosecute** or defend (a **lawsuit** or legal action); pursue (a legal case)."[10] Therefore, when litigation is selected as the desired dispute resolution alternative, the process will take place in a **court of law**. The vast majority of individuals associate litigation with **trials** and court hearings, when in reality approximately 90% of litigated cases never reach a courtroom, as they are often settled before going to trial.

Litigation is ultimately a distributive, zero-sum dispute resolution alternative, as **damages** are paid by one party and received by another party. In a zero-sum situation, what is lost or paid by one party is received by the **counterparty**, resulting in an overall net gain/loss of zero. The rules and regulations associated with litigation will vary from court to court based on the country where it is located. Variables such as court proceedings and customs, role and involvement of the **judge**, power of the **jury** (if a jury is present), enforcement of damages, and ambiguities of jurisdiction will be different across various legal systems and countries. Litigation is most commonly associated with the settlement of **tort** disputes, where one party has been wronged by another and wishes to receive damages in compensation for the wrongdoing.

While mediation and arbitration tend to occur very much "behind the scenes" due to the private nature of the two, litigation is a very public dispute resolution alternative. In the context of an international commercial business dispute, often businesses will try to "avoid litigation"—meaning they will either attempt to employ a different dispute resolution alternative, such as mediation or

---

[9] HG.org, LEGAL Resources, "Litigation Law", http://www.hg.org/litigation-law.html
[10] The Free Dictionary By Farlex, "Litigation", http://www.thefreedictionary.com/litigation

arbitration, or attempt to settle with the other party. There are several reasons for avoiding litigation, as discussed already, such as high costs, unfamiliar forum and jurisdiction, and the public nature of litigation. The publicity surrounding litigation is rarely positive, whether one is a defendant or a plaintiff.

For example, if you are a customer of an oil and gas company, you are likely going to question the integrity of the company, and, in turn, question the prospect of doing future business with them if you see that they are being sued for a **negligence** tort. Similarly, investors in corporations will be concerned about their investment, and oftentimes the stock price of a company—so long as it is publicly traded—will decrease following an unsuccessful lawsuit. Public image and reputation are also important components of running a successful business with longevity, and litigation can frequently be detrimental to both.

However, litigation is often the necessary dispute resolution alternative when it comes to complex commercial disputes, and the terms of litigation are typically included in a contract between the parties. This contract will often include things such as choice of law clauses, choice of forum clauses, and various types of jurisdiction. Courts do not allow parties to oust their jurisdiction, but they can try to tailor the trial, and exclude a jury trial. Such clauses can give one party an advantage over another party, for example if the choice of law and choice of forum are those of one party.

Jurisdiction

Jurisdiction is an issue that is frequently contested in cross-border disputes. It may not be an issue in purely domestic contracts located in federal type states. However, in places like the United States and Canada, there can be advantageous aspects to the laws of certain states and provinces. A vast majority of intellectual property cases are filed by plaintiffs in East Texas, and most class action lawsuits originate in certain states.

Simply put, if a court has **jurisdiction**, it can hear and decide a particular case, based on a variety of factors. This section discusses the many different subsets and varying types of jurisdiction. If a court has jurisdiction, it is described as being a "competent court." Consent to jurisdiction is an important component of the litigation process. A party is considered to expressly consent to a jurisdiction if any of the following things happen:

1. A party appears in court after a suit has commenced.
2. A party appoints an agent within a state to receive service of process documents.[11]
3. A party agrees to the personal jurisdiction of a particular court in a forum selection clause contained in the contract.

While jurisdiction is a key component of litigation, it can often be difficult to determine which court has jurisdiction in a particular case. Consider the following situation:

A laptop computer severely malfunctions, causing significant harm to its owner. The owner of the laptop then decides to sue the company from which they bought the laptop. Who has jurisdiction to hear the case in this scenario? This may be difficult since the laptop was designed in the United States (California), built in China, and then malfunctioned in Canada (Alberta). The following subset of jurisdiction laws and regulations will aid in determining the designated jurisdiction.

---

[11] The Convention on the Service Abroad of Judicial and Extrajudicial Documents in Civil or Commercial Matters, more commonly known as the Hague Service Convention is a multilateral treaty which allows for service of process of legal documents from one state to another, without having to use diplomatic or consular channels. There are 71 states that are part of the convention.

1. Territorial Jurisdiction

Territorial jurisdiction is most prevalently associated with **criminal law** and refers to the power of a court to hear and decide a case regarding a crime that has been committed or an event that has occurred "within their territory." If a court lacks territorial jurisdiction, then the **defendant** cannot be obligated or forced to pay damages to the **plaintiff** by that court.

2. In Rem *Jurisdiction*

In Rem **Jurisdiction** relates to the court's jurisdiction "concerning the status of a particular piece of property."[12] There are three main types of property that can be addressed in litigation:

  a. **Real property**: Real property is immovable or fixed property and refers to things, such as land and buildings.
  b. **Personal property**: Personal property is moveable property and refers to personal belongings, such as cars, electronics, furniture, and clothing.
  c. **Intellectual property**: In contrast to real and personal property, which refer to tangible things, intellectual property is intangible, referring to things such as ideas, creations, and inventions.

In Rem Jurisdiction gives a court the power to hear and decide the rights to ownership of these various types of property.

3. Subject Matter Jurisdiction

Subject Matter Jurisdiction is the ability of a court to hear and decide a case that is based on a particular subject matter. By definition, it is "the power of a court over the nature of a case and the type of remedy demanded."[13] For example, a criminal court that deals exclusively with criminal cases will not have subject matter jurisdiction to deal with a bankruptcy case. The details contained in the contract will often times determine who has subject matter jurisdiction.

In addition, subject matter jurisdiction can also be established through legislation. For example, in Canada, the Federal Court has jurisdiction over certain federally regulated matters, but cannot otherwise adjudicate on many other issues, which are left to the Provincial Superior Courts. There are three stipulations that enable the authority of the Federal Court over a given subject matter:

  a. *The subject matter must be assigned to Parliament under the Constitution; and*
  b. *There must be actual, existing and applicable federal law; and*
  c. *The administration of that law must have been conferred upon the Federal Court*

4. In Personam *Jurisdiction*

In Personam **Jurisdiction**, also known as Personal Jurisdiction, simply refers to the power of a court to hear and decide a case "against the person."[14] Translating the phrase *in personam* from Latin to English, we get "*directed toward a particular person.*" In the context of litigation, individual people and corporations are considered persons. In contrast to *In Rem* Jurisdiction, which only applies where the property is located, *In Personam* Jurisdiction can be exercised over a person regardless of where they are located.

---

[12] Legal Information Institute, Cornell University Law School, "In Rem", https://www.law.cornell.edu/wex/in_rem

[13] Legal Information Institute, Cornell University Law School, "Subject Matter Jurisdiction", https://www.law.cornell.edu/wex/subject_matter_jurisdiction

[14] Legal Information Institute, Cornell University Law School, "In Personam", https://www.law.cornell.edu/wex/in_personam

In order for a court to have *In Personam* Jurisdiction over a person, the person must have some sort of connection to the area and court. If this is not the case, then the defendant will **motion** to have the case dismissed. Connections can be things such as:

a. permanent residence,

b. carrying on business, or

c. receipt of notice of legal proceedings.

If an individual consents to *In Personam* Jurisdiction, this is also sufficient for a court. However, connection to a court is not always clear and can often be difficult to establish. In order for a court to have *In Personam* Jurisdiction, the defendant must have "minimum contacts" with the said court.

Minimum Contacts: Covenant for **In Personam** *Jurisdiction*

The doctrine of Minimum Contacts serves as a means of judging whether or not a court should have personal (*In Personam*) Jurisdiction over a defendant. Minimum Contacts can be demonstrated in a number of ways.

At the outset of a contract between two parties, minimum contacts can be established by including the proper contractual governing forum clause, which stipulates who has jurisdiction should a dispute arise, or a forum selection clause, which stipulates that litigation over a dispute will be held in a particular, pre-determined forum. These components of a contract are discussed in the chapter on contracts.

Where the contract is silent on who has *In Personam Jurisdiction*, establishing minimum contacts can be accomplished in other ways. The concept of minimum contacts and personal jurisdiction is dynamic and evolving, being refined, and adjusted as relevant cases arise. Courts will weigh and evaluate many criteria to determine if a person has minimum contacts sufficient to confer *In Personam Jurisdiction*. For example, minimum contacts with a forum state may be established if the defendant:

- *Has direct contact with the state,*[15]
- *Has a contract with a resident of the state,*[14]
- *Has placed their product into the stream of commerce such that it reaches the forum state,*[16]
- *Seeks to serve residents of the forum state,*[17]
- *Has satisfied the Calder Effects test and/or,*[18]
- *Has a non-passive website viewed within the forum state.*

The Calder Effects test is based on the Supreme Court of Canada case called *Calder v. Jones* and stipulates that minimum contacts can be established based on the effects of a tort or some other wrongdoing on the plaintiff in his place of residence. If such effects are sufficient to satisfy the Calder Effects test, the defendant can be tried in the plaintiff's place of residence.

---

[15] JUSTIA, Supreme Court of the United States, Mcgee v. International Life Insurance Co., 355 U.S. 220, 78 S.Ct. 199, Available at: (https://supreme.justia.com/cases/federal/us/355/220/case.html) (last visited Thursday March 3, 2016).

[16] JUSTIA, Supreme Court of Illinois, Gray v. American Radiator & Standard Sanitary Corp., N.E.2d 176: 761. 1961. Available at: (http://law.justia.com/cases/illinois/supreme-court/1961/35872-5.html), (last visited Thursday March 3, 2016).

[17] JUSTIA, U.S. Supreme Court, World-Wide Volkswagen Corp. v. Woodson, 444 U.S. 286, 100 S.Ct. 559; 62 L.Ed.2d 490. Available at: (https://supreme.justia.com/cases/federal/us/444/286/case.html) (last visited Thursday March 3, 2016).

[18] JUSTIA, U.S. Supreme Court, Calder v. Jones, 465 U.S. 783, 104 S.Ct. 1482; 79 L. Ed. 2d 804; 1984 U.S. LEXIS 41; 52 U.S.L.W. 4349; 10 Media L. Rep. 1401. Available at: (https://supreme.justia.com/cases/federal/us/465/783/) (last visited Thursday March 3, 2016).

In addition to the conditions listed above, courts will also evaluate more subjective criteria in determining whether the minimum contacts doctrine should give rise to *In Personam* jurisdiction. Most frequently, courts will consider the fairness and reasonability of making a defendant from a foreign place appear before a court in a different part of the world, whether it is a domestic or international dispute. In a case-by-case context, the requirements for establishing minimum contacts can vary greatly, as the facts and relevant criteria will change. As a result of this, it can be difficult to predict whether or not a court will attain *In Personam* Jurisdiction based on previous cases.

Jurisdiction and Litigation in the United States vs. Canada

While the process of litigation and the determination of jurisdiction, whether it be territorial, subject matter, *in rem* or *in personam* are in many ways quite similar from the United States to Canada, "there are some significant differences that American litigants and attorneys should bear in mind when navigating their way through a Canadian proceeding."[19] The main and most glaring difference between the two legal systems with respect to jurisdiction stems from the *structure* of the courts.

In the United States, a two-court system exists, which is made up of a Federal Courts and several State Courts. State Courts have two types of jurisdiction for trial courts:

1. **Limited**—these are usually trial courts and include municipal courts, magistrate courts, county courts, and justice of the peace courts.

2. **Specific**—includes municipal courts, magistrate courts, county courts, and justice of the peace courts.

Each type of jurisdiction specifies what types of cases can be heard in the court. Typically, trial courts with limited jurisdiction will hear cases with limited gravity or severity. These cases can include minor criminal offenses, juvenile cases, or traffic violations. Trial courts with specific jurisdiction have jurisdiction over some very particular aspects of the law. These trial courts will often hear matters of probate, family law, juvenile law, and small claims. In addition to trial courts with limited and specific jurisdiction, courts with general jurisdiction exist as well. These courts are likely to hear higher profile cases, involving more severe crimes or larger monetary amounts. The Federal Courts in the United States will hear cases that fall under Federal law, rather than State law. Examples of Federal Courts are Court of Federal Claims, Tax Court, and Bankruptcy Court.[20]

In contrast to the United States' two-court system, Canada employs a three-court system. The Canadian Court system is comprised of Superior Courts, Provincial Courts, and Federal Courts. There is a Superior Court in each Canadian Province and Territory, and these courts have the broadest jurisdiction, referred to as "inherent jurisdiction." This simply means that unless a **statute** stipulates otherwise, the Superior Courts can hear *any* kind of case. Superior Courts will typically hear the most severe civil and criminal cases. Less severe cases, such as minor criminal offences, juvenile cases, regulatory offences, and family law cases are *carved out* from the Superior Courts' inherent jurisdiction by provincial legislation and delegated to Provincial Courts. The provincial legislation will also stipulate the maximum monetary amount for minor civil cases—called "small claims"—that can be heard in Provincial Courts. Finally, the Federal Courts of Canada play a smaller role than the Federal Courts in the United States, and are limited very specific federally regulated issues.

---

[19] Lawson Lundell LLP, Mark Vesely, "The Top 10 Differences Litigating in Canada versus the U.S.A.", (last update July 2013), http://www.lawsonlundell.com/media/news/382_USCanadaLitigationDifferences2013.pdf

[20] http://www.dummies.com/how-to/content/getting-to-know-the-us-court-systems.html

Ethical Considerations 3.2

TransCanada v. United States of America

Kelly Cryderman and Shawn McCarthy, "TransCanada to launch NAFTA claim over Keystone rejection," *The Globe and Mail* [Calgary and Ottawa], January 6, 2016, http://www.theglobeandmail.com/report-on-business/industry-news/energy-and-resources/transcanada-files-lawsuit-over-keystone-pipeline-rejection/article28038526/

How do international corporations resolve disputes that arise when dilemmas span cross-border? Who decides where the case can be brought up? How is the case decided? How can bias be dealt with? Consider all these questions while reading the next case.

In early January 2016, TransCanada Corporation brought up a claim against the United States government in Houston federal court that stated the president's rejection of the Keystone XL pipeline was invalid and unconstitutional based on the fact that Congress did not give direct authorization to the annexation of the pipeline. TransCanada is seeking to invalidate the president's claim and ignite the project once more.

As well, TransCanada filed a notice of intent under the North American Free Trade Agreement (NAFTA) for arbitration not to reinstate the Keystone Xl pipeline, but to seek monetary compensation for damages due to the rejection of the project ($15 billion in damages).

Previous arbitrations under NAFTA have sided with the United States of America. In fact, the USA has never lost an arbitration case under NAFTA. Does this show a bias under the terms of the trade agreement? As well, because TransCanada has brought up a constitutional claim against the USA in Houston, Texas, how can TransCanada be assured that there will be no bias due to the fact that all key adjudicators will be American?

Decision Tree

Consider the following situation: CanCo has a sales contract to sell equipment to RussCo. RussCo believes that the products you sold were defective so they sue you in a foreign court, a Russian court. The Russian legal and political system is different from Canada's, and you are unfamiliar with their legal processes. For these reasons, it is important to weigh your options before making decisions on future actions. There is an orderly process that CanCo should follow to determine if they should defend the lawsuit. Remember by defending an action, CanCo would be submitting to the jurisdiction of Russia. On the other side of the coin, any plaintiff should follow the same decision process before bringing an action.

1. Is there a governing law clause (choice of law and choice of forum).
2. If the choice of law (governing jurisidiciton) is Russia then defend; if not, go to step 3.
3. Is there a reciprocal enforcement treaty between Canada and Russia. If yes, then one must defend, if not go to step 4.[21]
4. Does CanCo have significant assets in Russia? If so, they may be seized on the basis of a default judgment. If not, then one may not need to defend.

---

[21] *Reciprocal Enforcement of Judgments Act*, RSA 2000, Chapter R-6. The reciprocating jurisdictions include all provinces and territories within Canada and also Australia, and the States of Montana, Washington, and Idaho. Added to this is Arizona once Alberta declares Arizona a reciprocating jurisdiction. Such reciprocating legislation facilitates greater investment between the two places as there is greater certainty in the ability to enforce a money judgment by a judgment creditor.

5. If one does not defend, RussCo may try and enforce the foreign judgment in Canada. However, this allows CanCo to defend on its home turf, where it is more familiar with the laws.

6. One final note is irrespective of the above legal reasons to possibly not defend; CanCo may still want to defend for reputational reasons.

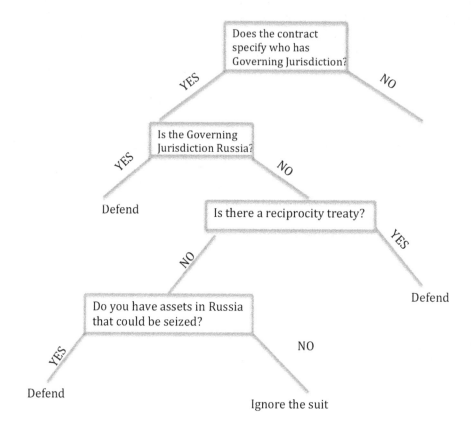

Jurisdiction and Court System in Russia

In Russia, the local courts of "general jurisdiction" form the foundation of the legal system.[22] The vast majority of administrative, criminal, and civil cases are heard here, as they act as courts of first instance—meaning that most cases are originally heard in these local courts. The bodies that act in a supervisory role for the local courts are the courts of regions, republics, provinces, and autonomous districts. Typically, these courts will act upon newly uncovered evidence, and rarely in the first instance. Above both the local courts and the regional and republic courts, lies the Supreme Court of Russia. "According to Pt 1, Art. 128 of the Constitution, judges of the Supreme Court are introduced by the President, and appointed by the Council of the Federation. A judge of the Supreme Court must be a Russian Citizen with a law degree and experience in the legal profession for 10 years." (Russian Law Online, Par. 2). While local courts serve as the foundation for the courts of general jurisdiction, the Supreme Court serves as the pinnacle of it. The Supreme Court can also hear administrative, criminal, and civil cases. In cases involving significant public interest, the Superior Court may serve as the court of first instance, similar to how the Supreme Court of Canada can receive "reference" cases from the government. In addition to being the peak of the general jurisdiction system, the Superior Court of Russia also maintains the "right of legislative initiative" (Russian Law Online, Par. 1), which gives it the ability to establish new laws.

---

[22] Russian Law Online, "Russia Through Lawyers' Eyes", "Courts of General Jurisdiction", http://www.russianlawonline. com/content/russia-court-system-courts-general-jurisdiction

Governing Law Clauses

Governing law is often used in a broader sense to refer to both a choice of law and/or a choice of forum clause. In the narrow sense, these two clauses are very different. For simplicity, governing law clauses will refer to both **choice of law** and **choice of forum** clauses. In congruence with choice of law clauses, there are choice of forum clauses. Oftentimes, both will be included at the outset of a contract, for matters of consistency and efficiency in dispute resolution. Including a choice of law clause alongside choice of forum clause in a contract will serve to greatly decrease ambiguity and stagnancy in dispute resolution, should a dispute arise.

Different Types of Clauses

There are usually two types of governing law clauses in a contract; choices of law and choice of forum clause. A distinction needs to be made between choice of law clauses and choice of forum clauses.

1. Choice of Law Clauses

Laws can vary greatly from place to place, so it is important for the parties involved to be aware of what law they will be subject to by including a choice of law clause in a contract. A choice of law clause indicates the law under which the parties have chosen to interpret their potential dispute. This is the law that will be applied to interpret the existence and validity of a contract.

In the context of international business, choice of law clauses are very important. Consider the following situation: A Canadian software company that is based in Vancouver enters into a contract with a Korean computer engineering company. Should a dispute arise in the future, under what jurisdiction should it be settled? It is not always easy to decide. Neither company has any significant connection to their counterparty's geographical location; however, both have an office in Southern San Francisco (Silicon Valley), a major technology hub. In this case, the parties can agree to include a choice of law clause in the contract that stipulates that the governing law of California will take precedence over the conflict of laws rules and that the parties agree to settle the dispute there. This is possible because both companies have a significant connection to the location, and it would be convenient for both parties.

2. Choice of Forum Clauses

Choice of forum clauses, also referred to as forum selection clauses, are included at the outset of a contract between two parties and stipulate where litigation would take place if any dispute were to arise in the future. Including a forum selection clause in a contract can help remove ambiguity and uncertainty in case of a dispute, as both parties will be well aware of how the dispute will be dealt with. There are various choices of forum clauses that fall under three main categories:

1. Particular Court: Parties can agree to use a particular court and jurisdiction in case of any disagreements or disputes. This power is subject to the parties following civil procedure standards for that jurisdiction, and if they chose an inappropriate court for their uses the local standards will be used to determine the appropriate court.

2. Dispute Resolution Process: Specific processes, such as mediation, arbitration, or special hearings can be predetermined by the parties.

3. Or a combination of both preselections, requiring a certain process to be used in a certain level of court/jurisdiction.

Consider the following situation: a Canadian oil and gas company and a Russian oil and gas company enter into a contract with one another over the sale of equipment. Should a dispute occur, a choice of forum clause is included in the contract. The clause stipulates that in the event of a dispute, the companies have agreed that the dispute resolution alternative will be litigation, and it will take place in Canada. This choice of forum clause might read something like this: "The parties submit all their disputes arising out of or in connection with this Agreement to the exclusive jurisdiction of the Courts of Alberta." Choice of forum clauses will be tailored to each individual contract to reflect the specifics and requirements of each individual situation.

While choice of forum clauses can be a very beneficial component of a contract for reasons of clarity and efficiency they provide in the event of a dispute, imbalance and disparity of bargaining power between companies can result in an uneven playing field. The company that has greater negotiating power can take advantage of its position and push for a choice of forum clause that is favorable to them. Oftentimes this will mean a clause that stipulates that disputes will be dealt with in their place of residence, rather than the whereabouts of their counterparty or a neutral location. While this imbalance of power can be relevant in these situations and can cause inequity in the drafting of a contract, including choice of forum clauses in contracts is a very effective way to counter "forum shopping" by the parties. Forum shopping is the strategy of attempting to have your case heard in a court that will result in the most favorable outcome for you. By including a choice of forum clause, the parties forestall forum shopping down the road.

A. Choice of Forum (Jurisdiction)

The parties may give exclusive, non-exclusive, or concurrent jurisdiction to a particular forum.

- **Exclusive jurisdiction**: The parties agree that the dispute will be resolved in only one jurisdiction—"exclusive jurisdiction" to a particular forum.
- **Non-exclusive jurisdiction**: The parties agree to one forum but not to the exclusion of others.
- **Concurrent jurisdiction:** The parties—allow disputes to be heard in more than one forum.

B. Forum Shopping

Forum shopping refers to the attempt by either a plaintiff or a defendant to have their case heard in a particular court that is more favorable to them than another court might be. While forum shopping is frowned upon and there are things such as choice of forum clauses that can help eradicate it, it is still prevalent in many cases. **Litigants** will actively seek out a specific venue, dispute resolution alternative, or an individual to hear their case, so long as they believe it will give them a better chance of winning the case or earning maximum damages.

Consider the following situation: An American company based out of New Mexico has a patent on a new type of a sunglass lens, and it has come to their attention that another sunglasses company in Illinois has been using the technology and marketing it as their own. The New Mexico Company has filed a lawsuit over patent infringement, and they have filed it in the District Court for the Eastern District of Texas. In this case, the New Mexico Company has gone "forum shopping" and chosen this venue because of its track record. In patent cases, this District Court, based in Marshall, Texas, has ruled in the Plaintiff's favor in just shy of 80% of the cases, compared to the 59% national average, making it a very attractive place to have a patent infringement case heard. While having the case heard in this location would be very favorable for the plaintiff, it is clearly less than ideal for the defendant in this case[23].

---

[23] The New York Times, "Business", "So Small a Town, So Many Patent Suits", Julie Creswell, (Published: September 24, 2006). http://www.nytimes.com/2006/09/24/business/24ward.html?_r=0

The defendant has several different options to combat forum shopping by the plaintiff. While the plaintiff usually retains the right to decide on the forum, the defendant has a right to file for **removal jurisdiction** through a "notice of removal," in order to have the case heard elsewhere. Removal jurisdiction refers to the moving of a lawsuit that has been filed at a State Court to the relevant Federal District Court within the same State. In order for a case to be removed, the case must have been eligible to be filed in the Federal Court in the first place.

Another strategy that a defendant can employ to combat forum shopping is requesting a change of **venue.** As explained below, the term "venue" simply refers to the location where a hearing will take place. A defendant will often request a change of venue when they believe that the location the plaintiff has selected is not the best location to hear the case based on factors such as the location or lack of jurisdiction. The location may create undue expense or create an unfair playing field from a biased jury in a jury trial. Changes of venue are common in high-profile cases where important details and information have become public knowledge and could very well cause a jury to issue a biased ruling either in favor of or against the defendant.

If a defendant believes that there is a more appropriate court to hear their case than the one selected by the plaintiff, then their request for a change of venue is referred to as *forum non conveniens*. However, we will discuss the *forum non conveniens* later in this Chapter. In the context of the dispute between the sunglasses companies located in New Mexico and Illinois, the plaintiff (New Mexico company) has selected a district court in Texas because of a high chance of the ruling being in their favor. The defendant (Illinois company) will more than likely file for removal jurisdiction or request a change of venue. This example will continue in our discussion of *forum non conveniens*.

Ethical Considerations 3.3

Governing Jurisdiction Advantages

At the beginning of the formation of a contract between two international parties, the jurisdiction of the governing body should be chosen so any contractual issue that arises is not the cause of long-term headaches and frustration. The chosen governing law may be known for favoring certain transactions over others and thus a jurisdiction may be chosen for their business friendly judgements or their lax environmental regulations.

Certain jurisdictions may have very different ideas concerning human rights or civil law such as marrying a woman in Saudi Arabia. Under Sharia law the husband could have up to four wives and in the event of a divorce, the courts will favor the husband. Custody will remain with the husband and settlements only going to the woman if there was an existing prenuptial agreement. In addition to this example there are many others where one party firmly decides on a jurisdiction that will clearly be in their favor should an issue occur.

Is choosing a governing law that will be an advantage to one party unfair? Should parties be bound by ethics and morals when deciding on a jurisdiction—or is more of a "survival of the fittest" approach more logical for corporations in the free market?

C. Venue

Venue, separate from jurisdiction, simply means the geographical area where a case is heard. It is defined as "the proper place to hold a civil or criminal trial, usually because important related events have taken place there." The terms forum and venue are often confused. Contractual devices that limit where suits are brought are often referred to as "forum selection clauses" or "choice of forum" regardless if it limits forum, venue, or both. Forum is "a court or other judicial body; a place of jurisdiction," while venue is "the territory, such as a country or political subdivision, over which a trial court has jurisdiction." Venue governs where, within a state/province, an action may be heard. In simple terms, forum is the court itself and venue is the geographical location of the trial.[24] While jurisdiction refers to a court's *ability* to hear and decide a case, venue focuses on *where* the case is to be heard. In terms of American law, available venues vary depending on which court has the jurisdiction to hear the case. If it is a Federal case, the decision of venue will be in which district to hear the case. If it is a case to be heard in a State Court, the decision of venue will be based on which county is most appropriate.

Venue selection is based on multiple factors. While oftentimes there are many different jurisdictions that are appropriate to hear a given case, one venue has to be selected. There are three main decision criteria when it comes to venue in general in regards to a judicial district.

1. *Where any defendant resides, if all are residents of the district state;*
2. *Where substantial part of events, omissions, or property, giving rise to the claim;*
3. *Where any defendant is subject to the court's personal jurisdiction, with respect to such action if no other district.*[25]

When the plaintiff files a lawsuit, they will choose a venue to hear their case at that time. Oftentimes, the defendant will exercise their right to file for a change of venue if they believe the selected venue to be inappropriate. Returning to our discussion of forum shopping, defendants can do so in a number of ways, including filing for removal jurisdiction or requesting a change of venue.

If it is decided that the selected venue is unfair to one party, then a case can be moved or dismissed based on *forum non conveniens*, which we will discuss later.

Choice of forum clauses that are included in contracts between parties also serve to identify an appropriate venue for litigation should a dispute arise. The concept of venue can be especially problematic in international business disputes, since the parties involved in a dispute are normally far apart geographically. If a forum or venue selection clause is not included in a contract, it can be difficult to identify where the case should be heard.

Consider the following situation: a manufacturing company in the United States sells goods to a Japanese company. The Japanese company defaults on their payment, claiming that they aren't obligated to pay because the goods arrived two days late, as they were delayed in China. The American company files a lawsuit and chooses an American court as the venue. Is this venue the most appropriate to hear the case? The American company files the suit in the United States, but they are suing a company based out of Japan, over an incident that has occurred in China. The Japanese company will more than likely request a change of venue in this case, or a court will likely decide that forcing the Japanese company to come all the way to the United States is unfair, and the case will be moved based on the *forum non conveniens* doctrine. *Sinochem International Co. Ltd. v. Malaysia International Shipping Corporation*,[26] illustrates this principle. Malaysia International Shipping Corporation (MISC) owned a vessel carrying steel coils for Sinochem International, a Chinese company. Sinochem sued in Chinese Admiralty Court, alleging that MISC had backdated a bill of lading, and sought to detain the ship in China. MISC sued in a Pennsylvania district court, accusing Sinochem of fraudulent misrepresentation. Sinochem argued that the District Court had no personal jurisdiction over the Chinese company, but the District court failed to rule and dismissed on the grounds of "forum non-conveniens." The

---

[24] Legal Information Institute, Cornell University Law School, "Venue", https://www.law.cornell.edu/wex/venue

[25] Legal Information Institute, Cornell University Law School, "Venue Generally", "Venue In General", https://www.law.cornell.edu/uscode/text/28/1391

[26] *Sinochem International Co. Ltd. v. Malaysia International Shipping Corporation*, 549 U.S. _ (2007)

Appeal Court overturned the decision of the District Court, but the US Supreme Court stated that the District Court has discretion to respond at once to a defendant's forum non-conveniens plead. The US Supreme Court said the District Court may dismiss the action before conclusively establishing subject matter or personal jurisdiction if it determines a foreign court is the more suitable court.

3. Forum Non Conveniens

Translated from Latin, *forum non conveniens* means "forum not agreeing" and is a legal doctrine giving courts the ability to refuse the hearing of a case. This refusal will happen if, despite a court having proper jurisdiction over a case, and despite an appropriate venue having been selected, it is believed there is a better court to hear the dispute. The doctrine stipulates that when there are multiple courts with appropriate jurisdiction to hear a case, the court with the closest connection to the incident, and the most overall convenient court should hear the case.

This conflict can happen domestically between courts in the same country, or internationally between courts of different countries, and arises when the parties involved reside in substantially different geographical locations. The decision on where a case should be heard will be based on two types of factors: private and public.

   i. **Private Factors:** The private factors considered are those that relate to the individual parties, and their interests and convenience.
   ii. **Public Factors:** The interest of the public in relation to the case is also considered when deciding where a case should be heard.

The doctrine of *forum non conveniens* was first formulated in the United States in the case called *Willendson v. Forsoket.*[27] In this case, a Pennsylvanian court refused to hear a suit for unpaid wages filed by a Danish seaman against a Danish sea captain. The court held that, "if any differences should hereafter arise, it must be settled by a Danish tribunal."[28] In essence, the Pennsylvanian court had no connection to the case or the parties involved, thus it was not convenient to hear the case there.

In the United Kingdom, the doctrine of *forum non conveniens* finds limited use, but the ideas and principles related to it are similar. The doctrine generally finds little recognition in Europe, as per the signed Brussels Convention, which lays down specific rules to decide which court has the jurisdiction to hear a case. Typically in Europe, it is believed that jurisdiction should be assigned based on the location of the defendant, as they should have the ability to defend the lawsuit in their "own" court. This is in contrast to the United States where it is the plaintiff who usually determines where the case will be heard.

A defendant in an international business dispute will almost always attempt to have their case heard in their location, rather than abroad, for a number of reasons. Some reasons include:

   • Uncertainty associated with foreign laws and procedures,
   • Inconvenience of frequent travel for pretrial obligations, and
   • Associated additional expenses, whether they be extra legal fees or travel costs.

4. Conflict of Laws

The term **conflict of laws** refers to a situation where laws of more than one jurisdiction potentially apply to a given dispute. As a general rule, courts typically apply and enforce their local laws. However, when there are multiple jurisdictions at play, a competent court may be called upon to apply the

---

[27] U.S. Supreme Court, Willensdon v. Forosket, 29 Fed Cas 1283 (DC PA 1801) (No 17, 682), Available at: (https://law.resource.org/pub/us/case/reporter/F.Cas/0029.f.cas/0029.f.cas.1283.4.pdf) (last visited Thursday March 3, 2016).

[28] PSBLAW, Journal of Consumer Attorneys Associations for Southern California, Pete Kaufman, "An inconvenient forum for whom?" (January 2013 Issue), http://www.psblaw.com/wp-content/uploads/2013/06/20130111112204624.pdf

laws of a different jurisdiction. In cross-border context, conflict of laws rules will determine what law should be employed to resolve a dispute.

The starting point in applying conflict of laws rules is the choice law clause. A choice of law clause will often be included in a contract between two parties, and will specify which choice of law the parties have agreed to apply to the resolution of any disputes between them. If there is a choice of law clause, the conflict of laws analysis will usually end there. However, if a choice of law clause is not included in a contract, a court faced with a conflict of laws will typically follow a two-part decision process:

1. The court will apply the law of the forum (lex fori) to all procedural matters (including, self-evidently, the choice of law rules); and

2. It counts the factors that connect or link the legal issues to the laws of potentially relevant states and applies the laws that have the greatest connection, i.e. the law of nationality (lex patriae) or residence (lex domicilii) will define legal status and capacity, the law of the state in which land is situated (lex situs) will be applied to determine all questions of title, the law of the place where a transaction physically takes place or of the occurrence that gave rise to the litigation (lex loci actus) will often be the controlling law selected when the matter is substantive, but the proper law has become a more common choice.[29,30]

Chapter Summary

Disputes are an inevitable part of international business. With cross-border transactions, however, comes greater risk and more complex challenges than purely domestic disputes. Concerns include that the other party will not deliver the goods, will not pay, or renege on their agreement. The time and resources involved in an international dispute are greater due to a lack of a global and streamlined legal or enforcement mechanism. Different jurisdictions require careful planning from the drafting of the transaction to the enforcement of rights between the parties.

Disputes can be resolved in a number of ways including traditional litigation as well as alternative methods such as mediation and arbitration. Alternative dispute resolution methods are growing rapidly as a preferred method for resolving international disputes. It is important to have a strong understanding of the various principles underlying the principles of alternative dispute resolutions.

In addition, structuring the transaction to avoid having to resolve disputes in unfavorable locations is paramount. Choice of law and choice of forum clauses allow parties to remove some of the uncertainty and potential expense if a dispute should arise.

Glossary

Ad Hoc Arbitration: A proceeding that is not administered by others and requires the parties to make their own arrangements for selection of arbitrators and for designation of rules, applicable law, procedures, and administrative support.[13]

Appeal: An application or proceeding for review by a higher tribunal.[16]

---

29 High Court of Australia, Dow Jones and Company v. Gutnick (2002) HCA 56; 210 CLR 575; 194 ALR 433; 77 ALJR 255 (10 December 2002), (last updated: 5 February 2003), Available at: (http://www.austlii.edu.au/au/cases/cth/HCA/2002/56) (last visited Thursday March 3, 2016).

30 Conflict of Laws, "Choice of Laws", https://en.wikipedia.org/wiki/Conflict_of_laws

Alternative Dispute Resolution: Procedures for settling disputes by means other than litigation; by arbitration, mediation, or mini-trials.[5]

Arbitral Tribunal: A body made up of one or more members that will hear the facts and make a final decision in an arbitration proceeding.

Arbitration: A process of settling an argument or disagreement in which the people or groups on both sides present their opinions and ideas to a third person or group.[2]

Arbitration Clause: Provision, included in certain types of contracts, requiring settlement of disputes through arbitration instead of litigation.[12]

Choice of Law Clause: A component of a contract that designates the jurisdiction under whose laws a dispute will be settled should one arise.

Contract: An agreement with specific terms between two or more persons or entities in which there is a promise to do something in return for a valuable benefit known as consideration.[11]

Counterparty: The other party or participant in an agreement, court case, deal, or negotiation.[24]

Court of Law: A court that hears cases and makes decisions based on statutes or the common law.[21]

Criminal Law: A body of rules and statutes that defines conduct prohibited by the government because it threatens and harms public safety and welfare and that establishes punishment to be imposed for the commission of such acts.[29]

Damages: Monetary compensation that is awarded by a court in a civil action to an individual who has been injured through the wrongful conduct of another party.[23]

Deadlock: A state in which progress is impossible, as in a dispute, produced by the counteraction of opposing forces.[15]

Defendant: A person or institution against whom an action is brought in a court of law; the person being sued or accused.[30]

Defense: The denial or pleading of the defendant in answer to the claim or charge that has been made.[18]

Dispute Resolution: The process of resolving disputes between parties.

Express Consent: Express consent is permission for something that is given specifically, either verbally or in writing.[10]

Forum Non Conveniens: A legal doctrine giving courts the ability to refuse to hear a case if it is deemed that there is a better court for the case to be heard.

Forum Shopping: The attempt by either a plaintiff or a defendant to have their case heard in a particular court that is more favorable to them than another court might be.

In Personam *Jurisdiction:* The power of a court to hear and decide a case against a person.

In Rem *Jurisdiction:* The power of a court to hear and decide a case regarding property.

Injunction: A court order by which an individual is required to perform, or is restrained from performing, a particular act.[9]

Institutional Arbitration: A situation where the parties avail themselves of established rules, protocols, arbitrator rosters, and administrative resources available through one of many arbitration bodies.

Intellectual Property: Intangible property encompassing things such as ideas, creations, and inventions.

Judge: A public officer authorized to hear and decide cases in a court of law; a magistrate charged with the administration of justice.[25]

Jurisdiction: The right, power, or authority to administer justice by hearing and determining controversies.[4]

Jury: A body of persons sworn to give a verdict on some matter submitted to them; especially a body of persons legally selected and sworn to inquire into any matter of fact and to give their verdict based on the evidence.[26]

Lawsuit: A process by which a court of law makes a decision to end a disagreement between people or organizations.[20]

Legal Action: A judicial proceeding brought by one party against another; one party prosecutes another for a wrong done or for protection of a right or for prevention of a wrong.[17]

Litigant: A person who is involved in a lawsuit; someone who is suing another person or is being sued by another person.[34]

Litigation: The act or process of bringing or contesting a legal action in court.[3]

Mediation: A settlement of a dispute or controversy by setting up an independent person between two contending parties in order to aid them in the settlement of their disagreement.[1]

Mediator: A person who attempts to make people involved in a conflict come to an agreement; a go-between.[8]

Motion: An application made to a court or judge for an order, ruling, or the like.[32]

Negligence: Conduct that falls below the standards of behavior established by law for the protection of others against unreasonable risk of harm.[28]

Negotiation: Mutual discussion and arrangement of the terms of a transaction or agreement.[7]

Personal Property: Moveable property, refers to personal belongings such as cars, electronics, furniture and clothing.

Plaintiff: A person who brings suit in a court.[31]

Prosecute: To institute legal proceedings against (a person) or to seek to enforce or obtain a right by legal process.[19]

Real Property: Immovable or fixed property, refers to things such as land and buildings.

Removal Jurisdiction: Removal jurisdiction, in the American context, refers to the moving of a lawsuit that has been filed a State court, to the relevant Federal District Court in the same State.

Settle/Settlement: A formal agreement or decision that ends an argument or dispute. Often an agreement on the amount of money one party will pay another.[6]

Statute: A law that has been formally approved and written down.[33]

Subject Matter Jurisdiction: The power of a court to hear and decide a case on a particular subject matter.

Territorial Jurisdiction: The power of a court to hear and decide a case regarding a crime or a wrong that has been committed within their territory.

Tort: A civil wrong which can be redressed by awarding damages.[27]

Trial: A proceeding in which opposing parties in a dispute present evidence and make arguments on the application of the law before a judge or jury.[22]

Tribunal: A special court or group of people who are officially chosen, especially by the government, to examine (legal) problems of a particular type.[14]

Venue: The geographical area where a case is heard.

Glossary Bibliography

http://legal-dictionary.thefreedictionary.com/mediation [1]

http://www.merriam-webster.com/dictionary/arbitration [2]

http://www.thefreedictionary.com/litigation [3]

http://dictionary.reference.com/browse/jurisdiction [4]

http://legal-dictionary.thefreedictionary.com/alternative+dispute+resolution [5]

http://www.merriam-webster.com/dictionary/settlement [6]

http://dictionary.reference.com/browse/negotiation [7]

http://www.oxforddictionaries.com/definition/english/mediator [8]

http://legal-dictionary.thefreedictionary.com/injunction [9]

http://whatis.techtarget.com/definition/express-consent [10]

http://legal-dictionary.thefreedictionary.com/contract [11]

http://www.businessdictionary.com/definition/arbitration-clause.html [12]

http://www.carrow.com/ad-hoc.html [13]

http://dictionary.cambridge.org/dictionary/english/tribunal [14]

http://dictionary.reference.com/browse/deadlock [15]

http://dictionary.reference.com/browse/appeal [16]

http://www.thefreedictionary.com/legal+action [17]

http://dictionary.reference.com/browse/defense [18]

http://dictionary.reference.com/browse/prosecute [19]

http://www.merriam-webster.com/dictionary/lawsuit [20]

http://www.thefreedictionary.com/court+of+law [21]

http://www.thefreedictionary.com/trial [22]

http://legal-dictionary.thefreedictionary.com/damages [23]

http://www.businessdictionary.com/definition/counterparty.html [24]

http://dictionary.reference.com/browse/judge [25]

http://www.merriam-webster.com/dictionary/jury [26]

https://www.law.cornell.edu/wex/tort [27]

http://legal-dictionary.thefreedictionary.com/negligence [28]

http://legal-dictionary.thefreedictionary.com/Criminal+Law [29]

https://www.vocabulary.com/dictionary/defendant [30]

http://dictionary.reference.com/browse/plaintiff [31]

http://dictionary.reference.com/browse/motion [32]

http://dictionary.cambridge.org/dictionary/english/statute [33]

http://www.merriam-webster.com/dictionary/litigant [34]

Bibliography

Arbitration Award. "Enforcement of Arbitration Awards, https://en.wikipedia.org/wiki/Arbitration_award

Chartered Institute of Arbitrators, (CIArb). "Dispute Resolution Clauses" "'Catch All' Dispute Resolution Clause", http://www.ciarb.org/docs/default-source/das/contract-clause.pdf?sfvrsn=4

Conflict of Laws. "Choice of Laws" https://en.wikipedia.org/wiki/Conflict_of_laws

Forum Selection Clause, https://en.wikipedia.org/wiki/Forum_selection_clause

HG.org, LEGAL Resources. "Litigation Law" http://www.hg.org/litigation-law.html

High Court of Australia, Dow Jones and Company v. Gutnick (2002) HCA 56; 210 CLR 575; 194 ALR 433; 77 ALJR 255 (10 December 2002), (last updated: 5 February 2003), Available at: (http://www.austlii.edu.au/au/cases/cth/HCA/2002/56) (last visited Thursday March 3, 2016).

http://www.dummies.com/how-to/content/getting-to-know-the-us-court-systems.html

International Arbitration Attorney Network, "Arbitral Institutions And Arbitration Courts." "Leading Arbitral Institutions and Centres." https://international-arbitration-attorney.com/arbitral-institutions-and-arbitration-courts/

International Chamber of Commerce. "Arbitration." (Recognition and Enforcement of Awards), http://www.iccwbo.org/products-and-services/arbitration-and-adr/arbitration/

International Chamber of Commerce. "Standard ICC Arbitration Clauses", http://www.iccwbo.org/products-and-services/arbitration-and-adr/arbitration/standard-icc-arbitration-clauses/

JUSTIA, Supreme Court of Illinois,. Gray v. American Radiator & Standard Sanitary Corp., N.E.2d 176: 761. 1961. Available at: (http://law.justia.com/cases/illinois/supreme-court/1961/35872-5.html), (last visited Thursday March 3, 2016).

JUSTIA, Supreme Court of the United States. Mcgee v. International Life Insurance Co., 355 U.S. 220, 78 S.Ct. 199, Available at: (https://supreme.justia.com/cases/federal/us/355/220/case.html) (last visited Thursday March 3, 2016).

JUSTIA, U.S. Supreme Court, Calder v. Jones, 465 U.S. 783, 104 S.Ct. 1482; 79 L. Ed. 2d 804; 1984 U.S. LEXIS 41; 52 U.S.L.W. 4349; 10 Media L. Rep. 1401. Available at: (https://supreme.justia.com/cases/federal/us/465/783/) (last visited Thursday March 3, 2016).

JUSTIA, U.S. Supreme Court, World-Wide Volkswagen Corp. v. Woodson, 444 U.S. 286, 100 S.Ct. 559; 62 L.Ed.2d 490. Available at: (https://supreme.justia.com/cases/federal/us/444/286/case.html) (last visited Thursday March 3, 2016).

Lawson Lundell LLP, Mark Vesely. "The Top 10 Differences Litigating in Canada versus the U.S.A." (last update July 2013), http://www.lawsonlundell.com/media/news/382_USCanadaLitigationDifferences2013.pdf

Legal Information Institute. "Alternative Dispute Resolution", Cornell University Law School, https://www.law.cornell.edu/lii/terms/documentation

Legal Information Institute, Cornell University Law School, "In Personam", https://www.law.cornell.edu/wex/in_personam

Legal Information Institute, Cornell University Law School. "In Rem", https://www.law.cornell.edu/wex/in_rem

Legal Information Institute, Cornell University Law School. "Subject Matter Jurisdiction", https://www.law.cornell.edu/wex/subject_matter_jurisdiction

Legal Information Institute, Cornell University Law School. "Venue", https://www.law.cornell.edu/wex/venue

Legal Information Institute, Cornell University Law School. "Venue Generally", "Venue In General", https://www.law.cornell.edu/uscode/text/28/1391

Out-Law.com, "Institutional vs. 'ad hoc' arbitration", (last updated August, 2011), http://www.out-law.com/en/topics/projects–construction/international-arbitration/institutional-vs-ad-hoc-arbitration/

PSBLAW, Journal of Consumer Attorneys Associations for Southern California. Pete Kaufman. "An inconvenient forum for whom?" (January 2013 Issue), http://www.psblaw.com/wp-content/uploads/2013/06/20130111112204624.pdf

Russian Law Online. "Russia Through Lawyers' Eyes", "Courts of General Jurisdiction", http://www.russianlawonline.com/content/russia-court-system-courts-general-jurisdiction

The Free Dictionary By Farlex, "Litigation", http://www.thefreedictionary.com/litigation

The New York Times. "Business", "So Small a Town, So Many Patent Suits", Julie Creswell, (Published: September 24, 2006). http://www.nytimes.com/2006/09/24/business/24ward.html?_r=0

U.S. Supreme Court. Willensdon v. Forosket, 29 Fed Cas 1283 (DC PA 1801) (No 17, 682), Available at: (https://law.resource.org/pub/us/case/reporter/F.Cas/0029.f.cas/0029.f.cas.1283.4.pdf) (last visited Thursday March 3, 2016).

World Intellectual Property Association. "What is Arbitration?" WIPO, http://www.wipo.int/amc/en/arbitration/what-is-arb.html

Finance

Learning Objectives

After reading this chapter, you will have an understanding of:

1. What acceptance is and the different risks associated with the different forms
2. What are the various ways that international transactions can be financed
3. What a letter of credit is and the types of versions of it that are available
4. The alternatives to a letter of credit and the different versions

Introduction to Finance

International trade finance is often a chicken and egg issue. Payment to the seller versus delivery of the goods to the buyer. This problem is magnified because the transaction crosses borders. If a seller requires payment in advance, sales may go down as buyers fear non-delivery of goods. Sellers likewise fear that if they ship the goods and trust the buyer to pay, they run a high risk. In order to alleviate this risk, an intermediary system has developed over the years, though the use of banks, who step in and provide various types of financing that attempts to address the concerns of both sellers and buyers. Such methods include letters of credit, credit insurance, export factoring, **forfaiting**, and other methods. This chapter will take a look at the various ways that are available to finance international transactions. Throughout the course of the chapter we will look at the different ways that typical letter of credit transactions will occur, and some alternative ways to carry out transactions without the use of letters of credit. To properly understand what a letter of credit is, we must first learn what drafts are and the history behind letters of credit in order to understand why they have such an impactful application in today's international marketplace.

Payment Methods of International Trade

There are a number of ways to actually complete an international transaction. Each has their own advantages and disadvantages to either party that must be weighed carefully when making the decision on which payment to agree upon. However, depending on the relative bargaining power that each party brings to the table, how the transaction is paid may not be as much of a negotiation as it is a dictation of how the transaction will occur.

Advance Payment

This payment method is probably the most preferable method to the seller. The buyer pays for the goods before they are shipped.[1] This is beneficial to the seller because they know that their efforts are already compensated and do not have to worry about incurring a loss due to lack of payment. This payment method is somewhat risky to the buyer because there are no guarantees that the goods will be shipped and the payment could put them in a financially risky situation.

Documentary Credit

A documentary credit, also known as a letter of credit is the most secure payment method for both the buyer and the seller in terms of risk sharing.[2] A letter of credit is a guarantee by a bank to pay the seller upon presentation of certain documents—the security in this transaction stems from the trustworthiness of the bank.

Documentary Collection

This method of payment is about as equally risky for both the buyer and seller as a letter of credit; however, this type of payment includes less of a transaction cost than the letter of credit.[3] In this scenario, the seller ships the goods but delivers the specified documents to the banks. Upon delivery, the buyer will pay the bank, which, in turn, pays the seller, and the buyer receives the specified documents. This method is most easily thought as an international "cash on delivery" system.

Direct Payment

This payment method is the most secure to the buyer and the most risky to the seller. In this case, money transfer from the buyer to the seller; this can be done either when the goods are received, or whenever the contract stipulates that payment be made. In this case the seller is completely reliant on the buyer to receive payment and there may be limited recourse the seller can seek for non-payment.

Ethical Considerations 4.1

International Finance Ethics

Woodhouse A.C. Israel Cocoa Ltd v. Nigerian Product Marketing Co Ltd [1972] AC 741, http://legalmax.info/conbook/index.htm#t=woodhous.htm

---

[1] Edward G. Hinkelman, "Introducing the Basic Terms of Payment." In *A Short Course on International Payments*, by Edward G. Hinkelman, 182. World Trade Press, 2002
[2] Ibid.
[3] Ibid.

Peace Palace Library, "International Finance Law Introduction," (n.d.), http://www.peacepalacelibrary.nl/research-guides/economic-and-financial-law/international-financial-law/

The goal of international finance law is to provide guidelines that international markets and transactions can rely upon to create financial stability. Each national jurisdiction must be aware of their financial environment to maintain their international trade standing, national interest, and standards. The most imminent threat is widespread globalization, developments in technology, and financial innovation.

An important aspect of finance law is agreeing upon the currency of the contract and the currency of payment. In the 1972 case of *Woodhouse A.C. Israel Cocoa Ltd. v. Nigerian Product Marketing Co. Ltd*, the two parties created a sales contract for coffee beans payable in Nigerian pounds. The seller, however, asked to send the invoice with pound sterling as the currency at demand. Since the pound sterling and Nigerian pound were of equal value at this moment, the buyer immediately accepted the delivery without objection. Soon after, the pound sterling's value fell drastically compared to the Nigerian pound, which caused the buyer to attempt to convert their contracts back to Kenyan shilling.

It was held that promissory estoppel could not be enacted due to the parties' agreement of currency prior to the delivery of the goods and that the buyer clearly knew what was implied with the currency change. If this case could not raise promissory estoppel, then was it unethical for the seller to maintain the currency change that ultimately benefitted that one party?

Bill of Exchange

Origins of Bills of Exchange

Historically, bills of exchange originated when merchants and traders in 14th and 15th century Europe wished to find a safer and more efficient way to receive payment for their goods rather than by utilizing gold or other forms of money. As more and more merchants bought into the idea that paper could be traded and used as payment instead of gold and other currency, laws had to be enacted in order to validate and enforce any disputes that arose. Bills of exchange became formally recognized by statute in 1822 in England under the *English Bills of Exchange Act* and in the United States in the *Uniform Negotiable Instruments Law* in 1866.

Bills of Exchange Today

Today, a bill of exchange is a specialized type of international draft commonly used to accelerate foreign money payments in many types of international transactions. Bills of exchange are widely used and despite their common history, there are different requirements for their content across different parts of the world. According to the *English Bills of Exchange Act*, in order for a bill of exchange to be valid, the following must be contained:[4]

- An unconditional order in writing
- Addressed by one person to another
- Signed by the person writing it

---

[4] Parliament of the United Kingdom, "*Bills of Exchange Act 1882*," August 18, 1882. http://www.legislation.gov.uk/ukpga/Vict/45-46/61

- With a requirement that the person whom it is addressed pay on demand or at a fixed or determinable future time
- A sum certain in money
- To the order of a specific person or to bearer

The English requirements for a bill of exchange are very similar to the requirements set out by the Uniform Commercial Code—which will be discussed in more detail later on in this chapter. However, according to the United Nations *Convention on Bills of Exchange and Promissory Notes*, in order for the bill of exchange to be valid, the words "bill of exchange" must appear on the instrument.[5]

Laws Governing Bills of Exchange

Until the middle of the 17th century, bills of exchange were governed by a single international law, the **lex mercatoria**. This law clarified that the bill of exchange was allowed to act as a *permutation pecuniae presentis cum absenti* (an exchange of money by one who is present with one who is absent).[6] Since bills of exchange were used exclusively for trade between distant places, it was exempt from the Christian Church's mandate that interest cannot be charged on loans.[7] Because of this exemption, bills of exchange rapidly became the way to do business with medieval banking.

Following this, the *Bills of Exchange Act* was created in 1882 in England, and is still in use today throughout many of its former colonies. Today, the *Bills of Exchange Act* continues to be a powerful force in the Commonwealth with revisions occasionally being made.

Bills of Exchange in Other Parts of the World

The United States' answer to a unified rulebook for negotiable instruments came in the form of the **Uniform Commercial Code (UCC)**, which was first established in 1952.[8] This act's goal was to create a clear set of rules and regulations related to sales and transactions of negotiable instruments across the United States. Revisions are made continuously to ensure that the act remains relevant.

Following World War 1 in 1930, the League of Nations created the Geneva Convention on the Unification of the Law Relating to Bills of Exchange (ULB), and two years later they also created the Geneva Conventions on Unification of the Law Related to Checks (ULC). The goal of these conventions was to create unified ruling on bills of exchange, and for the most part have successfully done so. A very large majority of Europe follows these guidelines and standards.

Currently there are no uniform worldwide rules governing bills of exchange exchange. However, there is a widely followed set of international rules governing the collection of checks, as set out by the International Chamber of Commerce (ICC) called the **Uniform Customs and Practice for Documentary Credits (UCP)**. Most domestic banks set out their policies in accordance with the ICC's rules, which makes the UCP the most common rules to be followed in the international community.

---

[5] United Nations, "*United Nations Convention on International Bills of Exchange and International Promissory Notes*," 1988. https://www.uncitral.org/pdf/english/texts/payments/billsnotes/X_12_e.pdf

[6] *Principles of Contract Law: A Compilation of Law Mercatoria?* November 22, 2012. http://blogs.law.nyu.edu/transnational/2012/11/principles-of-contract-law-a-compilation-of-lex-mercatoria/

[7] Ibid.

[8] For more information regarding the UCC, visit https://www.law.cornell.edu/ucc

Drafts

Draft Background

Drafts are an unconditional order to pay a certain sum of money. In their most basic form, a draft is a signed order to the **drawer** (signature of the person who issues the bill, in most cases the buyer), given to a **drawee** (the name of the person who is to pay, in most cases, a bank) who is in possession of money to which the drawer is entitled, to pay a sum of money to a third party, the **payee** (the name of the person who will be receiving the money), on demand or at a definite time in the future.[9] The most recognizable form of a draft is a check where the company who issued the check is the drawer, the bank where you deposit the check is the drawee, and you are the payee. Drafts come in several different forms but we will focus on a select few that are mainly used in international business transactions. In general a draft contains: an unconditional order to pay a definite sum of money, the name of the person who will be paying, the date that the payment will be made, where the payment will be made, the name of the person who will be paid, the place and date where the bill was issued, and the signature of the person who issued the bill.[10]

Sight Draft

As we had touched on previously, a draft is an unconditional order to pay a certain sum of money. A **sight draft** is a type of draft to be paid upon presentation or demand, it is known as a sight draft because it is payable "on sight."[11] Checks written on a demand deposit are an example of these types of drafts. For shipping transactions, sight drafts must be accompanied by the required shipping documents in order for the seller to be paid. The documents are then sent "for collection" to the buyer's bank where they act as agents for the seller and are authorized to accept or reject the shipment on the buyer's behalf. Unlike a time draft, where there is a short delay in payment after the buyer receives the goods, the sight draft is payable upon demand immediately.[12]

Time Draft

A draft that is payable at a future date or after the buyer has received and accepted the appropriate documents, is called a **time draft**.[13] One of the benefits to a time draft is that it can be used to allow an exporter to extend credit to a buyer who accepts the draft and receives documents as opposed to a sight draft, where there is a possibility of no such extension. In order for any draft to become an obligation to any of the parties, acceptance of the draft must occur first.

Acceptance

Acceptance turns non-binding documents into an unconditional order to pay. Under UCC, acceptance "may consist of the drawee's signature alone," which creates either bank or trade acceptance and is therefore an unconditional obligation to pay the draft on the due date.[14] Following acceptance, the draft is returned through the proper channels to the seller who then has a couple of options regarding what to do with the draft following acceptance. The seller can hold the draft until its maturity and receive full payment, or it can sell it at a discount to a local bank or commercial institution to receive immediate cash, although the cash will be at a discounted rate. As a general rule, the greater the

---

[9] *West's Encyclopedia of American Law, edition 2.* S.v. "draft." http://legal-dictionary.thefreedictionary.com/draft

[10] Ibid.

[11] Investopedia. *Sight Draft.* n.d. http://www.investopedia.com/terms/s/sight-draft.asp

[12] Ibid.

[13] Investopedia. *Time Draft.* n.d. http://www.investopedia.com/terms/t/time-draft.asp

[14] (§ 3-409. ACCEPTANCE OF DRAFT; CERTIFIED CHECK. 2002)

Time Draft

At sight _____ Date _____ City _____
(Indicate above whether payable on demand or other time limit)

Pay to the order of _____ Canada
(Name of exporter, exporter's bank or payee)

_____ Canadian Dollars

For value received and charged to the account of National Bank Letter of Credit No. _____

The transaction which gives rise to this
instrument is the:

☐ Import   ☐ Domestic Shipment

☐ Warehousing

Of _____

from_____ to _____

To: National Bank, N.A.
    Anytown, Canada
(Importer, Buyer, or Drawee)

_____
Drawer's Signature (Exporter)

Sight Draft

Date:

To:

Dear

Upon presentment, you are directed to debit our account and pay to the order of_____the
sum of Dollars ($_____).

_____
Account Name

By: _____
Authorized Signature

_____
Account Number

creditworthiness the buyer in the initial transaction, the higher the seller will be able to sell the draft for. There are two generally accepted ways in which acceptance can take place and they are banker's and trader's acceptance.

Banker's Acceptance

A **banker's acceptance** is a time draft that is accepted by a bank. With this acceptance, the bank has an unconditional obligation to pay the seller. The bank substitutes its own credit for that of the buyer in order to finance the seller. At maturation, the bank will then pay the holder of the draft the previously negotiated sum and then the buyer will reimburse the bank. As mentioned previously, the holder of the draft can then hold the draft until its maturation, or sell it at a discount. The issue of banker's acceptance came up in *Voest-Apline International v. Chase Manhattan Bank*,[15] where Voest-Alpine International argued that Chase Manhattan Bank had accepted fraudulent documents and thus Voest was due for payment as a beneficiary to a letter of credit. The court found that with the development of the Uniform Commercial Code, the elimination of a verbal acceptance, by virtue, also eliminated oral acceptance, and remanded the case for further consideration.[16] This is significant because this case further exemplified the UCC requirements that acceptance must be explicitly stated on the face of the documents.

Banker's Draft

At sight _____ Date _____ City _____ (Indicate above whether payable on demand or other time limit) Pay to the order of _____ Canada (Name of exporter, exporter's bank or payee) _____ Canadian Dollars For value received and charged to the account of National Bank Letter of Credit No. _____	

The transaction which gives rise to this instrument is the:

☐ Import ☐ Domestic Shipment

☐ Warehousing

Of _____

from_____ to _____

ACCEPTED

Date_____

National Bank, N.A.

PerAuthorized Signature

To: National Bank, N.A.
    Anytown, Canada
(Importer, Buyer, or Drawee)

Drawer's Signature (Exporter)

---

[15] *Voest-Alpine International Corp., v. Chase Manhattan Bank, 707 F.2d 680[1983]*, 1983 http://law.justia.com/cases/federal/appellate-courts/F2/707/680/230008/

[16] Ibid.

Trader's Acceptance

A **trader's acceptance** is a time draft that is accepted by a seller of merchandise. With this acceptance, the seller is the one who creates the draft. Depending on who the buyer is and the relationship that the buyer and seller have, a trader's acceptance can be riskier than a banker's acceptance. Because the seller is reliant upon the buyer to receive payment instead of a bank, the risk is generally higher with a trader's acceptance because the transaction is very reliant upon the buyer's credit as opposed to a bank's. As with a banker's acceptance, the draft can be held to maturity to receive full payment, or sold at a discount to receive immediate payment.

Negotiable Instruments

Under UCC Article 3, a **negotiable instrument** is a signed writing, containing an unconditional promise or order to pay a fixed sum of money, to order or to bearer, on demand or at a definite time.[17] Negotiable instruments are anything that can be traded or sold, though generally they take the form of promissory notes, bills of exchange or checks. Now, negotiation in this sense may not be what is typically thought of when the word negotiation comes to mind. With respect to negotiable instruments, negotiation simply means that the instrument is able to be transferred to another party.

Negotiable instruments serve two main purposes: a substitute for money, as well as acting as a financing or credit device. Additionally, when it comes to negotiable instruments, they can be made out to order or to bearer, each possessing their own qualities.

Made to Order

A negotiable instrument that is made out to order means that the instrument is made out to a named recipient, and unless you are the person who the instrument is made out to, you will not be able to cash it. Order papers can be transferred by the named payee to another party, and this is generally done in order to receive immediate payment as opposed to waiting for the completion of the task for which the instrument was made. The transferring of title in this case is called endorsement and is done so by the original payee signing their name on the back of the instrument, and naming a new payee. Interestingly, instruments that are made to order can be converted to bearer instruments by the original payee endorsing the instrument and naming the new payee "to bearer."

Made to Bearer

A negotiable instrument that is made to bearer simply means that whoever is in possession of the instrument has the ability to deposit the instrument and receive payment. A very commonly used example that might come to mind when thinking of negotiable instruments made to bearer would be bearer bonds. Having the negotiable instrument being made to bearer enables title to be transferred more easily because one simply needs to be in possession of the instrument in order to claim ownership—no endorsement is needed on the face of the instrument to transfer ownership. Bearer instruments do run the risk of unintentional ownership due to the fact that if the intended owner misplaces the instrument, anyone who finds the instrument is then entitled to the title of the goods. In order to minimize this risk, bearer instruments can be transformed into order instruments by endorsing the instrument and then naming a specific payee.

Promissory Notes

Promissory notes are a two-party transaction where the maker unconditionally promises to pay a definite sum of money in the future or on demand to the recipient, or payee. While promissory notes

---

[17] (§ 3-104. NEGOTIABLE INSTRUMENT. 2002)

are more formal than an IOU, they still not as reliable as a letter of credit or bank guarantee. If you are accepting a promissory note as a method of payment, it is very important that you are able to trust the other party issuing the note or be very confident that there is some other form of financial recourse available to you if the note is defaulted upon.

Promissory Note
(Term: Fixed Rate of Interest)
(Interest Only)

$1,000,000   Due: October 1, 2018

FOR VALUE RECEIVED the undersigned promises to pay on September 29, 2016 to or to the order of CanCo at 1039 Westboro Street, Toronto, Ontario, the principal amount of $1,000,000 in lawful money of Canada and to pay interest at the rate of 5% per year calculated monthly not in advance on the principal amount from time to time remaining unpaid, to be payable on the 1st day of each and every month commencing on the 1st day of September, 2016 up to and including the 1st day of October, 2020. Payments received will be applied firstly in payment of unpaid accrued interest and the balance if any in reduction of principal.

Upon default in payment of any payment when due under this Note, the entire unpaid balance of the principal amount and accrued interest will become immediately due and payable without notice or demand and the undersigned covenants to pay interest on it and on subsequent overdue interest at the above rate, both before and after judgment, until paid in full. The covenants to pay interest will not merge on the taking of a judgment or judgments with respect to any of the obligations stipulated for in this Note.

The undersigned waives demand and presentment for payment, notice of non-payment, protest, notice of protest, notice of dishonour, bringing of suit and diligence in taking any action.

DATED: August 13, 2016

By: _____
Authorized Signing Officer

Letter of Credit

Letter of Credit Background

Letters of credit are flexible banking instruments that are used around the world. In a broad picture, letters of credit substitute the name of the buyer with the name of the bank, opening up business opportunities for the buyer that previously may not have been available due to financial or other constraints. While in theory, almost all large banks can issue letters of credit, in practice, only a few banks actually issue letters of credit with these banks being located within international banking hubs. In order to clarify the general idea of letters of credit, it is helpful to use an analogy of a credit card company. When you buy something using your credit card, your credit card's reputation and bank account is used for payment instead of yours. While you still pay back your credit card company, you are sometimes able to purchase goods that you otherwise may not be able to because of the reputation of your credit card company. This is basically what letters of credit are used for when it comes to transactions. However instead of a credit card company, it is generally a bank that guarantees payment, but the principle of the transaction remains the same.

Types of Letters of Credit

There are many different variations created over the years of letters of credit. However, the basic purpose has not changed, and that is providing comfort to buyers and sellers in an international transaction, by essentially replacing the credit of the buyer with financial backing of a bank that issues the letter of credit. There are two basic types of letters of credit used:

1. *Commercial Letter of Credit.* The basic payment documents guaranteeing payment.
2. *Standby Letter of Credit.* A secondary payment device, which guarantees performance of a party.

Independent Principle

One of the central tenets of letter of credit law is the independent principle. A letter of credit is distinct from the underlying contract it is supposed to backstop. Any disputes concerning the beneficiary's performance of its obligations under the contract with the counterparty, or disputes between the issuing bank and the contract counterparty, have no bearing on the bank's obligation to pay the beneficiary if the documents presented conform to the letter of credit.

The fundamental principle governing documentary letters of credit and the characteristic which gives them their international commercial utility and efficacy is that the obligation of the issuing bank to honor a draft on a credit, when it is accompanied by documents which appear on their face to be in accordance with the terms and conditions of the credit, is independent of the performance of the underlying contract for which the credit was issued. Disputes between the parties to the underlying contract concerning its performance cannot as a general rule justify a refusal by an issuing bank to honor a draft which is accompanied by apparently conforming documents.[18]

Benefits of a Letter of Credit

There are benefits available to both the buyer and seller of goods in obtaining a letter of credit. To the seller, a letter of credit provides them with a financial guarantee that they will receive payment and allows them to finance production and exportation of their goods. To the buyer, a letter of credit enables them to do business with large companies that may not have done business with the buyer under normal circumstances. From a general standpoint, what really happens is that the buyer knows that they will be provided with goods and the seller knows that they will receive payment.

Letters of credit are also very good ways of financing deals. One of the reasons for this is that sometimes you cannot finance a deal through equity financing and in order to help the transaction proceed, a letter of credit will allow you to find the capital that is necessary. Additionally, a letter of credit can allow the manufacturer of the goods a way to finance production if there are large upfront costs associated with production. This can be done by red clause payments, which will be covered in more detail later. Basically, the buyer is giving a loan to the seller to minimize the upfront costs of production, but also the negotiability of a letter of credit can allow the seller to transfer title to the payment in exchange for immediate capital by selling the title to receive payment to another party.

---

[18] *Bank of Nova Scotia v. Angelica-Whitewear Ltd.*, [1987] 1 S.C.R. 59

Consequences of Not Obtaining a Letter of Credit

While it is generally advisable that letters of credit be used for most international transactions: it is not mandatory. However, the consequences of not obtaining the letter of credit can cause a breach of contract or even bankruptcy. When a buyer and seller enter into a contract that requires either party to obtain a letter of credit, the legal consequences of whether the contract is enforceable or not depends on one of two conditions of the contract. If the letter of credit was a condition precedent to the formation of the contract, failure to obtain a letter of credit will relieve the parties of their obligation to finance the transaction with a letter of credit. However, if the letter of credit was a condition for the performance of the contract and there was no letter of credit obtained, this results in a breach of contract because the contract already exists and the injured party is entitled to sue for damages. This concept is best explained in the following case, *Trans Trust S.P.R.L. v. Danubian Trading Co., Ltd.*[19] where the judge had to decide whether or not the letter of credit was a condition of the contract or condition precedent to the formation of a contract.

Trans Trust Sprl v. Danubian Trading Co., Ltd.[20]

Facts:

A British seller agreed to sell 1,000 tons of rolled steel sheets to a Belgian buyer and to have them delivered FOB Antwerp. In order for the British seller to carry out the contract, they contacted an American company, S.A. Azur.

The seller was under the impression that a condition of the contract was for the buyer to create a confirmed letter of credit with the Krediet Bank in Brussels, with its beneficiary being S.A. Azur. However, the buyer did not create this letter of credit, and when urged by the seller to do so, they did not comply. The British seller then sued the Belgian buyer for breach of contract, alleging that the buyer's failure to create a letter of credit constituted a breach of contract. The buyer's defense was that the letter of credit was a condition precedent to the contract, and without the letter of credit, there was no contract, and thus, no breach occurred.

Issue:

Was there a contract in this transaction?

Decision:

The trial judge held that there was a contract, and that one of the terms of the contract was that the buyer would immediately seek for the creation of a letter of credit, and since the buyer did not do so, they were liable for breach of contract.

Reasons:

Sometimes there are conditions that are condition precedents to the formation of a contract, that is, certain conditions must be fulfilled in order for the contract to actually be formed, and there are some conditions that are actually conditions within a contract, and their fulfillment is vital to the terms of the contract. It is very important to find out what type of condition the promise of opening a letter of credit was in this case.

When the buyers stated in a letter to the seller that "a credit will be opened forthwith," it did not appear to be a statement that was merely a contemplation of whether or not the buyer would be opening a letter of credit, but that the statement was a firm promise from the buyer to the seller that a credit would be opened forthwith. Because of this, the judge held that the formation of a letter of credit was not a condition precedent to the creation of a contract, but rather it was a condition contained within the contract.

---

[19] Trans Trust S.P.R.L. v. Danubian Trading Co., Ltd. [1952] 2 QB 297
[20] Ibid.

Parties to a Letter of Credit Transaction

There may be four or three parties in a typical letter of credit, depending on the circumstances of the transaction. In a domestic transaction, not as many parties are typically required, however the option is available to use the same process as you would in an international transaction. The number of parties in a transaction is largely reliant on a number of factors including relationship between the parties and where the parties are located.

- **Account Party**, or the buyer, is the party that applies for the letter of credit.[21] As shown previously, the actual application for a letter of credit can be a conditional term to the formation of the contract, or application may be required upon formation of the contract.

- **Issuing Bank** is the bank that actually opens the letter of credit.[22] The issuing bank is responsible for reviewing the documents provided by the beneficiary party to make sure that they meet the requirements of the contract before issuing payment. Generally, the issuing bank is the bank of the buyer.

- **Beneficiary** to the letter of credit is the seller of the goods or services.[23] The beneficiary has to submit the required documents to the issuing bank in order to be paid for their services or goods.

- **Advising Bank** is not required in a letter of credit transaction; however, it is very useful for the beneficiary to utilize one in an international transaction. The advising bank handles communication with the issuing bank and can ease the transaction between the buyer and seller. The advising bank is usually located in the beneficiary's city and their role is to advise the beneficiary and insure the beneficiary that the letter of credit is valid. This is usually accomplished because the advising bank has a relationship with the issuing bank. They also help ensure that the appropriate documents are collected and sent to the issuing bank.

- **Confirming Bank** is also optional in a letter of credit transaction. Irrevocable letters of credit can be confirmed or unconfirmed. An issuing bank that issues a confirmed letter of credit may require that a confirming bank confirm the letter of credit for the beneficiary, which means the confirming bank is obligated to ensure payment to the beneficiary.[24] The benefit to the seller of having a confirming bank is the possible lack of trust of the issuing bank's creditworthiness. Further, the seller may be uneasy about the country where the issuing bank is located. A confirming bank can provide the financial assurance that is required in order to facilitate the transaction.

Contracts in a Letter of Credit Transaction

Throughout the process of a letter of credit transaction, a number of contracts are made, each with their respective terms and conditions that must be fulfilled. While these contracts may differ with a different number of parties, the core goal of the contracts stays the same, which is to make sure that each party benefits from the transaction and crafting the contract to ensure that the level of risk is minimized.

- **Initial Contract (Transaction)**

  The initial contract is the sales contract which outlines the terms and includes the means by which the contract will be paid (in this case a letter of credit), naming the required documents of the transaction, and naming an advising bank, which is generally a bank in the seller's home country or one that the seller is very familiar with.

---

[21] *Understanding and Using Letters of Credit. Part 1.* 1999 https://www.crfonline.org/orc/cro/cro-9-1.html
[22] Ibid.
[23] Ibid.
[24] Ibid.

- **Issuing Bank/Buyer**

  The next contract is between the buyer and the issuing bank. This contract lays out the terms agreed upon in the previous contract, and the bank will use these terms when committing their documentary review of the letter of credit and the corresponding documents provided.

- **Advising (Confirming Bank/ Seller)**

  The third contract is between the advising (confirming) bank and the seller. This contract creates an obligation that the bank needs to pay the seller upon the proper presentation of documents that are given to the advising bank once the goods have been shipped to the buyer from the seller.

- **Banks (Advising [Confirming Bank]/Issuing Bank)**

  The final contract is between the advising (confirming) bank and the issuing bank. This contract outlines the obligations that the banks have to each other and reiterates the terms of the letter of credit.

The reason for so many contracts is to minimize the risk associated with the transaction. If the seller does not trust the buyer's bank, they may choose to hire the services of a bank that they are comfortable with in order to strengthen the trust in the transaction. Additionally, the seller's bank will also have a contract with the buyer's bank in order to guarantee payment. In order to clarify this example a little bit, illustrations have been provided along with a mock scenario in order to allow you to grasp a deeper understanding of the concepts.

Four-Party Transaction with a Letter of Credit

In this hypothetical scenario, the transaction will be between a Canadian company, the Seller (CanCo) and a buyer, a Russian company (RussCo). However, in an effort to make this transaction more realistic, CanCo will use a Cyprus subsidiary (CypCo) as the party to the transaction. CypCo will hire a Cyprus bank as its confirming bank. CypCo is the Seller and RussCo is the Buyer.

1. The Seller and the Buyer agree on terms of sale, one of which is the Buyer provide a letter of credit to guarantee payment.
2. The Buyer requests their bank open a letter of credit in favor of the Seller. This letter of credit includes all instructions to the seller concerning the equipment.
3. The Buyer's bank approves the letter of credit and forwards to its correspondent bank (Advising or Confirming Bank) in the Seller's area requesting confirmation and that they will perform the advising or confirming functions.
4. The Advising bank advises or confirms the letter of credit and forwards the original to the Seller (Beneficiary).
5. The Seller (Beneficiary) ships the goods and the other documents required by the letter of credit to the Buyer.
6. The Seller arranges with the freight forwarder to deliver the goods to the appropriate port or airport.
7. When the goods are loaded, the freight forwarder completes the necessary documents.
8. The Seller (Beneficiary) presents the documents required by the letter of credit to the advising or confirming bank to be examined for compliance and approval.

9. The confirming bank forwards payment to the Seller.

10. Issuing bank examines the documents for compliance. If they are in compliance, the issuing bank debits the Buyer's account and sends the funds to the confirming bank.

11. Issuing bank forwards the documents to the Buyer so the Buyer can claim the goods.

Generally, the shipping of documents will move faster than the shipment of goods so in all likelihood, the accounts will be settled by the time the goods arrive in Russia. If the documents are accepted in Russia, the Cyprus subsidiary will be paid by the Cyprus bank (confirming bank), who will be paid by the Russian bank (issuing bank), who will be paid by the Russian buyer. The illustration in Figure 4.1 is meant to help you understand how this transaction would occur if it happened as described above. The numbers display the order in which the action would occur.

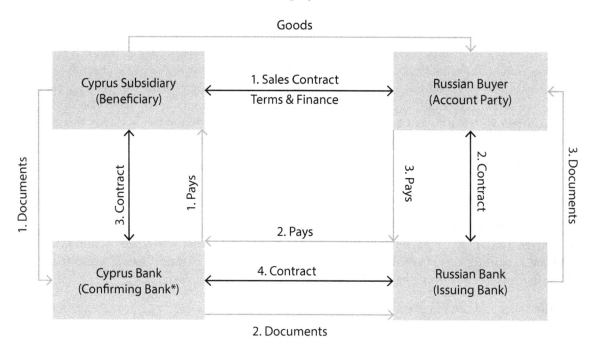

Figure 4.1: Four-Party Letter of Credit Process

Three-Party Transaction with a Letter of Credit

This scenario will build off of the one used for the four-party letter of credit transaction. For this example, we are again faced with a Cyprus subsidiary and Russian buyer, however, instead of two banks in the transaction, there will only be one. For the sake of the example, let's say that both the Cyprus subsidiary and Russian buyer both trust a Cyprus bank. The steps in this transaction will be very similar to the four-party transaction.

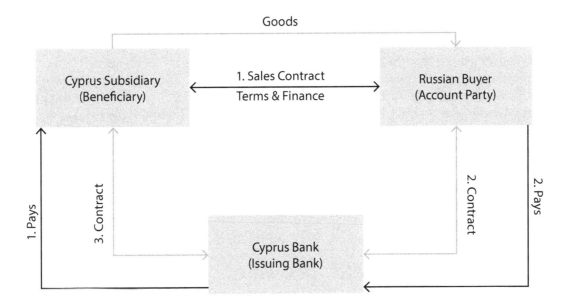

Figure 4.2: Three-Party Letter of Credit Process

Maurice O' Meara Co. v. National Park Bank of New York

Facts:

National Park Bank issued a letter of credit addressed to Ronconi and Miller, at the request of the account party, the Sun Herald. The letter of credit was taken out so that it would cover "the shipment of 1,322 tons of newsprint paper in 72 ½- inch and 36 ½-inch rolls to test 11-12, 32 lbs. at 8 ½ cents per pound net weight." The letter of credit did not require an independent testing certificate from a testing laboratory to accompany the documents. When Ronconi and Miller's invoice and documents arrived at the bank, it refused to pay because there was no way to verify the strength of the paper. Ronconi and Miller transferred their right to collect payment to Maurice O'Meara, who brought an action against the National Park Bank in order to be paid the full amount of the draft. Maurice O'Meara asserted that the bank had no legal right to test or inspect the paper since it wasn't required by the letter of credit.

Issue:

Was the bank right to refuse payment even though they did so for reasons not included in the letter of credit?

Decision:

National Park Bank's responsibility to pay under the letter of credit is completely separate from what is required by the contract. National Park Bank had no right to refuse payment even if they believed that the paper was not of the kind that was ordered as long as the documents presented were compliant with the terms set out in the letter of credit.

Reasons:

The extent of interest that the bank has to the letter of credit transaction is that to which the documents comply with the terms set out in the letter of credit. There is an appropriate legal remedy available to the buyer if the paper turned out to be different than the paper originally requested in the sales contract, but that is separate from the letter of credit. If there was a requirement in the letter of credit to have the paper be a certain strength, then the bank may be justified in requesting a test, but since the letter of credit had no such requirement, then the bank is not allowed to conduct any additional tests. If the drafts, when presented, were accompanied by the proper documents, then the bank is bound to make the payment under the letter of credit, regardless of whether it knew, or had any reason to believe that the paper delivered was not compliant with the terms set out in the letter of credit.

Laws Applicable to the Letter of Credit

There are two distinct sets of laws that are available to documentary transactions. One is mainly focused on harmonizing commercial transactions across the United States, and is called the Uniform Commercial Code (UCC), and the other is more focused on the rules that govern international letter of credit transactions called the Uniform Customs and Practice for Documentary Credits (UCP).

UCC

The goal of harmonizing commercial transactions across the United States has many practical purposes and has been widely successful with its implementation throughout the United States and its territories. The UCC came into force in 1952, and contains many different articles but the one that is most relevant to this chapter is Article 5, which relates to letters of credit. This Article sets out the definition, scope, requirements, and all other relevant information related to a letter of credit transaction in the United States.[25]

UCP

The International Chamber of Commerce handles the UCP with the most recent edition of the UCP being UCP 600, whose rules have been effective since July 1, 2007. The UCP is in use in virtually every nation in the world and the majority of letter of credits issued are subject to the rule of the most recent UCP revisions. In the terms of the UCP, letters of credit are considered to be irrevocable unless the letter of credit clearly states otherwise. An important revision contained within UCP 600 is that it replaced the phrase "reasonable time" of refusal or acceptance of documents to a maximum period of five banking days in order to clear up any discrepancies.[26]

Additionally, UCP 600 is moving towards substantial compliance, instead of strict compliance. Substantial compliance eases the requirement that documents be fully compliant—it allows for certain discrepancies.[27]

A key takeaway from this section is that while the UCC sets out rules for the United States, the UCP has almost universal acceptance, and has a much greater impact on international letters of credit than does the UCC.

---

[25] (U.C.C. - ARTICLE 5 - LETTERS OF CREDIT 1995)

[26] International Chamber of Commerce, "UCP 600," July 1, 2007 http://www.fd.unl.pt/docentes_docs/ma/mhb_ MA_24705.pdf

[27] Ibid.

Letters of Credit Characteristics

1. **Negotiable Instrument:** Generally letters of credit are negotiable instruments. Negotiable instruments is explained above. A beneficiary may direct the issuing bank to pay another bank named by the beneficiary. The new bank becomes a holder in due course of the letter of credit, and accepts the letter of credit for the specified value and in good faith without notice of any claims against it. This is on the assumption that the documents are in order, are presented and acceptable to the issuing bank. An exception is a straight negotiation, which means the issuing bank's obligation to pay is exclusive to the beneficiary of the letter of credit. Certain language in the letter of credit is required for a straight negotiation such as "we engage with you" or "available with ourselves." In a straight negotiation, the issuing bank's obligation to pay does not extend to a party that purchases the draft as a holder in due course.

2. **Revocable or Irrevocable:** Letters of credit may be revocable or irrevocable and the status is usually indicated on the face of the letter of credit.

   a. *Revocable:* These are very rare because they can be revoked or modified at any time and for any reason and without notification to the beneficiary. A revocable letter of credit is one by which the bank can revoke at any time; this type of letter of credit provides the seller with a very small amount of security.[28] A revocable letter of credit cannot be confirmed. The letter of credit cannot be revoked once it has been presented to the issuing bank, examined, and found to comply. At that point it becomes final and the draft must be honored.

   b. *Irrevocable:* Irrevocable letters of credit cannot be revoked or modified without the unanimous consent of the issuing bank, the confirming bank, and the seller/beneficiary. An **irrevocable letter of credit** is most commonly used in export transactions and by its very definition, cannot be rescinded for any reason.[29] It is generally advised to avoid revocable letters of credit, but there is one instance where they might be acceptable—in a transaction between a parent company and its subsidiary. If the required documents are presented and the documents conform to the terms and conditions of the letter of credit, the timing requirements are met, then the issuing bank will pay as required.

Confirmed and Unconfirmed Letters of Credit

Whenever a seller does business with someone, risks are involved. Generally, whenever the seller is concerned about the creditworthiness of the issuing bank in another country, or the stability of the economy in that region, or even the reputation of the company they are selling to, a seller may wish that the letter of credit be confirmed by a bank with which the seller is familiar. A **confirmed letter of credit** is one in which a second bank, usually one that the seller is comfortable with, joins the letter of credit transaction to add its guarantee of payment to the seller.[30] In this transaction, the documents will be shipped through the proper banking channels, and upon the presentation of the proper documents, the confirming bank pays the seller, the issuing bank pays the confirming bank, and the issuing bank is paid by the buyer. Since there are more parties in a confirmed letter of credit transaction, and because the banks are exposed to the risk of the transaction (non-payment), a confirmed letter of credit transaction is generally more expensive than an unconfirmed transaction.

---

[28] Edward D. Henkelman. "Standard Credits." *In A Short Course in International Payments*, by Edward D. Henkelman, 182. World Trade Press, 2002.

[29] Ibid.

[30] Ibid.

In an **unconfirmed letter of credit** transaction, only the issuing bank has the responsibility to honour the drafts presented to it for payment.[31] While unconfirmed letters of credit are generally safe to use between developed countries where the parties are familiar with each other. However, as a general rule, it is best to always use confirmed letters of credit.

Ten Rules Regarding International Letters of Credit:

1. *Facial Compliance*: Banks are not allowed to investigate the goods or have any access to the goods apart from the documents presented in the documentary transaction process. Facial compliance has the implication that banks cannot actually inspect the goods themselves to determine whether or not the goods are of a satisfactory condition to be paid or not. Even if there are problems with the goods, for the most part, as long as the documents are consistent with what is required, the banks are obligated to make payment.

2. *Layman's Terms:* The letter of credit may not include any industry-specific terms or any terms that an ordinary person would not be able to recognize or have any troubles discerning. The letter should be issued in as clear language as possible

3. *Strict Compliance*: Banks may reject documents for any discrepancy.[32]

   Recently, many legal experts have made the argument for a movement towards substantial compliance, where even if there are discrepancies present within the documents, as long as they fill their purpose, they should be interpreted as fulfilling their requirements.[33] Additionally, there are ways to still enforce the letter of credit even if there are major discrepancies contained within the documents presented to the bank.

   An example of a violation of strict compliance will be shown later with *Bank of Nova Scotia v Angelica Whitewear Ltd.,* where the Bank of Nova Scotia accepted a bill of lading that included an INCOTERM that was not consistent with what was required by the letter of credit.[34] An example of this related to the Canadian seller and Russian buyer would be if the agreed upon INCOTERM in the letter of credit is FOB Houston and the INCOTERM included in the bill of lading was CIF Dallas, the Russian bank would be expected to reject the documents on the basis that they do not comply with the letter of credit.

4. *Expiry Date:* A letter of credit must have an expiry date to be enforceable. If the letter of credit does not include an expiry date, it will not be considered enforceable and the seller will be without financial protection in the transaction.

5. *21 Day Rule:* UCP 600 21-day rule—the beneficiary party must deliver documents within 21 days of receipt (of bill of lading) to the issuing or advising bank, or the letter of credit automatically expires. If you are worried about this time restriction, in the contract you can specify how many days can pass before the letter of credit expires, and can be changed to fewer or more days, whichever both parties are comfortable with.

6. *Bank's Period of Review*: As per UCP 600, banks have a reasonable period to review documents,[35] which means no longer than five business days or three business days if you are following the UCC.[36]

---

[31] Ibid.

[32] *Letters of credit—strict compliance and the use of banking "shorthand".* September 23, 2013. http://www.incelaw.com/en/knowledge-bank/publications/letters-of-credit-strict-compliance-and-the-use-of-banking-shorthand

[33] International Chamber of Commerce, "UCP 600," July 1, 2007 http://www.fd.unl.pt/docentes_docs/ma/mhb_MA_24705.pdf

[34] *Bank of Nova Scotia v. Angelia Whitewear Ltd., [1987] 1 SCR 59,* March, 1987. https://www.canlii.org/en/ca/scc/doc/1987/1987canlii78/1987canlii78.html?autocompleteStr=bank%20of%20nova%20scotia%20v%2F%20&autocompletePos=4

[35] International Chamber of Commerce, "UCP 600," July 1, 2007 http://www.fd.unl.pt/docentes_docs/ma/mhb_MA_24705.pdf

[36] (Uniform Commercial Code n.d.)

7. **Presumption of Irrevocability**: UCP 600 and UCC Article 5 presumes that a letter of credit is irrevocable unless it clearly states on its face that it is revocable.

8. **Insurance Certificate**: The insurance certificate must not be dated later than date of loading and should be in the amount of CIF (cost, insurance, and freight) plus 10%. The concept of CIF plus 10% is that your insurance should cover the cost of your insurance, the cost of freight, and the 10% is considered the least amount that you might profit on the transaction.

9. **Commercial Invoice:** The commercial invoice must include the exact description of the goods shipped as found in the letter of credit.[37] This is due to the fact that banks have to comply with strict compliance, and if the amount of goods are substantially different, or the description of the goods are substantially different, the banks have the responsibility to reject the goods for non-compliance with the letter of credit.

10. **Transferability**: A letter of credit is presumed to be non-transferable unless it specifically states that it is a transferable credit.

Common Discrepancies found in Letters of Credit

1. Incorrect Grammar: Spelling errors and improper use of acronyms.

2. Incorrect Data: Information that does not comply with the terms and conditions of the letter of credit.

3. Inconsistency in Documents: Banks may reject letters of credit when the data in the document conflicts with that in the letter of credit. If the name of the company listed in the letter of credit is "CanCo International Inc." and the commercial invoice lists "CanCo Inc.", this is an inconsistency.

4. Late Shipment: Goods shipped after the permitted shipment date. Documents like the bill of lading must not be dated later than the latest date of shipment. Latest date of shipment is the date of the transport document, usually the bill of lading.

5. Expiry of the Letter of Credit: Banks will usually not accept documents presented after the expiration date of the letter of credit.

6. Missing Documents: The letter of credit calls for certain documents, and usually for so many originals and copies. If documents are missing or there are only two originals when three are required, this is a discrepancy.

7. Carrier Uncertain: The bill of lading needs to be signed by the master or the master's agent and needs to have the carrier named.

8. Late Presentation: The 21 day rule.

9. Incorrect Description of the Goods: The description on the documents must match the letter of credit description.

10. Partial Shipment: Must be clear that a partial shipment is allowed and clearly stated on the documents.

11. Draft: Draft is drawn incorrectly or for wrong amount, or not signed or endorsed.

12. Invoice: Description does not match the letter of credit, including being in the same language.

13. Incorrect Endorsement: Certain documents must be properly endorsed, such as the insurance document, the bill of lading and the bill of exchange.

---

[37] *Understanding and Using Letters of Credit. Part 1.* 1999 https://www.crfonline.org/orc/cro/cro-9-1.html

14. Credit Amount: The credit amount is insufficient to cover the shipment.
15. Multimodal bill of lading:
    a. Multimodal bill of lading presented when the letter of credit calls for port-to-port, or simply "ocean" bill of lading. Is acceptable if "on board" notation includes the name of the vessel and the port of loading.
    b. Multimodal bill of lading presented when shipping terms are FOB, and does not indicate inland freight has been prepaid or otherwise fails to meet requirements of port-to-port shipment.

16. Documents fail to show license numbers, the letter of credit number, or other identification numbers required by the letter of credit.

Obligation of Banks

While banks have somewhat limited obligations in a letter of credit transaction, the duties that they do have are very important. The main priority of banks in a letter of credit transaction is the rule of strict compliance.

Strict Compliance

Strict compliance means that banks are not allowed to check out the physical contents inside the containers shipped, they can only look at the paperwork and see if it is in compliance with the letter of credit requirements.[38] If the documents appear to be in order and there are no major discrepancies, then the bank is forced to pay.

There are many facets in the general rule of strict compliance, and in UCP 600, there was a movement towards substantial compliance—where the terms in the letter of credit and in the documents provided to the bank do not have to be completely similar and the revisions now allow for minor discrepancies.[39] However, in the case that major discrepancies appear on the documents, it is required that the letter of credit be amended to accommodate the discrepancies and approved by the issuing bank, the confirming bank (if applicable), and the beneficiary.

According to UCP 600, if banks are made aware of a major discrepancy, and have had "a reasonable time to examine the documents and determine... whether to take up or to refuse the documents," the new rule provides that if the bank failed to have worked in a timely manner or failed to return the documents to the person who presented them that there is an implied acceptance.[40] So, according to the new rules, failure of action implies that you agree with the documents presented.

According to the UCP, "banks assume no liability or responsibility for the form, sufficiency, accuracy, genuineness, falsification, or legal effect of any documents.[41]" This means that even if the banks are aware that the goods shipped are fraudulent, if the shipping documents appear to be legitimate, the issuing bank must pay the seller. But what if the underlying transaction is fraudulent; can the banks refuse to pay then? The answer is that it depends on the type of letter of credit that the buyer initially applied for. If the letter of credit is revocable, then the banks are able to avoid payment, however, if it is an irrevocable letter of credit, numerous passages in the UCP suggest that the bank will be forced to pay.

---

[38] *Letters of credit—strict compliance and the use of banking "shorthand"*. September 23, 2013. http://www.incelaw.com/en/knowledge-bank/publications/letters-of-credit-strict-compliance-and-the-use-of-banking-shorthand
[39] International Chamber of Commerce, "UCP 600," July 1, 2007 http://www.fd.unl.pt/docentes_docs/ma/mhb_MA_24705.pdf
[40] Ibid.
[41] Ibid.

Bank of Nova Scotia v. Angelica Whitewear Ltd.[42]

Facts:

At the request of Angelica Whitewear Ltd. ("Whitewear"), the Bank of Nova Scotia opened an irrevocable letter of credit in order to create an agreement with a foreign supplier, Protective Clothing Co. ("Protective").

Whitewear took issue with the payment of two drafts that were presented in order to receive payment under the letter of credit by the confirming bank, Shanghai Commercial Bank Ltd. ("Shanghai Commercial"), Protective's advising bank on this transaction. The first draft was paid by the Bank of Nova Scotia on July 26, 1974 and charged to Whitewear's account. On August 2, 1974, when Whitewear was able to take a look at the documents that were provided to the Bank of Nova Scotia, Whitewear noticed that the signature on the inspection certificate accompanying the draft appeared to have been forged. Days later, Whitewear brought a couple of discrepancies on the face of the documents accompanying the second draft for a Protective invoice. Whitewear held that these discrepancies constituted a violation of the terms and conditions of the letter of credit and asked the Bank of Nova Scotia to refuse payment of the second draft. The discrepancies that Whitewear noticed were: the inspection certificate referred to a letter of credit of Shanghai Commercial instead of the Bank of Nova Scotia's letter of credit, the quantity of merchandise shown in the inspection certificate did not closely correspond to the quantity shown in the invoice, and the bills of lading accompanying the draft for invoice called for freight prepaid delivery to Vancouver (the letter of credit was to be CIF Montreal).

In the months following, the Bank of Nova Scotia initiated an action against both respondents (Angelica Corporation had guaranteed Whitewear's liabilities to the appellant) for the balance owed to the Bank of Nova Scotia by Whitewear. Whitewear's defence was that the drafts were improperly paid by the Bank of Nova Scotia and made a cross-demand for damages. The basis for the countersuit by Whitewear was that the first draft never should have been paid and the prices in the second draft were allegedly inflated. The Superior Court dismissed Whitewear's cross-demand and maintained the Bank of Nova Scotia's action. Then the defendants only appealed the portion of the judgement in respect to the inflated prices which were only contained in the second draft (so the fraudulent signature from the first draft didn't matter), to which the Court of Appeal allowed the appeal. The Court of Appeal upheld the defendant's contention based on the fraud in the transaction, but did not deal with the contention on the non-compliance with the terms and conditions of the letter of credit.

Issue:

Were the discrepancies large enough to warrant a breach of strict compliance?

Decision:

The Court of Appeal held that the appeal should be dismissed.

---

[42] *Bank of Nova Scotia v. Angelia Whitewear Ltd.*, [1987] 1 SCR 59, March, 1987. *https://www.canlii.org/en/ca/scc/doc/1987/1987canlii78/1987canlii78.html?autocompleteStr=bank%20of%20nova%20scotia%20v%2F%20&autocompletePos=4*

Reasons:

With regard to the second draft, there was no evidence establishing that the alleged price inflation was brought to the attention of the Bank of Nova Scotia in a timely manner before the payment of the second draft. The Bank of Nova Scotia's knowledge of the fraud and quality of goods in the first draft does not influence whether or not it had any knowledge of alleged fraud when it came to the second draft. Since nothing was brought to the Bank of Nova Scotia's attention for the second draft in a timely enough manner, it was allowed to assume that there was nothing wrong with the second draft.

For two of the discrepancies, there are no grounds for finding that the draft was improperly paid by the Bank of Nova Scotia. The first instance of a discrepancy between the references to the bank's letter of credit was still clear enough to figure out that the same goods were being referenced. The second discrepancy between the quantities of the goods included was not large enough to justify a material refusal of payment.

However, the Bank of Nova Scotia was not justified to accept the documents and pay the second draft because of the discrepancy between the shipping terms in the bill of lading and the letter of credit. Regardless of the fact that the goods came to Whitewear at no additional cost, a documentary non-compliance cannot be fixed even if the underlying contractual terms are completed.

Sztejn v. Henry Schroder Banking Corp.[43]

Facts:

The plaintiff and his business partner contracted to purchase a quantity of hog bristles from Transea Traders, Ltd. ("Transea") who was located in Lucknow, India. In order for the transaction to occur, the plaintiff contracted J. Henry Schroder Banking Corporation ("Schroder"), asking Schroder to issue an irrevocable letter of credit, whose beneficiary is Transea.

The letter of credit reached Transea through Schroder's correspondent bank in India, and Transea then loaded the pre-arranged quantity of material onto a steamship, created the necessary documents in order to comply with the letter of credit. However, the plaintiff alleges that Transea did not actually load the 50 cases with hog bristles; instead the plaintiff alleges that Transea loaded the 50 cases with cow hair and other similarly worthless material. Following this, the complaint says that Transea drew a draft under the letter of credit to the order of the Chartered Bank of India, Australia, and China ("Chartered Bank"), and then presented the draft for payment. The Chartered Bank then presented the documents to Schroder for payment and the plaintiff brought an action seeking to enjoin payment in this fraudulent transaction.

Issue:

Can a letter of credit's payment be enjoined when there is a fraudulent transaction and the plaintiff has brought it to the attention of the bank before the drafts or documents have been presented for payment?

---

[43] *Sztejn v. Henry Schroder Banking Corp 31 N.Y.S.2d 631 [1941] http://uniset.ca/other/cs4/31NYS2d631.html*

Decision:

Schroder was allowed to enjoin payment and the plaintiff was allowed to nullify the contract.

Reasons:

Since it was brought to Schroder's attention that there was active fraud in the transaction before Schroder was presented with the documents or drafts, the principle of independence of Schroder's obligation under the letter of credit should not be extended to protect a dishonest seller, so Schroder is not forced to pay the draft that covers a transaction that is plausibly fraudulent. Note that if Schroder had knowledge of fraud in the transaction, if they were unaware, Schroder still would have had to comply with facial compliance.

Typical Documents Required in a Letter of Credit

The documents required in a documentary transaction can vary, as it is generally up to the parties to determine what documents they require. Documents are vital in the process for both the buyer and seller, for payment and delivery. Some documents represent payment, and others represent delivery. Banks deal with documents and not goods, so documents represent goods. These documents can be divided into different groups as follows:

1. Transport Documents
   a. Bill of Lading: Discussed above.

2. Insurance Documents
   Usually just one document, but can be an insurance policy, insurance certificate, or an open cover. Usually has to be for a minimum of CIF.

3. Financial Documents
   a. Bill of Exchange (Draft): Discussed above.
   b. Commercial Documents
   c. Transaction Contract (Sales Contract)
   d. Commercial Invoice: An itemized account issued by the beneficiary, addressed to the applicant, which describes the goods, unit price, shipping terms, payment terms, delivery date, shipping charges, insurance coverage, etc. Usually, if required, certified by a chamber of commerce.
   e. Packing List: Usually more detailed than the commercial invoice, and helps identify the contents of each package or container.
   f. Inspection Certificate: If a letter of credit calls for an inspection certificate, it usually specifies who must issue the certificate. These are usually used to protect the buyer against receiving substandard goods, as the inspection is usually done by a reputable independent third party. The certificate indicates the goods have been examined and found to be as ordered.

4. Official Documents
   a. Certificate of Origin: Certifies as to the country of origin of the goods described. They are often required by the customs department of the importing country to determine if any preferential duty will be applied. Often these are issued by chambers of commerce.
   b. Consular Invoice: Prepared by the beneficiary on forms provided by the buyer or local consulate office and are stamped and signed by a consular officer. They usually require the value of the goods be shown. Purpose is to control and identify the goods.

Types and Conditions of Letters of Credit

Sometimes, a standard letter of credit will not be enough in order to complete a transaction. In that case, modifications must be made to the letter of credit in order to help the parties complete the transaction. The following section is by no means an exhaustive list on the different conditions available in letters of credit, but it features the most prominent ones.

Transferable Credits

A **transferable letter of credit** can be used in multiple business transactions.[44] The beneficiary to the letter of credit is able to transfer part of the letter of credit to other sub-beneficiaries. The usefulness in a transferable letter of credit is that it allows for a type of middleman relationship. In this case, the middleman, or main beneficiary, buys the goods from the supplier and is able to use the buyer's letter of credit to fund the transaction.[45] The charge is simply taken out from the account and can be split up with many suppliers. Each seller takes his or her profit from the account of the letter of credit. For example, if the Russian buyer wanted multiple suppliers, and did not have the time or resources to find them themselves, they could hire an intermediary to facilitate the transactions. The Russian buyer would take out a transferable letter of credit and name the intermediary as the main beneficiary, who has the power to pay each supplier from the initial letter of credit.

Red Clauses

A **red clause letter of credit** is one where the buyer extends an unsecured loan to the seller.[46] The reason that this could happen could be because the seller needs the capital in order to start producing the product that they will be making for the buyer and the value of the loan is normally taken off the selling price to the buyer. In a most basic sense, a red clause credit is a way of providing financing to the seller from the buyer. If we were to apply this to the Russian buyer and Canadian seller (via their Cyprus subsidiary), this would be used for any of the start-up costs that the Canadian firm may experience while producing Russia's goods. The red clause draft can be up to the full extent of the letter of credit as well. There are no limits in the extent to which that can be advanced.

Revolving Credits

A **revolving letter of credit** can be used for ongoing business transactions and eliminates the need for re-application at the end of every transaction.[47] As draws are taken from the letter of credit account, repayment of the debt refills the account to its full amount until the expiration of the credit. This type of credit can be irrevocable or revocable, and can revolve regarding the balance of the credit, or by date. Revolving credits are used in cases where a buyer and a seller have an arrangement where the buyer wishes to be continually shipped goods and both parties find it more convenient to continually use one letter of credit to handle the transactions as opposed to a number of letters of credit.[48] Relating back to the textbook-wide example, in business this type of letter of credit could be used if the Canadians and Russians have a continuous and trusting relationship that are willing to use one letter of credit for the length of their relationship.

---

[44] Edward D. Henkelman. "Special Letters of Credit." In *A Short Course in International Payments*, by Edward D. Henkelman, 182. World Trade Press, 2002.

[45] Ibid.

[46] Ibid.

[47] Ibid.

[48] Ibid.

Back-to-Back Letter of Credit

In a **back-to-back** letter of credit transaction, a party uses an existing, non-transferable letter of credit, which it is the beneficiary of, in order to open a second letter of credit.[49] The first letter of credit is used as collateral for the second letter of credit. In essence, this is very similar to the seller transferring all or part of the first letter of credit that it is entitled to a final supplier that will provide goods or services to the original seller. Relating back to the textbook-wide example, let's pretend that in order for the Canadian exporters to create the gas valves for the Russian buyers, the Canadian sellers require a source of raw materials in order to produce these valves. The way a back-to-back letter of credit would work would be that the Canadian seller would be the original beneficiary in the letter of credit transaction with the Russian buyer. Since the Canadian buyer is now guaranteed payment via the letter of credit, they are able to use the guaranteed money from the original letter of credit in order to open another letter of credit with their supplier for the raw materials required to produce the gas valves. In order to illustrate this concept, an illustration has been provided in Figure 4.3.

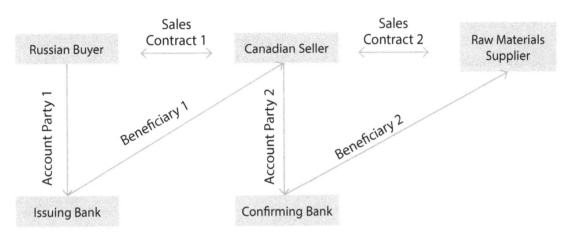

Figure 4.3: Back-to-Back Letter of Credit Illustrated

Standby Letter of Credit

A **standby letter of credit,** which also known as a "non-performing letter of credit," is a letter of credit whose main purpose is to ensure that performance is guaranteed throughout the course of a contract.[50] Whereas a commercial letter of credit is a payment mechanism for a particular international trade transaction, a standby letter of credit serves as a secondary or back-up means of payment. Where a commercial letter of credit is paid when things go right, a standby letter of credit is paid when things go wrong, and it is hoped that the issuing bank will not be called upon to fund the standby letter of credit.

A standby letter of credit can only be drawn on if the customer has failed to perform some required action, as specified in the letter of credit, and before the credit's expiration date. It acts as type of guarantee, usually under construction or service contracts, or as security in any other type of contract. The upside to standby letter of credits is that they do not necessarily even need to be used and the conditions in a contract can be used to determine whether or not the letter of credit will be triggered or not.

In a more general sense, a standby letter of credit protects the buyer by allowing them to receive payment in the case that the seller either defaults on a payment of a debt or fails to meet the performance of an obligation. The upside to a standby letter of credit is that it is very flexible and can be modified to suit your best interests. For example, if you are an individual who contracts a construction company

---

[49] Ibid.

[50] Pritchard, Justin. *Standby Letter of Credit*. February 5, 2015. http://banking.about.com/od/LettersOfCredit/fl/Standby-Letter-of-Credit.htm

to build you an office building, in order to minimize your risk associated with the transaction, you can ask the construction company to have a standby letter of credit and in case of the project running too long or a poor job, you can receive payment from the construction company.

Another example could be in a sale of goods. If you are a buyer, you could ask the seller to take out a standby letter of credit so that if the seller defaults on their performance either through unsatisfactory quality of goods or for other reasons discussed in the letter of credit, you may be entitled to payment in lieu of the goods you wanted to receive. Please note that standby letters of credit are invoked when a company fails to perform its specified tasks, hence why it is called a standby, whereas a regular letter of credit is related to the performance of certain tasks

Other examples of when standby letters of credit are useful include:

- Contracts where a level of quality is required, if the level of quality is not achieved, then the construction company will have to pay the party for whom the project was built.
- Repayment of loans, if the party who is required to pay back the loan is unable to, they may be required to substitute a standby letter of credit in order to guarantee repayment.
- Secure countertrade commitments, if you do not trust the other party in a countertrade arrangement, you could ask for a standby letter of credit so in the case that the other party does not perform as they were asked, you will be entitled to some sort of compensation.

Lac du Bonnet (Rural Municipality) v. Lee River Estates Ltd.[51]

Facts:

The Rural Municipality of Lac du Bonnet ("R.M") and Lee River Estates Ltd. ("Lee River") entered into a development agreement for the development of a cottage lot sub-division. As part of the development agreement, Lee River was required to install and construct services within the sub-division that were compliant with the standards outlined in the development agreement. Lee River was required to provide a letter of credit as part of the agreement, which they did, from Astra Credit Union ("Astra").

Later, the R.M. called the letter of credit, and demanded payment of funds from the letter of credit. After the demand for payment had occurred, Lee River disputed the calling of the letter, as did Astra, who refused to pay any funds.

Issues:

Is the R.M. entitled to payment under a letter of credit issued by the Astra against the credit of Lee River?

Decision:

The R.M. was granted authority in calling the letter of credit held by Astra.

Reasons:

One of the distinguishing features of the letter of credit is the "autonomy" of the credit transaction, its independence from the underlying commercial transaction. Enforcement of a letter of credit does not require that the beneficiary first prove that the customer has defaulted on its obligations from the underlying contract, and in this case, this issue is not even relevant. In order to figure out if the R.M. was justified to call the letter of credit, one must look at the letter of credit itself to see if the R.M. was justified to do so. Here is the excerpt from the letter of credit that is relevant:

---

[51] *Lac du Bonnet (Rural Municipality) v. Lee River Estates Ltd., 1999 CanLII 14224 (MB QB), 1999 http://canlii.ca/t/1qwtq*

"The municipality may call upon it in whole or in part by a written demand signed by the secretary-treasure (*sic*). The letter of credit is renewed from year to year unless the Credit Union gives 30 days advance notice of its intention not to renew. The expiry date will be September 1, 1993."

Two features of the letter are very important. First, all that is required in order for the R.M. in order to call the letter of credit is a written demand signed by the secretary-treasurer. Secondly, the letter of credit is irrevocable. This letter of credit is clear that the R.M. is entitled to immediate payment upon complying with the terms of the letter. There may be proper legal recourse that Lee River could pursue against R.M. in terms of breach of contract, however, it cannot attempt to stop payment under this letter of credit.

Itek Corp. v. First National Bank of Boston[52]

Facts:

The First National Bank of Boston ("FNBB"), as requested by Itek Corp., issued numerous letters of credit to a beneficiary, the Bank of Melli Iran ("Melli"). These letters of credit acted as standby letters of credit and were created as part of a contract between Itek and Iran's Imperial Ministry of War. The content of the contract said that Itek would make and sell high-technology optical equipment to the Ministry of War. The contract stipulated that Itek was to provide two types of guarantees, the first being a down payment guarantee, which gave the Ministry of War a right to reclaim their down payment until an equivalent monetary value had been done on the project, and the second was a good performance guarantee, whose objective was to protect the Ministry of War against breach of contract.

Bank Melli, an agency of the Iranian government, issued the guarantees to the Ministry of War. In addition to these guarantees, Melli also ordered Itek to provide it with standby letters of credit in Melli's favour. The underlying sales contract contained a *force majeure* clause that said if the contract "is cancelled due to *force majeure*, all bank guarantees of good performance of work will be immediately released."

The construction was uneventful until Iran's government collapsed in early 1979. In April 1979, the United States government suspended Itek's export license, who then cancelled the contract in accordance with the *force majeure* clause in the contract.

Issue:

Do the circumstances surrounding Melli's calls on the FNBB's letters of credit establish fraud in the transaction?

Decision:

Melli was without a plausible legal basis for calling the letters of credit and that its call upon them, in the circumstances revealed in this record, constituted "fraud." The injunction was properly issued.

Reasons:

If Melli has no plausible or colorable basis under the contract to call for payment of the letters, its effort to obtain the money is fraudulent and payment can be enjoined.

---

[52] *Itek Corp. v. First National Bank of Boston 730 F.2d 19 (1st Cir. 1984)*, 1984. http://law.justia.com/cases/federal/appellate-courts/F2/730/19/345301/

Optional Parties in a Letter of Credit Transaction

Freight Forwarder

A **freight forwarder** is a person or company who coordinates the movement of goods, secures the bill of lading, and completes other documentation as required by the letter of credit. It is not unnatural for international business transactions that the shipment of goods requires multiple forms of transportation and freight forwarders handle the whole supply chain. Freight forwarders in international business transactions are also required to have the knowledge of processing and preparing customs forms and various other activities that are associated with international transportation. The advantage to hiring a freight forwarder is that they are most likely very familiar with the different customs operations in the countries that the goods are being shipped through and will be able to make the transaction move as efficiently as possible. Generally the exporter and their freight forwarder will sign a power of attorney form that gives the forwarder the ability to sign documents in the name of the exporter.

Surveyors

Sometimes it is not feasible for an employee of the buyer to come to where the seller is shipping their goods to inspect the goods for any defects prior to transportation. In order to combat this problem, many companies hire *surveyors*, who act as agents for the buyer to inspect the goods and make sure that they are in the condition that is required by the contract.[53] This can not only ease distrust about the original state of the goods in the transaction, but can also provide both parties with a more transparent claim against the shipping provider in case of a mishap during the process of shipping the goods. For example, if the surveyor inspects the goods and clears them before they are loaded into a sea can and the goods emerged damaged when extracted from the sea can, the shipping company will be held liable for the damaged goods as well as whichever party was responsible for the shipment, as laid out in by the INCO term in the contract.

Alternative Methods of Guaranteeing Performance

While a letter of credit is widely used, it is by no means the only way to facilitate an international transaction. There are many less common methods that will be covered in this section.

Performance Bond

A **performance bond** is that which insures performance by a contractor, and acts as security for job completion.[54] The most similar comparison that can be made between a performance bond and an example from earlier this chapter would be a standby letter of credit, where if a contractor fails to live up to its obligations, the contractor is forced to pay compensation for the breach of contract. Performance bonds are most commonly used in real estate and land development industries where a contractual breach is foreseeable (no matter how likely). Performance bonds can only be used to the full amount of the bond, and no other form of monetary compensation will be available through the performance bond. However, no depending on the contract, other means of compensation may be available.

---

[53] *The Role of the Marine Surveyor. January 10, 2013 https://www.bimco.org/Education/Seascapes/Maritime_Matters/2013_10_01_The_Role_of_the_Marine_Surveyor.aspx*

[54] *What is a Surety Bond? n.d. https://www.bryantsuretybonds.com/what-is-a-surety-bond*

Bid Bonds

A **bid bond** is a bid that a contractor issues to a project owner in hopes of gaining a contract.[55] Bid bonds are generally required at most auctions and are either fully or partially forfeited if the execution of the contract falls through. Bid bonds generally go along with performance bonds as part of the contractual process and are an essential part of the transaction. An advantage about bid bonds is that they can convey the seriousness of the contractor and their willingness to undertake the project.

Credit Surety

A **credit surety** happens when a guarantor promises to pay a certain party (i.e., Party A) if another party (i.e., Party B), does not comply with the terms of their (Party A and B's) agreement.[56] It is very important for Party A to make sure that guarantor actually has the funds to be able to pay Party A if a breach does occur, and they have to trust that the guarantor will actually make a payment if Party B does not comply with the terms set out in the contract.

Retention Fund

In a broad sense, when it comes to a **retention fund**, payment for the product is withheld until a certain action or condition of the contract has been fulfilled.[57] For example, a certain percentage of the payment could be withheld until the installation of some type of equipment and that equipment is fully operational. With this type of payment it is very important to specify what equipment qualifies in terms of installation and what needs to be done for the equipment to be considered fully operational (i.e., output per hour, etc.)

Demand Guarantee

For a **demand guarantee**, one party is entitled to a previously agreed upon sum of money if the other party does not perform according to agreed upon specifications.[58] An example of this could be related to a shipment of bicycles. If the importer asks for a demand guarantee, the exporter has to go to the bank to ask for a demand guarantee, and if the exporter does not live up to the terms and conditions set out in the contract, the importer is then able to go to the bank and demand the set out sum of money to which it is entitled. There are many reasons why a demand guarantee could be enacted, such as non-performance, late performance, or unsatisfactory performance. If you are an importer, you would want the demand guarantee conditions in the contract to be as broad as possible; whereas if you were the exporter, the narrower the terms in the demand guarantee, the better off you would be.

Factoring and Forfaiting

In order to increase the immediate cash flow to a firm, a number of options can be taken to do so, the most prominent being factoring and forfaiting.

---

[55] Ibid.
[56] Ibid.
[57] *Explaining retention funds.* September 9, 2014. http://www.stanlib.com/newsatstanlib/Documents/African_Bank/ ABIL_Retention_Funds.pdf
[58] *Bank Guarantees.* n.d. http://www.letterofcredit.biz/Bank-Guarantees.html

Factoring

Factoring occurs when an outside source, which could be a bank or another party, buys a negotiable instrument from the seller.[59] The acquiring party pays a discounted rate for the draft but the incentive to the seller is that they will receive immediate cash flow instead of what the terms laid out in the contract. The additional benefit to the seller is that they do not have to deal with the risk associated with the transaction. As soon as they sell the draft to the buyer, the risk of non-payment is transferred to the buyer.

Forfaiting

Forfaiting is very similar to factoring; however the sale of the account receivables is for longer-terms than are the terms for factoring.[60] Another difference between factoring and forfaiting is that forfaiting also includes the selling of promissory notes. A forfaiting arrangement generally is agreed upon before the conclusion of the sales contract, which allows the exporter to take the forfaiting discount cost into their sales price.

Countertrade

Countertrade occurs when goods and services are used to acquire other goods and services. Countertrade is a non-monetary transaction, although a monetary valuation can be used in order to determine what a fair amount of goods or services might be, or for bookkeeping reasons.[61] While there are a number of different ways to participate in countertrade, only the most prominent will be featured in this section.

Barter

Barter occurs when goods or services are exchanged for other goods or services without the use of cash to help the transaction.[62] One key component of bartering is that it is vital to know the cash values of what you are bartering for and what you are willing to give up. If you overvalue the other party's products, or undervalue your products, you could come away from the transaction with a net loss.

Buyback

Buyback occurs when a firm offers to construct a building in another country, and in exchange for a cheaper contract price, the constructing firm will take a portion of the output.[63] Buyback agreements are generally long-term and usually occur in the production of industrial plants or factories where production occurs. So, in terms of the textbook-wide example, if for instance, the Russian buyers were looking to have a gas valve production facility in Russia, the Canadian company could offer to cheaply build the production facility in exchange for a certain percentage of the production facility's gas valves.

Counter Purchase

Counter purchasing happens when there is an agreement between two firms to buy each other's products in order to avoid a direct payment from one party to the other.[64] For example, company A will buy company B's products in June, in return company B will buy company A products in July.

---

[59] *Factoring and Forfaiting.* December 30, 2009. http://www.export.gov/finance/eg_main_018104.asp
[60] Ibid.
[61] *What are the various forms of countertrade?* 2011 http://www.londoncountertrade.org/countertradefaq.htm
[62] Ibid.
[63] Ibid.
[64] Ibid.

Offset Agreement

An **offset** agreement seems complicated at first, but truthfully isn't too complex. An offset agreement is one between a high-priced seller and a buyer in another country. The seller agrees to buy products, whether it is the raw materials, or something else from the buyer's country in order to help offset the large balance sheet deficit that would be experienced by the buyer's country.[65] It does not have to even be the sale of raw materials; the seller could also shift production to the buyer's country in order to minimize the balance sheet deficit for that country. Simply put, an offset agreement minimizes the balance sheet deficit in the buyer's country by providing some sort of economic stimulus to the buyer's country.

Tolling

In a **tolling** transaction, a supplier provides himself with the raw material and hires capacity of the factory to turn it into finished goods.[66] Following the transition to finished goods, the supplier then sells the goods to a buyer. Throughout the production process the supplier holds title over the goods until they are finally bought. This type of transaction is especially useful if the supplier has access to the raw materials but lacks the capacity to refine them into more valuable final products. This type of transaction can best be illustrated by either a crude oil supplier who lacks the capacity to refine the crude oil into gasoline or other similar products but hires a refinery to help the supplier make the crude oil into another product that is more valuable to the supplier.

Swap

A **swap**, also known as a switch, or switch trading is a form of countertrade where one company sells its obligation to make a purchase in another country to a different company.[67] For example, if two countries (i.e., Country A and Country B), wish to participate in countertrade, they might offer each other goods and services in order to create a transaction. Now, if Country A does not need or want the goods that Country B is willing to sell, Country B has the option to sell the goods to Country C, who will then pay Country A for the initial shipment of goods to Country B.

Production Sharing

Production sharing is most commonly used in resource extraction industries between the government and private industry.[68] In this type of agreement, a contract is signed between the government and a private company who extracts resources that relates to how much of the resource each party gets to receive once it is extracted.

Chapter Summary

Although there is a common history for all letters of credit, there are no universal rules governing letters of credit and bills of exchange. In the United States, the Uniform Commercial Code is widely accepted and has achieved almost country-wide acceptance. Article 5 of the Uniform Commercial Code pertains to letter of credit transactions and the whole code is constantly revised in order for it to remain as relevant as possible in today's marketplace. Internationally, the Uniform Customs and Practice for Documentary Credits is the most widely accepted code for letter of credit transactions,

---

[65] Ibid.

[66] Ibid.

[67] Ibid.

[68] Dr. Irinia Paliashvili *The Concept of Production Sharing.* September 14, 1998. http://www.rulg.com/documents/The_Concept_of_Production_Sharing.htm

with its most recent edition being UCP 600. One major transition that is noticed in UCP 600 is the move toward substantial compliance, where the documents presented and the letter of credit do not have to be exact replicas and allows for minor discrepancies in a letter of credit transaction.

Letters of credit are the most typical ways to finance international business transactions, although they are by no means the only way to do so. In a typical letter of credit transaction, there will be four parties: the account party, the beneficiary, the advising/confirming bank, and the issuing bank. While there generally is a principle of independence assumed between the underlying contract and the letter of credit, there are some conditions contained within the underlying contract that can influence the letter of credit (see: Itek Corp. v. First National Bank of Boston).

A letter of credit can be tailored to perform many different duties. A standby letter of credit is useful because it can be used to guarantee performance and can be used to enforce standards during the course of the performance as well. There are also alternatives to a standard letter of credit such as a transferable letter of credit, red clause letter of credit, or revolving letters of credit. Each form has its own benefits and displays the versatility of a letter of credit.

Apart from a letter of credit, there are a number of ways to guarantee performance or payment of services that are contracted. Different bonds and guarantees can be formed to fulfill the same function that a letter of credit would be used in, and with possibly less costs associated with the transaction, although there is a risk of non-performance and successful use of these bonds may be reliant upon the relationship between the buyer and seller as well as the geographical location of the parties.

Countertrade can be used when both parties wish to trade goods or services without the direct use of money in the contract. The benefits to countertrade include that there is no actual money being transferred so you might actually be able to improve your financial position by being a shrewd negotiator. There are quite a few different transactions that can be conducted through countertrade, and it is really up to the negotiating skills of the parties in order to find the best agreement.

Glossary

Acceptance: The acknowledgement by the person on whom the bill is drawn

Account Party: Party who applies to a bank to open a letter of credit

Advance Payment: Payment that is made to the seller before the goods are shipped

Advising Bank: Handles communication with the issuing bank and enables the letter of credit transaction, the advising bank has no obligation to pay the seller. You generally use an advising bank when you trust the issuing bank

Back-to-Back Letter of Credit: A party uses an existing, non-transferable letter of credit, which it is the beneficiary of, in order to open a second letter of credit

Banker's Acceptance: Time draft that is accepted by a banker/bank

Barter: Goods or services are exchanged for other goods or services without the use of cash to help the transaction

Beneficiary Party: Seller of the goods or services in a letter of credit transaction

Bid Bond: Bid that a contractor issues to a project owner in hopes of gaining a contract

Buyback: Firm offers to construct a building in another country, and in exchange for a cheaper contract price, the constructing firm will take a portion of the output

Confirmed Letter of Credit: Four party transaction where a confirming bank acts as a second guarantee to the initial letter of credit

Confirming Bank: Similar to an advising bank but it has an obligation to pay under the letter of credit

Counter Purchase: Agreement between two firms to buy each other's products in order to avoid a direct payment from one party to the other

Countertrade: Goods and services are used to acquire other goods and services

Credit Surety: A guarantor promises to pay a certain party if another party defaults on the party's agreement

Demand Guarantee: One party is entitled to a previously agreed upon sum of money if the other party does not perform according to agreed upon specifications

Direct Payment: Money transfer happens from the buyer to the seller

Documentary Collection: Similar to a letter of credit, however there are no guarantees by the bank for payment

Documentary Credit (Letter of Credit): Guarantee by a bank to pay the seller upon presentation of certain documents

Draft: An order to pay a sum certain in money, signed by a drawer, payable on demand or at a definite time, to order or bearer.

Drawee: Party who is in possession of money to which the drawer is entitled

Drawer: Signature of the person who issued the bill

Facial Compliance: Banks are only required to review documents and compare them with the requirements of the letter of credit for conformity

Factoring: An outside source buys a negotiable instrument from the seller

Forfaiting: Similar to factoring, but the items sold are for longer terms than factoring

Freight Forwarder: Person or company who coordinates the movement of goods, secures the bill of lading, and completes other documentation as required by the letter of credit

Irrevocable Letter of Credit: Most commonly used in export transactions and by its very definition, cannot be rescinded for any reason

Issuing Bank: Bank that actually opens the letter of credit

Lex mercatoria: "Merchant law," commercial law used in medieval Europe

Negotiable Instrument: Signed writing, containing an unconditional promise or order to pay a fixed sum of money, to order or to bearer, on demand or at a definite time

Negotiation: Ability to transfer legal title from one party to another

Offset agreement: Minimizes the balance sheet deficit in the buyer's country by providing some sort of economic stimulus to the buyer's country.

Payee: The name of the person who will be receiving the money

Performance Bond: Insures performance by a contractor, and acts as security for job completion

Production Sharing: A contract is signed between the government and a private company who extracts resources that relates to how much of the resource each party gets to receive once it is extracted

Red Clause Financing: Buyer extends an unsecured loan to the seller

Retention Fund: Product is withheld until a certain action or condition of the contract has been fulfilled

Revocable Letter of Credit: Bank can revoke at any time

Substantial Compliance: Documents presented are allowed to have a certain amount of discrepancies without compromising obligations

Sight Draft: Draft is to be paid upon presentation or demand

Standby Letter of Credit: Main purpose is to ensure that performance is guaranteed throughout the course of a contract

Strict Compliance: Banks may reject documents for any discrepancy

Surveyor: Agents for the buyer inspect the goods and make sure that they are in the condition that is required by the contract

Swap: Where one company sells its obligation to make a purchase in another country to a different company

Time Draft: A draft that is payable at a future date or after the buyer has received and accepted the appropriate documents

Tolling: Supplier provides himself with the raw material and hires capacity of the factory to turn it into finished goods

Trader's Acceptance: Time draft that is accepted by a seller of merchandise

Transferable Credit: Can be used in multiple business transactions

Unconfirmed Letter of Credit: Only the issuing bank has the responsibility to honour the drafts presented to it for payment

Uniform Commercial Code (UCC): United States' unified rulebook for negotiable instruments

Uniform Commercial Code Article 5: Article of the UCC that is related to letters of credit

Uniform Customs and Practices for Documentary Credits (UCP): Rules that govern international letter of credit transactions

Bibliography

2002. § 3-104. *NEGOTIABLE INSTRUMENT*. https://www.law.cornell.edu/ucc/3/3-104.

2002. § 3-409. *ACCEPTANCE OF DRAFT; CERTIFIED CHECK*. https://www.law.cornell.edu/ucc/3/3-409.

n.d. *Bank Guarantees*. Accessed February 18, 2016. http://www.letterofcredit.biz/Bank-Guarantees.html.

Bimco. 2013. *The Role of the Marine Surveyor*. Janurary 10. https://www.bimco.org/Education/Seascapes/Maritime_Matters/2013_10_01_The_Role_of_the_Marine_Surveyor.aspx.

Export.Gov. 2009. *Factoring and Forfaiting*. December 30. http://www.export.gov/finance/eg_main_018104.asp.

Henkelman, Edward G. 2002. *A Short Course in International Payments*. World Trade Press.

Hinkelman, Edward D. 2002. "Special Letters of Credit." In *A Short Course in International Payments*, by Edward D. Henkelman, 182. World Trade Press.

Hinkelman, Edward G. 2002. "Introducing the Basic Terms of Payment." In *A Short Course in International Payments*, by Edward G. Hinkelman, 182. World Trade Press.

Investopedia. n.d. *Sight Draft*. Accessed February 20, 2016. http://www.investopedia.com/terms/s/sight-draft.asp.

—. n.d. *Time Draft*. http://www.investopedia.com/terms/t/time-draft.asp.

Kurt, Daniel. n.d. *Banker's Acceptance 101*. http://www.investopedia.com/articles/investing/062013/bankers-acceptance-101.asp.

2013. *Letters of credit - strict compliance and the use of banking "shorthand"*. September 23. http://www.incelaw.com/en/knowledge-bank/publications/letters-of-credit-strict-compliance-and-the-use-of-banking-shorthand.

London Countertrade Roundtable. 2011. *What are the various forms of countertrade?* http://www.londoncountertrade.org/countertradefaq.htm.

Paliashvili, Dr. Irina. 1998. *The Concept of Production Sharing*. September 14. http://www.rulg.com/documents/The_Concept_of_Production_Sharing.htm.

2012. *Principles of Contract Law: A Compilation of Law Mercatoria?* November 22. http://blogs.law.nyu.edu/transnational/2012/11/principles-of-contract-law-a-compilation-of-lex-mercatoria/.

Pritchard, Justin. 2015. *Standby Letter of Credit*. February 5. http://banking.about.com/od/LettersOfCredit/fl/Standby-Letter-of-Credit.htm.

STANLIB. 2014. *Explaining retention funds*. September 9. http://www.stanlib.com/newsatstanlib/Documents/African_Bank/ABIL_Retention_Funds.pdf.

1995. *U.C.C. - ARTICLE 5 - LETTERS OF CREDIT.* https://www.law.cornell.edu/ucc/5/.

1999. *Understanding and Using Letters of Credit, Part 1.* https://www.crfonline.org/orc/cro-9-1.html.

n.d. *Uniform Commercial Code.* https://www.law.cornell.edu/ucc.

n.d. *What is a Surety Bond?* Accessed February 18, 2016. https://www.bryantsuretybonds.com/what-is-a-surety-bond.

West's Encyclopedia of American Law, edition 2. S.v. "draft." from http://legal-dictionary.thefree-dictionary.com/draft

CHAPTER 5

Liability of Carriers of Goods and Passengers

Learning Objectives

After reading this chapter, you will have an understanding of:

1. The rules governing international air carriers of cargo and passengers
2. The purpose and history of the rules governing international air carriers
3. The rules governing international marine carriers of cargo and other merchandise
4. The purpose and history of the rules governing international marine carriers
5. How different sections of the conventions governing international carriers (both air and marine carriers) are applied in practice and in court

Introduction

The transportation of goods, whether by land, sea, or air, creates potential liabilities. The major question is who is liable when goods are damaged, destroyed, or lost. Possibilities are the seller, the buyer, or the carrier. Liability may be contractual or tortious. Contractual liability may be limited under privity of contract, by exclusion clauses within the contract, or by rules of a statute or treaty the parties agreed upon.

Carriers have a great deal of potential liability with regards to international carriers of goods, and after being found liable, the subsequent payment of damages for air and marine carriers of internationally sold goods and services can be quite a monetary outlay. Carriers here refer to the many forms of transportation on which internationally sold and distributed goods are loaded onto and moved from country to country. Carriers can take the form of ships, airplanes, trucks, trains, and other transportation vehicles. This text will take focus on two particular groups of transportation vehicles, or carriers, used to take internationally sold goods from sellers to buyers: marine carriers and air carriers.

The myriad of different issues and potential pitfalls facing international carriers is astounding; whether it's an international marine carrier's liability with regards to cargo during an intense typhoon, or an international airline's liability with regards to their passengers (and their passengers' cargo or belongings) during flight, there have been an incredible number of lawsuits brought against international carriers. This chapter will examine the liability of international carriers of goods through both air and marine transport. At all times someone has title to the goods and another has possession. Carriers may be the actual carrier (the carrier in possession of the goods) or the legal carrier (carrier under contract) or both. The actual carrier can only be sued in tort because they have no contract, but the legal carrier can be sued in both contract and tort.

Similar to incoterms, international transport of goods gives rise to the ongoing issue of standardized international rules to alleviate uncertainty. This is done through using international conventions. These conventions set forth the rules for liability and the limits of liability. The application of different carriage liability rules in an international transport of goods transaction is potentially overwhelming. Different conventions will apply if it is by land, sea, or air. In addition, different conventions or rules may apply for different modes of transport. In ocean carriage there are three potential regimes: the Hague Rules, the Hague-Visby Rules, or the Hamburg Rules. One must first determine which regime applies. Just to add to the complexity, not all states are parties to the conventions.

The final piece in the puzzle is the role of insurance. Buyers and seller have to take out proper cargo insurance given the fact that the noted conventions limit the carrier's liability. Such insurance policies have to cover various modes of transport. This usually requires different and overlapping insurance policies covering different modes, different types of losses, and different types of coverage.

Types of Transportation:

1. Air
2. Sea
3. Other

Air Carriage

For the most part, international air carrier liability is governed by internationally recognized and ratified conventions, starting specifically with the **Warsaw Convention** of 1929, and more recently with the **Montreal Convention** of 1999. The Montreal Convention has replaced the Warsaw Convention in numerous countries across the world, which was made easier by the creators' efforts to mimic the style and purpose of the Warsaw Convention. The various conventions will be examined, in particular, the marine carrier's liabilities for the goods they carry, the potential pitfalls and subsequent damages. For marine carriers, the Hague Rules, created post World War I, are the original uniform international governing rules used to reduce uncertainties in the laws governing the liability of ocean carriers for damage or loss of goods at sea. Again, there will be a thorough exploration of both the history of the Hague Rules and the application of them, as well as commentary on a few other protocols and amendments that followed the Hague Rules. Finally, we will conclude with a brief overview of all that is captured in this chapter.

International Air Carrier Liability

Just as another reminder, a good place to start before we begin examining the liability for carriers of internationally bought and sold goods (in this case specifically air carriers) is to define what exactly a carrier means in this context. As an example, imagine a situation whereby a microchip manufacturer in California has sold a mass shipment of computer chips to a computer manufacturer in Beijing, China. Neither the microchip producer, nor the computer manufacturer, specializes or even dabbles in the international transportation of goods; thus, an opportunity for companies or persons with a competitive advantage in transporting goods across the globe arises. These international transportation companies typically employ either a wide variety of transportation vehicles and personnel required to operate them, or they specialize in the logistical side of the transportation journey for internationally bought and sold cargo while finding independent contractors who will provide the physical infrastructure required to move the goods from the seller's location to the buyer's. These specialized international transportation entities are the "carriers" of purchased goods governed by international sales contracts.

A very logical question quickly arises when examining the use of, and purpose of, international carriers; if an accident or problem should arise during the transportation journey, who is on the hook for any damages to the goods or cargo (or in the case of air carriers as we are looking at, passengers)? A multitude of different circumstances and situations affect not only the potential liability of air carriers but also the question of jurisdiction with regards to air carriage accidents. Is the passenger flying domestically or internationally? Is the flight in question within 12 nautical miles of the American shoreline? Has the accident taken place over land or over water? These questions are just a small sample of the many different possible circumstances that can affect an international air carrier liability lawsuit. While we are only examining liability for international transportation with regards to international passengers and damages to cargo arising from international air transport, domestic flights have many of the same pitfalls and questions as international flights.[1]

Beginnings of International Air Transportation

The Wright Brothers first took a passenger on board an aircraft in May of 1908, and questions of liability with regards to air transportation have been a heavily debated topic of conversation ever since. The liability of international air carriers was especially important during the infancy of the air travel industry; governments across the world were worried about the survival of the industry before it ever even got off the ground (pun intended). What would happen if an airplane full of patrons crashed and there was a never-before-seen loss of life? Would airline lawsuits be so incredibly punitive that entrance into the industry wasn't worth the potential liability? Global leaders saw the world of aviation and air travel as the future of transportation and were strongly motivated to protect the industry and by extension the airlines and carriers of both domestically and internationally bought and sold cargo, as well as domestically and internationally travelling passengers. This landscape gave rise to the creation and ratification of the Warsaw Convention of 1929, which created a common ground and common rules for international passenger and cargo carriers. The Warsaw Convention was the first step in protecting international air carriers and we will now take a more in-depth look at the history and application of this agreement, followed by its next of kin, the Montreal Convention of 1999 which replaced the Warsaw Convention in a multitude of countries where ratified.

Conventions

1. The Warsaw Convention (1929)[2]

Since the inception of the Warsaw Convention air carrier liability has been governed by internationally recognized conventions. The Warsaw Convention was the first of its kind, and although it has been amended by a few protocols over the past 90 years it is still in effect in some countries for a variety of reasons and uses. The Warsaw Convention essentially standardized air travel and air carrier procedures; in the Warsaw Convention there is commentary and direction on how to issue and how to handle baggage claim forms, cargo receipts, passenger tickets, and other transport documents. Because insurance companies were scared to insure new air carriers and because governments across the globe saw the

---

[1] Inbound Logistics. 2013. *Trasnportation Liability: Busting Seven Common Myths*. January. Accessed February 2016.
    www.inboundlogistics.com/cms/article/transportation-liability-busting-seven-common-myths
[2] n.d. Wikipedia The Free Encyclopedia. Accessed January 2016. https://en.wikipedia.org/wiki/warsaw_convention

importance of the survival of the air industry (and didn't want it to be wiped out in one large-scale air disaster), the Warsaw Convention was a necessary stepping stone to create a sort of safety net for air carriers, specifically international air carriers. The Warsaw Convention protected air carriers and airlines from liability and from having to pay immense damages for passenger injury or death in a few different ways. First and foremost, the Warsaw Convention declared that air carriers were not liable for any accidents causing either passenger or cargo harm if they were able to prove that "all necessary methods" were taken to avoid the accident in question. Second, and almost as important, the Warsaw Convention placed a strict limitation on the dollar amount of air carrier liability in the case of an accident. In the 1920s and 30s it made sense to arrive at the liability cap by pegging the value of any particular nation's currency to the value of gold, so this is what the Warsaw Convention did. There was a cap of $9.07 per pound for damaged luggage or cargo in the United States until the late 1990s, and the limit for damage payments resulting from any injury to an airline customer was capped at $75,000 (including litigation fees and costs).

Clearly, these damage caps don't accurately reflect the possible losses of international airline passengers; no one can reasonably claim that the death of a family member is properly reflected in a $75,000 payment. Recently the international air carrier liability cap has become a serious subject of debate and has been debated with more vim and vigor than ever before, with most people in agreement that these limits are in no way fair to the wronged individual. The liability of a reckless and negligent driver of a vehicle that crashes and results in a wrongful death to another party has no cap, with some damage payments exceeding hundreds of thousands or even millions of dollars. Under the Warsaw Convention, the only way for a plaintiff (or the wronged individual/family/party) to recover a dollar amount greater than the Warsaw cap was to prove that the damages (or injury/death to a passenger) were directly caused by the international air carrier's "willful misconduct," which was (and is) an incredibly difficult standard to meet and hurdle to jump over. It requires the plaintiff to not only prove the wrongdoing of the air carrier, but to prove that the wrongdoing was the cause of some sort of affirmative, or willful, action.

The Warsaw Convention clearly had a very high standard of proof required to increase the monetary liability limit of international air carriers, and one such example of a plaintiff succeeding in their claim for damages over and above the Warsaw caps was in the case of a Pan Am flight that crashed over Lockerbie, a town in Scotland. Airline security, after receiving warning of a bomb, failed to take any action and in fact actively ignored the bomb claim and took no steps to substantiate it in any way. The sum of the circumstances led to the plaintiff winning their claim. It was in the face of that antiquated international air travel landscape that finally, in 1997, everyone (including the international airline industry), agreed they would voluntarily increase the monetary damage limits. And in 1999, in the face of this new international air carriage liability landscape, the Montreal Convention was completed. Passengers and shippers were as a result given much greater rights against air carriers (note: shippers in this context simply mean persons or entities that required the movement of goods that are bought and sold internationally).

2. The Montreal Convention (1999)[3]

Seventy years after the conception of the Warsaw Convention there was a greater and even more substantial change in international air transportation law and liability. The full title of the Montreal Convention was the "Montreal Convention for the Unification of Certain Rules for International Carriage by Air," but it will herein be referred to simply as the Montreal Convention. The idea behind the Montreal Convention was quite simple: it would replace the Warsaw Convention, which had many outdated rules and other flaws (not the least of which was the monetary liability limits). Although the Warsaw Convention does still act as the international air carrier law for some countries, more than 95 have replaced it and ratified the Montreal Convention. One thing to note about both the Montreal and Warsaw Conventions is that although they apply to international air carrier liability, they do not

---

[3] Wikipedia. n.d. Wikipedia the Free Encyclopedia. Accessed January 2016. https://en.wikipedia.org/wiki/montreal_convention

apply to or govern lawsuits brought against third parties related to international air carriers (such as the company providing the air carrier's food, the manufacturer of a defective airplane, private security firms, and other passengers). Normally, these cases are tried by ordinary state tort law or whatever other jurisdiction in which the lawsuit is heard.

For example, imagine a situation wherein an airline stewardess provided an international passenger with an abnormally hot cup of coffee which was then, as a result of the stewardess's turning around too quickly and catching the mug handle on her uniform, spilled on the passenger resulting in horrible third degree burns. In this situation the stewardess (and by extension the airline) will be protected and governed by the Montreal Convention. However, should the passenger come to the correct conclusion that the reason the coffee mug caught on the stewardess's uniform was a direct result of the uniform manufacturing company's design flaw and they chose to sue the uniform manufacturer, the manufacturer will not be protected by the Montreal Convention and the lawsuit will be tried under ordinary state law.

Just as the Warsaw Convention had commentary on transport documentation and the issuance and controls surrounding such documentation, the Montreal Convention updated these commentaries to better reflect our modern and globalizing economic landscape, such as the advent of the Internet and incredible evolution of electronic communication. Airline insurance was a very important feature of the new Montreal Convention; all international airlines were now lawfully required to be insured for their possible losses in the countries that the Montreal Convention governs. The Montreal Convention loosened some of the stringent standards placed by the Warsaw Convention with regards to recovering damages for international airline liability, be it from passenger injury or cargo and baggage loss.

Basically, the new Montreal Convention eliminated the previous requirement of proving willful neglect by the air carrier to obtain more than $75,000 in damages, which should eliminate or reduce protracted litigation. Finally, something that hits home to many of us who frequent the international airline industry, the Montreal Convention included commentary on flight delays, and the rights of ticket holders with regards to flight delays. Airlines are now liable for delays in transporting persons, baggage, or cargo. However, should the international carrier prove that there were reasonable measures taken to avoid the delay (or that the delay was unavoidable), then they are freed from liability. The damage cap on liability of international air carriers for delays is 4,694 SDRs per passenger as of 2010 (SDRs will be expanded on shortly).

Ethical Considerations 5.1

Airline Compensation Documents

Friederike Wallentin-Hermann v. Alitalia—Linee Aeree Italiane SpA, C-549/07, (2008), http://curia.europa.eu/en/actu/communiques/cp08/aff/cp080100en.pdf

The flight delay compensation regulation puts into place various rules regarding compensation to passengers if they happen to have their flight cancelled, delayed greatly, or are denied boarding. The entitlements that passengers enjoy has been in effect since 2005 and applies to most individuals departing from a nation that recognizes this treaty and have complied with airline rules such as maintaining check-in times. The compensation that passengers have available includes items such as cash compensation, refunding, rerouting, and accommodations. However, Article 5 constitutes that an air carrier does not have to compensate passengers if they have evidence that the cancellation was due to extraordinary circumstances that could not have been prevented even if the airline performed all reasonable measures.

In Wallentin-Hermann v Alitalia—Linee Aeree Italiane SpA of 2008, the European Court of Justice sided with the plaintiff stating that technical issues that fall under aircraft maintenance cannot be considered extraordinary circumstances. The court affirms that the cancellation from mechanical problems must lie beyond the aircraft's control. The controversy stirs when we deal with what exactly lies inside or outside their actual control and thus, the subject continues to be litigated in a number of European Union states.

Upon whose judgment is it that a passenger's compensation may be taken away? The cancellation of a flight may cause an individual a great deal of hardship getting to their final destination. Should compensation be greater for someone who paid a higher ticket price?

One other defining feature (and perhaps the most important feature) of the Montreal Convention is the fact that the creators and contributors modelled the new agreement after the Warsaw Convention. This was incredibly important as it allowed, and still allows, common law court decisions and precedents to continue to have substance and meaning even after the Warsaw Convention was no longer the law governing international air carrier liability. Basically, it allowed courts across the world to continue to use their precedents and court decisions with regards to the Warsaw Convention and international air carrier liability when seeing new international air carrier liability cases that are now governed by the Montreal Convention. It allowed the case laws that were decided under the Warsaw Convention to continue to hold and apply to future air carrier liability decisions.

Montreal Convention, Article 1

Article 1 of the Montreal Convention states the following:

> The Convention applies to all international carriage of persons, baggage, and cargo by aircraft in which the place of departure and the place of destination, whether or not there be a break in the carriage or a transhipment, are situated either within the territories of two countries, or within the territory of a single country if there is an agreed stopping place within the territory of another state, even if that state is not a country. Carriage between two points within the territory of a single country without an agreed stopping place within the territory of another state is not international carriage for the purposes of this Convention.
>
> Carriage to be performed by several successive carriers is deemed, for the purposes of this Convention, to be *one undivided carriage* if it has been regarded by the parties as a *single operation,* whether it had been agreed upon under the form of a single contract or of a series of contracts, and it does not lose its international character merely because one contract or a series of contracts is to be performed entirely within the territory of the same state.[4]

To summarize, the Montreal Convention was explicitly referring to internationally ticketed passengers, and even more specifically to internationally ticketed passengers who are travelling between two countries that have both ratified the Montreal Convention. Also, in situations where a passenger is ticketed for a round trip flight beginning and ending in a country that uses the Montreal Convention the Montreal Convention will apply, even if there will be passage through countries and regions that have not accepted the Montreal Convention as the law governing international air carrier liability. In most other situations, the Montreal Convention will not apply, and any plaintiff will have to try their case using state or local law.

One intriguing situation occurs when passengers have an international journey scheduled, but it includes a domestic transfer. For example, imagine a passenger ticketed for a round-trip journey from Los Angeles to Paris, but they must transfer flights in New York before completing the trip; does the Montreal Convention apply if an accident occurred in between the Los Angeles to New York flight? The determining factor will be whether or not the passenger in question was engaged in a "continuous" international journey. If they are, they will be covered by the Montreal Convention, but passengers on the same flight

---

4 Peterson, Douglas H. 2014. *International Business Transactions B LAW 444*. Toronto: Nelson Education Ltd.

who are not engaged in a continuous international journey would not be covered by the Montreal Convention should an accident occur. The Montreal Convention is supposed to apply in situations where all sections of an international trip are booked on the same ticket (international and domestic sections), and will probably still apply when the flights are purchased separately should the intention of the traveler clearly be international travel. A famous case of this exact situation playing out is in Robertson v. American Airlines Inc.[5] A flight passenger purchased two round trip tickets, on different days, for an international journey; one round trip ticket was on British Airlines and was for travel between London and Denver, while the other round trip ticket was for travel between Denver and Washington D.C. on American Airlines. While on the domestic leg of the journey the passenger in question was burned quite badly by dry ice, which was accidentally given to them by a stewardess. Because the court stated that "it is unlikely that a layover of [a length of three hours] (which was the total scheduled length of the passengers layover) would even have given time to leave the airport, and the record confirms that Robertson had no purpose in Denver that day other than to make the plane connection," they ruled that both of the flights were part of an undivided international carriage. Unfortunately for the plaintiff this meant that the Warsaw Convention and its two-year statute of limitations would be applied and the case would have to be dismissed.

Comprehensive Case 1: El Al Israel Airlines Ltd. v. Tseng (525 US155 (1999))[6]

Facts:

While in the process of boarding an international flight, the plaintiff Tseng was asked some common questions by an airport security guard about her travel plans. Not finding her responses suitable and having some level of suspicion, the security guard took Tseng to a private security room for a routine pat down and body search. Nothing was found, and Tseng was allowed to continue onto her flight. Although no bodily injury was sustained, Tseng sued the airline in question (El Al) under NY law on charges of false imprisonment and mental injuries for assault. The basic question this case answers is the following: should a plaintiff, when unsatisfied with the remedies afforded under the Convention governing international air carrier liability, be able to find better alternatives under state law?

Court Decision:

The airline removed the case to a federal district court, which then dismissed the case. The district court's decision determined that the only remedy for Tseng was under the Warsaw Convention and because the Warsaw Convention did not award damages unless there was physical injury, Tseng didn't qualify. On appeal to the US Court of Appeals the decision was that Tseng, who did not qualify for any remedies under the Warsaw Convention, could in fact then seek damages under local law for an injury sustained during an international journey. Of course, El Al appealed this decision to the Supreme Court.

The Supreme Court reversed the Court of Appeals decision; it stated that: "we… hold that recovery for a personal injury suffered on board an aircraft or in the course of any of the operations of embarking or disembarking (loading the plane and unloading the plane) if not allowed under the Convention, is not available **at all**." Judge Ginsburg of the Supreme Court made this decision under the premise that the internationally agreed upon Warsaw Convention would lose some of its power and the regulation of international air carrier liability would become even more litigious and murky than it already was.

---

5 Ibid.
6 Cornell University Law School. n.d. *Legal Information Institute*: Open Access to Law Since 1992. Accessed February 2016. http://www.law.cornell.edu/supremecourt/text/525/155

Conclusion:

The Warsaw Convention's purpose and premise was that it alone governs the liability of carriers with respect to passengers and their baggage. Article 17 of the Warsaw Convention states that the conditions to receive damages for personal bodily injury while onboard an international flight are that the carrier is liable for death or bodily injury if the accident took place on board the plane (or while embarking/disembarking, as mentioned above). Not only did a routine body search not constitute an accident, but American common law also had previously set precedent that the purpose of the Warsaw Convention is for "uniformity of rules governing claims arising from international air transportation" (Eastern Airlines Inc. v. Floyd, 499 US 530, 111 S.Ct. 1489 (1991)).[7] To provide the desired uniformity and regulation the Warsaw Convention explicitly stated that it should apply to all international transportation and that there is an array of explicitly stated liability "rules" laid out in the Warsaw Convention. Due to all of these facts, the Supreme Court believed that the Court of Appeals decision would essentially undermine the Warsaw Convention and would lead to unfounded litigation being filed against air carriers. Also, since Tseng's injuries were not a result of an accident per say, but rather an internal reaction to usual airport operations, there was no grounds for a lawsuit to be filed. In the end, it was decided that a passenger could not seek damages under state law when the claims don't satisfy the Warsaw Convention's conditions for international air carrier liability, and the US Court of Appeals decision was reversed.

Montreal Convention, Article 17

Article 17 of the Montreal Convention states the following:

- The carrier is liable for damage sustained in case of **death or bodily injury** (i.e., physical injury) of a passenger upon condition only that the **accident** which caused the death or injury **took place on board the aircraft or in the course of the operations of embarking or disembarking.**[8]

The standard requirement to hold an international air carrier of passengers liable for damages to the passenger is a three-pronged requirement.

The Montreal Convention's conditions for seeking damages for personal peril are in fact three-fold; there must be either death or bodily injury sustained, the injuries must result from an accident on the part of the international air carrier, and the injuries must have been sustained while in the act of boarding the plane/beginning the international journey (embarking), while on the plane, or while disembarking. These criteria raise immediate questions: what constitutes bodily injury? Is an accident an act that is willful or negligent or simply a mistake made? What exactly is the definition of embarking or disembarking an international air carrier? The amount of lawsuits brought through courts around the world that hinge on these three criteria is astounding, and luckily for us it has provided a massive base of knowledge in terms of international common law and court precedents.

Death or Bodily Injury

The first criteria that must be satisfied to be awarded damages from an international air carrier is quite straightforward: there must be death or bodily injury to a passenger. Psychological injury does

---

[7] Ibid.
[8] Ibid.

not qualify, most likely because it acts as a control to reduce the possibility of creative lawsuits that in essence would just clog up the judicial system. The one key piece of information to provide in terms of this first international air carrier liability criteria is there are still stringent limitations on the amount of monetary damages that could be awarded under the Montreal Convention should death or bodily injury be found to have occurred (and the other two criteria must also be satisfied), although the limits are updated from the Warsaw Convention. The Warsaw Convention, as mentioned previously, chose to limit liability based on an amount arrived at by taking the currency of any participating country relative to the value of gold, at the time a widely held international standard of account. This system was actually quite effective and accepted until the last 50 years when the value of gold lost and currencies were no longer pinned to it. Under the Montreal Convention this idea of damage limitation was maintained, however the measurement of it was altered; now, damage limits are determined on the basis of "special drawing rights" (herein referred to as SDRs). SDRs are an amount that can be easily converted into any participating country's currency and is determined by the International Monetary Fund based on a variety of factors. It is periodically updated and can easily be found online. For example, on February 19, 2016, one SDR is worth $1.40 American Dollars. The Montreal Convention does also call for the international air carrier liability limit to be periodically updated and reviewed as well.

In the simplest description possible, the Montreal Convention's limits for international air carrier liability is a two-tiered system. First, any international carrier is liable for damages as a result of death or bodily injury arising out of an accident (that can be proven) in an amount no greater than 113,100 SDRs per passenger (or $158,340 American) without any regard to the international air carrier's fault. This is the first tier in the liability system. The second tier states that the international air carrier is liable for damages over and above this cap, without any limit, unless the carrier itself can show that the damages were not a result of any negligence on its part. Stated another way, the actual fault of the international carrier only matters for damages over the 113,100 SDR base cap.

Air Carriers and Accidents

The second criteria that must be satisfied when seeking damages from international air carriers for death or bodily injury is that the injury was the result of an "accident." The logical question then becomes: what constitutes an accident? Essentially, the accident can't be a commonplace international air travel occurrence or must be the result of an abnormal air transport happening. Also, the accident must be external to the passenger; this essentially means that an abnormal internal reaction of a passenger to a routine external event does not qualify as an accident. For example, in the case of Air France v. Saks[9] the passenger took a routine international flight and exited the aircraft without complaint. Days later it was concluded that at some point during the flight the air pressure changes resulted in the passenger losing all hearing in the left ear. The trial court and US Court of Appeals had differing conclusions with the case eventually being heard by the Supreme Court. The Supreme Court determined that international air carrier liability only arises if injury is caused by "unexpected or unusual" circumstances that are "external" to the plaintiff. Although this precedent explicitly left room for flexibility in the determination of fault in international air travel accidents it also explicitly stated that a "passenger's own internal reaction to the usual, normal and expected operation of an aircraft" cannot constitute an accident, even if the internal reaction wasn't routine or normal. So while an international air carrier accident may be constituted or triggered by a terrorism threat, a necessary crash landing, or the breaking of an airplane seat resulting in injury, any individual person's internal accident resulting from routine external airline operations does not trigger liability. This precedent was accepted by the British House of Lords in 2005, also while hearing a case involving the formation of blood clots in the legs of flight passengers.

---

[9] Ibid.

Another feature of the Montreal Convention with regards to international air carrier liability for accidents is that the air carrier has another defense for the accident criteria beyond proving that the accident in question either didn't take place or wasn't an accident. Comparative negligence means that if a plaintiff contributed to causing the accident in question by partaking in some form of negligence themselves, then they will not be able to collect damages (to the extent that their negligence caused the accident). Put another way, if the international air carrier can prove that either the entire accident, or the severity of it, was affected and altered by the plaintiff's negligence then the carrier will be released wholly or partly from their liability. As an example, imagine an airplane with a cord running through the middle of the cabin. At the beginning of the flight, the flight attendants explicitly state that the cord is present and that there is to be no running on board the aircraft. There are also signs posted throughout the aircraft stating the presence of the cord and reiterating the no running rule. Near the end of the flight, a man decides he must use the washroom and needs to make it back to his seat to see the conclusion of his in-flight movie; the man gets out of his seat, runs to the washroom, trips on the cord, and breaks his nose. This passenger would not be able to receive the full damage limit that the Montreal Convention allows (113,100 SDRs) and likely wouldn't receive any damages, as the accident and injury occurred as a result of his own willful negligence.

International Air Travel Embarking and Disembarking

The final criteria to be satisfied when seeking damages from international air carriers for injuries that result from an accident is that the accident and injury took place either while physically on board the aircraft, or while in the process of embarking or disembarking on the international journey. It is quite obvious whether or not a passenger is physically on board an aircraft when an accident resulting in physical injury takes place, but the situation becomes unclear when determining whether or not the passenger was embarking or disembarking. Factors that courts consider when determining whether or not a passenger was in fact in the operation of embarking or disembarking are pretty standard; how physically close was the plaintiff to the boarding gate or to airline security when the incident occurred, whether the plaintiff was under the control of the airline or security official at the time of the incident, and what the activity of the plaintiff was at the time of the incident. There have been cases tried where incidents occur long distances from the location of departure or for incidents occurring in airport corridors and moving sidewalks. The majority of these cases find the international air carrier in question not guilty for obvious reasons. When the plaintiff is in the process of boarding or exiting the aircraft, though, the international air carrier is definitely responsible and liable for any accidents resulting in physical injury.

Unfortunately, most international air carrier liability cases hinging on the criteria of a passenger embarking or disembarking on their international journey are much more complicated. Normally when inside the airport and shopping, dining, or collecting baggage at a baggage claim an international air carrier is free from any liability. This makes sense, as most people would agree that these acts and locations are not consistent with a plaintiff embarking or disembarking on their international journey. However this is not always the case; Singh v. North American Airlines[10] was a case wherein a passenger was forcibly detained and imprisoned for the possession of illegal drugs in his baggage after an international flight. It was several months later that it was discovered that the plaintiff's international air carrier's employees had planted the drugs and framed the plaintiff for their own gain. Once Singh sued, the district court determined that this did in fact constitute an accident in terms of the Montreal Convention because the airline employees in Guyana (one of the airports the plaintiff landed at) handled baggage and the process of checking bags and obtaining bag tags in Guyana was

---

[10] Ibid.

definitely a part of embarking on the international journey. The court went even further stating that it did not matter that the damages occurred later while the plaintiff was imprisoned because the "accident itself (the airline employees framing Singh) took place on board the aircraft or in the course of any of the operations of embarking or disembarking."

As evidenced above, there is a lot of room for determining whether or not physical injury of an international air carrier's passenger actually triggers liability and the subsequent payment of damages. There are damage limits, should the air carrier not be at fault for the accident, but no damage cap if it is clear that the international air carrier was in fact at fault. There is room for interpretation when determining whether or not a plaintiff was in fact embarking or disembarking on their international journey, as well as when determining whether or not the action resulting in a passenger's injury was actually an "accident." Although there have been a wealth of cases already tried and decided resulting in common law precedents around the world, there are still new cases tried frequently that require the intense consideration of the application of the Montreal Convention to international air carrier liability when determining passenger damages.

Montreal Convention and the Types of Afforded Damages

General tort law allows for a variety of different damages and remedies to be sought for personal injuries or death; there are economic damages (monetary costs) that are the result of the injury, and there are also non-economic damages such as pain and suffering that must be assigned a monetary value. For example, in the case of a car crash, the plaintiff may sue for economic damages such as their medical costs, as well as for non-economic damages such as compensation for the nightly nightmares that have plagued them since the crash. As evidenced by this example, plaintiffs in general tort law could seek several types of damages in one single case such as damages to cover a loss of income, recovery and rehab costs, damages for mental anguish and physical pain, loss of companionship (should the plaintiff have lost a loved one). Occasionally even punitive damages which are explicitly meant to teach the defendant a lesson and make an example of the situation so as to dissuade as strongly as possible the events that led to the event from happening.

All of these potential damages may be sought out by an individual who is the victim of an accident while on a flight from Vancouver to Toronto (a domestic Canadian flight). The question that we are asking here, though, is what sort of damages are afforded to plaintiffs in international air carrier cases? Are they afforded the same possible retributions as as plaintiffs in domestic air liability claims. The answer to these questions was clearly determined in a well-known 1983 case against Korean Air Lines. During a flight from South Korea to the U.S. one of Korean Air Lines' flights was shot down by a Soviet Union jet fighter (apparently because the Korean Air airplane strayed into Soviet controlled airspace). 269 passengers died in the crash. In Zicherman v. Korean Air Lines Co. Ltd.[11] the US Supreme Court stated that "the law of the Convention does not affect the substantive questions of who may bring suit and what they may be compensated for. Those questions are to be answered by the domestic laws selected by the courts of the contracting states." Basically, the Supreme Court said that in airline disaster cases the damages that are compensable depend on the state or federal law that is applied under conflict-of-law rules. For most airline accident litigation these cases would be tried under state law but in the United States there is the presence of a federal statute that governs accidents or disasters on the high seas called the US Death on the High Seas Act.

---

[11] Ibid.

US Death on the High Seas Act and PunitiveDamages for International Air Carriers

The Death on the High Seas Act (herein referred to as the DOHSA) is a US marine law enacted by the United States Congress. Its original intent was to "[recover] damages against a ship-owner by a spouse, child, or dependent family member of a seamen killed in international waters" in wrongful death cases caused by "negligence or unseaworthiness." Now it also applies to cases arising out of airline disasters over the high seas that occur beyond the 12-nautical miles of American waters. The DOHSA permits plaintiffs to seek both economic damages and damages for the loss of a deceased airplane patron's "care, comfort, and companionship." It does not allow for non-economic losses such as pain and suffering, mental anguish, or punitive damages.

The exclusion of punitive damages as a type of damage that is afforded to international travelers who are victims of accidents onboard a plane over the high seas isn't actually restricted to those individuals whose cases are tried under the US DOHSA. The Montreal Convention itself never allows for punitive damages to be recovered either. In a case related to the Korean Airlines case referenced above, a US Court of Appeals went against a jury decision awarding punitive damages to the plaintiff in excess of $50 million.

Other Types of Damages

In jurisdictions where non-economic damages for personal emotional distress are a possible remedy, they may only be a remedy for a plaintiff in an international air carrier lawsuit governed by the Montreal Convention if the emotional distress is actually caused by a physical injury. Imagine a situation wherein a plane was forced to crash land (for reasons other than the international carrier's negligence). There may be passengers suffering from anxiety and nightmares, and these individuals may seek legal remedies and non-economic damages. If a plaintiff also had suffered a physical injury (such as a sprained toe) the court would allow for damages to cover the physical injury but not for the mental anguish, as the physical injury merely accompanied the mental anguish and didn't cause it. Courts have decided cases and set precedents that conclude that "an air carrier cannot be held liable under Article 17 when an accident has not caused a passenger to suffer death, physical injury, or physical manifestation of injury."

Jurisdiction and Statute of Limitations Issues

One of the most difficult areas of international air carrier liability law is determining where exactly a case should be tried. Often defendants that are onboard a single aircraft have wildly different final destinations as well as places they call home. Lawsuits stemming from a single accident are often filed in different cities, states, and even countries. In the United States alone some cases are heard in state court while plaintiffs of the exact same accident may be tried in federal court. In certain specific situations cases may even be consolidated for the purpose of finding the international air carrier is in fact liable, and then the trials for each person's damages are held separately.

Luckily for us, the Montreal Convention spells out exactly where lawsuits against international air carriers (that are governed by the Montreal Convention) can be brought; a plaintiff can only bring an international air carrier liability lawsuit governed by the Montreal Convention in countries that are using the Convention as law, and only in the country where the flight tickets were purchased, the country of the plaintiff's final destination, the country where the international air carrier is incorporated, or the country of the plaintiff's residence (if the carrier operates or conducts business there). The reasons for the need of these rules are simple; it would be unfair to have injured persons be forced to try cases in countries that are incredible distances away from their own.

In terms of time limitation issues, the Montreal Convention is quite straightforward: all lawsuits seeking damages must be brought within two years from the date of arrival at the destination, or two years from the date on which the aircraft ought to have arrived, or two years from the date on which the international carriage stopped.

Damages for Personal Belonging and Cargo Losses

Fortunately for international air carriers, the Montreal Convention didn't update many of the Warsaw Convention commentaries on liability for loss to cargo and baggage. One important note on baggage damage lawsuits is that their statute of limitation is different than for personal injury. Where baggage and cargo suffer damages, a carrier must be notified no more than seven days after the receipt of checked baggage and 14 days from the date of receipt in the case of air cargo.

Baggage and cargo losses have different remedies allowed under the Montreal Convention. Damage sustained to cargo under the control of an international carrier results in a liability not in excess of 19 SDRs per kilogram of cargo (unless a shipper has declared otherwise on an airway bill). The damage cap is broken so to speak if the damaged cargo is a result of an intentional act by the international carrier or its employees, or from a reckless act with knowledge that damage would probably come about due to the reckless action. International carriers will not be held liable, though, for damage resulting from defective cargo, packaging, or an act of war or public authority (like a customs officer). Damage sustained to baggage (or lost/delayed baggage) only holds a carrier liable to a limit of 1,131 SDRs (as of 2010) for each passenger (unless, again, the passenger has declared a higher value).

Sea Carriage

"The emergent use of these cargo-carrying containers marks a significant technological stride within the maritime industry, and their use seems certain to expand in years to come because of the substantial advantages they provide over conventional modes of ocean carriage for shippers and carriers alike." (Matsushita Electric Corp v. S.S. Aegis Spirit, 414 F. Supp. 894 (w.D. Wash. 1976)).[12]

The case went on to expand further, claiming that the efficiency and economic advantages provided by this new form of packaging would drive the demand for containerized shipping. In terms of efficiency the case specifically pointed out that handling, loading, stowing, and discharging cargo contained in these massive sea containers would be much easier than when small groups of goods are packaged together and each package has to be handled individually. Another advantage of containerization is the increased protection against the elements they provide the owner of the goods being transported. One other key feature of containerization is the amount of money international marine carriers can save by making this their primary form of packaging goods; labor cost (typically quite high for international marine carriers) can be cut substantially due to the use of machines that only require a single operator to handle the large containers.

Unfortunately, despite all the positive impacts of containerization on international marine transportation there will always still be damaged and loss cargo for international shippers. In the case of damaged goods shippers, cargo owners, and insurers expect the international carrier of the goods to compensate them for the loss. This section of the chapter will explore how and why international marine carrier liability is provided protection under the law.

---

[12] Ibid.

Liability Uncertainties

Before technological advancements made it possible to track and monitor ships and their containers over entire international journeys, internationally transported marine cargo would be under sole control and watch of marine carriers. Without cameras and other tracking devices there was no way to prove how or why cargo was damaged after an international journey. Governments realized the importance of marine transportation and needed to advocate for international trade, and by extension they needed to advocate for shippers of international goods to use international marine carriers for transportation. The result was staggering; both the United States and England declared that marine carriers would essentially be the insurers of the goods they were carrying. Put another way, carriers were held "absolutely liable" for all damage to cargo in their possession (with a few exceptions). Slowly, marine carriers became more powerful; ships became faster and international trade grew exponentially. Bills of lading are contracts between a shipper of goods (the owner of the goods) and marine carriers, and as the power of individual carriers grew they began tailoring their bills of lading to reduce or even eliminate their liability with regards to damage of shipped cargo. Some carriers were so bold as to include clauses that even freed them from their own negligence. This led to a period of great uncertainty surrounding internationally shipped goods, international marine carriers, and the liabilities connecting the two.

Harter Act (1892)[13] and the Hague Rules (1924)[14]

1. Harter Act

The first real answer to the uncertainties surrounding international marine carriers and their potential liabilities came with the advent of the Harter Act, a US statute pertaining to merchandise transported between American and foreign ports (although the act is currently partially superseded by the US Carriage of Goods by Sea Act (1936). Today, the Harter Act still applies to the carriage of goods that isn't governed by the Carriage of Goods by Sea Act, including the period before loading of the goods and after discharge (i.e., during warehousing) unless the bill of lading expressly makes the Carriage of Goods by Sea Act applicable to these situations also. A key feature of the Harter Act was that it voided clauses in bills of lading that relieved a marine carrier of liability for damages resulting from the carrier's own negligence and also voided clauses attempting to lessen the carrier's obligations to exercise due diligence to provide seaworthy ships. Finally, the Harter Act relieved a carrier of liability for errors in navigation or ship management (should the owner of the vessel exercise due diligence).

2. Hague

In 1924, the Hague Rules were introduced (formally referred to as the "International Convention for the Unification of Certain Rules of Law relating to Bills of Lading, and Protocol of Signature"). The purpose of the Hague Rules was simple: it imposed minimum standards on international marine carriers, and provided increased protection to the owners of cargo being transported. Previously, international marine carriers were governed by common law wherever a dispute occurred; with the implementation of the Hague Rules, there was a formal standardized collection of laws to govern international marine carriers. One important note, though, is that the Hague Rules should not be seen as a "consumer's charter" of sorts because the Hague Rules actually favored the carriers when disputes arose.

The reason the Hague Rules was so ground-breaking was that it represented the very first attempt by international world leaders to find a workable and logical solution to the problems facing internationally shipped goods using international marine carriers. As the marine carriers sought to implement

---

[13] US Legal. n.d. US *Legal Definitions*: Harter Act Law & *Legal Definition*. Accessed January 2016. definitions.uslegal.com/h/harter-act/

[14] —. n.d. Wikipedia *the Free Encyclopediea*. Accessed January 2016. https://en.wikipedia.org/wiki/hague_rules

more and more clauses to reduce their own liability inside their bills of lading, cargo owners were losing any control over the safekeeping of their merchandise. The Hague Rules established minimum mandatory liability for the international marine carriers and finally dealt with this problem of carriers excluding their own liability in transportation contracts. The Hague Rules also stated that the owner of the goods being transported was actual liable for the cost of damaged goods unless they could prove that the transportation vessel wasn't properly manned, up kept, or generally seaworthy. Basically, the international marine carriers could avoid liability for damages resulting from human error (provided they exercised due diligence). The Hague Rules actually still govern an incredibly large percentage of world trade and are still in use by almost all major trading countries. It should be noted that although the Hague Rules have been updated by two protocols, and amended very slightly to become the Hague-Visby Rules, the basic liability provisions stated above remain unchanged.

3. The Rotterdam Rule[15]

Similar to the Hague Rules, the Hague-Visby Rules, and the Hamburg Rules, the Rotterdam Rules are the latest attempt by the international community to create uniformity in shipping contracts. The Rotterdam Rules are a radical and extensive set of laws and legislations, and if it does become effective it will replace the Hague Rules and become the largest change in marine transport law in over 90 years. The full title of the Rotterdam Rules is the "United Nations Convention of Contracts for the International Carriage of Goods Wholly or Partly by Sea," and it was first introduced for signing and implementation in 2008 (although it can't come into force until one year after the date that it is approved and ratified by 20 signatory nations). Basically, the purpose of the Rotterdam Rules is to establish a more modern, comprehensive, and uniform set of legal rules to govern shippers, carriers, and consignees under contract for shipments involving international transport.

Specifically, the Rotterdam Rules attempt to address two specific ongoing problems. First, the overlap and conflict existing with three conventions in place. Imagine a basketball league where some teams play by NBA rules, some NCAA rules, and other FIBA rules. This is the state of affairs today. Second, it addresses many of the outdated rules that have not kept up with technology or modern international business practices.

As of November 2015 the Rotterdam Rules have only been ratified by three states and is not yet in force. It is unlikely that the Rotterdam Rules will ever come into force as certain states believe the existing state of affairs, where some rules are carrier friendly and others are more cargo friendly, provides them with a competitive advantage. The Rotterdam Rules modify the definitions and duties and liabilities of the parties. For example, the traditional language so widely used in shipping, specifically the terminology of bills of lading, sea bills etc., is replaced with a more legalistic and simplified approach. It opts for terms such as negotiable transport document and non-negotiable transport document. The Rotterdam Rules have yet to come into effect, and most likely won't in the near future. However, be aware that there is a movement to update the international marine carrier liability governance.

Carriage of Goods by Sea Act (1936)[18]

In 1936 the US implemented an Act to codify the Hague Rules and apply to every single bill of lading that governs the international carriage of goods by sea to or from American ports. This was known as

[15] —. n.d. Wikipedia *The Free Encyclopedia*. Accessed January 2016. https://en.wikipedia.org/wiki/rotterdam_rules

[16] Mandelbaum, Samuel Robert. 1996. "Creating Uniform Worldwide Liability Standards for Sea Carriage of Goods Under the Hague, COGSA, Visby and Hamburg Conventions." *University of Denver Transportation LawJournal*, Spring.

[17] Ibid.

[18] Radzik, Edward, and Gerard White. n.d. *Understanding the Carriage* of Goods by Sea Act. Presentation, New York: McDermott & Radzik, LLP; Hill Rivkins & Hayden LLP.

the Carriage of Goods by Sea Act, or COGSA. An important feature of COGSA is that it technically only governs the part of an international marine carriage journey from the time goods are loaded onto the vessel until they are unloaded (although this time period can be extended with explicit provisions in any bill of lading). Another key feature of COGSA is that it does not allow for any clauses to reduce the mandatory minimum liabilities that are laid out in the Act. Put another way, an international marine carrier cannot reduce their liability via provisions past the point of mandatory liability laid out in the Act. If a carrier is liable for a specific piece of defective hardware resulting in damaged goods under COGSA, but inputs a clause into their bill of lading that releases them from this liability, the clause is null and void. Yet another important feature of the Act is that it increased the amount that carriers have to pay cargo owners for damages that take place during transit to US $500 per package (or per customary freight unit).

1. Historical Developments

When COGSA came into effect, it should be noted that the majority of cargo was still shipped in small boxes and bags. As merchandise owners realized the efficiency of pallets, carriers argued that their "per package" liability limit should now be applied per pallet, thus reducing their liability, and some courts did agree. As international trade evolved further, shipping containers and containerized freight became the norm; seeing another opportunity to reduce liability, international marine carriers again argued that these extremely large containers should represent one package and thus be subject to the "per package" liability limits. Even though some containers were valued at over $500,000, carriers wanted to reduce their liability to the US $500 per package limit for each container, and again some courts did agree. Seeing the issues created by COGSA led other governments to address this imbalance by amending the Hague Rules (in 1968) with the Visby Amendments, eliminating the "per package" limitation and instead introduced a "per kilogram" limitation. This led to litigation concerning liability limits to become non-existent outside of the US. Unfortunately, Congress failed to pass the Visby Amendments and so the COGSA "per package" limitations lives on in America.

2. Exemptions

An international marine carrier governed by COGSA is protected considerably from damage resulting from negligence in managing the ship or from fire and storms. The carrier will be liable, though, for failure to use due diligence in providing a seaworthy transport vessel at the beginning of an international transportation journey. A vessel is "seaworthy" if it is reasonably fit to carry the cargo it has undertaken to carry on the international journey. International carriers are generally not liable for damage to cargo from errors in navigation, mismanagement of the transport vessel, acts of god, and acts of war among others. Below lists the liability exceptions for international marine carriers:[19]

- Act of God
- Perils, dangers, and accidents of the sea or other navigable waters
- War, hostilities, armed conflict, piracy, terrorism, riots, and civil commotions
- Quarantine restrictions; interference by or impediments created by governments, public authorities, rulers, or people including detention, arrest, or seizure not attributable to the carrier or any person referred to in article 18
- Strikes, lockouts, stoppages, or restraints of labor
- Fire on the ship

[19] United Nations Commission on International Trade Law. 2008. "United Nations Convention on Contracts for the International Carriage of Goods Wholly or Partly by Sea."

- Latent defects not discoverable by due diligence
- Act or omission of the shipper, the documentary shipper, the controlling party, or any other person for whose acts the shipper or the documentary shipper is liable pursuant to article 33 or 34
- Loading, handling, stowing, or unloading of the goods performed pursuant to an agreement in accordance with article 13, paragraph 2, unless the carrier or a performing party performs such activity on behalf of the shipper, the documentary shipper or the consignee
- Wastage in bulk or weight or any other loss or damage arising from inherent defect, quality, or vice of the goods
- Insufficiency or defective condition of packing or marking not performed by or on behalf of the carrier
- Saving or attempting to save life at sea
- Reasonable measures to save or attempt to save property at sea
- Reasonable measures to avoid or attempt to avoid damage to the environment
- Acts of the carrier in pursuance of the powers conferred by articles 15 and 16

COGSA requires written notice be given to the carrier at the port of discharge should damage be found upon delivery. If the damage is visible, the notice must be given at the time that the goods are taken from the carrier (or before this act). If damage isn't visible, but is later noted, written notice must be given within three days from the time that the goods are taken from the carrier. The reason these rules are important is because, should the time limits not be met, it will be argued by the carrier that the goods were delivered in good condition and were only damaged afterwards, and this is the presumption of the court. The statute of limitations for filing claims under COGSA is one year.

3. Per Package Limitation[20]

Briefly mentioned above, COGSA provides that carriers have a per package liability limit of $500. The term "per package" is slightly flexible and can also be taken to mean "per customary freight unit." At the advent of COGSA, simple packages were the normal way for goods to be transported internationally and domestically. Over time the shape, size, and material used to package internationally transported goods has changed over and over again. Rather than have a different rule and liability limit for each and every different unit of transport, the per unit damage cap applies to the customary (or normal) unit of transport for the goods being internationally carried (this could be crates, pallets, containers, etc.). The only way for this limit to be lifted or raised is for the owner of the goods in question to state as much on the bill of lading. Basically, the owner must input a clause into the bill of lading (which governs the goods) stating that the potential liability limit under COGSA has been raised to whatever monetary amount that is agreed upon by both parties to the contract. If the quantity of packages can be easily and clearly determined on the bill of lading, and if those packages documented on the bill of lading are handled and transported into ocean containers, then the $500 per package limitation applies to each individual package and not to the number of large ocean containers. This is one of the most litigious topics in international marine carrier liability law, as carriers and merchandise owners alike try to maximize their well-being by minimizing the cost on themselves for damaged goods.

How do you determine if a particular object is a COGSA package. Courts will take a broad view that a package consists of preparation that facilitates an items handling. A narrow view looks at the plain meaning of the word package. [1]

---

[20] Recupero, Patricia Ryan. 1973. "The Shipper's Right to Recover Under COGSA for Damage to Containerized Cargo." *Boston College Law Review* Volume 15, Issue 1 Number 1, Article 2.

Containers

Generally, when a bill of lading clearly and unambiguously describes a unit of packaging that can be reasonably construed as a package, a court will accept the bill of lading's package definition as a COGSA package. Litigation arises, however, when bills of lading are unclear, imprecise, or ambiguous. When a court finds ambiguity in the bill of lading it will enter into a relatively fact-intensive analysis based on the "best indication of the parties intent." [2] COGSA pre-dates containers so it does not address whether containers are packages, and no clarification has taken place about this. The Rotterdam Rules however have addressed this issue. As a general rule if the bill of lading lists the container as a package it will be treated as a package. However, if what is inside the container could reasonably considered to be a package, then the container is not a package, but the smaller item within the container. The rule therefore followed sometimes is that a package is the smallest item described as such or that could reasonably be described as such on the bill of lading.

Shipping Pallets

Pallets are much more acceptable to courts as a COGSA package. When the bill of lading explicitly lists pallets as packages, or the shipper uses the pallets in a manner consistent with a package's purpose, the pallet is considered a COGSA package. The Rotterdam Rules and the Hague-Visby Rules narrow the application limitation to pallets. [3]

Customary Freight Unit

The customary freight unit (CFU) liability limitation is applied to goods not shipped in packages. The liability is USD $500 "per customary freight unit." Such goods that fall within this category include bulk cargo, bulk goods, and unpackaged equipment. Courts look specifically to the "unit by which the freight was calculated in the particular case" by the shipper and the carrier. Courts have to analyze in detail the bill of lading to determine the party's intent.

The following case illustrates the approach to determine what constitutes a package or customary freight unit.

Comprehensive Case 2: Z.K. V Arch (776 F. Supp. 1549 (1991))[21]

Facts:

The MV Archigetis was an international marine carrier during the 1980s, and in 1987 was contracted to ship five large yachts from Taiwan to the United States. Each yacht had a corresponding clean negotiable bill of lading that they were shipped under, but these bills of lading were purchased by the plaintiff from the shipper of the yachts (or the owner of the yachts in Taiwan) while the yachts were in transit. Explicitly stated on each of the five bills of lading was the fact that only one unit was being shipped (per bill of lading), that the yacht was being shipped at the yacht owner's risk (in this case the plaintiff, Z.K. Marine, an importer of yachts for sale in the United States), that the value could be declared with prior notice, and that the liability limit for loss was limited to $500 per package or per customary freight unit. The yachts were known to be properly secured and fastened at the outset of the international carriage journey, however during transit a single yacht was lost while the other four had some level of damage. As is to be expected, the plaintiff wanted total compensation for the loss of one yacht and the damage to four others, however the defendant/international marine carrier claimed that the liability on their part was limited to $500 per yacht.

---

[21] Ibid.

Court Decision:

The international marine carrier's argument centered on COGSA (the governing agreement in this situation) and the explicitly laid out damage limits present on the bills of lading. As mentioned previously, the bills of lading clearly documented that "one unit" was being transported per bill of lading. And even if the yachts couldn't each be considered a single package, the defendant maintained that each yacht must be considered a single customary freight unit because the freight charges paid were based on a single customary freight unit, and a yacht was used as the basis of a single freight charge. A court agreeing with the international marine carrier would therefore agree that their liability is limited to $500 per yacht.

The plaintiff, on the other hand, had a few different arguments as to why the international marine carrier's liability cap of $500 per unit should be lifted. At first it was argued that the terms explicitly stated on the bills of lading should be unenforceable. Their reasoning was the fact that there was never an opportunity to declare a higher value for the yachts on the bills of lading (as they were purchased while already in transit). The plaintiff argued that there was no space on the bill of lading to even declare a higher value; however, when the court examined the bills of lading it was noticed that explicitly on the bills was stated that the "value of goods may be declared provided merchant gives prior notice and agrees to pay greater freight ad valorem bases see clause 18 on back hereof." It just so happens that clause 18 limits the potential damage payments of the international marine carrier to $500 per package unless a higher value is declared. Also, the court determined that although there wasn't a specific space on the bills of lading for declaring a higher value there was definitely extra free space to declare a higher value somewhere on the document.

When the court determined that there was in fact space to declare a higher value for the yachts being transported, the plaintiff slightly altered their argument; now they claimed that even if the bills of lading did provide an opportunity to increase the potential damage caps they had no physical opportunity at all to do so, because they purchased the negotiable bills of lading while the yachts were already in transit. Unbeknownst to them, though, was the fact that purchasers of bills of lading also purchase the rights that the original shipper (in this case in Taiwan) had negotiated. Essentially, all rights (for anybody) to declare a higher value for the yachts was nulled at the point when the yachts were placed onto the ship.

The plaintiff's final argument was that a single yacht doesn't constitute a single package and therefore shouldn't be limited by the per package damage caps stated on the bills of lading. The way that the yachts were secured and stored on board the marine carrier's vessel, the plaintiff argued, didn't constitute a package under the letter of the law. Unfortunately for the plaintiff, though, is the fact that the law sees a package as any class of cargo, no matter the weight or size, which has been prepared for transport by adding some packaging that facilitates the handling but doesn't necessarily enclose or fully package the goods.

In the end, the court held that a single yacht, under these circumstances, constituted a single package and would be governed by the $500 per package liability limit pursuant to COGSA. The purchasers of the bills of lading also purchased the statutes and clauses explicitly agreed upon in the bills of lading, and this included the liability limit of $500 per customary freight unit.

Conclusion:

Normally, COGSA's defining per package liability limitation doesn't apply to goods above deck. But, due to the circumstances surrounding the yachts in this court case, as well as the provisions in the bill of lading explicitly stating that they would be governed by COGSA and the $500 per package liability limit, the court found that the monetary damage payments with regards to the yachts would be limited at $500.

Exceptions to the Package Limitation

There are three exceptions to the package limitation:

1. Fair Opportunity Doctrine
2. Unreasonable Deviation
3. Fundamental Breach

1. Fair Opportunity Doctrine

The Fair Opportunity Doctrine states, "a carrier may limit its liability under COGSA only if the shipper is given a fair opportunity to opt for a higher liability by paying a corresponding greater charge." If the carrier fails to provide this opportunity then the limitation liability of USD $500 per package or customary freight unit is invalidated. The question is what then constitutes fair opportunity. Usually it requires some positive act of notice to the shipper of the opportunity, in other words, providing a clear place to fill in a higher value on the bill of lading.

2. Unreasonable Deviation

Unreasonable deviation by the carrier will also void the package limitations. Interestingly, an unreasonable deviation is also in and of itself a fundamental breach, therefore the last two exceptions work together. Unreasonable deviation traditionally was a geographical deviation—wandering off the regular and usual course of voyage. However, there are obvious exceptions to the geographical deviation, such as emergencies, war, pirates, mechanical failures, or other reasonable reasons. In addition, efforts to save life or property at sea is also an exception and COGSA specifically states within it that a "reasonable deviation" is not a breach of contract. Over time unreasonable deviation was expanded from mere geographical deviation to include "quasi-deviation." On deck stowage of goods is considered quasi-deviation without prior written contractual consent of the shipper, or showing some general custom.

3. Fundamental Breach

Fundamental breach is very close to the unreasonable deviation doctrine. In essence, deviation and quasi-deviation are subsets of fundamental breach, but applied narrowly. As in other areas of law, the distinction between ordinary breach and fundamental breach is grey.

Due Diligence Required Under COGSA

Under COGSA a carrier is required (before, at, and during the time of the international voyage) to exercise due diligence. The following diagram shows the three areas that COGSA requires carriers to exercise due diligence.

Also specified under COGSA are the rights and immunities of both the carrier of goods being transported as well as the actual ship being used for transportation. Carriers may use a myriad of defenses in court to reduce or avoid paying monetary damages. Some of the defenses which are used are claims that a loss is the result of an uncontrollable cause (i.e., a shipboard error, natural forces, external human forces, or the fault of the owner of the goods being shipped), their personal freedom from negligence, the amount of liability being maxed out at the value of cargo, and the fact that cargo which they are moving is inherently dangerous (such as flammable or explosive cargo).[22]

We will now take a closer look at the seaworthy requirement under COGSA.

---

[22] Canadian Manufacturers & Exporters. 2003. *Transportation Best Practices Manual.* May. Accessed February 2016. www.tw.gov.nl.ca/publications/bestpracticesmanual.pdf

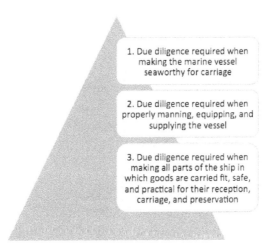

1. Due diligence required when making the marine vessel seaworthy for carriage

2. Due diligence required when properly manning, equipping, and supplying the vessel

3. Due diligence required when making all parts of the ship in which goods are carried fit, safe, and practical for their reception, carriage, and preservation

Seaworthy Requirement

As mentioned above, under COGSA a carrier is responsible for damage arising from unseaworthiness that is caused by a failure to exercise due diligence when making the ship seaworthy. For this requirement the burden of proving the exercise of due diligence is actually on the carrier. To determine the relative seaworthiness of a ship there is a standard test that is used: due diligence requires care by a reasonable prudent vessel owner, so was the vessel reasonably fit for the international carriage journey it is contracted to undertake? An example of when a ship would be unseaworthy is when the international marine carriage vessel Master is improperly trained or when there is a fault in the carrier's equipment on board that should have been recognized.

Burden of Proof Required Under COGSA

The last point to be made with regards to international marine carrier liability governed by COGSA is with the burden of proof when claiming damages in a lawsuit. Under COGSA there is a presumption of liability after a plaintiff establishes a claim of damages which is accepted until proven otherwise. This is starkly different than the common law ruling which put a heavy requirement on the plaintiff in an international marine carriage lawsuit to persuade and produce evidence proving the damages they are claiming. The disadvantage of this previous common law ruling is that the facts and evidence needed by the plaintiff to properly prove their damages are under the control of the defendant (i.e., the international marine carrier).

When suing for damages to cargo the plaintiff has the burden of establishing any reasonable case against the international marine carrier. They can prove that the damaged cargo in question was given to the carrier in satisfactory condition but was returned in damaged condition. If the well-being of the cargo when given to the carrier isn't obvious then the plaintiff is required to provide additional information or testimony. An example of this would be when the carrier receives goods already boxed up and has no way of knowing the condition of the goods upon receipt. Normally at the conclusion of the international journey when the cargo is released from the carrier's possession there will be a survey report taken that documents the condition of the cargo, and this is an extremely valuable document for the plaintiff in an international marine carriage lawsuit.

The next step in a lawsuit governed by COGSA must be taken by the defendant, or in this case the international carrier of goods. In terms of carrier requirements (to be held not liable) when being sued under COGSA they must prove that either due diligence was taken when preparing for and partaking on the international carriage journey or that the damage falls within the exceptions explicitly stated under COGSA. Also, the carrier must prove what proportion of the damage to cargo was the result of an exception under COGSA if that is their defence.

If the carrier proves they engaged in proper due diligence, the burden shifts back to the owner of the goods, to prove that the carrier was negligent.

Conclusion

International carrier liability is still evolving and changing by the day, as evidenced by the wealth of information and litigation that has been brought under the topic of international carrier liability law in this chapter. There is still much debate and a wealth of issues and potential litigation pitfalls that must be addressed. Hopefully better knowledge of international carriers of goods, and their responsibilities and liabilities with regards to the goods (or passengers) that they carry, has been gained through the reading of this chapter.

Bibliography

Business Dictionary. n.d. *Business Dictionary*. Accessed February 2016. http://www.businessdictionary.com/definition/Hague-rules.html

Canadian Manufacturers & Exporters. 2003. *Transportation Best Practices Manual*. May. Accessed February 2016. www.tw.gov.nl.ca/publications/bestpracticesmanual.pdf

Cornell University Law School. n.d. *Legal Information Institute: Open Access to Law Since 1992*. Accessed February 2016. http://www.law.cornell.edu/supremecourt/text/525/155

Dictionary.com. n.d. *Dictionary.com*: Accessed February 2016. http://dictionary.reference.com/

Encarta. n.d. Encarta Dictionaries.

Inbound Logistics. 2013. *Transportation Liability: Busting Seven Common Myths*. January. Accessed February 2016. www.inboundlogistics.com/cms/article/transportation-liability-busting-seven-common-myths

Lexology. n.d. *Lexology: Federal Court of Appeal Rules on Liability of International Air Carriers*. Accessed January 2016. http://www.lexology.com/library/detail.aspx?g=80c56131-7a57-42ae-9362-ac3f8636dfd9

Mandelbaum, Samuel Robert. 1996. "Creating Uniform Worldwide Liability Standards for Sea Carriage of Goods Under the Hague, COGSA, Visby and Hamburg Conventions." *University of Denver Transportation LawJournal*, Spring.

Oxford University Press. n.d. *Oxford Dictionaries*.

Peterson, Douglas H. 2014. *International Business Transactions B LAW 444*. Toronto: Nelson Education Ltd.

Quizlet. n.d. *Quizlet: International Business Law Cases*. Accessed February 2016. https://quizlet.com/37605078/international-business-law-cases-flash-cards/

Radzik, Edward, and Gerard White. n.d. *Understanding the Carriage of Goods by Sea Act*. Presentation, New York: McDermott & Radzik, LLP; Hill Rivkins & Hayden LLP.

Recupero, Patricia Ryan. 1973. "The Shipper's Right to Recover Under COGSA for Damage to Containerized Cargo." *Boston College Law Review* Volume 15, Issue 1 Number 1, Article 2.

Trade Ready. 2012. *TradeReady.ca International Trade Matters*. November 27. Accessed February 2016. www.tradeready.ca/2012/fittskills-refresher/legal-aspects-of-international-transportation-of-goods/

United Nations. 2006. *United Nations Conference On Trade And Development: Carriage of Goods by Air, a Guide to the International Legal Framework*. General, United Nations.

US Legal. n.d. *US Legal Definitions: Harter Act Law & Legal Definition*. Accessed January 2016. definitions.uslegal.com/h/harter-act/

Wikipedia. n.d. *Wikipedia the Free Encyclopedia*. Accessed January 2016. https://en.wikipedia.org/wiki/montreal_convention

—. n.d. *Wikipedia The Free Encyclopedia*. Accessed January 2016. https://en.wikipedia.org/wiki/warsaw_convention

—. n.d. *Wikipedia The Free Encyclopedia*. Accessed January 2016. https://en.wikipedia.org/wiki/rotterdam_rules

—. n.d. *Wikipedia the Free Encyclopediea*. Accessed January 2016. https://en.wikipedia.org/wiki/hague_rules

World Shipping. n.d. *World Shipping: Partners in Trade, Cargo Liability*. Accessed January 2016. http://www.worldshipping.org/industry-issues/cargo-liability

CHAPTER 6

Incoterms

Learning Objectives

After reading this chapter, you will have an understanding of:

1. The purpose and history of International Commercial Terms
2. The meaning and objective of each of the specific International Commercial Terms included in the Incoterms® 2010 publication
3. The proper use and application of each of the specific International Commercial Terms included in the Incoterms® 2010 publication
4. How to avoid some common pitfalls when using Incoterms in trade contracts

Incoterms Section

Diagrams

Please note that where there is an overlap on any of the diagrams below, with regards to the risk or cost responsibility between the buyer and seller in a contract, there exists a "grey area" of sorts within the requirements of that specific Incoterm. For example, the FCA term the delivery point, or point where the cost and risk transfer from the seller to the buyer, can vary anywhere from the seller's premises to the point of export before a border crossing such as an airport, wharf, or road terminal. Because the specific delivery point can be agreed upon between the buyer and seller and will be different depending on the specific contract, there exists a "grey area" under the FCA Incoterm and this is the reason for the overlap in Figure 6.2 FCA Diagram.

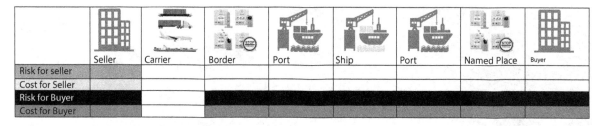

	Seller	Carrier	Border	Port	Ship	Port	Named Place	Buyer
Risk for seller								
Cost for Seller								
Risk for Buyer								
Cost for Buyer								

Figure 6.1: EXW Diagram

	Seller	Carrier	Border	Port	Ship	Port	Named Place	Buyer
Risk for seller								
Cost for Seller								
Risk for Buyer								
Cost for Buyer								

Figure 6.2: FCA Diagram

	Seller	Carrier	Border	Port	Ship	Port	Named Place	Buyer
Risk for seller								
Cost for Seller								
Risk for Buyer								
Cost for Buyer								

Figure 6.3: CPT Diagram

	Seller	Carrier	Border	Port	Ship	Port	Named Place	Buyer
Risk for seller								
Cost for Seller								
Risk for Buyer								
Cost for Buyer								

Figure 6.4: CIP Diagram

*Note: The seller is obligated to buy insurance to cover the transportation of the goods between the carrier and the destination named place under CIP but not CPT.

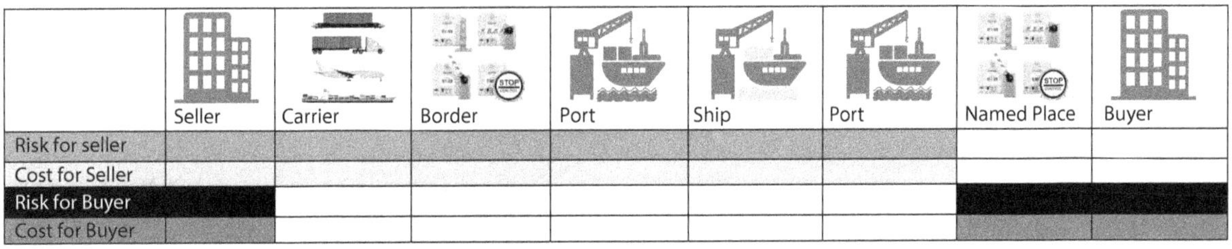

	Seller	Carrier	Border	Port	Ship	Port	Named Place	Buyer
Risk for seller								
Cost for Seller								
Risk for Buyer								
Cost for Buyer								

Figure 6.5: DAT Diagram

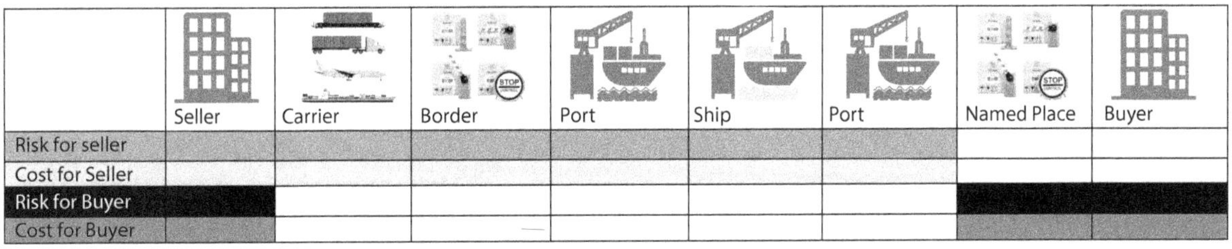

	Seller	Carrier	Border	Port	Ship	Port	Named Place	Buyer
Risk for seller								
Cost for Seller								
Risk for Buyer								
Cost for Buyer								

Figure 6.6: DAP Diagram

*Note: Under DAT the Seller is obligated to unload the goods at the named place of destination. Under DAP it is the buyer's obligation.

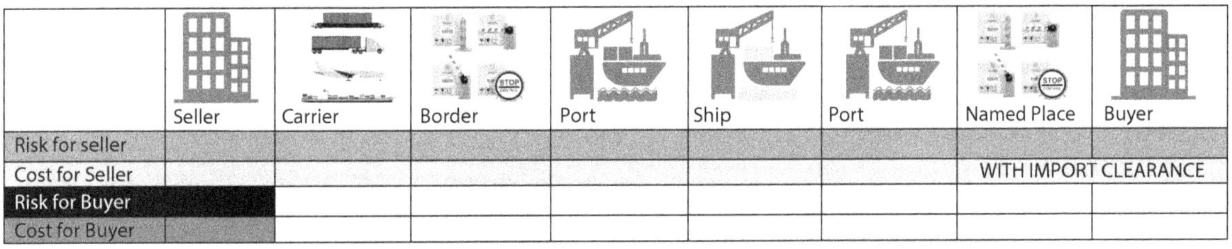

	Seller	Carrier	Border	Port	Ship	Port	Named Place	Buyer
Risk for seller								
Cost for Seller								WITH IMPORT CLEARANCE
Risk for Buyer								
Cost for Buyer								

Figure 6.7: DDP Diagram

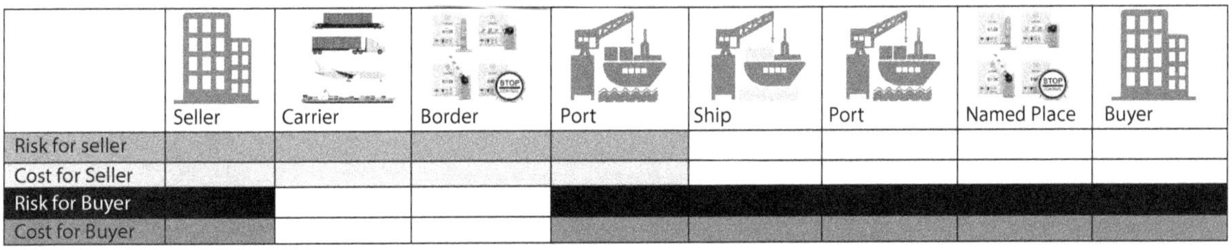

	Seller	Carrier	Border	Port	Ship	Port	Named Place	Buyer
Risk for seller								
Cost for Seller								
Risk for Buyer								
Cost for Buyer								

Figure 6.8: FAS Diagram

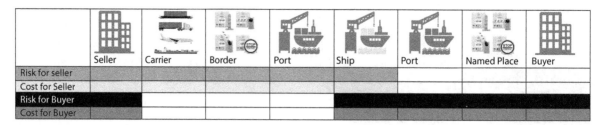

Figure 6.9: FOB Diagram

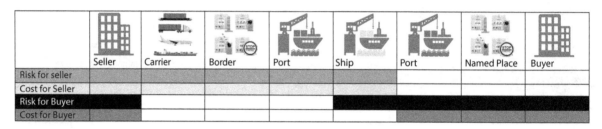

Figure 6.10: CFR Diagram

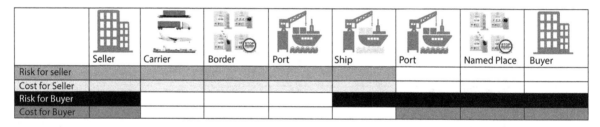

Figure 6.11: CIF Diagram

*Note: Under CIF the seller is obligated to buy insurance to cover the transportation of the goods between the carrier and the destination port, but not under CFR.

Liability of Internation Carriers of Goods and Passengers Section

Figures by Doug Peterson

The Warsaw Convention of 1929	standardized air travel and carriage procedures
	commentary on baggage claim forms, cargo receipts, passenger tickets, and other transport documentation
	declared international air carriers exempt from liability if "all necessary methods" were taken to avoid an accident
	limitation on monetary liability set at $9/pound for damaged cargo and $75,000 for passenger injuries

Figure 6.12: Warsaw Convention Diagram

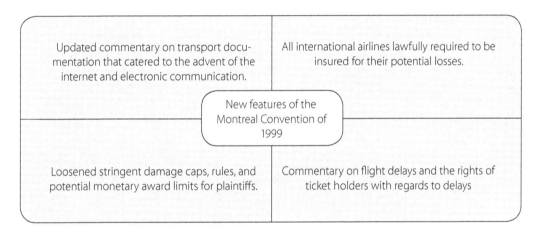

Figure 6.13: New Features of the Montreal Convention

Figure 6.14: International Air Carrier Liability Standards

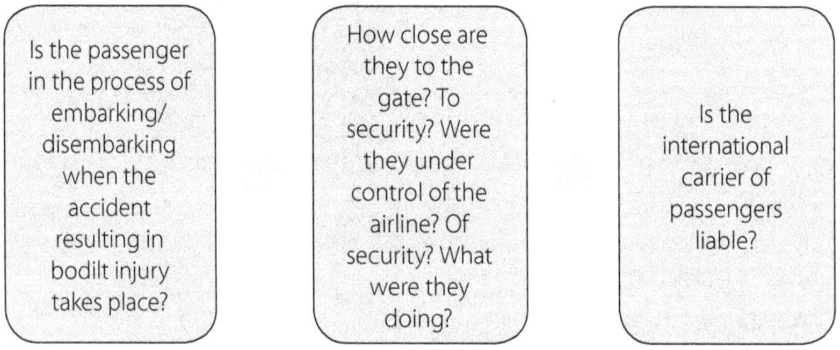

Figure 6.15: International Air Travel Embarking/Disembarking Determination

International Marine Carrier Governing Conventions and Their Respective Features

	Hague-Visby Rules	Hamburg Rules (won't be explored)	Multimodal Convention*
Transport Documentation	Bill of Lading	Any (including sea waybill)	Multimodal Document
Negotiable Transport Document	Yes	Optional	Optional
Basis of Carrier's Liability	Must act with due diligence in providing persons or corporations with a seaworthy vessel	Carrier must prove that all reasonable measures were taken to avoid the damages in question	The multimodal transport carrier must prove that all reasonable measures were taken to avoid the damages in question
Limitation of Carrier's Liability	666.67 units of account (monetary value decided by some pegged standard such as the value of gold) per package of goods being transported, or 30 units of account per kilogram of gross weight, whichever is **higher**	835 SDRs per package of goods being transported, or 2.5 SDRs per kilogram of gross weight	920 SDRs per package of goods being transported, or 2.75 SDRs per kilogram, or the higher amount provided under national law
Statute of Limitations	1 year	2 years	2 years (but notice within 6 months)

*Please note that this convention has yet to come into force

Figure 6.16: Different International Marine Carrier Conventions Compared

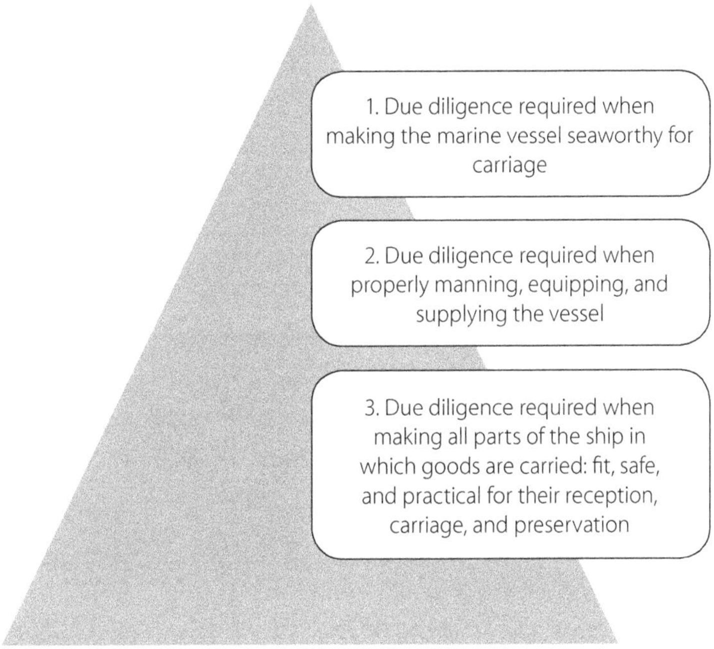

Figure 6.17: Due Diligence Requirements Under COGSA

Introduction

The idea behind International Commercial Terms (Incoterms) is simple; they are a way to standardize international trade contracts in all parts of the world and eliminate any unnecessary confusion or liability for any parties in the contract.[1] The main benefit of using Incoterms is the reduced risk in an international commercial transaction. Since countries have different laws, business cultures, and languages, Incoterms are international in nature, which allows both parties to comprehend them without misconception. The uncertainty of different interpretations of terms in different countries can be avoided or at least reduced to a considerable degree. Incoterms are structured with three letters that specify the seller's (exporter) and buyer's (importer) obligations. Incoterms focus on two key aspects of the transaction.

1. **Terms and Conditions**: Which party—buyer or seller—is responsible for arranging and paying for transport (and associated activities such as loading and unloading), import and export procedures, insuring the goods etc.
2. **Transfer of liability:** At what point in the journey does responsibility for the consignment transfer from the seller to the buyer? This is important since goods can be lost or damaged in transit, and this determines which party has responsibility for the goods.

There is no confusion with regards to rules of transportation from point A to point B. By using Incoterms, the buyer and seller have clarity in defining their obligations and responsibilities. However, Incoterms do not cover all the aspects of the commercial transaction; therefore a contract should be taken into consideration for other specific issues. An international body periodically updates and adjusts the contractual trade terms also known as Incoterms® 2010 publication as deemed necessary. There are 11 terms used under the most recent revision. In addition to creating clarity in transport obligations, it alerts parties to the transaction who bears transportation costs. These terms determine the costs of the transport of goods, which can vary greatly depending on the Incoterm used. Sellers

---

[1] Export.Gov. 2015. *Export.Gov: Helping U.S. Companies Export.* August. Accessed November 2015. http://www.export. gov/faq/eg_main_023922.asp

need to budget accordingly to ensure transportation costs do not erode any profit from the sale. Buyers have a corresponding risk and need to be equally diligent in the choosing of an Incoterm.

This chapter will discuss each Incoterm and analyze the point where the risk and cost transfers from seller to buyer. We will begin with a general overview of the Incoterms and then move onto each of the 11 terms published under Incoterms® 2010 individually to provide a more thorough description of each.

What Incoterms Do

- Incoterms dictate the exact delivery terms between the parties
- Incoterms help the sales contract by defining the respective obligations, costs, and risks involved in the delivery of the goods from the seller to the buyer
- Incoterms determine when the risk of loss passes from the seller to the buyer
- Incoterms apply to the contract of sale

What Incoterms Do Not Do

- Determine when title passes from seller to buyer—this is determined by the sales contract
- Constitute a contract
- Evoke any payment terms
- Address price payable, currency or credit terms
- Apply to service contracts
- Define contractual rights or obligations (except for delivery) or deal with remedies for breach of contract
- Protect parties from their own risk or loss, cover the goods before or after delivery
- Specify details of transfer, transport, and delivery of the goods (container loading is NOT considered packing and must be addressed in the sales contract)
- Incoterms do not apply to the contract of carriage

Incoterms are not law and there is no default Incoterm if one is not stated. Incoterms have always been primarily intended for goods crossing international borders, hence the name international commercial terms. However, they can and often are used in domestic sales.

Overview of International Commercial Terms

Incoterms have been in existence since its implementation in 1936 by the International Chamber of Commerce (ICC). The idea behind creating Incoterms was to produce a few simple and easily understandable trade terms that could fit into any international sales contract depending on the needs and wants of the seller and buyer of the goods being sold. Their main purpose is to eliminate confusion and conflicts that may arise with regards to the different risks and obligations of each party in the international sales contract; they determine and define the transportation costs and the risks with regards to damage to the goods being sold as they are passed from the seller to the buyer in the transportation journey governed by the contract.[2]

---

[2] International Chamber of Commerce. 2011. *ICC: We are the world business organization.* Accessed November 2015. http://www.iccwbo.org/products-and-services/trade-facilitation/incoterms-2010/

The terms also provide a set of international rules for the interpretation and enforcement of the most commonly used trade terms and practices in foreign trade as international trade gives rise to many disputes. This in turn allows individuals and corporations to draft general sales contracts for use in trade with different trading partners in various countries without requiring a new sales contract to be agreed upon and drafted each time there is a sale of goods. Each Incoterm is defined by the varying degree to which the seller and buyer in the sales contract is responsible for goods sold under contract during the transportation journey or varying degree of the seller's risk, as well as who is responsible for the costs associated with the different parts of the transportation journey. They are continually reworked, updated, and republished by the ICC due to the rapid and continual expansion of global trade and the changing transportation landscape facing international buyers and sellers of physical goods. The last two updates by the ICC were in 2000 and 2010. The terms are recognized internationally and although they are most commonly used in contracts for the international sale of goods requiring transport they have also, over the past several years, been adopted for use in contracts governing domestic sales and the subsequent transportation of goods as well. The use of any Incoterms defines an international sales contract in the sense that it defines the respective obligations, costs, and risks of the buyer and seller of the goods governed by the contract during the transportation journey of the goods to their end destination. When using Incoterms in any sales contract, whether domestic or international, even though Incoterms are used globally and are accepted globally, they do not supersede the laws governing contracts and contract terms in any particular country.

The most recent set of Incoterms came into effect on January 1, 2011. There was an emphasis by the ICC on the need for transportation insurance in the face of growing international piracy concerns, as well as handling the digitalization of trade and the corresponding conflicts and confusion that arise from increased technological advancement. Incoterms® 2010 consists of 11 different trade terms, reducing the 13 used in Incoterms® 2000. Previously, the trade terms were divided into five categories but with the publication of Incoterms® 2010 the ICC decided to subdivide the terms into only two different categories: **Rules for Any Mode of Transportation and Rules for Sea and Inland Waterway Transport**. The larger group of seven rules (Rules for Any Mode) can be used in any international trade contract and apply regardless of the method of transport for the goods. The smaller group of four rules (Rules for Sea) are only applicable only to sales contracts that solely involve transportation of the goods over water. We will now dive deeper into Incoterms® 2010 and give a description of each of the 11 specific terms under the publication as well as explain some of the subtle differences between them.

One of the aims of the Incoterms 2010 was to encourage the use of correct Incoterms for containerized goods, which is the common method today of shipping goods. Use of the traditional Incoterms such as CIF and CFR for containerized goods exposes the exporter to unnecessary risks. The tsunami in Japan in 2011 dramatically illustrated this when exporters suffered avoidable losses when their containers were washed away while in the container terminal.

In general, the use of "transport by sea or inland waterways only" rules should only be used for bulk cargos (oil, coal, etc.) and non-containerized goods, where the exporter can load the goods directly onto the vessel. Where the goods are containerized, the "any transport mode" rules are more appropriate.[3] There is a critical difference between these two groups of rules with respect to the point at which the risk passes from the seller to the buyer.

³ Wikipedia. 2014. *Wikipedia The Free Encyclopedia*. Accessed October 2015. https://en.wikipedia.org/wiki/Incoterms

Incoterms® 2010 Examination and Analysis

The key to properly using any of the 11 Incoterms is to first take a close look at the specific situation the buyer or seller faces; consider any limitations, such as the amount of money available for financing the transportation and the modes of transportation available. This analysis will allow the party to choose the most appropriate Incoterm. If you always approach the use of Incoterms in this way, you won't be caught unintentionally obligated to perform any additional actions or make any additional payments that you haven't planned for.

An additional feature to consider when choosing which specific Incoterm to use in a trade contract is that the price or cost of the product/shipment being sold under contract will be affected by the specific Incoterm that is chosen to govern the transportation journey. As a general rule, the more responsibility or risk that an Incoterm places on the seller or buyer in the contract, the more favorable the price is for that party; for example, if choosing the EXW Incoterm (which places much more responsibility and risk on the buyer of the goods sold under contract than the seller) the price of the shipment should be more favorable to the buyer than if the chosen Incoterm is DAT (which places more risk on the seller of the goods under contract). To some degree, the market landscape facing the parties to a contract will also drive the choice of a specific Incoterm; for example, if exporters in a certain geographical location desperately need business they will be more willing to take on an Incoterm that will cost them relatively more because they are essentially paying for the security of having additional, locked-in business.

Basic Overview of Incoterms

There are three different ways to group Incoterms:

1. **Two Types of Incoterms.** The 11 rules are divided into two groups based on mode of transportation.

Sea or Inland Waterways only	Any Transport Mode
EXW Works	**FAS** Free Alongside Ship
FCA Free Carrier	**FOB** Free On Board
CPT Carriage Paid to	**CFR** Cost and Freight
CIP Carriage & Insurance Paid to	**CIF** Cost Insurance and Freight
DAT Delivered at Terminal	
DAP Delivered at Place	
DDP Delivered Duty Paid	

2. **Prepaid Terms vs. Collect Terms.** The 11 rules are divided into two groups based on whether or not the term is prepaid or collected.

Collect Terms	Prepaid Terms
EXW Works	**CFR** Cost and Freight
FCA Free Carrier	**CIF** Cost Insurance and Freight
FAS Free Alongside Ship	**CPT** Carriage Paid to
FOB Free On Board	**CIP** Carriage & Insurance Paid to
	DAT Delivered at Terminal
	DAP Delivered at Place
	DDP Delivered Duty Paid

3. **Letter Groups**

One useful way of initially classifying and thinking about the different Incoterms is by considering the following question: Who is responsible for the main carriage of the goods sold under contract (and payment for the main carriage of the goods) during the transportation journey: the buyer or the seller? If the seller is responsible for the main carriage of the goods then where does the risk associated with carrying the goods pass from the seller to the buyer, before the main carriage or after it? By looking at the 11 Incoterms under this light we see four distinct groups[4]:

Group	Incoterms	Responsibility
Departure	EXW	Buyer responsible for all of the carriage
F Group	FCA	Main carriage unpaid
	FAS	Buyer arranges for and pays for the main carriage
	FOB	
C Group	CPT	Seller arranges for and pays for the main carriage
	CIP	Risk passes before the main carriage
	CFR	
	CIF	
D Group	DAT	Seller arranges for and pays for the main carriage
	DAP	Risk passes after the main carriage
	DDP	

Each group's letter makes up the first letter of the Incoterm.

Rules for Any Mode of Transport

EXW—Ex Works

Overview

- Minimum responsibility on seller; maximum responsibility on buyer
- Seller makes goods available at specified place, usually seller's factory or depot
- Buyer responsible for loading goods, export procedures, onward transport, costs arising after collection of the goods

Using EXW in a sales contract means that the seller has delivered the required goods and thus loses both the risk (in terms of damage, stolen, or lost goods), as well as the responsibility for paying the costs associated with transporting the goods to their final destination, when it places the goods at the disposal of the buyer at the seller's premises or at another place named explicitly in the contract.[5] The seller's premises refers to the place where the goods first begin their transportation journey. EXW specifically is most commonly used for the international sale of goods by buyers and sellers in Europe because of the absence of strict borders due to the presence of the European Union. Another defining feature of EXW is that the seller of the goods does not need to load the goods on any collecting vehicle, even on their own premises, nor does it need to clear the goods for export where such clearance is applicable. Both of these obligations fall on the buyer of the goods when using EXW in the sales contract. In many real cross-border transactions, though, this rule can present practical difficulties. Specifically, the exporter or seller of the goods may need to be involved in export reporting and

---

[4] Mantissa E-Learning. 2011. *IncotermsExplained.com*. Accessed October 2015. http://www.incotermsexplained.com/
[5] Ibid.

clearance processes and cannot realistically leave these responsibilities to the buyer. Trading parties often turn to the Free Carrier Incoterm to more easily resolve a situation such as this because there is more legal leeway granted in determining the location at which the obligations and risks associated with the goods are transferred when the exact location isn't explicitly stated. One other thing to be aware of: although the seller is not obliged to load the goods onto any carrying vehicle, if the seller does load the goods anyway, it is at the buyer's risk!

FCA—Free Carrier

Overview
- Any transport mode
- Flexible rule suitable for all situations where buyer arranges main carriage
- Seller delivers goods, cleared for export, to a named place, main carriage unpaid
- Named place can be freight forwarders depot, inland clearance depot, terminal, or seller's premises
- Seller responsible for export clearance
- Buyer assumes all risks and costs after goods delivered at named place
- FCA best for containerized goods where buyer arranges for main carriage

FCA is a very flexible rule that is suitable for all situations where the buyer arranges the main carriage of the goods during the transportation journey. Using FCA means that the seller must deliver the goods to a carrier (or another person appointed by the buyer) at the seller's premises or another explicitly named place.[6] The parties to the sales contract are well advised to specify as clearly as possible the point, within the named place of delivery that the transfer of goods actually takes place, as the risk passes to the buyer at that specific point. This is why we see an overlap of cost and risk at the carrier section of Figure 6.1. Under FCA the seller may arrange a pre-carriage of the goods being sold from seller's premises to an explicitly named place of delivery, which can be a terminal, transport hub, forwarder's warehouse, or any other similar location. In this situation the delivery of the goods being sold is completed and the transfer of risk associated with the goods takes place when the pre-carriage transport vehicle arrives at the named place ready for unloading; in other words, the carrier appointed by the buyer is responsible for unloading the goods (note: if there is more than one carrier of the goods for the buyer, then risk transfers on delivery to the first carrier). When the named place of delivery in the sales contract is the same location as the seller's premises, then the seller is responsible for loading the goods onto the buyer's truck or other carriage vehicle; this is an important difference from EXW.

In all situations under FCA, the seller is responsible for export clearance and the buyer assumes all risks and costs associated with the goods under contract after the goods have been delivered at the named place. FCA is the term of choice for a contract governing containerized goods where the buyer arranges for the main carriage during the transportation journey.

CPT—Carriage Paid To

Overview
- All forms of transport and multimodal transport
- Seller delivers goods to carrier and pays for main carriage to named place
- Seller does not pay for insurance

---

[6] Ibid.

- Named place can be freight forwarder, terminal, or inland clearance depot
- Risk transfer at point where carrier takes charge of goods

When using the Carriage Paid To Incoterm, the seller of the goods has the responsibility of arranging and paying for the carriage of the goods all the way to the named place of destination, but not for insuring the goods from any risks all the way to the named place of destination.[7] CPT also states that delivery of the goods is complete, and therefore risk transfers from the seller to buyer, at the point where the goods are taken in charge by a carrier. This point should be agreed upon and explicitly stated by the buying and selling party within the sales contract to eliminate any confusion or possible conflict should the goods become damaged at some point during the transfer (this is the reason we see an overlap once again in Figure 6.2, as well as the overlap in Figure 6.3 relating to the CIP Incoterm). Basically, using CPT means that the seller delivers the goods, and loses the risks associated with them, when they arrive to a carrier (or another person explicitly appointed in the contract) at the agreed upon place (if any such place is agreed upon by the parties) and that the seller must contract for and pay the costs of carriage necessary to bring the goods to the named place of destination (other than insurance). Under CPT be careful of terminal handling charges by the terminal operator. Such charges may or may not be included in the carrier's freight rates, so buyer needs to check whether CPT price includes terminal handling charges. Buyer should also ensure that insurance coverage starts for the main carriage when the carrier takes charge of the goods. This needs to be stipulated in the commercial contract, as this is not necessarily the same place referred to in the Incoterm.

CIP—Carriage and Insurance Paid To

Overview
- All forms of transport and multimodal transport
- Seller delivers goods to carrier and pays for main carriage to named place
- Seller pays for insurance of journey
- Only requires minimal level of insurance (sales contract may require more insurance coverage)
- Named place can be freight forwarder, terminal, or inland clearance depot

Using CIP the seller is responsible for arranging for the carriage of the goods being sold (and paying for it) to the named place of destination and for insuring the goods during their transportation journey.[8] Using CIP also means that the seller has to deliver the goods to the carrier (or another person appointed by the buyer) and thus loses the risks associated with them when they arrive at an agreed upon place for the carrier before the main carriage portion of the transportation journey. To repeat, the buyer must contract for insurance coverage against the seller's risk of loss or of damage to the goods during the entire carriage to the named place of destination. CIP and CIF (Cost Insurance and Freight) are the only two that place an obligation on the seller to arrange for insurance for the transportation of the goods (also note that this insurance actually covers the buyer's risk because under CIP risk will pass from the seller to the buyer before the main carriage). This is the only defining difference between CPT and CIP and should be the deciding factor between these two terms when choosing between them; do you need the seller to pay for insurance for the transportation journey? The buyer should note that under CIP the seller is required to obtain only minimal insurance coverage. Should the buyer wish to have more insurance protection it will need to either expressly agree with the seller in the contract or arrange for its own extra insurance coverage. Same issue of terminal handling charges applies here as with CPT above.

---

[7] Ibid.
[8] Ibid.

DAT—Delivered At Terminal

Overview

- All forms of transport and multimodal transport
- Seller delivers goods to named place; goods unloaded from ship, truck, rail, at the named place
- Seller assumes all costs and risks to point delivered at the terminal
- Seller does not clear goods for import

Under DAT the seller is responsible for arranging for the carriage of the goods (and paying for it) to the named place of destination. In addition, the transfer of risk does not pass to the buyer until the seller has unloaded the goods at the named destination.[9] Using DAT specifically means that the seller has delivered the goods when they are unloaded from the arriving carriage vehicle and are placed at the disposal of the buyer at an explicitly named terminal at the named port or place of destination. "Terminal" in this case includes a place, whether covered or uncovered, such as a quay, warehouse, or container yard, a road, rail, or air cargo terminal. The place for delivery should be specified as precisely as possible within the sales contract, as many ports and transport hubs are very large. The seller bears all risks involved in bringing the goods to, and unloading them at, the terminal at the named port or place of destination. Note that under DAT the buyer is responsible for import clearance and any applicable local taxes or import duties associated with the goods. If the specified terminal is a clearance depot or a similar location, then use of this rule is straightforward as the goods can be delivered before clearance is required. If customs procedures take place before complete delivery by the seller (as defined under the Incoterm in the contract) at a border, then the goods can often be given a pre-clearance or transit status and still be considered completely delivered before clearance is required. However, sometimes complications can arise if the goods have to go through a clearance point before complete delivery by the seller. Clearance of the goods may require close liaison between the carrier and the buyer of the goods in the contract and when this goes awry there can be delays and disputes about additional charges. This is an appropriate Incoterm for container operations where seller bears responsibility for main carriage.

DAP—Delivered At Place

Overview

- All forms of transport and multimodal transport
- Seller delivers goods to named place ready for unloading from ship, truck, rail, etc.
- Seller assumes all costs and risks to point of unloading
  - DAT—seller is responsible for unloading
  - DAP—buyer is responsible for unloading
- Buyer responsible for import clearance, local taxes, and import duties
- Can be used to replace Incoterms 2000 DAF, DEX, and DDP

---

[9] Ibid.

When using the DAP Incoterm, the seller is responsible for arranging for the carriage of the goods (and paying for it) as well as for bringing the goods, ready for unloading from the arriving carriage vehicle, to an explicitly named terminal at the named place of destination before the risks associated with the transportation of the goods passes to the buyer.[10] This is the defining difference between DAT and DAP, as under DAT the seller is responsible for physically unloading the goods at the named place, not just bringing them to the named place of destination ready for unloading. The seller bears all risks involved in bringing the goods to the named place of destination but the buyer is still responsible for import clearance and any applicable local taxes or import duties under DAP. This rule can often be used to replace the Incoterms 2000 terms Delivered At Frontier (DAF), Delivered Ex Ship (DES), and Delivered Duty Unpaid (DDU). Note that just like DAT if the specified terminal at the named place of destination is a clearance depot or a similar location, then the use of this rule is straightforward as the goods can be delivered before clearance is required. If customs procedures take place before complete delivery by the seller at a border, then the goods can often be given a pre-clearance or transit status and still be considered completely delivered before clearance is required. However, sometimes complications can arise if the goods have to go through a clearance point before complete delivery by the seller. Clearance of the goods may require close liaison between the carrier and the buyer of the goods in the contract and when this goes awry there can be delays and disputes about additional charges.

DDP—Delivered Duty Paid

Overview

- All forms of transport and multimodal transport
- Seller delivers goods, ready for unloading from the conveyance, to a named place
- Seller has costs and risks to named place
- Seller clears goods for import, pays taxes, and duties
- Maximum responsibility for seller, minimum responsibility for buyer

DDP in a sales contract means the seller is responsible for arranging for the carriage (and associated payment) of the goods, as well as for delivering the goods to the named place of destination before the risk transfers to the buyer.[11] The goods must also be cleared for import and with all applicable taxes and duties paid by the seller, such as GST. Put another way, using this Incoterm means the seller has completed delivery of the goods and transfers the risk associated with the goods when the goods are placed at the disposal of the buyer (already having been cleared for import) on some form of transport, ready for unloading, at the named place of destination. Under DDP the seller bears all the costs and risk associated with bringing the goods to the place of destination. They also have an obligation to clear the goods not only for export but also for import, to pay any duty for both export and import, and to carry out all customs formalities. DDP places the maximum obligation on the seller and is the only rule that requires the seller to take responsibility for import clearance and the payment of taxes and import duty. These defining requirements can be highly problematic for the seller because in some countries the import clearance procedures are quite complex and bureaucratic and so it is most likely best left to the buyer who has local knowledge.

---

[10] Ibid.

[11] Ibid.

Rules for Sea and Inland Waterway Transport

FAS—Free Alongside Ship

Overview

- Sea and inland waterways only
- Seller delivers goods alongside ship
- Seller clears for export; main carriage is unpaid
- Buyer responsible for loading goods onto ship
- Should not be used for containers (use FCA instead)

The use of this Incoterm is restricted to contracts governing the sale of goods transported by sea or inland waterway. This Incoterm should be used for situations where the seller has direct access to the vessel for loading, for example bulk cargos or non-containerized goods. Using FAS means the seller has delivered the goods (cleared for export), and the risk is transferred when the goods are placed alongside the vessel of transport (i.e. on a quay or a barge) nominated by the buyer at the named port of shipment.[12] The risk of loss of or damage to the goods passes from the seller to the buyer when the goods are alongside the ship and the buyer begins to bear all costs related to the transportation of the goods from that moment onwards (this is why we see an overlap at the port in Figure 6.7). The buyer is responsible for loading the goods on the vessel of transport as well as for all the costs from that point on. This Incoterm should be only used when the seller has direct access to the vessel for loading, especially for bulk cargo or non-containerized goods.

FOB—Free On Board

Overview

- Sea and inland waterways only
- Seller delivers goods cleared for export, loaded on board the vessel at the named port
- Risk transfers from seller to buyer once goods have been loaded on board
- For containers use FCA instead

FOB is restricted to contracts governing the sale of goods transported by sea or inland waterway. In practice this Incoterm should be used for situations where the seller has direct access to the vessel for loading, for example bulk cargos or non-containerized goods. When using FOB the seller has completed delivery of the goods when they are cleared for export and are loaded on board the transportation vessel at the named port of shipment (this is the reason for the overlap at the ship in Figure 6.8).[13] Once the goods have been loaded on board the shipping vehicle, the risk associated with the transportation of the goods transfers to the buyer who also bears all costs thereafter.

---

[12] Ibid.

[13] Ibid.

Aside on FOB and Container Traffic[14]

By far the biggest problem with FOB is its continued incorrect application to container traffic. The majority of container traffic is not delivered directly to a wharf; rather it is staged. The notion of FOB relies on delivering the goods alongside the ship to be loaded onto the vessel directly from the delivery vehicle. This is rarely the case in practice, as increased security measures in place at ports across the world make it very unlikely a delivery vehicle will get anywhere near the transport water vessel with a container.

One basic responsibility under FOB is for the seller to pay for all charges until the goods have been loaded onto the carriage vessel at the agreed port. This includes the loading charges. In a situation where the buyer wishes the seller to provide transport documentation, FOB may create a sort of double charging issue for the buyer, depending on how the carrier issues the invoice. Sometimes, carriers will separate loading charges at origin from unloading charges at destination. However this sometimes is not the case; sometimes carriers will only issue a total invoice charge. This circumstance calls for the buyer to pay for both the unloading and loading charges because the loading charges at origin cannot be determined. Thus, a double charging of sorts takes place.

It must also be remembered that the term FOB was coined at least two centuries before containers became a reality. It seems a misapplication that a term invented 200 years ago suddenly becomes "the norm" while containers that the Incoterm is governing in a contract have only been around for 50 years. The incorrect use of FOB for container traffic complicates the issue of who is responsible for bearing which charges, particularly port charges, as the lines of responsibilities become blurred. A better choice would be to use FCA for sea container traffic. Lastly, in relation to FOB it should be noted that the ship's rail under the current publication of Incoterms is no longer the risk transfer point (as it was in the past). Now the seller has to deliver the goods on board before any risk is transferred to the buyer.

Obviously, there is not just one problem with the use of FOB for container traffic. First, as mentioned above, it needs to be understood that FOB was around long before maritime container transport was invented. The main issue since container traffic became the norm has been the risk transfer point between the seller and buyer of goods sold under a contract governed by FOB. The Incoterms themselves are partly at fault, as they have been somewhat unclear over the years. Incoterms 2000 stated:

> The delivery point under FOB, same under CFR and CIF, has been left unchanged… in spite of a considerable debate. To deliver the goods "across the ship's rail" may seem inappropriate in many cases, it is nevertheless understood by merchants and… takes account the goods and the available loading facilities.

Unfortunately, this is exactly why this term is not well understood and is the reason that problems arise. The current Incoterms publication makes it quite clear that FOB is not preferred for container traffic because in practice the container is part of multiple movements and not just one transfer onto the sea vessel. Many containers are not delivered directly from the exporter's premises to the wharf but rather go through third parties like container packing warehouses, freight forwarders, containers parks, etc.

Prudent risk management practices would have the risk transfer when the seller loses control of the goods by handing them over to a third party. When using FCA, CPT, and CIP (the recommended multimodal answers to FOB, CFR, and CIF) this is indeed the case.

---

[14] Tkachuk, Heather. 2013. "Best Environmental Technologies Discussion Draft 2." Research Project, Edmonton, 1-10

CFR—Cost and Freight

Overview

- Sea and inland waterways only
- Seller delivers goods loaded on board ship, cleared to export, and pays for main carriage to named port
- Seller does not pay insurance
- Appropriate for general or bulk cargo but not for containers—use CPT instead

CFR is restricted to contracts governing the sale of goods transported by sea or inland waterway. In practice this Incoterm should be used for situations where the seller has direct access to the vessel for loading, for example bulk cargos or non-containerized goods. Under CFR the seller arranges and pays for the transportation journey to named port of destination. However, the seller has completed delivery of the goods and thus transfers the risk associated with transporting the goods when they are cleared for export and loaded on board the shipment vehicle (once again, this is the reason for the overlap in Figure 6.9).[15] The risk transfers from the seller to the buyer once the goods have been loaded on board (or before the main carriage takes place). Note that the seller is not responsible for insuring the goods for the main carriage portion of the transportation journey.

CIF—Cost, Insurance, and Freight

Overview

- Sea and inland waterways only
- Seller delivers goods loaded on board ship, cleared for export, pays for main carriage to named port
- Seller pays for insurance
- Appropriate for general or bulk cargo, should not be used for containers—use CIP instead

CIF is restricted to contracts governing the sale of goods transported by sea or inland waterway. In practice this Incoterm should be used for situations where the seller has direct access to the vessel for loading, for example bulk cargos or non-containerized goods. Using CIF means that the seller has completed delivery of the goods once they are cleared for export and are on board the shipment vehicle (again, this is the reason for the overlap in Figure 6.10).[16] The risk of loss or damage to the goods passes from the seller to the buyer when the goods are delivered on board the transportation vessel. The seller must contract for and pay the costs and freight necessary to bring the goods to the named port of destination. The seller is also required to contract for insurance to cover against the buyer's risk of loss or of damage to the goods during the carriage. The buyer should note that under CIF the seller is required to obtain only minimal insurance coverage. If the buyer wishes to have more insurance protection it will need to either expressly agree to this with the seller within the sales contract or to buy its own extra insurance. Incoterms only require a minimal level of insurance coverage, although the sales contract may call a higher level.

---

[15] Ibid.
[16] Ibid.

Incoterms in Practice

It cannot be stressed enough that the first step to properly using any of these 11 Incoterms in a contract is to critically examine the restrictions and limitations facing your international sales agreement. If you do not carefully examine the specific situation facing both parties to the contract before using any of the Incoterms you may find that either the buyer or seller of the goods under contract is contractually obligated to do something that was completely unintentional and is more than likely completely unwanted. It should be noted while there is no obligation for the seller to do so under Incoterms® 2010, it is acknowledged that sellers may wish to meet the demands of buyers even though a specific Incoterm may require different action. The reason is the presence of deeply entrenched customs in different industrial sectors and countries around the world that are directly opposed to certain features of certain Incoterms, such as who pays for specific expenses during the transportation journey of a specific good. Also, when using any of the above Incoterms in a contract, buyers and sellers should be very careful to note when they refer to a "named place"; if these locations are not explicitly and specifically stated within the sales contract, disagreements and conflicts are more likely to arise.

Incoterms

Carapanayoti & Co. v. E. T. Green Ltd., 1 Q.B. 131 (1958)

Michael G. Rapsomanikas, *Frustration of Contract in International Trade Law and Comparative Law* (Duquesne Law Review (1979-1980) 551-605, 2006), http://www.cisg.law.pace.edu/cisg/biblio/rapsomanikas.html

In 1956, *Carapanayoti & Co. v. E.T. Green Ltd* included a contract for the sale of Sudanese cottonseed cake that was to be shipped from Port Sudan CIF to Belfast. The contract included standard clauses in the event of extraordinary circumstances and a provision stating that in the event of a blockade or hostilities preventing performance, the contract would be canceled. Once the Suez Canal closed down, the seller refused to ship and claimed frustration, and the Queen's Bench Division upheld the claim of frustration.

It can be said that a CIF contract places heavy risk of non-shipment on the seller even when extenuating circumstances render the shipment impossible. The best form of protection is through a clause that will excuse their liability—but even so, there is a heavy burden on the seller to anticipate every possible risk to have full protection. Conversely, if the seller is exempt from risks that then fall to the buyer, they could potentially drive up the price of the transaction. Is it ethical to force a seller into choosing between paying higher costs or assuming all risk of unforeseen events? Should parties be granted a natural right to cancel a contract that, at no one's fault, physically cannot be performed?

Incoterms 2010 vs the Uniform Commercial Code (UCC)

The UCC has certain trade terms defined within it, such as FOB and CIF. It contains shipment and delivery provisions that are similar to those of Incoterms 2010. They even have the same three-letter abbreviations. However, their definitions are totally different. The most problematic is FOB, which can have a number of different meanings within the UCC, which do not match the ICC definition. This is further complicated with variations between different US states. In 2004 there was a major revision of the UCC, which abolished these terms. However, many states failed to adopt the 2004 revision; so in these states the former UCC revision remains law. Companies also out of habit continue to use such terms. US companies and those dealing with US companies must ensure they quote Incoterms 2010, to avoid any confusion.

Common Mistakes Made When Using Incoterms[17]

Below is a list of common mistakes that can be easily avoided but are often made by both importers and exporters when using Incoterms® 2010:

- Using a traditional "sea and inland waterway only" rule such as FOB or CIF for containerized goods instead of using a similar "all transport modes" rule such as FCA or CIP.
  - This exposes the exporter or seller to unnecessary risks. A dramatic recent example was the Japanese tsunami in March 2011, which wrecked the Sendai container terminal. An immense amount of goods awaiting dispatch were damaged or destroyed. Exporters who were using the wrong rule found themselves responsible for losses that could have been avoided!
- Making assumptions about the passing of the title to the goods based on the Incoterms rule in use. The Incoterms are silent on when "title" passes from seller to buyer; this needs to be defined separately in the sales contract.
- Failure to specify the port/place with sufficient precision, for example stating "FCA Chicago," which could refer to many places within a wide area.
- Attempting to use a term such as DDP without analyzing whether the seller can undertake all the necessary formalities in the buyer's country, for example paying VAT.
- Attempting to use EXW without thinking through the implications of the buyer's requirements to complete export procedures; in many countries it will be necessary for the exporter to communicate with the authorities in a number of different ways and thus it wouldn't make sense to use EXW.
- Using CIP or CIF without determining whether the level of insurance in force matches the requirements of the commercial contract; these Incoterms only require a minimal level of coverage, which may be inadequate depending on the specific contract.
- Where there is more than one carrier there is sometimes a failure to think through the implications of the risk transferring to the first carrier; from the buyer's perspective this may turn out to be a small haulage company in another country so retribution may be difficult in the event of loss or damage.
- Failure to establish how terminal handling charges are going to be treated at the point of arrival. Practices of different carriers vary substantially. Some carriers absorb terminal handling charges and include them in their freight charges while others do not.
- Where there is a payment with a letter of credit or a documentary collection there is sometimes a failure to align the Incoterm with the security requirements applicable to the payment or the requirements of the banks.
- When DAT or DAP is used with a "post-clearance" delivery point there is sometimes a failure to think through the liaison required between the carrier and the customs authorities; this can lead to delays and extra costs.

Practical Application

Going back to our example. CanCo has entered into a sales contract with RussCo. Within the sales contract there will be a clause setting out an Incoterm. The transportation route will see the goods transported from Edmonton, Canada by truck to Houston. From Houston by sea to St. Petersburg. What are the various obligations of each party under the agreement in light of the use of an Incoterm? As a starting example the Incoterms is: **FOB HOUSTON Incoterms 2010.**

---

[17] Ibid.

Note the three elements:

- A three-letter abbreviation—FOB stands for "Free On Board."
- A precisely-defined place. For the FOB Incoterm, this is the place of destination to which the seller has contracted to transport the goods.
- The applicable edition of the Incoterms rules—here Incoterms 2010. (Parties could use earlier editions but must specifically state so).

Parties will incorporate Incoterms into the contract of sale, and it is important an express reference is made to the current version of the Incoterms. A failure to refer to the most current version may create a dispute as to whether or not the parties intended to incorporate the current version or an earlier version.

Other Issues of Concern

1. **Non Containerization**: If one does not use a container, but instead uses crates (bulk cargo) unless the seller controls the bulk cargo, there could be a potential delay in the loading of the cargo or the cargo will be mixed in with someone else's cargo, referred to as co-packing, or stuffing (the loading of a container). The problem is two fold:

   a. Controlling the loading of the goods: The goods may not be loaded until there is enough cargo for that container.

   b. Controlling the timing of when the goods shipped: The goods won't ship until the container is stuffed fully.

2. **Fumigation:** Improper stamping of certain products can hold up a container for fumigation. For example, an exporter's goods are stuffed into a container along with another third party's goods, those goods being wood. As wood, the third party's goods should have been stamped as "fumigated"; however, the third party failed to properly label their goods. In situations of improper labelling or lack of proper labelling, then the whole container, which contains your goods, may be contaminated and held or worse destroyed.

3. **Country of Origin**: Important that proper export documentation is used. If there is co-packing of goods and some goods lack proper documentation to the country of origin, it could hold up the whole container.

Ethical Considerations 6.4

Transport of Goods to a Foreign Nation (Transportation)

The author of this textbook had a case years ago that included the transportation of goods into a country via sea and then land. Upon arrival into the country, the contract stipulated that the sellers were to continue transporting the items inland to their final destination. It so happened that there was no road for the trucks to use inland to their destination. The buyer of the deal did not disclose that there was no useable road.

Should a seller be able to walk away from the shipment without getting to their drop off point since vital information was withheld? Not disclosing information—silence—may be unethical but it is not illegal in all countries. There is an expectation that parties negotiate in good faith and disclose all relevant information, but it is not required. Should parties be forced to speak up about all issues they are aware of? Is there a duty of good faith on the buyer to disclose certain information?

Conclusion

Incoterms can be an incredibly useful tool when drafting international sales contracts; they quickly define whether the buyer or seller is responsible for the risks and costs associated with the transportation journey of the goods. Most Incoterms are relatively straightforward and easily understandable; however problems can arise when using an Incoterm in a sales contract before carefully thinking what using that term actually means and what it requires. The language in which the Incoterms are written is quite complex and this is one area that requires thorough examination and practice to gain comfort while choosing which Incoterm suits your particular situation.[18] Without adequate and proper planning there may be unintended consequences of using an Incoterm because there may be binding contractual obligations that arise that are extremely unfavorable or even impossible to complete for one of the parties to the contract. Again, as long as you survey the situation being governed by the sales contract before choosing the appropriate Incoterm to use, you will find great success in the use of Incoterms® 2010.

Glossary [19] [20] [21]

Buyer/Seller Premises: The location at which goods sold under a contract governed by Incoterms begin their transportation journey (seller's premises) or end their transportation journey (buyer's premises).

Containerize: Pack into or transport by ocean container.

Incoterms: The Incoterms rules or International Commercial Terms are a series of pre-defined commercial terms published by the International Chamber of Commerce (ICC). They are widely used in International commercial transactions or procurement processes.

Mode of Transport: Mode of transport (or means of transport or types of transport or transport modality or form of transport) is a term used to distinguish substantially different ways to perform transport.

Obligation: An act or course of action to which a person is morally or legally bound; a duty or commitment.

Bibliography

Business Dictionary. n.d. *Business Dictionary.* Accessed February 2016. http://www.businessdictionary.com/definition/Hague-rules.html

Dictionary.com. n.d. *Dictionary.com:* Accessed February 2016. http://dictionary.reference.com/

Encarta. n.d. *Encarta Dictionaries.*

Export.Gov. 2015. *Export.Gov: Helping U.S. Companies Export.* August. Accessed November 2015. http://www.export.gov/faq/eg_main_023922.asp

---

[18] Ghana Shipping Guide. n.d. *Incoterms 2010: Transfer of Risk From The Seller To The Buyer.* Accessed December 2015. http://ghanashippingguide.com/2014/12/understanding-the-commercial-term-you-use-for-your-international-trading/

[19] Dictionary.com. n.d. *Dictionary.com:* Accessed February 2016. http://dictionary.reference.com/

[20] Encarta. n.d. *Encarta Dictionaries.*

[21] Oxford University Press. n.d. *Oxford Dictionaries.*

Ghana Shipping Guide. n.d. *Incoterms 2010: Transfer of Risk From The Seller To The Buyer.* Accessed December 2015. http://ghanashippingguide.com/2014/12/ understanding-the-commercial-term-you-use-for-your-international-trading/

International Chamber of Commerce. 2011. *ICC: We are the world business organization.* Accessed November 2015. http://www.iccwbo.org/products-and-services/trade-facilitation/ incoterms-2010/

Mantissa E-Learning. 2011. *IncotermsExplained.com.* Accessed October 2015. http://www.inco-termsexplained.com/

MIQ Logistics: Intelligent Global Solutions. 2015. *New Incoterms Effective January 1 2011.* MIQ Logistics.

Peterson, Douglas H. 2014. *International Business Transactions B LAW 444.* Toronto: Nelson Education Ltd.

Rohlig Logistics. n.d. *Insurance Liability, Assumption of Risks and Costs, Pursuant to Incoterms 2010.* Accessed December 2015. http://www.rohlig.com/infocenter/incoterms-2010.html

SeaRates.com. 2012. *Incoterms 2010: ICC Official Rules for the Interpretation of Trade Terms.* Accessed October 2015. http://www.searates.com/reference/incoterms

Tkachuk, Heather. 2013. "Best Environmental Technologies Discussion Draft 2." Research Project, Edmonton, 1-10.

Wikipedia. 2014. *Wikipedia The Free Encyclopedia.* Accessed October 2015. https://en.wikipedia.org/wiki/Incoterms

CHAPTER 7

Intellectual Property

Learning Objectives

After reading this chapter, you will an understanding of:

1. The purpose of intellectual property in business
2. The various forms of intellectual property
3. How intellectual property is protected
4. The benefits of intellectual property transfer agreements
5. What entities exist to protect and govern intellectual property internationally

Take a quick look around the room at the different items that surround you and what do you see? You might see a computer, clothing, books, and other common items. What you might not know is that each of these "everyday" items is associated with intellectual property. **Intellectual property** is a series of rights that are given to a person to protect the expression of their ideas.[1] This protection encourages innovation and creativity. Whether it be the software that your computer uses, the name of the brand on your clothing, or the contents of the book that you are reading, each are protected under intellectual property.

In our example, CanCo has applied for and has been granted a patent on a processing unit and method for separating hydrocarbons from feedstock material. In addition CanCo has a trademark for their company name "CanCo" and for their machine which is called CleanCan. In addition, CanCo, has copyrighted specific software which is used in the operation of the CleanCan machine.

There are various categories under intellectual property that provide different forms of protection for different types of creations. There are patents, trademarks, copyrights, industrial designs, and trade secrets.[2] Each of these explores a very important aspect of expression and creation.

---

[1] Canadian Intellectual Property Office, "A Guide to Patents", Government of Canada, (Quebec: last update Jan 2016) https://www.ic.gc.ca/eic/site/cipointernet-internetopic.nsf/eng/h_wr03652.html#understandingPatents.
[2] Don Tomkins, "A Brief Introduction to Patents and Related Intellectual Property Rights" (presentation, University of Alberta School of Business, Edmonton, AB, November 14, 2008).

Intellectual property is both a vital component as well as an obstacle for any successful business, both domestically and internationally. Intellectual property is created and enforced domestically but various international treaties provide protection in other countries. A company can go from bust to boom due to the success of one piece of intellectual property. This gives companies incentive to create new ideas that will make them leaders in their industries. Companies also have the option to license the use of their intellectual property to other businesses in different geographic areas. This provides companies with an easy way to expand their business abroad with little investment risk and provides income through various forms of intellectual property transfers such as licensing.

This chapter will focus on the various types of intellectual property, how they are created, how they are protected domestically and abroad, and how businesses benefit through licensing transactions.

Patents

Definition of a Patent

Simply, a **patent** is a government-approved monopoly that entitles the patentee the right to prevent others from making, using, or selling the invention claimed in a patent. The patentee has the right automatically to use, create, or sell its invention within a limited period of time.[3] A patent is an invention or an improvement on an existing invention, in fact, 90% of patents are for improvements to existing patents. However, the granting of a patent in one country does not automatically grant you a patent in another country. The monopoly only exists in the place where the patentee has registered its invention.[4] In Canada, under the *Patent Act,* an invention is considered to be "any new and useful art, process, machine, manufacture or composition of matter, or any new and useful improvement in any art, process, machine, manufacture or composition of matter."[5] From this extensive definition it is clear that in Canada there are a number of types of inventions that are considered patentable including:

1. **Art**: This term has been defined as the application of knowledge to effect a desired result. An act or series of acts performed by some physical agent upon some physical object and producing in such object some change either of character or condition.[6]

2. **Process**: A process is the application of a method to a material or materials. Even if the product produced is not patentable, the process may be.

3. **Machine**: A mechanical embodiment of any function or mode of operation designed to accomplish a particular effect.

4. **Manufacture**: A product made by a machine or hand, industrially, mass-produced, by changing the character or condition of material objects.[7]

5. **Composition of Matter**: A combination of substances or ingredients, a fluid, a gas, a solid, as a chemical union or physical mixture.[8]

---

[3] Canadian Intellectual Property Office, "A Guide to Patents", *Government of Canada,* (Quebec: last update Jan 2016) https://www.ic.gc.ca/eic/site/cipointernet-internetopic.nsf/eng/h_wr03652.html#understandingPatents.

[4] Ibid.

[5] Canadian Intellectual Property Office, "What is a patent?", *Government of Canada,* (Quebec: last update Dec 2015) http://www.ic.gc.ca/eic/site/cipointernet-internetopic.nsf/eng/wr03716.html?Open&wt_src=cipo-patent-main.

[6] *Lawson v. Canada (Commissioner of Patents)* (1970), 62 C.P.R. 101 (Ex. Ct.) at p. 109.

[7] *Harvard College v. Canada (Commissioner of Patents),* [2002] 4 S.C.R. 45.

[8] David Vaver, *Intellectual Property Law: Copyright, Patents, Trade-Marks,* 2nd ed. (Toronto: Irwin Law, 2011) at 294.

In practicality, an invention is usually one of the following:

    a. A product (a zipper)

    b. A process (a method for making zippers)

    c. A machine (a machine for making zippers)

    d. A composition (a chemical composition used in lubricants for zippers)

In the United States, under the *America Invents Act (AIA),* any person who "invents or discovers any new and useful process, machine, manufacture, or composition of matter, or any new and useful improvement thereof, may obtain a patent."[9] Although this definition is similar or if not the same as the Canadian definition under the *Patent Act,* there are still differences in what is categorized as a patent. In the United States there are three types of patents:[10]

- *Utility Patents*, which are any inventions, discoveries or improvements to any of the classes described under the *America Invents Act.*

- *Design Patents* are new, original, and ornamental designs for any good.

- *Plant Patents* are for a new and distinct plant species that have been invented or discovered and asexually reproduced.

In the United States, patent subject matters is as follows:

1. **Process**: An act, or series of acts or steps. "A process is a mode of treatment of certain materials to produce a given result. It is an act, or a series of acts, performed upon the subject-matter to be transformed and reduced to a different state or thing."[11]

2. **Machine**: A concrete thing, consisting of parts, or of certain devices or combination of devices.[12]

3. **Manufacture**: An article produced from materials, prepared or raw, by giving the materials a new form, quality, properties, or combinations, by hand or machinery.

4. **Composition of Matter**: Compositions of two or more substances, whether gases, fluids, powders or solids.

When a person registers their patent they are then entitled to a maximum of 20 years of protection. During this time period the patentee is able to use, reproduce, license, or even sell the rights to the patent to another party. The incentive of financial profit in exchange for inventiveness encourages research and development, and sequentially benefits society as a whole.[13]

---

9 United States Patent and Trademark Office, "General Information Concerning Patents", *Government of the U.S.* (Virginia: last update Oct 2014) http://www.uspto.gov/patents-getting-started/general-information-concerning-patents.

10 Ibid.

11 *Gottschalk v. Benson,* 409 U.S. 63, 70, 175 USPQ 673, 676 (1972); *Cochrane v. Deener,* 94 U.S. 780, 788, 24 L. Ed. 139, 1877 Dec. Comm'r Pat. 242 (1876);

12 Canadian Intellectual Property Office, "A Guide to Patents", Government of Canada, (Quebec: last update Jan 2016) https://www.ic.gc.ca/eic/site/cipointernet-internetopic.nsf/eng/h_wr03652.html#understandingPatents.

13 Canadian Intellectual Property Office, "A Guide to Patents", *Government of Canada,* (Quebec: last update Jan 2016) https://www.ic.gc.ca/eic/site/cipointernet-internetopic.nsf/eng/h_wr03652.html#understandingPatents.

Ethical Considerations 7.1

2015: The Year for Patent Lawsuits

Joe Mullin, "Trolls made 2015 one of the biggest years ever for patent lawsuits," *ars technica*, January 5, 2016, http://arstechnica.com/tech-policy/2016/01/despite-law-changes-2015-saw-a-heap-of-patent-troll-lawsuits/

Alice Corp. Pty. Ltd. v. CLS Bank Intern., 134 S. Ct. 2347—Supreme Court 2014, https://scholar.google.ca/scholar_case?case=7784134755284986738&hl=en&as_sdt=6&as_vis=1&oi=scholarr&sa=X&ved=0ahUKEwjSjuTEqqjLAhWHKWMKHSoVDkcQgAMIGygAMAA

"Patent trolls" are shell companies without assets that are filing for patents, which are far too similar to existing patents from real companies. In 2015 there were more patent lawsuits filed than any other year in America's history. In the case of *Alice Corp. v. CLS Bank* (2014) Alice Corp. filed for patents that exhibited the same ideas from CLS Bank, but had a few additional computer language phrases added to differentiate the two. The US Supreme Court held that Alice Corp.'s claims were invalid and should not have been granted patents. The hope was to have software patents abolished altogether, but the court stated they will still allow patents for new ideas that will improve the computer's functions or enhance current technological processes.

Prior to the 2014 court decision, patent trolls would privately ask for hundreds of thousands of dollars because the infringers knew they had little chance of losing a court case and the amount they were asking would be less than legal fees of a trial. Now settlements are less than $100,000 due to the uncertainty of how the court will rule on the case. Is it unethical for an individual to patent their new technology that was based on existing concepts with only a few minor changes? How material must the differences be to avoid patent lawsuits? Should regulatory bodies be stricter with allowing patents, especially software related patents?

Patentability

In countries like Canada and the United States it is clear that not all inventions are approved for a patent. There are three requirements that the invention must have in order to be deemed patentable.

1. *Novelty*: The invention must be considered novel or new but this does not mean that the invention has to be "brand new."[14] As long as the invention has not been previously made known to the public and no one currently in the world has a published patent application or patent for it then it is deemed novel. For example, if someone was to invent a new process of changing car tires from old rims to new rims, the inventor would have to search to see if a similar process has been already disclosed to the public.[15] If not then the invention would most likely be deemed new. Disclosures made in private, such as an internal document within CanCo that is not disclosed to the public, would not count.

2. *Utility*: An invention must be considered useful in order to be patentable. This occurs when the invention can be used for some pre-determined purpose. The threshold of utility is fairly low, so usually if the invention works then it is useful. The new invention of changing tires on rims would be considered useful because it serves a distinct function and solves a problem.

---

[14] Ibid.

[15] Ibid.

3. *Inventive (Non-Obvious)*: The invention, which is a new development or an improvement on a previous piece of technology, must be non-obvious, often referred to as "inventive ingenuity" or "inventive step." The improvement must not be the obvious next step to the existing invention. The invention must have not been obvious to a person in the specific industry.[16] In order for the tire invention to be considered "inventive" it must be determined that a reasonable person in the automotive field would not have thought of this improvement with the previous technology.[17] This may be difficult to determine, as experts in the field must be consulted. In *Apotex Inc. v. Sanofi-Synthenlabo Canada Inc.*,[18] the Supreme Court of Canada affirmed the test for non-obviousness as was set forth in the ground setting 1985 English case of *Windsurfing International Inc. v. Tabur Marine (Great Britain) Ltd*:[19]

   (i) Identify the notional "person skilled in the art" and the relevant common general knowledge of that person;

   (ii) Identify the inventive concept of the claim in question or if that cannot readily be done, construe it;

   (iii) Identify what, if any, differences exist between the matter cited as forming part of the "state of the art" and the inventive concept of the claim or the claim as construed;

   (iv) Viewed without any knowledge of the alleged invention as claimed, do those differences constitute steps that would have been obvious to the person skilled in the art or do they require any degree of invention?

Subject Matter

The list of inventions that will be approved to be patented may be very extensive but there are still specific areas that are excluded from patent protection. They include:

- Scientific principles and abstract theorems, which may include mathematical formulas, and laws of nature.[20]

- Inventions that already receive protection under other areas of intellectual property. This may include computer programs or software, as they are under copyright protection.[21]

- An idea cannot be patented, unless it is in a tangible form. For example if you have an idea on how to further develop a washing machine but have done nothing in the form of creating this idea then you cannot claim this as a patent.

- Clothing cannot be patented and that is the main reason why no matter what store you walk into the same style of clothing will be available no matter what the brand is. The reason is that clothing does not fit underneath the requirements for a patent, as it is usually not new and is considered obvious.[22] Aspects of clothing like the brand name and the logo can be protected under other areas of intellectual property.

---

[16] Mario Theriault, "Have an Invention? We can help", *Theriault & Company,* (New Brunswick: accessed Jan 2016) http://www.patentway.com/faqs.

[17] Canadian Intellectual Property Office, "A Guide to Patents", Government of Canada, (Quebec: last update Jan 2016) https://www.ic.gc.ca/eic/site/cipointernet-internetopic.nsf/eng/h_wr03652.html#understaning Patents.

[18] *Apotex Inc v Sanofi-Synthelabo Canada Inc,* [2008] 3 S.C.R. 265

[19] *Windsurfing International Inc. v. Tabur Marine* (Great Britain) Ltd., [1985] RPC 59 (CA)

[20] Supreme Court Judgments, "Monsanto Canada Inc. v. Schmeiser, [2004] 1 S.C.R. 902, 2004 SCC 34", *Supreme Court,* (Ottawa, last update May 2004), paragraph 133, http://scc-csc.lexum.com/scc-csc/scc-csc/en/item/2147/index.do.

[21] World Intellectual Property Organization, "Patenting Software", *WIPO,* (Switzerland: Accessed Jan 2016), http://www.wipo.int/sme/en/documents/software_patents_fulltext.html.

[22] Canadian Intellectual Property Office, "What is a patent?" *Government of Canada,* (Quebec: last update Dec 2015) http://www.ic.gc.ca/eic/site/cipointernet-internetopic.nsf/eng/wr03716.html?Open&wt_src=cipo-patent-main.

Business Methods

Until recent years business methods in Canada and the United States were recognized as not being able to fit the requirements for a patent but lately, Federal Court decisions have altered this belief and now business methods, although still difficult to obtain, are patentable in both countries. In the United States, *Bilski v. Kappos,*[23] was a groundbreaking case on whether or not business methods were patentable. The patent claim in this was ultimately rejected but it was not rejected on the grounds that business methods aren't patentable but because the claim was merely an abstract idea, which is not included under the patent requirements.[24] The *Bilski* decision lead to the approval of many well-known patents such as Amazon.com's "One-Click" claim. In Canada, approval for business methods was established in *Amazon v. Canada.*[25] Amazon tried to get its claim for a "One-Click" patent for years but was ultimately rejected until it was brought before the Federal Court of Appeal, where the judge ruled in its favor. This forced the Commissioner of Patents to re-examine the claim and this ultimately lead it to be approved. The judge claimed, "There is no basis for the Commissioner's assumption that there is a 'tradition' of excluding business methods from patentability in Canada."[26] Along with this it was stated that Amazon's claim was not just an idea but had practical application, which fits the requirements of a patent.[27]

Application Process

The patent application process is unique in the sense that protection only arises when the patent has been granted. Merely inventing something does not give the inventor rights of protection.

In Canada, the inventor needs to register their invention at the Canadian Intellectual Property Office. Canada uses a first-to-file system, which means whoever registers first gets the patent. Canada switched in 1989 from a first-to-invent system to a first-to-file system.[28]

The United States has long been a country that utilizes the first-to-invent system but on March 16, 2013, there was an amendment to the *America Invents Act* that changed the United States to a first-to-file system.[29] This improved the efficiency and fairness of patent approvals, and provided clear expectations of what is expected to obtain a patent, which results in a more user-friendly system.[30]

The process of preparing a patent application is similar in both countries as they both follow three distinct steps.

---

[23] *Bilski v. Kappos, 561 U.S. 593 [2010]*, 2010. http://www.supremecourt.gov/opinions/09pdf/08-964.pdf.

[24] United States Patent and Trademark Office, "Interim Guidance for Determining Subject Matter Eligibility for Process Claims in View of Bilski v. Kappos,"*Government of the U.S.,* (June 2010) http://www.uspto.gov/sites/default/files/patents/law/exam/bilski_guidance_27jul2010.pdf

[25] *Canada (Attorney General) v. Amazon.com, Inc., 2011 FCA 328 (CanLI),* November 2011. Ihttp://www.canlii.org/en/ca/fca/doc/2011/2011fca328/2011fca328.html.

[26] Ibid., para 60.

[27] Gowlings, "Business Method Patents: How Prepared are You?" Gowlings Law Firm, (2012) http://www.gowlings.com/knowledgeCentre/publicationPDFs/Business-Method-Patents-How-Prepared-are-You.pdf.

[28] Smart & Biggar, "First-to-File comes to America: What innovative Canadian companies should know," *Smart & Biggar Law Firm,* (Toronto: March 2013), http://www.smart-biggar.ca/en/articles_detail.cfm?news_id=729.

[29] Ibid.

[30] World Intellectual Property Organization, "The Global Impact of the America Invents Act", *WIPO,* (December 2011), http://www.wipo.int/wipo_magazine/en/2011/06/article_0002.html.

1. **Specification (Disclosure)**: During this step the inventor describes the specifics of the invention as if someone wanted to replicate the invention. Also, the inventor discloses the application of the invention and the issues that it solves. Along with this the inventor must describe how this particular invention is different from prior art.[31] The disclosure may also contain examples of experiments that are carried out to show how the invention works. In order for a patent to grant, the invention must be described in enough detail for a person of skill in the art to make and use the invention. This part of the application is vital because once the patent expires the general public will be able to build, use, and sell the invention, so they need to be able to know how they can replicate it properly. For CanCo the specifications would be a clear and complete description of the invention and its usefulness. In particular, a processing unit and method for separating hydrocarbons from feedstock material.

2. **Drawing**: This step is exactly what you think it is. The inventor provides an illustration of the makeup of the invention, so it is clear what it will be. The drawings are described in detail in the disclosure. In some cases drawings may not be relevant, for example in pharmaceutical applications; however, graphs or other figures may be provided to show the results of experiments carried out. For CanCo, the drawings would have a brief description, usually through diagrams showing the flow for the system of processing hydrocarbon feedstock, the input and output systems, the processing unit of the system, various views (side views, bottom views, top views, etc.) of the processing system.

3. **Claims**: This is the most important aspect of the application process because this is when the inventor will define the rights that are being sought after.[32] Claims must be clear and concise but you do not need an enabling disclosure in the claims. The claims are interpreted with reference to the description and the description must provide an enabling disclosure. The balance of the claims is not to be too detailed that it is easy for a competitor to invent around your claims, but not too broad that they are not novel over what is publically known. If claims are too vague, they may not be patentable, in other words, they may not be considered novel and inventive, but being vague does not necessarily mean one will infringe on another person's patent. Infringement is restricted to making, selling, using a product that falls within the claims of another person's patent. **Enabling Disclosure** is also important because your description in this step must be clear, and concise so that a skilled person is able to make, use and sell the invention after the patent has expired.[33] The most important primary claims are usually first, followed by secondary claims. For CanCo, the claims would embody what protection is being sought, generally the processing unit for separating hydrocarbons from feedstock material.

The importance of the application can't be stated enough and it is important that the application is prepared by a patent agent who has a background preparing applications in the technical field of the invention. If the specifications, drawings, and claims are not in line with the requirements, then the patent seeker will not benefit. In the Supreme Court decision of *Teva Canada Ltd. v. Pfizer*, Pfizer experienced the impact that not being "clear" in the application process can have.[34]

---

[31] Don Tomkins, "A Brief Introduction to Patents and Related Intellectual Property Rights" (presentation, University of Alberta School of Business, Edmonton, AB, November 14, 2008).

[32] Ibid.

[33] European Patent Office, "Enabling disclosures," *European Union*, (last update January 2015), http://www.epo.org/law-practice/legal-texts/html/guidelines/e/g_iv_2.htm.

[34] *Teva Canada Ltd. v. Pfizer Canada Inc., 2012 SCC 60, [2012] 3 S.C.R. 625*, November 2012. https://scc-csc.lexum.com/scc-csc/scc-csc/en/item/12679/index.do.

Teva Canada Ltd. v. Pfizer (2012)[35]

Facts:

Pfizer discovered from tests that sildenafil could treat men that suffer from erectile dysfunction. In 1994, Pfizer sought a patent claiming a wide range of compounds are used in treating erectile dysfunction even though only sildenafil, more commonly known as Viagra, is used in the treatment.[36] Sildenafil was included in claim 7 of 7 claims but it was not disclosed that sildenafil was the actual compound that treated erectile dysfunction. Pfizer received the patent but in 2006, Teva Canada, a generic drug manufacturer, submitted an application to Health Canada to allow for the manufacture of a generic version of sildenafil. Pfizer stated that approving the application would violate the patent that they had in place and Teva should wait until 2014, when Pfizer's patent would expire.

Issue:

Although Pfizer had been benefitting from patent protection in regards to sildenafil, Teva claimed that the patent was invalid because it was obvious and improperly disclosed the terms of the patent. Therefore, Teva should be allowed to manufacture the generic version of the drug immediately.

Decision:

The Supreme Court of Canada came to the conclusion that Pfizer's patent was indeed invalid because Pfizer failed to disclose in clear terms what the invention was.

Reasons:

The Court had to determine whether or not the patent met the requirements of disclosure according to the *Patent Act*.[37] The Court stated that even though there are claims for lots of compounds it doesn't matter because a skilled reader of patents would know that the important compound would be in the last claim. However, in Pfizer's patent it was not clear whether the true compound was in claim 6 or 7 because they were the only ones that did not have more than one compound. The Judge concluded by saying, "the disclosure failed to state in clear terms what the invention was" leading to the conclusion that Pfizer's patent was invalid.[38] A skilled person trying to replicate the invention would have to do a series of investigations in order to truly understand what the correct compound was due to the ambiguous terms.

The date of the filing of the finished patent application is termed as the priority date.[39] This is officially when the patent process begins. Subsequent applications may be filed within one year of the priority date, and such subsequent applications will obtain initial priority date. If no subsequent applications are filed then the priority date is the filing date of the application. If the patent seeker does obtain the patent, then the filing date is used as the first day of the 20-year monopoly.[40] The actual process of getting a patent approved typically takes upwards of 3–10 years or more from the date of filing, although ways of fast tracking the process are available. Even though an application has been filed it does not mean that it will be examined. In Canada, the inventor has 5 years to request examination.[41] If exami-

---

35 Ibid.

36 Ibid [3].

37 Ibid [69].

38 Ibid [80].

39 Canadian Intellectual Property Office, "A Guide to Patents," *Government of Canada*, (Quebec: last update Jan 2016) https://www.ic.gc.ca/eic/site/cipointernet-internetopic.nsf/eng/h_wr03652.html#understandingPatents.

40 Ibid.

41 Ibid.

nation is not requested then the application is considered abandoned. However, once an examination has been requested the process may still take up to 2 years to complete due to the amount of applications being processed. Once an application has been filed for 18 months the patent office releases information to the public by publishing the application.[42] During this time the original inventor does not have protection but can label its invention as "patent pending" to warn other users that once the patent is granted they will be infringing.[43] Since the patent pending label is only considered a warning, the inventor cannot enforce their rights over their invention because they have yet to receive any.[44] The infringer can continue to use the invention but they do so at a risk because once the information has been disclosed and the patent granted, the patent holder could sue all those who have been infringing from the time of disclosure to the present.

There are cases when an inventor has an idea but is also aware that others may be creating a similar idea, so in this case they can file a provisional application.[45] This allows the inventor to get something on file and maintain priority. Then from the date of filing the inventor has one year to finish the application.[46]

Appendix A

Patent Application Process

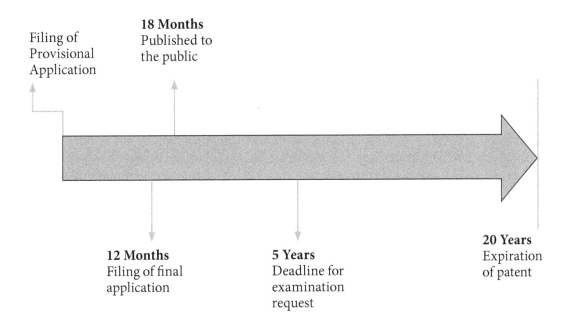

Filing of Provisional Application

18 Months
Published to the public

12 Months
Filing of final application

5 Years
Deadline for examination request

20 Years
Expiration of patent

Doug Peterson

---

[42] Ibwid.

[43] Kozlowski & Company, "Patents Frequently Asked Questions (FAQS)," *Kozlowski & Company*, (2015), http://www.kozlowskiandcompany.com/patent-faqs.html#7.

[44] Ibid.

[45] United States Patent and Trademark Office, "Provisional Application for Patent," *Government of the U.S.* (last update January 2015), http://www.uspto.gov/patents-getting-started/patent-basics/types-patent-applications/provisional-application-patent.

[46] Ibid.

According to the *Patent Act,* when an individual creates an invention they are the owner and therefore, are entitled to the rights.[47] This usually only pertains to independent contractors. When an independent contractor creates an invention the company which contracted them has to seek permission in order to use the rights that pertain to the invention.[48] This can be changed through a contract. Within the contract the company can add stipulations such as the ability to have non-exclusive access to the invention along with a royalty free clause, so the company does not have to make payments to the contractor.[49]

Ownership in reference to inventions created during the course of employment is not deliberated in the *Patent Act.*[50] Instead it is through the Courts that distinction regarding ownership of patentable inventions is discussed.[51] In *Techform v. Wolda,* the Court stated, "The mere existence of an employment relationship does not disqualify employees from patenting inventions made during the course of their employment."[52] However, there are exceptions to this when there is a written agreement stating the terms of ownership and if the employee's purpose was to invent.[53]

As previously discussed a commissioned employee whose primary purpose is to invent would not be considered the owner of the invention since he or she would be compensated for their work.[54]

In all situations if the employer wants ownership of the patentable invention then they need to provide clarification within the employment agreement to mitigate ownership issues from arising. They should use a grant clause that would describe the rights and conditions that the employee would have regarding the invention.[55] More specifically a reservation of rights clause would be beneficial to the employer because they can stipulate what rights belong to each of the parties. It is also beneficial to obtain an executed assignment from the inventor(s) to the employer assigning the rights to the invention and any patent applications or patents that result from the invention just before or soon after a patent application has been filed.

Infringement of Patent Protection

Patent infringement is as simple as someone making, using, or selling another's invention without the patent owner's permission.[56] When an inventor is granted a patent they are given specific rights to the invention that last up to 20 years and if anyone claims those right then they are infringing. There are several remedies for infringement and they include:

- **Injunction**: The Court orders the infringer to stop making use of the patent.[57]
- **Damages**: This could be anything from the amount lost by the plaintiff, the amount gained by the infringer or even just legal fees.[58]

---

[47] Michele Ballagh, "Intellectual Property: Who OWNS it?" Ballagh Edward LLP, (last update: October 2009), http://www.ballaghedward.ca/uploads/pub_uploads/intellectual-property-ownership-2-.pdf.

[48] Ibid.

[49] Nolo Law Firm, "Who owns Patent Rights? Employer or Inventor?" *Nolo Law Firm,* (2015), http://www.nolo.com/legal-encyclopedia/who-owns-patent-rights-employer-inventor.html.

[50] Michele Ballagh, "Intellectual Property: Who OWNS it?" *Ballagh Edward LLP,* (last update: October 2009), http://www.ballaghedward.ca/uploads/pub_uploads/intellectual-property-ownership-2-.pdf.

[51] Ibid.

[52] *Techform Products Ltd. V. Wolda, [2001] CanLII 8604,* October 1, 2001. http://www.canlii.org/en/on/onca/doc/2001/2001canlii8604/2001canlii8604.html.

[53] Ziad Katul and Colleen Zimmerman, "Canada: Patent Ownership in Canada," *Borden Ladner Gervais LLP,* (last updated April 2006) http://www.mondaq.com/canada/x/39282/Patent/Patent+Ownership+in+Canada.

[54] Nolo Law Firm, "Who owns Patent Rights? Employer or Inventor?" *Nolo Law Firm,* (2015), http://www.nolo.com/legal-encyclopedia/who-owns-patent-rights-employer-inventor.html.

[55] Ibid.

[56] United States Patent and Trademark Office, "About Patent Infringement?" *Government of the U.S.* (January 2015), http://www.uspto.gov/patents-maintaining-patent/patent-litigation/about-patent-infringement.

[57] National Paralegal College, "Remedies for Patent Infringement," *National Paralegal College,* (2016), http://national-paralegal.edu/public_documents/courseware_asp_files/patents/Patents2/Remedies.asp.

[58] Ibid.

Trademarks

Definition of a Trademark

If you were to think about running shoes what comes to mind? One of your first thoughts might be the style that you prefer or the brand that you like to buy. Whether we like it or not our lives revolve around seeing brands or product names. These can be considered trademarks. A **trademark** is distinguishing words, symbols, or designs that are used to distinguish a product or service offered by one person from that of others.[59] Trademarks can be considered one of the most important aspects of intellectual property because a person's trademark for a particular good is often a reflection of the quality of the good. This is normally referred to as goodwill and has great value to a company and is also a major asset. This is why companies are so eager to obtain a unique trademark and protect it from unauthorized use to maintain consumer's perceptions.

The word CanCo, although a generic example for the purposes of this text, could be a trademarked word, and the logo of CanCo, is also a separate trademark. In addition, CanCo could trademark the machine they patented, in this case they have trademarked CleanCan and a corresponding logo.

Types of Trademarks

Canada and the United States share views on what a general trademark is and the protection that it provides. In both countries registration of a trademark is not mandatory but most times it is recommended in order to receive the maximum amount of protection. However, there are differences in the types of trademarks that are recognized in each country. Both countries believe that the following are categorized as trademarks:

- *Certification Marks*: This is used to mark the quality or origin of the product.[60] An example would be the "UL" certification mark that is seen on most appliances and electronic products. This mark shows to the consumer that the product has been tested and found safe to use.
- *Word Marks*: Anything from brand names to slogans, i.e. Nike's "Just do it."
- *Design Marks*: One of the most visual forms of a trademark, such as logos and symbols, i.e. Nike's Checkmark.[61]

Canada differs from the United States in that it recognizes a **distinguishing guise** as a basic category of a trademark.[62] This includes product shapes or the very distinct packaging that the product comes in.[63] One of the most common examples of a distinguishing guise is the Coca Cola bottle. Like other forms of trademarks, a distinguishing guise can be registered in Canada but only if it can be proved that the distinguishing guise has been well established and used in Canada so as to have become distinctive.[64] Also, by trademarking the distinguishing guise it can't limit the development of any art or industry, so you can only get a monopoly in the guise if there are other ways for the industry to still be competitive.[65] For example, Coca-Cola was able to get a distinguishing guise trademark because there are other ways that bottles can be made, therefore, this does not hinder competition.

---

[59] Canadian Intellectual Property Office, "A guide to trademarks," *Government of Canada*, (last update December 2015), http://www.ic.gc.ca/eic/site/cipointernet-internetopic.nsf/eng/h_wr02360.html.

[60] Ibid.

[61] Ibid.

[62] Jonathan Burkinshaw and Justine Wiebe, "Canada," *World Trademark Review*, no. 20 (2009) : 1-3, accessed February 1, 2016, http://www.bereskinparr.com/files/file/docs/tm_wtr_tradedresspro_jw_jb_0809.pdf

[63] John McKeown, "What is a Distinguishing Guise?" *GSNH LLP*, (August 2013), http://www.gsnh.com/what-is-a-distinguishing-guise/.

[64] Jonathan Burkinshaw and Justine Wiebe, "Canada," *World Trademark Review*, no. 20 (2009): 1-3, accessed February 1, 2016, http://www.bereskinparr.com/files/file/docs/tm_wtr_tradedresspro_jw_jb_0809.pdf

[65] Ibid.

Unlike Canada, the United States Patent and Trademark Office categorizes trademarks and service marks as different things.[66] A **service mark** is essentially the same thing as a trademark but rather than distinguishing a particular product it is distinguishing a specific service.[67]

Alternates to Trademarks

1. **Trade Names**: A trade name is simply the name of a particular business. It is the name under which a sole proprietorship, a partnership, or a corporation does business, often referred to using "dba" or "doing business as" or "operating as." To a degree it is an assumed name or fictitious name.[68] Like a trademark for a particular good or service, a trade name is vital for the survival and success of any business as it adds a sense of protection by defending the business' reputation.[69] A trade name can be registered in certain jurisdictions, but a trade name does not give you the same protective rights as a trademark. In addition, whereas trademarks are federally protected, trade names are generally protected and registered on a provincial/state wide basis. Businesses must be careful not to assume that a registered tradename gives them a right to use a name for any purpose related to business. If one uses a trade name to identify services or goods, then it is functioning as a trademark, but now risks infringing on another trademark. A tradename can be registered as a trademark but only if it is used to identify goods or services.

2. **Corporate Names**: A corporate name is the legal name under which the company is known by.[70] A corporate name can be registered either provincially/state or federally. A corporate name that is registered federally allows the company to conduct business anywhere in the country.[71] However, there are particular criteria in which a corporate name has to abide by in order to be approved. A corporate name cannot be confused with other corporate names or trademarks.[72] Although a corporate name is separate from a trademark it can also be considered a trademark as well.[73] By filing a corporate name as a trademark the corporate name will receive more protection across the country.

3. **Domain Names**: A domain name is basically an Internet address.[74] As the Internet and technology in general continues to become a central part of our lives, the importance of a domain name will also continue to grow in importance. Unlike a regular trademark, when a domain name is registered it is registered throughout the world.[75] For example, if you were to search google.com from any country in the world the results would be the same, since there is only one domain name made available.

Domain names are filed with the Internet Corporation for Assigned Names and Numbers (ICANN). A domain name in and of itself is not the same thing as a trademark. Use of a domain name merely acts as an informational part of the domain name holder's internet address does not qualify as trademark use. Unlike tradenames and trademarks, which are domestic, domain names are international. To qualify as a trademark, the domain name must function as a trademark. A domain name can qualify as a trademark when it is used in connection with a website that offers services to

---

[66] United States Patent and Trademark Office, *"General FAQs," Government of the U.S.* (last update December 2014), http://www.uspto.gov/learning-and-resources/general-faqs.

[67] Ibid.

[68] Canadian Intellectual Property Office, "What's in a Name?" *Government of Canada,* (last update June 2015), https://www.ic.gc.ca/eic/site/cipointernet-internetopic.nsf/eng/wr00058.html.

[69] Ibid.

[70] Ibid.

[71] Ibid.

[72] Innovation, Science and Economic Development Canada, "Choosing a name ..." (last update June 2011), https://www.ic.gc.ca/eic/site/cd-dgc.nsf/eng/cs01191.html.

[73] Ibid.

[74] Oyen Wiggs Green & Mutala LPP, "Domain Names," *Oyen Wiggs Green & Mutala LPP,* (2016), http://www.patentable.com/what-we-do/domain-names/.

[75] Ibid.

the public. It must serve as an indicator of source, not merely as an informational part of an Internet address. Examples of this are sites conducting e-commerce.

Complications frequently arise concerning companies with similar names but in different industries. For example, there could be three companies in different geographic locations, one being called Western Beets, another Western Boats and the last being Western Clothing. If Western Beets registered the domain name of western.com first, they would secure the name over Western Boats and Western Clothing who may also have also tried to obtain the domain name of Western.com. Western Beets would be the company with the rights to that name, so the other two companies would have to register for something a little bit different.

Another issue that may arise is if Western Beets was going to register its domain name of western.com and discovered that another person had already obtained western.com but had no intent to use it.[76] This type of person is referred to as a **cyber-squatter**," which means they have no real intent to use the domain name but are hoping to sell the rights to the highest bidder or are merely preventing others such as their competitors from using it.[77] Cyber-squatters might also be using the good name of a company to attract Internet traffic to its site to sell unrelated goods. In this case, Western Beets can either negotiate a fair price for the domain name, or seek trademark infringement proceedings. Western Beets would have to prove that the current domain owner registered in bad faith, has no real interest in the domain name, and that the domain name is too similar to Western Beets' trademark.[78]

Included in the World Intellectual Property Office (WIPO), there is a Uniform Domain Name Dispute Resolution Policy (UDRP) in place to help determine disputes regarding domain names.[79] Whether it be due to cyber-squatting or multiple parties having legitimate claims for the same domain name, UDRP provides clarification to who should be allowed access to the name.[80] Resolution services through the WIPO are faster and cheaper than litigation in regular courts. The decision is binding and the name will either be transferred to the claimant or the claimant will be denied its claim.[81]

Uzi Nissan, in 1991 incorporated "Nissan Computer Corp." and then in 1994 filed for the domain name of nissan.com for his business.[82] This business revolved around the sale of computer hardware, maintenance, and networking. At this time Nissan Motors was still known as Datsun.[83] In 1999, Nissan Motors was seeking legal action claiming that Nissan Computer was infringing on Nissan Motor's trademark and therefore diluting it.[84] Courts later determined that Nissan Computer was entitled to maintain the nissan.com domain name and was not diluting Nissan Motor's mark.[85] Nissan Computer Corp. has every right to the name and since they were the first to file for it, are the true owners.

Ethical Considerations 7.2

Domain Squatting

Domain squatting, also known as cybersquatting, is registering or using a domain name with bad faith intentions such as profiting from a brand that belongs to another person. The party that has

---

[76] Ibid.
[77] Ibid.
[78] Ibid.
[79] World Intellectual Property Organization, "Frequently Asked Questions: Internet Domain Names," (last update 2016), http://www.wipo.int/amc/en/center/faq/domains.html#7.
[80] Ibid.
[81] Ibid.
[82] Uzi Nissan, "We've Been Sued," *Nissan Computer*, (last update 2009), http://www.nissan.com/Lawsuit/The_Story.php.
[83] Ibid.
[84] Ibid.
[85] Ibid.

taken the internet domain has no right or true permission to use the cyberspace and will generally then attempt to sell the rights back to the entity that rightfully should hold the domain at a higher than normal price.

Cleankeys, a technology company designing touch keyboards that are slim with an easy to clean protected surface, wanted to register their domain in the states making it cleankeys.com. However, that domain was taken by another figure. The company gained the rights to cleankeys.ca while they settled the matter of who owns the cyberspace they should rightfully own. The organization found that a man in China arbitrarily took cleankeys.com without having a company or any ties to such a name. He squatted on the domain and wanted to sell the rights back to the rightful company at an inflated price.

A recent example of domain squatting is. Donald Trump, 45th President of the United States of America during the 2016 election. His campaign tactics were as creative as they were fascinating. In January of 2016 there was notice that Jeb Bush, another candidate for the presidency until he dropped out of the race in February 2016, did not renew the rights to his domain name—jebbush.com. Trump took action quickly, bought the rights, and made the site redirect to donaldtrump.com. An interesting tactic, but is it unethical? Should Bush have the rights to share his platform in our digital society? Should he have legal remedy to correct the situation, along with other victims of cybersquatting?

Ethical Considerations 7.3

Trademark Squatters

Scott Baldwin, "Don't Sit and Wait: Stopping Trademark Squatters," *Inventors Eye* vol. 4, no. 1 (2013), *http://www.uspto.gov/custom-page/inventors-eye-don-t-sit-and-wait-stopping-trademark-squatters*

Trademark squatting, also known as bad faith trademark filing, is an issue faced by many companies that are expanding their business internationally. A company's trademark is vital to help it distinguish itself from competitors and provides brand recognition to the customers. A downfall is that trademarks are territorial and the protection they provide is contained within the registered country. Unfortunately, many companies find their trademark has already been registered in the market they are attempting to enter. The situation parallels domain squatting where the infringing party will generally hold onto the intellectual property rights until the true company can pay an inflated price to retain their own trademarks.

Many of the individuals that conduct bad faith trademark filing do it simply as a blockade to the company and to make a profit over the process, such as the Canadian high school student Mike Rowe that registered MikeRoweSoft.com spurring a legal battle with Microsoft. The clear trademark infringement was intentional and unethical as the student has no connection to Microsoft and its brand is directly associated with the trademarked name. Should registering individuals be required to prove their connection to the trademark they are filing before being granted the IP rights? Should the unethical act come with harsher legal punishments to deter future trademark squatting? What governing body would regulate the infringements?

Non-Traditional Trademarks

Another type of trademark that is common in the United States but still not considered "registrable" in Canada is a **non-traditional trademark**.[86] This simply constitutes elements that are not words,

---

[86] International Trademark Association, "Nontraditional Trademarks," *International Trademark Association*, (last update 2016), http://www.inta.org/TrademarkBasics/FactSheets/Pages/NontraditionalTrademarksFactSheet.aspx.

designs, certifications, or anything else that normally fits into a category of a trademark.[87] This could include sounds, scents, tastes, motions, or even the texture of a good. Sounds are the only aspects that are registrable in Canada but overtime more applications for other areas of non-traditional trademarks are slowly being accepted in Canada.[88]

Exclusions from Trademark Protection

You can trademark most names or slogans but like other forms of intellectual property there are some things that are still not protected under trademark law. These include the following

- *Certain names and surnames*: In majority of cases, names cannot be used as a trademark but there are some situations where it has been allowed, such as Ford Motor Company. In order for a name to be considered eligible for trademark protection it must be proven that the name or surname is well known and is associated with another meaning than merely just the name of an individual.[89]

- *Deceptively misdescriptive words*: You cannot mislead the consumer by suggesting the quality of the product or the service is one thing but really it is something completely different. An example would be calling a fertilizer "all-organic" when in fact it is not organic at all.

- *Clearly descriptive words*: A word used to describe a general characteristic of a good or service can't be trademarked because it is expected that is the case.[90] An example would be trademarking "creamy milk chocolate." All good milk chocolate should be considered creamy.

- *Place of origin*: You can't use the origin of a good as a trademark. The monopoly on that name would be unfair to others.[91] Just think if there was a company that had the trademark for "Florida Oranges." Would you want to buy oranges from another company? Or the one where Florida is actually in the name? Also, you can't use a location as a trademark if the good isn't actually from the location.[92] This could mislead people to belief that the good you are selling is actually from the location and therefore of a higher quality. If you saw someone selling "French Wine" but later found out it was from Nebraska, would you not be disappointed?

- *Words in foreign languages*: An example would be using "kuruma," the Japanese word for car, or "gelato" Italian for ice cream.

- *Anything that is morally offensive, obscene, scandalous or racial in nature*

- *Something that is considered confusing due to a current registered trademark*: This is the most prominent area in which court cases arise.

- *Confusing something to be associated with a Government entity*: An example would be thinking that a courier service is part of Canada Post.

---

[87] Ibid.
[88] Jonathan Burkinshaw, Susan Keri, "Non-traditional marks in Canada," *Intellectual Property Magazine*, March 2011, http://www.bereskinparr.com/files/file/docs/IPM_Mar_2011-SK_JB.pdf.
[89] Canadian Intellectual Property Office, "A guide to trademarks," *Government of Canada*, (last update December 2015), http://www.ic.gc.ca/eic/site/cipointernet-internetopic.nsf/eng/h_wr02360.html.
[90] Ibid.
[91] Ibid.
[92] Ibid.

Moseley v. V Secret Catalogue, Inc., 537 U.S. 418 (2003)[93]

Facts:

Victor and Cathy Moseley opened a new lingerie and adult novelty store in Fort Knox, Kentucky in 1998 called "Victor's Secret."[94] An army colonel who discovered the store became upset that this store was using Victoria's Secret's name to obtain business, so he notified V Secret Catalogue, Inc. regarding the infringement.[95] Victoria's Secret in turn sued Victor's Secret for trademark infringement and more specifically tarnishment and dilution of its trademark. The Moseleys quickly changed the name of their business to "Victor's Little Secret" but this did not satisfy Victoria's Secret.[96]

Issue:

Victoria's Secret claimed that Victor's Secret was too similar of a name to its own and because of that people were associating Victoria's Secret's well-known reputation with Victor's Little Secret. Also, Victoria's Secret claimed that they were world renowned for offering high-quality, sophisticated products, meanwhile, Victor's Little Secret sold cheap adult novelties that if associated with Victoria's Secret would cause Victoria's Secret's reputation to diminish or dilute.

Decision:

After many years of bouncing between the different courts and due to an amendment to trademark legislation, the US Supreme Court granted judgement in favor of Victoria's Secret, and ordered an injunction against the use of Victor's Little Secret.[97]

Reasons:

Until Congress passed the Federal Trademark Dilution Revision Act (FTDRA) in 2006, the Courts had come to the conclusion that although the trademarks were clearly similar, dilution could not be proved because there was no proof of actual economic damages.[98] However, due to the FTDRA, the Courts determined that actual proof did not have to exist but the mere likelihood of dilution was sufficient. This enables companies to more easily protect their famous trademarks from tarnishment and dilution.

Obtaining a Trademark

In Canada and the United States, it is *recommended* that an individual register their trademark in order to receive protection, since it is a first-to-file system. Registration is not however *required* in order to use a trademark.

Registering through the Register of Trademarks is the only method that enables the trademark holder to have full trademark protection, based on the first-to-file format. In Canada, this protection is valid for 15 years from the date of filing and unlike patents is renewable every 15 years.[99] However, in the United States the protection duration is 10 years, and renewable with optional 10-year periods.[100] Once you obtain the trademark you can use the registered trademark symbol®, which

---

93 Moseley v. V Secret Catalogue, Inc., (01-1015) 537 U.S. 418, (2003), 259 F. 3d 464, 2003, *Cornell Law School,* (last update March 4, 2003), https://www.law.cornell.edu/supct/html/01-1015.ZO.html.

94 Ryan Davis, "Victor's Little Secret Strikes Out in Trademark Case," *Law 360,* (last update May 2010), http://www.law360.com/articles/169784/victor-s-little-secret-strikes-out-in-trademark-case.

95 Ibid.

96 Ibid.

97 Ibid.

98 Ibid.

99 Canadian Intellectual Property Office, "A guide to trademarks," *Government of Canada,* (last update December 2015), http://www.ic.gc.ca/eic/site/cipointernet-internetopic.nsf/eng/h_wr02360.html.

100 US Government, "How do I register a U.S. trademark?" *Government of the U.S.* (2016), http://www.stopfakes.gov/learn-about-ip/trademarks/how-do-i-register.

provides notice to others that the trademark is protected.[101] The protection that you are entitled to is federally regulated, which means you can exercise the associated rights anywhere in Canada.[102] If you don't renew your trademark it enters the public domain and your right to it ceases to exist.

Unregistered trademarks are usually referred to as common law trademarks. This trademark is obviously not registered, so it uses a first-to-use system. Once a trademark has been in use in a particular geographic area for a certain amount of time and has gained a reputation it receives limited protection.[103] This can be difficult to prove, as there may not be an exact date in which the trademark was considered "known," so a registered trademark would more likely than not receive priority over the unregistered mark. Unlike a registered trademark, which is entitled to protection across the country, a common law trademark receives protection only in the geographic area in which it exists.[104] The mark that is used to determine a common law trademark is ™.[105] Sometimes companies will use a common law trademark at first to test the effectiveness of the mark prior to paying the fees for registration, which is one of the main reasons why people choose common law trademarks over registered.

Trademark Infringement

Trademark infringement is simply the unauthorized use of another party's trademark or the use of a similar trademark that is causing confusion or deception.

1. **Passing Off**: Passing off occurs when one party deceives the public by misrepresenting the goodwill of another company, usually in the form of deceiving the public that the product or service originated from them.[106] If a company represents its business, goods, or services with a confusingly similar or identical mark to someone else's mark, the tort of passing off has potentially occurred. Although recognized as a common law tort, passing off is also specifically prohibited in the Canadian Trademark Act. It is acceptable to have a similar trademark if the two marks are for different goods or services.

   Example: TOYO Tire & Rubber Co. has a registered Canadian trademark (TMA192714) for TOYO in relation to tires, and Mazda Motor Corporation also has a registered trademark (TMA470836) for TOYO, but in relation to machine tools.

   It is advisable that to the degree a business can considering marketing issues, to try and create distinct marks. The more generic the name the more likely it will infringe on another mark. It also lacks distinctiveness. For example there are approximately 5000 trademarks that have the word *best* in them, ranging from Best Bagels, Best Drycleaners, Best Environment, etc. There are over 400 trademarks with the word *tracker* in them.

2. **Confusion**: Confusion is another form of infringement and is also grounds for opposing another's attempt to register a trademark. The test of confusion is one of first impression.[107]

When you are shopping on the Internet and come across an amazing deal on Oakley Sunglasses do you often think that it is probably too good to be true? Chances are yes, it is too good to be true and

[101] Ridout & Maybee LLP, "Trade-marks," *Ridout & Maybee LLP,* (2016), http://www.ridoutmaybee.com/Page.asp?PageID=924&ContentID=685.

[102] Ibid.

[103] Megan Grainger and Cynthia Rowden, *"Canada,"* Bereskinparr LLP, (last update December 2008), http://www.bereskinparr.com/files/file/docs/tm_wtmr_cr_mlg1208.pdf.

[104] Ibid.

[105] Ridout & Maybee LLP, "Trade-marks," *Ridout & Maybee LPP,* (2016), http://www.ridoutmaybee.com/Page.asp?PageID=924&ContentID=685.

[106] *Edward Chapman Ladies Shop Ltd. v. Edward Chapman Ltd.* 2007 BCCA 370.

[107] *Rowntree Co. Ltd. v. Paulin Chambers Co. Ltd.* (1967), 54 C.P.R. 43, p. 47.

what you are experiencing is one of the most popular forms of trademark infringement, knock-offs. A knock-off is simply a cheap imitation of the original good.[108] It may function and appear as if it is the real thing but it most likely lacks the marks that would distinguish it as the original product.[109] Continuing with the Oakley Sunglasses example, the sunglasses may appear identical to a real pair of Oakley's but the only real difference besides the quality of the material is the name or mark on the glasses. Instead of saying Oakley's it might say Foakley's. Copies are similar to knock-offs in that they are almost exact replicas of the original but the main difference is that copies portray themselves as being the original good.[110] The consumer might think they are buying "real" Oakley sunglasses because it says "Oakley" along the side but in fact it is a copy or more commonly known as a fake.[111] Although it might be clear to the trademark holder that infringement is occurring, it is not a clear-cut case for the Court. In *Best Cellars, Inc. v. Wine Made Simple*, Best Cellars was suing Wine Made Simple for infringing on its trademark for its unique store layout.[112] The Court had to determine the distinctiveness of the trademark, and what the likelihood of confusion was. Even though the consumer may be aware of a registered mark, their imperfect recollection may cause them to mistake one mark for another. The Court stated "it is not sufficient if confusion is merely possible" because in all cases there could be confusion depending on the person, so in order to truly determine confusion, eight steps were set out by the court. The court uses an objective test of "the somewhat-hurried consumer":

1. *Strength of the Trade Mark*: How distinct is the mark or to what degree is it used?[113]

2. *Similarity*: How similar are the two trademarks being discussed?

3. *Proximity in the Market Place*: Are the goods or services being provided in a geographic area where consumers will come into contact with both?

4. *Bridging the Gap*[114]: If the plaintiff sold its goods within the market that the defendant is selling its good would confusion arise?

5. *Actual Confusion based Evidence*: Is there actual testimonial based evidence from consumers regarding confusing the two products?

6. *Bad Faith*: Did the defendant act in bad faith by creating a similar trademark to capitalize on an already established reputation?

7. *Quality of Product*: Is the quality of the product sold by the defendant of an inferior quality that might allow consumers to believe the plaintiff's quality is also low?

8. *Relevant Consumer Groups*: Are the consumers of the plaintiff and the defendant in fact the same and are they unable to tell the difference between the two products?

---

[108] HG, "Is it Illegal to Buy Counterfeit or Knockoff Designer Goods?" (last update 2016), https://www.hg.org/article.asp?id=31573.

[109] Ibid.

[110] Ibid.

[111] Ibid.

[112] *Best Cellars, Inc. v. wine Made Simple, Inc., 320 F. Supp. 2d 60 (S.D.N.Y. 2003)*, March 2003. http://law.justia.com/cases/federal/district-courts/FSupp2/320/60/2468888/.

[113] Ibid.

[114] Ibid.

Honeywell International Inc. v. Shanghai Gerritt Turbo System Ltd. (2015)

Facts:

Honeywell International Inc. is an American multinational company that produces a wide range of scientific technology in the United States and across the globe.[115] Honeywell's Garrett Turbocharger is a well-known trademark in almost all jurisdictions. In 2006, a Chinese manufacturer tried to obtain the trademark "Galitt" for its own turbocharger. Honeywell immediately rejected this claim because Honeywell stated that "Galitt" was far too similar to its own trademark, Garrett, and would cause confusion in the marketplace.[116]

Issues:

Honeywell argued that the Garrett Turbocharger had been a world-renowned brand for the last 60 years for being a high-quality product, so confusion would arise in the marketplace and Honeywell's reputation would diminish.[117] Also, Honeywell claimed that the Chinese Manufacturer was acting in bad faith by trying to capitalize on the already established reputation of Honeywell.[118]

Decision:

After nine years of litigation, the Supreme People's Court of China ruled on August 30, 2015 that the Chinese manufacturer was in fact infringing on Honeywell's rights.[119]

Reasons:

China's highest court decided that the Garrett brand was indeed well known within China and the rest of the world and because of that had a strong reputation. The Court agreed with Honeywell that the Chinese manufacturer was willingly acting in bad faith and trying to take advantage of Honeywell's reputation by using a similar sounding trademark.[120]

Christian Louboutin is a world-renowned designer, known for his red sole shoes, which he received trademark protection for in 2008.[121] However, in 2011, French fashion designer YSL designed a shoe that utilized a red sole, which was similar to that of Louboutin's. Louboutin then sued YSL for trademark infringement.[122] After an 18-month case a New York Judge determined that Louboutin's trademark for a red sole shoe was valid since the color was being used in a specific pattern or placement; however, the protection does not extend to shoes that are entirely red, so YSL can only use a red sole shoe if the rest of the shoe is also red.[123]

---

[115] Honeywell, "Our Company", *Honeywell, 2016,* http://honeywell.com/About/Pages/our-company.aspx.

[116] Honeywell, "Press Releases", *Honeywell, 2016,* https://honeywell.com/News/Pages/Honeywell-Wins-Trademark-Battle-Before-Chinas-Supreme-Court.aspx.

[117] Ibid.

[118] James Anderton, "People's Court of China Rules in Favor of Honeywell over Local Manufacturer", *Engineering,* (last update September 2015), http://www.engineering.com/AdvancedManufacturing/ArticleID/10646/Peoples-Court-of-China-Rules-in-Favor-of-Honeywell-over-Local-Manufacturer.aspx.

[119] Ibid.

[120] Ibid.

[121] Ella Alexander, "YSL Closes Louboutin Court Case," *Vogue,* (last update October 2012), http://www.vogue.co.uk/news/2011/04/20/christian-louboutin-sues-yves-saint-laurent-for-red-sole-shoes.

[122] Ibid.

[123] Ibid

Trademark Dilution

Another way that trademark infringement occurs is through trademark dilution. Dilution is the weakening of a "famous" trademark's capacity to be distinguished from other goods or services.[124] An important aspect of dilution is the reputation or the recognition that the trademark possesses.[125] If the trademark is not considered well known it is hard to prove trademark dilution, since the concept of dilution was originally developed to add additional protection to famous trademarks.[126] There is an important distinction between trademark infringement and trademark dilution. Infringement occurs when someone other than the trademark owner uses the mark in a way that is likely to cause consumer confusion. Dilution, by contrast, occurs when someone other than the trademark owner uses the mark, usually in connection with noncompeting goods, and thereby causes the association between the mark and the goods or services to decrease. Dilution is the opposite of infringement; it seeks to protect the mark from association in the public's mind with wholly unrelated goods and services. The more remote the good or service associated with the junior use, the more likely it is to cause dilution rather than infringement.

Trademark dilution occurs in one of two ways:

1. **Tarnishment**
2. **Blurring**

Tarnishment

Tarnishment occurs when the trademark is linked to products of a lower quality and therefore the distinctiveness of the trademark is reduced.[127] The mark is weakened through unsavory, inappropriate, or unflattering associations. Examples include using a similar mark, a term that plays on one's mark, association with sexual or offensive content, subject matter critical of the mark owner, its business practice, philosophies, and beliefs. "Enjoy Cocaine" is a common example often cited as tarnishment. Tarnishment has to be balanced against free speech rights that exist such as section 2 of the Canadian Charter of Rights or the US Constitution and can be considered a "fair use" exception to liability. A case of tarnishment could be argued if a famous trademark was somehow being associated with a racially offensive organization. Consumers might start believing that the famous trademark supports the racist organization and therefore will be less willing to buy the goods of the trademark. A prime example of tarnishment is when Mattel sued MCA records for the 1997 song "Barbie Girl" sung by the Danish band, Aqua. Mattel argued the song's lyrics tarnished the reputation of Mattel's trademark, and turned Barbie into a sex object, referring to her as a "Blonde Bimbo."[128]

Blurring

Blurring is the more traditional form of dilution, when one uses an identical or similar mark in connection with goods and services that may be completely different from and unrelated to the goods and/or services of the plaintiff's goods and/or services. It detracts from the consumer's strong association with the famous mark. Blurring occurs when a famous trademark loses its selling power, often referred to as basic dilution. Blurring is the whittling away of distinctiveness caused by the unauthorized use of a mark on dissimilar products. Examples would be Tylenol snowboards, Buick aspirin,

---

[124] International Trademark Association, "Trademark Dilution," *International Trademark Association,* (last update April 2015), http://www.inta.org/TrademarkBasics/FactSheets/Pages/TrademarkDilution.aspx.
[125] Ibid.
[126] Ibid.
[127] Ibid.
[128] *Mattel v. MCA Records,* 296 F. 3d 894 (9th Cir. 2002)

Harry Potter drycleaners, or DuPont shoes. In each example consumers would be confused that such products were associated with those particular companies. Even though these companies are completely different, people would no longer just associate Buick, Harry Potter or DuPont with vehicles, books, or chemicals but with other such products. This could negatively affect such companies' buying power and distinctiveness.

There are several criteria that determine what constitutes a distinctive and famous mark:

1. Duration and extent of the use of the mark
2. Duration and extent of advertising of the mark
3. Geographical area in which the mark has been used
4. Degree of distinctiveness of the mark
5. Use of the mark by third parties
6. Registration of the mark

Once it is decided that a mark is famous, the next step is to determine the use of the famous mark causes dilution. Factors include:

- The degree of similarity between the mark and the famous mark
- Degree of inherent or acquired distinctiveness of the famous mark
- Extent to which famous mark is engaging exclusive use of the mark
- Degree of recognition of the famous mark
- Whether the user of the mark intended to create an association with the famous mark
- Any actual association between the mark and the famous mark

Remedies

The remedies are the same for passing off as they are for confusion. Possible remedies are:

1. An interim/interlocutory injunction.
2. Permanent injunction—an injunction would be the first step in enforcing one's rights to a trademark.
3. Damages.
4. Accounting of profits-the defendant has to 'share' its profits from the infringed trademark with the rightful owner.[129]
5. Delivery of and destruction of infringing products or advertising materials.[130]

    A registered mark provides the strongest protection for a trademark. Trademark registration provides *prima facie* evidence of ownership. Registration defeats the innocent infringer defense and puts others on notice of your intention to defend your mark. Registration also helps in a dispute as the registered owner does not need to prove ownership; the onus is on the challenger.

---

[129] MaRs, "Trademark infringement and the Trade-marks Act in Canada," (last update July 2011), https://www.marsdd.com/mars-library/trademark-infringement/.
[130] Ibid.

Copyrights

Definition of a Copyright

Like the name suggests, copyright has to deal with "the right to copy."[131] **Copyright** provides protection for authors pertaining to particular works that they have created and allows only the authors the right to copy these works. Often copyright is referred to as "artistic works." An important aspect of copyright is what it protects. As with patents, an idea is not eligible for copyright protection. What is protected is the expression of the idea. This is the reason why there are so many Hollywood blockbusters about World War II. The idea of World War II and the many stories behind it are not protected but how they are expressed or portrayed in a film is protected.

Similar to other forms of intellectual property, copyright is essential to business. In fact there are many businesses that are in operation solely because of the copyrights that they posses, such as book publishers, or the music industry. Even businesses that aren't primarily focused on copyrights as their main "product" rely on copyrights to help promote their business.[132] Advertising in its many forms is a type of copyright, as is photographs, and instruction manuals. CanCo would seek to obtain a copyright on the software it has in connection with the operation of its CleanCan machine.

Copyright Owner vs. Author

There is an important distinction between an author and an owner. The creator of a work (such as the author of a book, the photographer, the painter) is generally the owner of the copyright. Some general exceptions apply, just because you wrote it, painted it, or recorded it, doesn't mean you own it. The person who has the legal right to publish, modify, and republish a work is the owner. The above general rule can be modified at any time by contract.

> **Assigned Rights**: An author may assign the ownership to a publishing company. The author of this textbook, *Douglas H. Peterson*, may assign the ownership to Kendall Hunt Publishing Company.
>
> **Employment**: Ownership becomes complicated when an employee creates a work during the course of employment.[133] If a work is created by an employee in the course of employment, the employer owns the copyright. Generally, in this situation the owner of the work is the employer unless otherwise stipulated by the parties.[134]
>
> **Works for Hire**: If the work is created by an independent contractor and the contractor signs an agreement that the works shall be "made for hire," the commissioning person or organization will usually own the copyright.

Forms of Copyright Expression

There are seven different ways in which copyrights can be expressed:

1. *Literary Works*: Anything in writing including, textbooks, stories, instruction manuals, poems, lyrics, software, exams, even contracts.

---

[131] Canadian Intellectual Property Office, "A guide to copyright," *Government of Canada,* (last update December 2015), http://www.cipo.ic.gc.ca/eic/site/cipoInternet-Internetopic.nsf/eng/h_wr02281.html.

[132] Queensland Government, "What are some examples of copyright works?" *Queensland Government,* (last update 2015), https://www.business.qld.gov.au/business/support-tools-grants/tools/intellectual-property-info-kit/browse/copyright/examples.

[133] Gil Zvulony, "Who Owns Copyright at Work?" *Zvulony & Co,* (last update December 2010), http://zvulony.ca/2010/articles/intellectual-property-law/copyright-law/copyright-at-work/.

[134] Ibid.

2. *Dramatic Works*: Anything that is expressed in an action, such as films, screenplays, videos, DVD's, choreography, plays etc.[135]

3. *Musical Works*: Anything that involves music, including compositions, harmonies, melodies, sheet music.

4. *Artistic Works*: This can be photography, maps, drawings, sculptures, engravings, charts, blueprints, or paintings.

5. *Performances*: The performance of any of the above works including the reading of a literary work.

6. *Sound Recording*: This pertains to the literal recording of the sound and not the lyrics or the performance of the sound.[136] An example would be if you recorded a performance of Mozart, you would have the copyright of the recording but not of the actual performance. Such forms as records, cassettes, compact discs, digital mp3s etc.

7. *Broadcasting*: A broadcaster has the rights to the communication signal that it broadcasts.[137] For example, you can't record or rebroadcast NFL games without the NFL's permission.

American Broadcasting Cos., Inc., v. Aereo, Inc. (2013)[138]

Facts:

On March 1, 2012, several broadcasting corporations, including CBC, NBC, ABC and Fox filed suit against Aereo, Inc. Aereo, which at the time was exclusively in New York City, was offering a service that allowed subscribers the ability to watch and record live television through the Internet. The broadcasters claimed that because Aereo did not have a license to transmit their programs it was infringing on their rights to transmit their works publicly.

Issue:

The broadcasters claimed that Aereo did not have permission to transmit their programs, so Aereo was violating copyright law. Aereo argued that it merely provided the equipment and that the subscribers had the ability to choose for themselves what they wanted to watch.

Decision:

The US Supreme Court ruled that Aereo was definitely violating the rights of the broadcasters and ordered an injunction.

Reasons:

The Supreme Court determined that the service that Aereo was providing was very similar to that of a cable service. A cable service, under licence, transmits performances to the public. The Court said "Aereo "perform[s]" petitioners' copyrighted works "publicly," as those terms are defined by the Transmit Clause,"[139] meaning that Aereo is infringing on the rights of the broadcasters and must stop. The Court also claimed that the judgement is purely based on the *Copyright Act* and they hope that this decision does not hinder advances in technology.

---

[135] Canadian Intellectual Property Office, "A guide to copyright," *Government of Canada*, (last update December 2015), http://www.cipo.ic.gc.ca/eic/site/cipoInternet-Internetopic.nsf/eng/h_wr02281.html.

[136] Ibid.

[137] Ibid.

[138] *American Broadcasting Cos., Inc., et al. v. Aereo, Inc., 134 S. Ct. 2498*, October 2013. http://www.supremecourt.gov/opinions/13pdf/13-461_1537.pdf.

[139] Ibid 21-22.

Exclusions from Copyright Protection

Essentially as seen from the list above almost anything that is either written, drawn, or performed in any way is eligible for copyright protection but yet there are still some things that don't make the cut. As referred to earlier, ideas can't be protected through copyright. In order for something to be eligible for copyright it must be fixed in a tangible medium.[140] Also, slogans, short phrases, titles, and factual information can't be protected through copyright.[141] Some of these, like slogans are, in fact, protectable under other areas of intellectual property law.[142]

Copyright Protection

The *Copyright Act* governs copyright law in Canada. Through the *Copyright Act* the rights that individuals receive in association with their copyrights is described. Also, in the *Act* the rights of individuals pertaining to what they can do with someone else's copyright without infringing upon it are also given. On June 29, 2012, Royal Assent was received for several significant amendments to the *Copyright Act*, which is referred to as *Bill C-11: The Copyright Modernization Act.*[143] On January 2, 2015, the *Act* fully came into practice.[144] As the name of the *Bill* suggests, the purpose of the amendments were to align Canada's copyright practices with that of modern technology. Some important amendments to the *Act* include:

- A person who already owns or has a license to use a copy of a work is allowed to make copies for backup purposes.[145] Along with this a person can change the format of the work and the time that the work is viewed.[146] As long as the use is for non-commercial purposes then you can ideally upload your favorite CD to your computer, download a song on iTunes and put it on your phone, and record a TV show and watch it at a later time. All of these things can be now done without any fear of infringing on the author's' rights.

- It is not considered infringement for a person to use an existing published work in the creation of a new work as long as it is for a private, non-commercial purpose.[147] Also, the source of the published work needs to be referenced. An example of this is something that most people have been doing already with YouTube. A person can now mash together several movie or music clips and not be infringing on the author's copyright.

- The Fair Use Doctrine has also received considerable amendments through the *Copyright Act*. Fair Use Doctrine is using or copying a work for private uses such as education, private study, research, reporting, parodies and satires.[148]

- This *Act* now provides limited liability for Internet providers for the actions of their customers. The term "Notice and Notice" is used to describe this provision because now when an Internet user illegally infringes a copyright owner's rights by illegally downloading a movie or a song, the owner can now indirectly communicate with the infringer through the Internet provider.[149]

---

[140] Bitlaw, "Works Unprotected by Copyright Law," *Bitlaw,* (2015), http://www.bitlaw.com/copyright/unprotected.html.

[141] Ibid.

[142] Ibid.

[143] UBC, "Bill C-11: The Copyright Modernization Act," *UBC,* (2016), http://copyright.ubc.ca/guidelines-and-resources/support-guides/bill-c-11-the-copyright-modernization-act/#pufde.

[144] Ibid.

[145] Parliament of Canada, "Chapter 20," *Government of Canada,* (2016), http://www.parl.gc.ca/HousePublications/Publication.aspx?DocId=5697419&File=45#7.

[146] Ibid 29.22.

[147] Ibid 29.21

[148] Oyen, Wiggs, Green, and Mutala LLP, "The Copyright Modernization Act: Big Changes to Copyright Law in Canada," *Oyen, Wiggs, Green and Mutala LLP,* (last update March 2013), http://www.patentable.com/the-copyright-modernization-act-big-changes-to-copyright-law-in-canada/.

[149] UBC, *"Bill C-11: The Copyright Modernization Act," UBC,* (2016), http://copyright.ubc.ca/guidelines-and-resources/support-guides/bill-c-11-the-copyright-modernization-act/#pufde.

The copyright owner will send a notice to the Internet provider and the Internet provider will then notify the infringer of what they have done and inform them if they don't stop legal action could prevail. During this process the Internet provider does not release the infringer's personal information, as the copyright owner is only aware of an IP address that is infringing on its right.[150] The Internet provider is to retain as a record for six months that a notice was delivered to the infringer just in case the copyright owner decides to pursue legal action. The *Act* has set statutory damages in these cases and they will range from $200 – $5,000 if the case is non-commercial.[151]

The amendments to the *Copyright Act* try to deal with the presence of the Internet and technology in general, as it is getting easier for just about anybody to infringe on copyrighted works. These amendments give more flexibility for individuals to use their legally obtained works and for copyright owners to better enforce their rights.

Requirements for Copyright Protection

The requirements for copyright protection are essentially universal wherever you go in the world. Whether you go to Australia, the United States, or Canada, you will find similar criteria for protecting your copyright:

1. *The work must be original*: The required amount of originality for a work is very small. Essentially, as long as the work is created by an author (not copied) with a minimum amount of creativity then the originality requirement will be met.[152] The concept of originality refers not to uniqueness or novelty, but to a work originated from the author. The bar for originality is very low and although beneficial to artists, is potentially bad for business. The more original a work, the less exact the copying has to be to constitute infringement. The less original a work, the more exact the copying must be to constitute infringement.

Feist Publications, Inc. v. Rural Telephone Service (1991)[153]

Facts:

Rural Telephone Service Co. provided a telephone service to several areas within Kansas. It provided a directory, which included the names, telephone numbers, and addresses of people within the specified areas. Feist Publications also created a book that used the information from Rural's directory but also included more information in order to cover an even greater geographic area.[154] Rural sued for copyright infringement claiming Feist used the information without Rural's consent.

Issues:

Rural claims that since the information was taken from their copyrighted book (directory) that Feist in fact infringed on their rights. Feist claims that permission to use the information in the book was not needed because the information is considered public and not original.

---

[150] Ibid.

[151] Ibid.

[152] Harvard Law, "The Requirements for Copyright Protection," *Harvard Law School,* (2016), http://cyber.law.harvard. edu/cx/The_Requirements_for_Copyright_Protection-JA.

[153] *Feist Publications, Inc. v. Rural Telephone Service Co., 499 U.S. 340 (1991)*, https://www.law.cornell.edu/copyright/ cases/499_US_340.htm.

[154] Ibid.

Decision:

The US Supreme Court found that Feist is free to use the information, as it does not infringe on Rural's protected work.[155]

Reasons:

The Supreme Court found that although the directory was protected, the names, telephone numbers, and addresses included in the directory were not considered original, as they were mere facts.[156] Also, since Rural was not the original compiler of the information, Rural has no rights pertaining to the information. Since Feist merely took the information from the directory and not the style or layout of the book itself, then Feist did not infringe.

2. *The work must be in a fixed medium*: As with other forms of intellectual property, an idea can't be protected. The work must be "fixed in a tangible medium of expression."[157] This could be anything from a story written on a piece of paper to an audio recording of a song. A song or story in my head is not protected until such time as I put it into a fixed form.

3. *Must be connected to Canada*: The connection to Canada can be anything from the work being created in Canada, by a Canadian, or by a resident who is a part of a recognized treaty.

Registering a Copyright

Copyright is unique in the sense that once the work has been created it automatically receives copyright protection and registration is not required.[158] As long as the criteria for a copyright have been met then the mere creation of the work is enough. The symbol of copyright protection is © and may be used even if the copyright is not registered but either way there is no requirement to use the symbol.[159] The question often arises, why would someone bother to register? The main incentive to register would be that your copyright would be protected across the country and it would prove that you own it. In the United States, copyright registration is even more important than in Canada because in order to bring about a lawsuit regarding copyright infringement the copyright owner must have the work registered.[160]

Typically, the owner of the copyright is the creator or the author of the work. However, there are circumstances when there are exceptions such as when a work is created created under an employment contract.[161] In this case the employer would be the official owner of the copyright and not the employee.

Rights of a Copyright Owner

Duration

One of the main differences between Canada and the United States regarding copyright owner's rights has to do with duration. Canada is unique as it has a shorter duration for copyright than other countries like the United States and the United Kingdom. In Canada, the copyright owner has rights during

---

155 Ibid.

156 Ibid.

157 Daniel Tysver, *Obtaining Copyright Protection, Bitlaw*, (2015), http://www.bitlaw.com/copyright/obtaining.html.

158 Ibid.

159 Mary Bellis, "Copyright Notice and the Use of the Copyright Symbol," (last update December 2014), http://inventors. about.com/od/copyrights/a/CopyrightNotice.htm.

160 Stanford University, "Copyright Registration and Enforcement," *Stanford University,* (2015), http://fairuse.stanford. edu/overview/faqs/registration-and-enforcement/.

161 Innovation, Science and Economic Development Canada, "About Copyright," (last update November 2013), https:// www.ic.gc.ca/eic/site/icgc.nsf/eng/07415.html#p3.

the duration of the author's life, or if joint authors, after the death of the last surviving author, plus 50 years.[162] In countries like the United States and the United Kingdom, the duration is the author's life, plus 70 years.[163] This enables the owner and whoever the rights pass on to the ability to enjoy the rights of the work. After this time period has expired the work then enters the public domain, which means they can be accessed by anyone.

In Canada, the corporation itself cannot be the author of the work because corporations can technically last forever.[164] This would cause an unfair perpetual monopoly on the work and wouldn't allow the work to eventually enter the public domain. The distinction between author and owner is important. The author can be the owner, but an owner may not be the author. The duration of copyright is based on the life of the author, not the owner.

Appendix B

Copyright Protection Duration

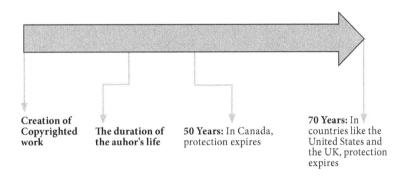

Creation of Copyrighted work

The duration of the auhor's life

50 Years: In Canada, protection expires

70 Years: In countries like the United States and the UK, protection expires

Doug Peterson

Bundle of Rights

The rights associated with a copyright are often referred to as a bundle of rights, a common way to explain the property rights associated with copyright, such rights granted by copyright acts. Such rights are acquired when original works are created. Such bundle of rights can be separated out and licensed or sold. Canada and the United States both give copyright holders certain rights that pertain to their works and they include:

- *The right to produce*: The ability to create the work in any form.
- *The right to reproduce*: The ability to reproduce the created work in any form. The original owner is the only one that is allowed to reproduce the work.
- *The right to translate*[165]: The ability to translate the work into any language and any form. An example would be translating an English-speaking film into a French novel.
- *The right to publish*: The ability to publish the work if it is unpublished.
- *The right to publicly perform*: The ability to perform the work in any form.[166]
- *The right to authorize someone else to exercise these rights*.[167] The ability to authorize any other person to use the work and the rights associated with it.

---

162 Ibid.
163 United States Copyright Office, "Duration of Copyright," *Government of the U.S.* (last update August 2011), http://www.copyright.gov/circs/circ15a.pdf.
164 Ibid.
165 Canadian Internet Policy and Public Interest Clinic, "Copyright Law", (last update September 2008), http://www.copyright.gov/circs/circ15a.pdf.
166 Daniel Tysver, "Rights Granted under Copyright Law," *Bitlaw*, (2015), http://www.bitlaw.com/copyright/scope.html.
167 Canadian Internet Policy and Public Interest Clinic, "*Copyright Law,*" (last update September 2008), http://www.copyright.gov/circs/circ15a.pdf.

Moral Rights

Another aspect of copyright that is unique only to copyright is the concept of moral rights. **Moral rights** are the rights given to the copyright author to prevent others from modifying the work in anyway without prior permission.[168] The moral rights reside with the author not the owner, although they may be the same person. In Canada, moral rights exist during the author's lifetime plus 50 years but in the United States moral rights end at the death of the author, so in Canada the moral rights last as long as the actual copyright protection does.[169] Moral rights are not transferable and exist with the author even after the possession of the work has been transferred to another person but the author can choose to waive its moral rights.[170] Moral rights include:

1. *The right of attribution*: This refers to the author's right to have their name with the work, use a pseudonym or to remain anonymous.[171] An example would be the author of a book has the right to have their name on the book.

2. *The right of integrity over the work*: The author has the right to prevent modification of the work if it will harm their reputation.[172] Merely, modifying the work is not enough to warrant infringement of moral rights, as the author has to prove that their reputation has been damaged due to the modification.

3. *The right to be associated with the work*: The author has the right to prevent anyone from using their work in association with anything that could cause damage to their reputation.[173] An example would be if the book was being promoted and sold at a fast food restaurant but the book was about healthy eating.

Copyright Registration

Each work in which copyright subsists should be marked with a notice. The notice should display the copyright symbol © followed by the name of the owner of the copyright, and followed by the year in which the work was published. This notice is to be displayed in such manner and location as to give reasonable notice of a claim of copyright in the work. The notice will defeat an innocent infringer defense. For example © Kendall Publishing Inc, 2016.

Innocent Infringer Defense

In both Canada and the United States, it is well established that innocent intention is not a defense in copyright matters and that ignorance as to the existence of a copyright is not a defense in an infringement suit. The exception is when where there is no registered copyright, and that the defendant was not aware of the existence of the copyright in the infringed work at the date of the infringement. Typically, innocent infringement involves actions by third parties without your knowledge or consent. For example, a website developer you hired uses copyrighted images without getting the necessary authorization, you may have a claim of innocence. If one successfully proves the innocent infringement they will not be liable for damages but could still be prohibited from further copying.

---

[168] Harvard Law School, "Moral Rights," *Harvard Law School,* (last update March 1998), https://cyber.law.harvard.edu/property/library/moralprimer.html.

[169] Philip Kerr, "Copyright Law in Canada," (2016), http://users.trytel.com/~pbkerr/copyright.html.

[170] Ibid.

[171] Zvulony & Co, "What are Moral Rights?" *Zyulong & Co.* (last update December 2010), http://zvulony.ca/2010/articles/intellectual-property-law/copyright-law/moral-rights-author-rights/.

[172] Ibid.

[173] Ibid.

Copyright Infringement and Exemptions

Infringement occurs when an unauthorized person uses the rights that are exclusively given to the author of the copyright. Like trademark infringement, the remedies for copyright infringements are similar. Injunctions, damages, accounting of profits, destruction of infringing goods are all examples of common remedies used against copyright infringement.[174]

There are several exemptions that normally may constitute copyright infringement but do not and they include:

- *Fair Use Doctrine*: Use that is for the purpose of private study, research, education, reporting, satire, and parodies.

- *First Sale Doctrine*: The copyright owner's right to remuneration does not exist after the first sale of the protected work.[175] Therefore, once the work has been sold, the buyer has exclusive rights to the work as long as the buyer doesn't infringe on the author's rights. An example would be a library, since the library buys the books and therefore has the right to loan the books to its members.

- *Computer Software*: The owner of legally obtained computer software is able to reproduce a single copy of the software for backup purposes.[176]

- *Public Domain*: Works where copyright has expired, or is ineligible for copyright protection, or whose creator waived copyright protection are within the public domain and can be used without infringement.[177] Just because something is in the public sphere does not necessarily mean it is in the public domain.[178] For example, an original piece by Mozart may be in the public domain but if the New York Orchestra performed that same piece in 2005, then the recording of that performance is not within the realm of the public domain, but the performance is. Therefore, you would have to pay for the copyright, in other words, buy the recording. A bootleg recording of a performance that is in the public domain may have copyright protection, even though the underlying performance within the recording does not. Protection in this regard is done through a contract: those attending the performance are under the terms of the contract that they may not record the performance.

- *YouTube:* Due to the amendments to the *Copyright Act* in 2012, it is permissible for a person to use existing published copyright material to create their own work.[179] This is only allowed if it is for non-commercial purposes and the original source is given. YouTube is full of videos where people use popular songs as background music. In most cases these videos are not giving proper credit to the artist but it isn't in the interest of the artist to track down all these infringers. For an example if someone were to create a video using Aerosmith's "Walk This Way" and the creator followed the appropriate guidelines and cited the source of the song there would be no issues. However, if this video became popular and started to generate royalties from YouTube then there might be an issue.

---

[174] Bereskin & Parr, "Remedies for Trademark and Copyright Infringement in Canada," *Bereskin & Parr LLP,* (last update march 2009), http://www.bereskinparr.com/Article/id76.

[175] Rich Sim, "The First Sale Doctrine," *Nolo Law Firm,* (2015), http://www.nolo.com/legal-encyclopedia/the-first-sale-doctrine.html.

[176] Philip Kerr, *"Computer software Law in Canada,"* (2015), http://users.trytel.com/~pbkerr/computer.html.

[177] Ryerson University, "Copyright Basics," *Ryerson University,* (2016), http://library.ryerson.ca/copyright/resources/general-copyright-information/copyright-basics/.

[178] Ibid.

[179] Anthony Pranata, *"Posting Videos on YouTube—Copyright Infringement or Not? The "Mash-Up" Provision,"* Mondaq, (last update June 2014), http://www.mondaq.com/canada/x/320054/Copyright/Posting+Videos+On+Youtube+Copyright+Infringement+Or+Not.

- *Creative Commons*: Allows authors to make their work available to the public but still possesses copyright protection.[180] This enables users to use the work under certain conditions, such as you must give credit to the original author, it has to be for a non-commercial use, and your creation must follow these conditions.[181]

Copyright Collectives

Most states have copyright collectives. Such collectives act for owners of copyright. These collectives collect royalty payments from users of copyright works and then distribute the royalties to the copyright owners. These copyright collectives usually grant licenses to copyright users as a licensing body. In Canada the copyright collective is SOCAN, the Society of Composers, Authors and Music Publishers of Canada.

Industrial Design

Definition of Industrial Design

In Canada, **industrial design** is referred to as the "features of shape, configuration, pattern or ornament, or any combination of these features applied to a finished article."[182] Industrial design and patents are often times confused for each other. As described earlier in this chapter patent law protects the functionality of an invention but industrial design protects the invention's appearance. In some situations you might want to apply for both a patent and industrial design protection for your invention.

In order to successfully obtain industrial design protection the design must be original and novel.[183] To be original, the designer would have to prove differences between his design and prior art.[184] Novelty will arise if there are no other identical or similar registered designs in existence. Also, the design can't have been disclosed anywhere one year prior to the filing date.[185]

Basic examples of protectable designs could be a pattern on wallpaper, or the specific design of a container, or the decoration applied to piece of clothing.[186] However, you can't register a method or an idea for doing something. Also, the materials that you used in something and the function can't be registered.[187] For example you can't register the fact that a bottle is made of glass or the way a couch works.

In the United States, industrial design is referred to as a **design patent** and has some difference from the industrial laws in Canada. The patent system in the United States is broken up into two kinds of patents. There are utility patents, which is what is referred to in Canada as a patent. There are also

---

[180] UBC, "Creative Commons Guide," *UBC,* (2016), http://copyright.ubc.ca/guidelines-and-resources/support-guides/creative-commons/.

[181] Creative Commons, "Attribution-NonCommercial-ShareAlike 2.5 Canada," *Creative Commons,* (2016), https://creativecommons.org/licenses/by-nc-sa/2.5/ca/.

[182] Canadian Intellectual Property Office, "A guide to industrial designs," *Government of Canada,* (last update February 2016), http://www.ic.gc.ca/eic/site/cipointernet-internetopic.nsf/eng/h_wr02300.html?Open&wt_src=cipo-id-main&wt_cxt=learn#understandingID.

[183] Don Tomkins, "A Brief Introduction to Patents and Related Intellectual Property Rights" (presentation, University of Alberta School of Business, Edmonton, AB, November 14, 2008).

[184] Ibid.

[185] Ibid.

[186] Canadian Intellectual Property Office, "A guide to industrial designs," *Government of Canada,* (last update February 2016), http://www.ic.gc.ca/eic/site/cipointernet-internetopic.nsf/eng/h_wr02300.html?Open&wt_src=cipo-id-main&wt_cxt=learn#understandingID.

[187] Ibid.

design patents. Design patents have a similar definition to industrial designs, "the subject matter which is claimed is the design embodied in or applied to an article of manufacture and not the article itself."[188] Like the difference between industrial designs and patents, utility patents and design patents have similar differences, since utility patents protect the functionality of the invention and design patents protect the visual appearance of the invention. A significant different between design patents and industrial designs are the duration in which they can be protected for. In Canada, industrial designs are protected for five years with an optional five-year renewal.[189] However, design patents are eligible for 14-years of protection.[190]

Industrial Design Registration Process

Similar to patents, in order for an industrial design to be considered protected it needs to be registered. Merely creating the design does not constitute protection like trademarks and copyrights.

In the application, a description of the design along with a drawing or photograph of the design with the finished article is to be included.[191] As long as the design meets the requirements for protection, meaning it is original and novel then the registration will be complete. It is important to register the design within a one-year span of the design being disclosed.[192]

The marking of industrial design is a capital D within a circle. There is no requirement for this marking to be on the particular design but it is beneficial for it to be. If the design is infringed upon but no marking is found the court can only award an injunction, but not damages.[193] However, if the design is infringed and the marking appears on the design then in this case the Court may be able to award compensatory damages, in addition to an injunction.[194]

Trade Secrets

Definition of a Trade Secret

In Canada, there is no official intellectual property law process that gives protection to trade secrets. **Trade secrets** are valuable assets that provide a business with a competitive edge over its competitors due to the secretive nature of the information.[195] Famous examples are the secret formula in Coca-Cola drinks or the algorithm that Google uses for its search engine. Both Coca-Cola and Google rely on these secrets in order to be competitive. Can you imagine if this information was public? Why would you bother spending money on the "real" Coke when cheaper brands taste exactly the same?

---

[188] United States Patent and Trademark Office, "Definition of a Design," *Government of the U.S.* (last update November, 2015), http://www.uspto.gov/web/offices/pac/mpep/s1502.html.

[189] Don Tomkins, "A Brief Introduction to Patents and Related Intellectual Property Rights" (presentation, University of Alberta School of Business, Edmonton, AB, November 14, 2008).

[190] United States Patent and Trademark Office, "Allowance and Term of Design Patent," *Government of the U.S.* (last update November 2015), http://www.uspto.gov/web/offices/pac/mpep/s1505.html.

[191] Canadian Intellectual Property Office, "A guide to industrial designs," *Government of Canada*, (last update February 2016), http://www.ic.gc.ca/eic/site/cipointernet-internetopic.nsf/eng/h_wr02300.html?Open&wt_src=cipo-id-main&wt_cxt=learn#understandingID.

[192] Ibid.

[193] Bereskin & Parr, "Industrial Design," *Bereskin & Parr LLP*, (2016), http://www.bereskinparr.com/Section/About-Intellectual-Property/Industrial-Design.

[194] Ibid.

[195] Canadian Intellectual Property Office, "What is a trade secret?" *Government of Canada,* (last update December 2015), https://www.ic.gc.ca/eic/site/cipointernet-internetopic.nsf/eng/wr03987.html.

Even though there is no official intellectual property law protection for trade secrets, there are still certain criteria that must be met to ensure the 'secret' really is a trade secret and they include the following:

1. Not generally known to the public or the industry
2. An economic advantage is the result of the secret
3. Reasonable efforts to maintain secrecy

CanCo has never registered a patent for the formula of the materials they put into the CleanCan machine, only the process of the machine. The secret formula of the materials is a trade secret of CanCo.

Protection and Infringement

Although there is no protection for trade secrets under intellectual property, legal action can still arise if the secret is "slipped" due to breach of confidence.[196] In order for breach of confidence to be considered the following three elements must be established:

1. The information conveyed was in fact confidential,
2. The "secret" was conveyed to the party in a circumstance in which a duty of confidence arises, and
3. The party to whom it was conveyed misused the confidential information.

If a party is in fact trying to steal a trade secret, the plaintiff does not have to prove to the Court what the trade secret is. Also, the party that attempted to steal the trade secret can't use the defense of ignorance. The Court in these cases gives the plaintiff or the trade secret holder the benefit of the doubt.

Comparing Areas of Intellectual Property

The distinct role that each area of intellectual property plays in business and within society is evident. Although each component of intellectual property is different, there is still a lot of overlap between the different areas. The creation process of all types of intellectual property is quite similar in that all property must exhibit some form of originality. Protection cannot be achieved if the property has already been created or is too similar to an already existing piece of property. In some cases when someone creates intellectual property it can be protected under all areas of the law. For example if someone created a new type of couch, they could potentially get a patent for the couch; a trademark for the name of the couch; a copyright for the instruction manual; and a industrial design for the pattern of the couch. No matter how different the types of intellectual property are, they are also very similar and can be strongly connected.

Trademarks and copyrights are similar in that both do not need registration in order to receive some sort of protection.[197] Although, it is recommended along with other types of intellectual property to register the property in order to avoid potential legal complications. Trademarks are unique as they're the only type of property that is considered renewable.[198] Patents, copyrights, and industrial designs all have an expiry date in which the protection ends.[199] Trademarks can be renewed every 15 years in order to maintain protection.[200] Patents and industrial designs are often times

---

[196] Canadian Intellectual Property Office, "Protect your innovation", *Government of Canada,* (last update January 2016), http://www.ic.gc.ca/eic/site/cipointernet-internetopic.nsf/eng/wr03586.html#secret.

[197] Canadian Intellectual Property Office, "A guide to trademarks," *Government of Canada,* (last update December 2015), http://www.ic.gc.ca/eic/site/cipointernet-internetopic.nsf/eng/h_wr02360.html.

[198] Ibid.

[199] Don Tomkins, "A Brief Introduction to Patents and Related Intellectual Property Rights" (presentation, University of Alberta School of Business, Edmonton, AB, November 14, 2008).

[200] Ibid.

confused due to their similarities. In the United States, industrial design or design patents, as it is more commonly referred, is included as a category under patent law.[201] Also, both patents and industrial designs both focus on the protection of an original and novel good. The main difference is patent protection focuses on the functionality of the good and industrial design focuses on the appearance of the good.[202]

Appendix C

Comparing and Contrasting the Types of Intellectual Property					
Types of Intellectual Property	Requirements	Examples	Need to Register?	Duration of Protection	Renewable
Patent	Novel, inventive, useful	Couch	Yes	20 years from filing date	No
Trademark	Distinctive, well-known	Name of the couch	No	15 years from registration date	Yes, every 15 years and every 10 years in United States
Copyright	Original, minimal creativity, fixed, connected to Canada	The instruction manual	No	Author's life plus 50 years	No
Industrial Design/Design Patent	Original, novel	The pattern of the couch	Yes	10 years from the filing date. Design patent is for 14 years.	No
Trade Secrets	Efforts to maintain secrecy, economic value, not known to the public	Methods for potential improvement of current couch	No, since it is a secret	Until it is no longer a "secret"	No

Doug Peterson

Transfer of Intellectual Property

Reasons for Transferring Intellectual Property

So far in this chapter we have learned that intellectual property can be a major asset to any business through the rights that it possesses. What we haven't talked about yet is what other things businesses can do with their intellectual property. Obviously businesses have the right to create and use their intellectual property but an ever-growing part of the business world is transferring the rights that are associated with intellectual property to another party.

---

[201] Ibid.
[202] Ibid.

There are two main ways in which a business can transfer intellectual property rights and they are through licensing and assignment. **Licensing** is very common as this is when an intellectual property owner gives limited permission to another person to use the specified rights of the intellectual property for a designated amount of time.[203] An **assignment** differs from a license because when intellectual property is transferred in an assignment it is done so permanently.[204] The buyer or the transferee obtains all the rights associated with the property.

The reason why businesses decide to license their property is simple. It gives them an economic advantage to do so. Licensing allows the property owner to enter new markets, limit infringement on its property and of course gain more profits.[205] In international business there is always a risk when entering a foreign market. By licensing the property to a foreign firm in a foreign market the business is able to mitigate most of the risks associated with international business, as there is limited direct investment taking place. Title does not pass, just possession, which enables the owner to terminate the license if there is a breach in the contract. For example, a software company in the United States wants to enter the market of Vietnam but has concerns with succeeding there due to a lack of knowledge of the culture. The risky option would be to invest capital in establishing an office and beginning to market the software; however, the other option is simply to license the software to a company already established in Vietnam with a working knowledge of the market. This then enables the US Company to gain a presence in the country and observe whether their product can succeed there without investing precious resources.

Although risk is mitigated through licensing intellectual property there are still risks associated with transferring rights to other parties. Probably the most significant risk is losing control of the intellectual property rights and a competitor is established. Along with the establishment of a competitor is the creation of the gray market.[206] **Gray markets** are formed when goods are supposed to be sold within foreign markets but are instead imported back into the company's domestic market without the company's authorization. These goods are legitimate intellectual property bearing goods but because the licensor's agreement with the licensee was too vague or the licensee sold the goods to a third-party that didn't have a "covenant not to compete clause", the goods are re-entering the market and competing with the licensor at lower prices.[207] An example would be if a US company sold basketballs in the Philippines for $5.00 USD instead of the $15.00 USD they cost in the United States. A company in the Philippines then bought a large amount of these balls and in turn sold them to consumers in the United States for $10.00 USD per ball. These basketballs were not supposed to re-enter the US market and now that they are they are hurting domestic sales and therefore creating a gray market.

Transfer Arrangements

When a business is looking to license its intellectual property rights to another party there are a few questions in which it should consider. The most important being what rights will be given to the licensee? This is important because this will determine whether the licensee will have all the rights pertaining to the property or if the licensor will retain some of the rights for itself. The licensee will more often than not request an **exclusive license** to the property.[208] As the name suggests, this enables the licensee and only the licensee to have all the rights pertaining to the property. Not even the licensor can use the property if these rights are given. Through exclusive rights the licensor will receive

---

[203] European IPR Helpdesk, "Commercializing Intellectual Property: License Agreements", *European Union*, 2013, https://www.iprhelpdesk.eu/sites/default/files/newsdocuments/Licence_agreements_0.pdf

[204] Ibid.

[205] Ibid.

[206] Christopher Dolan, "IP: Gray market goods spell trouble for companies", *Inside Counsel*, last update August 2011, http://www.insidecounsel.com/2011/08/23/ip-gray-market-goods-spell-trouble-for-companies.

[207] Ibid.

[208] Rowena Borenstein, Donald Cameron, "Key Aspects of IP License Agreements", *Ogilvy, Renault,* 2003, http://www.jurisdiction.com/lic101.pdf.

the most royalty fees but with this there is a lot of risk as well, since they are giving up control of the property and its future in the market.[209]

A **non-exclusive license** is the opposite in that the licensor retains its rights and is able to license its property to as many licensees as it wants to.[210]

In the middle of an exclusive license and a non-exclusive license there is a sole license. A **sole license** gives the licensee the same rights as an exclusive license but the licensor is able to retain rights for itself, meaning it is able to use the property as well.[211]

Common Licensing Clauses

Once the degree in which the intellectual property rights will be transferred is determined there are other conditions that need consideration and they include:

1. *Technology transfer laws*: Depending on the technology and the country in which the licensor resides, there might be regulations in place on what can be transferred. There are prior-approval schemes, which is typically used by protectionist governments and here the licensor needs prior approval from the government before any transfer arrangements can be finalized. There are also notification registration schemes, which require the licensor to notify the government of the arrangement.

2. *Duration clause*: This will prohibit the use of the property once the fixed time period has expired.[212]

3. *Confidentiality clause*: This allows limitations to be put on what personnel have access to the property. This is used to avoid the exploitation of the property by third parties.

4. *Forum selection clause*: This sets out the location where legal proceedings will occur if there is any breach in contract.[213]

5. *Grant clause*[214]: This will describe the rights and conditions that the licensee will receive in regards to the use of the property.

Other License Agreement Considerations

Along with the previously discussed clauses there are other clauses in which the licensor might want to utilize and they include:

1. *Territorial clause*[215]: This limits where the licensee can use the property. This is common when there are several licensees for the same property.

2. *Covenant not to compete*[216]: Once the licensing contract has expired the licensee can't compete with the licensor.

3. *Reservation of rights clause*: The licensor reserves any rights that are not expressly transferred by the license.

---

[209] Ibid.
[210] Ibid.
[211] Ibid.
[212] Ibid 8.
[213] Ibid.
[214] European IPR Helpdesk, "Commercializing Intellectual Property: License Agreements", *European Union*, 2013, https://www.iprhelpdesk.eu/sites/default/files/newsdocuments/Licence_agreements_0.pdf
[215] Rowena Borenstein, Donald Cameron, "Key Aspects of IP License Agreements", *Ogilvy, Renault*, 2003, http://www.jurisdiction.com/lic101.pdf.
[216] "Covenants' Not to Compete in Intellectual Property Transactions", *Lott & Friedland*, accessed February 2016, http://www.lfiplaw.com/articles/convenants_not_to_compete_in_ip_transactions.htm.

4. *Indemnification clause*: This clause would limit the liability of the licensor in the case of legal proceedings. The licensee would have to pay the expenses of the licensor.

5. *Royalty clause*: The calculated amount that the licensee would pay to the licensor for the use of the property. This can be done through guaranteed consideration (scheduled payments), or momentum royalties (royalty paid when the licensee makes money through the license).

6. *Hybrid clause*: Typically royalties are only paid during the duration of the intellectual property's protection. A hybrid clause extends the royalty payments beyond the duration of the protection.[217] Royalties made beyond the protection time period are not enforceable.

7. *Best efforts clause*: This clause is important in exclusive licenses because this requires the licensee to reach particular benchmarks or goals and there are repercussions for failure to meet these goals. This lowers the risk of the licensor when giving all its rights to the licensee.

8. *Termination clause:* This sets the conditions for what will conclude the license agreement.

9. *Non-partnership and independent contractor clause*: This is a vital part of the agreement because it sets out the fact that the licensee is not acting as an agent for the licensor.

Examples of a License Agreement Here — With Annotations

Kimble v. Marvel Entertainment (2015)[218]

Facts:

In 1990, Stephen Kimble obtained a patent for a toy that enables the user to shoot web-like strings from the palm of the hand. Naturally, Marvel Entertainment was attracted to this invention because of its famous character, Spider-Man. The two parties tried to negotiate a contract for the use of the property but no deal was finalized. Marvel was then sued by Kimble in 1997 because Marvel had developed a toy called a "Web Blaster" that was similar to Kimble's invention.[219] Marvel and Kimble settled and Marvel purchased Kimble's patent and agreed to pay 3% royalties on all future sales of the patent.[220] No end date was set for the royalties as both parties assumed consumers would eventually stop buying the invention.

In 2008, the two parties disagreed regarding the royalty payments and Kimble sued for breach of contract.

Issues:

Kimble sued Marvel because Marvel no longer wanted to make royalty payments and were therefore in breach of contract. Marvel argued that since the patent had indeed expired, the Brulotte Rule comes into affect. The Brulotte Rule states an agreement in which the patent owner is still receiving royalty payments even after the patent has expired is unlawful. This means Marvel does not have to pay royalties to Kimble anymore.

---

[217] Gwen Peterson, "Patent Licensing Considerations", *Association of Corporate Counsel,* last update August 2013, http://www.acc.com/legalresources/quickcounsel/qcplc.cfm.

[218] *Kimble et al. v. Marvel Entertainment, LLC 576 U.S., 135 S. Ct. 2401 (2015)*, October 2015, http://www.supremecourt.gov/opinions/14pdf/13-720_jiel.pdf.

[219] Ibid.

[220] Ibid.

Decision:

On June 22, 2015, the US Supreme Court came to the conclusion that the Brulotte Rule is still applicable, so Marvel no longer had to make royalty payments to Kimble.

Reasons:

The decision by the Supreme Court found that the Brulotte Rule is still applicable and stated, "We would prefer not to unsettle stable law."[221] Also, the Courts determined that by enforcing hybrid clauses and forcing parties to pay royalties post-expiration would in fact take away inventions from the free market and essentially this "runs counter to the policy and purpose of the patent laws."[222] Therefore, even though it might be in a contract, the Courts will not enforce royalty payments after the patent has expired.

International Protection for Intellectual Property

Reasons for the Existence of International Protection

Organizations everywhere are always looking for ways to protect their assets and seeing that intellectual property can be one of the most important assets that businesses own, protecting those rights seems essential. Intellectual property rights are created and enforced domestically. Any intellectual property rights created in Canada only receive protection in Canada and must be enforced in Canada according to the various intellectual property laws of Canada. Various international treaties provide protection in other countries.

When you register your intellectual property it only receives protection in the country that it is registered, so you must register your property in every country in which you want protection. This can cause concern to organizations because "don't countries have different requirements and rules concerning intellectual property?" There may be slight differences in criteria and terminology in different countries but the majority of foreign markets that you would want to enter are part of international organizations that protect intellectual property.[223] This allows businesses to enter various markets and register their property without fearing that they might lose their rights.

There are many different organizations, treaties, and conventions that govern the use and enforcement of intellectual property abroad.

World Intellectual Property Organization (WIPO)

The World Intellectual Property Organization or WIPO is a specialized branch of the United Nations that regulates the treaties and conventions that provide protection for intellectual property.[224] WIPO is headquartered in Switzerland and encompasses 188 member states. All member states of the United Nations are entitled to be part of WIPO but it is not mandatory. As someone who is seeking to register their intellectual property you will most likely not interact directly with WIPO, but you will deal with one of the 26 treaties that are part of WIPO.[225] WIPO strives to continually improve international protection for the rights of patents, trademarks, copyrights, and industrial designs.

---

[221] Ibid 14.

[222] Ibid 19.

[223] United States Patent and Trademark Office, "Protecting Intellectual Property Rights (IPR) Overseas", *United States Government*, last update October 2015.

[224] World Intellectual Property Organization, "What is WIPO?", *WIPO*, last update 2016, http://www.wipo.int/about-wipo/en/.

[225] Ibid.

Paris Convention for the Protection of Industrial Property

The Paris Convention was one of the first international agreements signed to protect intellectual property. The Paris Convention was signed in 1883 and since that time many revisions have taken place but the Paris Convention is still used today.[226] The Paris Convention protects "industrial property," which includes patents, trademarks and industrial designs. National treatment is an important aspect of the Paris Convention and this refers to the fact that each member state must provide protection to other member states, as if they were nationals.[227] The Paris Convention also includes right of priority, which means if someone who is a part of the Paris Convention files an application in a state that is also part of the Paris Convention, then the applicant has a certain time period to register in any of the other States and it will be deemed to be the first day of filing. [228]

Berne Convention

The Berne Convention was signed in 1886 and focuses on the protection of copyrights.[229] Like the Paris Convention, the Berne Convention agrees that all States must offer the same protection to other States as it does it own nationals. Also, the Berne Convention states that although each State is responsible for copyright protection in its own area, each State must provide minimum standards for protection.[230] The Berne Convention was also where it was decided that for a copyright to receive protection it does not have to been registered but must be in a "fixed" medium.[231]

Universal Copyright Convention (UCC)

The Universal Copyright Convention or the UCC was originally signed in 1952 but was later revised in 1971.[232] Its primary focus is the protection of copyrights internationally. The UCC was originally created because they deemed that the Berne Convention only benefited already economically productive countries and the main difference being the duration in which authors get to benefit from their work. [233] The Berne Convention states that it is the author's life plus a minimum of 50 years. The UCC however, differs only allowing the author's life plus 25 years.[234] Many states are part of the Berne Convention and the UCC. The United States is part of both but Canada is only part of the Berne Convention.[235]

Patent Cooperation Treaty (PCT)

The Patent Cooperation Treaty or the PCT was established in 1970 and is in use to help those seeking patent protection internationally.[236] This international patent system allows patent seekers to submit one application and receive protection in any of the 148 countries that are part of the treaty.[237] From the initial date of

---

[226] World Intellectual Property Organization, "Summary of the Paris Convention for the Protection of Industrial Property (1883)", *WIPO*, last update 2016, http://www.wipo.int/treaties/en/ip/paris/summary_paris.html.

[227] Ibid.

[228] Ibid.

[229] World Intellectual Property Organization, "Summary of the Berne Convention for the Protection of Literary and Artistic Works (1886)", *WIPO*, 2016, http://www.wipo.int/treaties/en/ip/berne/summary_berne.html.

[230] Ibid.

[231] Ibid.

[232] UNESCO, "Universal Copyright Convention", *United Nations Educational, Scientific, and Cultural Organization*, 2016, http://www.unesco.org/new/en/culture/themes/creativity/creative-industries/copyright/universal-copyright-convention/.

[233] Lloyd Duhaime, "Universal Copyright Convention", *Duhaime*, last update January 2012, http://www.duhaime.org/LegalResources/IntellectualProperty/LawArticle-591/Universal-Copyright-Convention.aspx.

[234] Ibid.

[235] Ibid.

[236] World Intellectual Property Organization, "PCT FAQS", *WIPO*, last update April 2015, http://www.wipo.int/pct/en/faqs/faqs.html.

[237] Ibid.

filing an application in any jurisdiction, the inventor has 12 months to file an application with the PCT.[238] The PCT is essentially composed of two different phases. The first phase is often referred to as the "international phase" and this is because at this time the application is considered singular and only reviewed by the PCT.[239] The PCT at this step of the process examines the application and conducts a search of prior art regarding the invention on an international scale.[240] Also, the search examines any documents that could disallow the patent in a particular jurisdiction. This step is advantageous to inventors because if the application passes the international phase, inventors can be sure that their application will most likely be accepted by individual jurisdictions. However, inventors have the option to have the PCT conduct a supplementary international search, which would further confirm that the application is firm.[241] Inventors have 19 months from the initial date of filing to have this optional supplementary search done.[242]

The second phase is considered the "national phase" and this is when the single application is then sent to individual jurisdictions.[243] Applicants have up to 30 months to decide on which foreign jurisdictions they would like to seek protection for their patents.[244] The PCT itself does not grant the patent, as "international patents" do not exist.[245] Each jurisdiction has the authority to approve the patent application for protection within its area based on its own patent requirements.

Appendix D

PCT Timeline

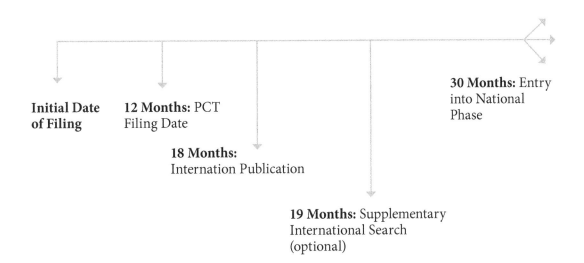

Initial Date of Filing

12 Months: PCT Filing Date

18 Months: Internation Publication

19 Months: Supplementary International Search (optional)

30 Months: Entry into National Phase

Doug Peterson

Rome Convention

The Rome Convention was signed in 1961 due to the increase in the use of technology in violating the rights of performers, producers of phonograms, and broadcasters. Essentially, performers' producers of phonograms and broadcasters were given the right to put limitations on the use of their works if

---

[238] World Intellectual Property Organization, "Summary of the Patent Cooperation Treaty (PCT) (1970), *WIPO*, (last update 2016), http://www.wipo.int/treaties/en/registration/pct/summary_pct.html.

[239] Ibid.

[240] Ibid.

[241] Ibid.

[242] Ibid.

[243] Ibid.

[244] Ibid.

[245] Ibid.

their consent was not already given.[246] For example if Sam was at a concert and decided to record the show and later air in on TV this would infringe on the performer's rights. The performer did not consent for their performance to be on TV.

Trade Related Aspects of Intellectual Property Rights (TRIPS)

TRIPS was established under the World Trade Organization (WTO) and is eligible for all members of the WTO. TRIPS is the most comprehensive international agreement in existence due to the fact that it provides minimum standards of protection for all forms of intellectual property.[247] TRIPS still follows the Paris Convention and the Berne Convention but it also fills in the gaps that these older Conventions were missing, such as the term of a patent.

Appendix E

Comparing and Contrasting the International Protection				
International Organizations, Treaties, Conventions	The Date it was Signed	Membership Amount	Types of Intellectual Property Protected	Importance
Paris Convention	March 30, 1883, last amended in 1979	176 parties	Patents, trademarks, industrial designs	National treatment, rights of priority
Berne Convention	September 9, 1886. Last amended in 1979	169 parties	Copyrights	National treatment, minimum standards, must be fixed
Uniform Copyright Convention	1952, last amended in 1971	100 parties	Copyrights	No longer significant
Patent Cooperation Treaty (PCT)	June 19, 1970, last modicifcation in 2001	148 parties	Patent	Able to submit one application to receive foreign protection
Rome Convention	October 26, 1961	92 parties	Copyright	Protects rights of performers, producers, and broadcasteres for unconsented works
TRIPS	January 1, 1995	158 parties	All Types	Minimum standards for all forms of IP

Doug Peterson

---

[246] World Intellectual Property Organization, "Summary of the Rome Convention for the Protection of performers, Producers of Phonograms and Broadcasting Organizations (1961)", *WIPO*, 2016, http://www.wipo.int/treaties/en/ip/rome/summary_rome.html.

[247] World Health Organization, "TRIPS", *WHO*, 2016, http://www.who.int/trade/glossary/story091/en/

Chapter Summary

Intellectual property is a bundle of rights given to a person to protect the expression of their ideas. Intellectual property is a broad term as it encompasses patents, trademarks, copyrights, industrial designs, and trade secrets. Each one of these forms of intellectual property possesses specific rights that protect them against unauthorized use.

Patents are inventions that are considered new, inventive, and useful. The patent holder is enabled to have a government-approved monopoly that lasts 20 years. Patents need to be registered in order to receive protection. Trademarks are words, symbols, or designs that are used to associate a product with a particular company. Trademarks are different from patents in that they do not have to be registered in order to receive protection. A trademark lasts 15 years but can also be renewed every 15 years after the date of filing. A copyright provides protection for author's original and creative works. These works can be literary, musical, dramatic, artistic, performances or broadcasts. Copyrights are similar to trademarks in that they don't have to be registered, as creation of the work in a tangible form is enough. Copyright protection in Canada last the span of the author's life plus 50 years. Industrial designs are like patents in that they need to be registered in order to have protection. Also, industrial designs protect the appearance of an invention rather than the functionality of it.

Intellectual property right owners are able to license or transfer their rights to other parties if they wish. They may choose to do this to reap economic benefits or to enter a foreign market with minimal risks.

Due to the fact that any person must register their property in each country they want protection, there are international treaties in place that help govern the use and protection of intellectual property abroad. These treaties and conventions enable equal treatment of intellectual property among all members.

Glossary

Assignment: When a party purchases the rights to intellectual property they also receive all the rights that pertain to the property.

Blurring: When a trademark is so similar to a famous trademark that the famous trademark is losing selling power because of confusion.

Copyright: Provides protection for authors pertaining to their works, which could include literary works, dramatic works, musical works, artistic works, sound recordings, broadcast transmissions and performances.

Cyber-Squatter: A person who obtains a domain name with no real intent to use it but are hoping to sell the rights to the domain name to the highest bidder or are trying to prevent their competitors from using it.

Design Patent: Similar to that of an "industrial design" as a design patent protects the rights of new, original ornamental designs that are featured on a good.

Distinguishing Guise: The distinct shape or packaging of an article of manufacture.

Domain Name: The name that is used as an Internet address.

Enabling Disclosure: The description must be clear, and concise so that a skilled person could make, use and sell the invention once the patent has expired.

Exclusive License: A license that enables the licensee to have all the rights pertaining to the property and prevents the licensor from using the property or licensing the rights to any other parties.

Fair Use Doctrine: Using copyrighted materials for the purpose of private study, research, education, reporting, satire, and parodies; without infringement occurring.

First Sale Doctrine: Once the copyrighted work is sold, the author's right to remuneration does not exist in potential future transactions.

Gray Market: When goods that are sold in foreign markets are then imported back into the domestic country and sold without the authorization of the intellectual property owner.

Industrial Design: The features of shape, configuration, pattern or ornament, or any combination of these features applied to a finished article.

Intellectual Property: The rights that are given to a person in order to protect the expression of their ideas.

Licensing: When an intellectual property owner gives limited permission to another party to use the rights of their intellectual property for a designated time period.

Moral Rights: Rights that are given to authors that prevent others from modifying their work in anyway without their permission.

Non-Traditional Trademark: A type of trademark that does not follow the requirements of trademark law because it contains elements that are not words, designs, or certifications.

Non-Exclusive License: The licensor retains the rights to the property and is able to license the property rights to as many parties as they see fit.

Patent: A government-approved monopoly that allows the patent holder the right to use, create, or sell its invention within a limited period of time.

Public Domain: Once intellectual property has expired they enter the public domain, so anyone can access and benefit from their use.

Service Mark: The distinguishing words, symbols, or designs that are used to associate a service offered by one person from that of others.

Solo License: The licensee receives all the rights pertaining to the property but the licensor is still able to make use of the property.

Specification: A step in the patent application process in which the inventor describes the invention so a skilled person could replicate the invention.

Tarnishment: When the trademark is linked to products of a lower quality and therefore the distinctiveness of the trademark is reduced.

Trademark: The distinguishing words, symbols, or designs that are used to associate a product or service offered by one person from that of others.

Trademark Dilution: The weakening of a well-known trademark's capacity to be distinguished from other goods or services.

Trade Name: The name that a business uses to represent itself.

Trade Secret: A valuable asset that provides a business with a competitive edge over its competitors due to the secretive nature of the information.

Utility Patent: Similar to the definition of a "patent" as a utility patent is the right for the patent holder to use, create, or sell its invention within a limited period of time.

Bibliography

Alexander, Ella, "YSL Closes Louboutin Court Case," *Vogue,* (last update October 2012), http://www.vogue.co.uk/news/2011/04/20/christian-louboutin -sues-yves-saint-laurent-for-red -sole-shoes.

American Broadcasting Cos., Inc., et al. v. Aereo, Inc., 134 S. Ct. 2498, October 2013. http://www.supremecourt.gov/opinions/13pdf/13-461_l537.pdf.

Anderton, James, "People's Court of China Rules in Favor of Honeywell over Local Manufacturer", *Engineering,* (last update September 2015), http://www.engineering.com/AdvancedManufacturing/ArticleID/10646/Peoples-Court-of-China-Rules-in-Favor-of-Honeywell-over-Local-Manufacturer.aspx.

Ballagh, Michele, "Intellectual Property: Who OWNS it?" *Ballagh Edward LLP,* (last update: October 2009), http://www.ballaghedward.ca/uploads/pub_uploads/intellectual-property-ownership-2-.pdf.

Bellis, Mary, "Copyright Notice and the Use of the Copyright Symbol," (last update December 2014), http://inventors.about.com/od/copyrights/a/CopyrightNotice.htm.

Bereskin and Parr, "Industrial Design," *Bereskin & Parr LLP,* (2016), http://www.bereskinparr.com/Section/About-Intellectual-Property/Industrial-Design.

____."Remedies for Trademark and Copyright Infringement in Canada," *Bereskin & Parr LLP,* (last update march 2009), http://www.bereskinparr.com/Article/id76.

Best Cellars, Inc. v. wine Made Simple, Inc., 320 F. Supp. 2d 60 (S.D.N.Y. 2003), March 2003. http://law.justia.com/cases/federal/district-courts/FSupp2/320/60/2468888/.

Bilski v. Kappos, 561 U.S. 593 [2010], 2010. http://www.supremecourt.gov/opinions/09pdf/08-964.pdf.

Bitlaw, "Works Unprotected by Copyright Law," *Bitlaw,* (2015), http://www.bitlaw.com/copyright/unprotected.html.

Borenstein, Rowena and Donald Cameron, "Key Aspects of IP License Agreements", *Ogilvy, Renault,* 2003, http://www.jurisdiction.com/lic101.pdf.

Burkinshaw, Jonathan and Justine Wiebe, "Canada," *World Trademark Review,* no. 20 (2009): 1-3, accessed February 1, 2016, http://www.bereskinparr.com/files/file/docs/tm_wtr_tradedresspro_jw_jb_0809.pdf

Burkinshaw, Jonathan, and Susan Keri, "Non-traditional marks in Canada," *Intellectual Property Magazine,* March 2011, http://www.bereskinparr.com/files/file/docs/IPM_Mar_2011-SK_JB.pdf.

Canada (Attorney General) v. Amazon.com, Inc., 2011 FCA 328 (CanLI), November 2011.

Canadian Intellectual Property Office, "A guide to copyright," *Government of Canada,* (last update December 2015), http://www.cipo.ic.gc.ca/eic/site/cipoInternet-Internetopic.nsf/eng/h_wr02281.html.

____."A guide to industrial designs," *Government of Canada,* (last update February 2016), http ://www.ic.gc.ca/eic/site/cipointernet-internetopic.nsf/eng/h_wr02300.html?Open&wt_src=cipo-id-main&wt_cxt=learn#understandingID.

_____. "A Guide to Patents", *Government of Canada,* (Quebec: last update Jan 2016) https://www.ic.gc.ca/eic/site/cipointernet-internetopic.nsf/eng/h_wr03652.html#understandingPatents.

_____. "A guide to trademarks," *Government of Canada,* (last update December 2015), http://www.ic.gc.ca/eic/site/cipointernet-internetopic.nsf/eng/h_wr02360.html.

_____. "Protect your innovation", *Government of Canada,* (last update January 2016), http://www.ic.gc.ca/eic/site/cipointernet-internetopic.nsf/eng/wr03586.html#secret.

_____. "What is a patent?", *Government of Canada,* (Quebec: last update Dec 2015) http://www.ic.gc.ca/eic/site/cipointernet-internetopic.nsf/eng/wr03716.html?Open&wt_src=cipo-patent-main.

_____. "What is a trade secret?" *Government of Canada,* (last update December 2015), https://www.ic.gc.ca/eic/site/cipointernet-internetopic.nsf/eng/wr03987.html.

_____. "What's in a Name?" *Government of Canada,* (last update June 2015), https://www.ic.gc.ca/eic/site/cipointernet-internetopic.nsf/eng/wr00058.html.

Canadian Internet Policy and Public Interest Clinic, "Copyright Law", *(*last update September 2008), http://www.copyright.gov/circs/circ15a.pdf.

"Covenants' Not to Compete in Intellectual Property Transactions", *Lott & Friedland,* accessed February 2016, http://www.lfiplaw.com/articles/convenants_not_to_compete_in_ip_transactions.htm.

Creative Commons, "Attribution-NonCommercial-ShareAlike 2.5 Canada," *Creative Commons,* (2016), https://creativecommons.org/licenses/by-nc-sa/2.5/ca/.

Davis, Ryan, "Victor's Little Secret Strikes Out in Trademark Case," *Law 360,* (last update May 2010), http://www.law360.com/articles/169784/victor-s-little-secret-strikes-out-in-trademark-case.

Dolan, Christopher, "IP: Gray market goods spell trouble for companies", *Inside Counsel,* last update August 2011, http://www.insidecounsel.com/2011/08/23/ip-gray-market-goods-spell-trouble-for-companies.

Duhaime, Lloyd, "Universal Copyright Convention", *Duhaime,* last update January 2012, http://www.duhaime.org/LegalResources/IntellectualProperty/LawArticle-591/Universal-Copyright-Convention.aspx.

European IPR Helpdesk, "Commercializing Intellectual Property: License Agreements", *European Union,* 2013, https://www.iprhelpdesk.eu/sites/default/files/newsdocuments/Licence_agreements_0.pdf

European Patent Office, "Enabling disclosures," *European Union,* (last update January 2015), http://www.epo.org/law-practice/legal-texts/html/guidelines/e/g_iv_2.htm.

Feist Publications, Inc. v. Rural telephone Service Co., 499 U.S. 340, 1991. https://www.law.cornell.edu/copyright/cases/499_US_340.htm.

Gowlings, "Business Method Patents: How Prepared are You?" *Gowlings Law Firm,* (2012) http://www.gowlings.com/knowledgeCentre/publicationPDFs/Business-Method-Patents-How-Prepared-are-You.pdf.

Grainger, Megan, and Cynthia Rowden, *"Canada," Bereskinparr LLP,* (last update December 2008), http://www.bereskinparr.com/files/file/docs/tm_wtmr_cr_mlg1208.pdf.

Harvard Law, "The Requirements for Copyright Protection*," Harvard Law School,* (2016), http://cyber.law.harvard.edu/cx/The_Requirements_for_Copyright_Protection-JA.

____. "Moral Rights*," Harvard Law School,* (last update March 1998), https://cyber.law.harvard.edu/property/library/moralprimer.html.

HG, "is it Illegal to Buy Counterfeit or Knockoff Designer Goods?" (last update 2016), https://www.hg.org/article.asp?id=31573.

Honeywell, "Our Company", *Honeywell,* 2016, http://honeywell.com/About/Pages/our-company.aspx.

____."Press Releases", *Honeywell,* 2016, https://honeywell.com/News/Pages/Honeywell-Wins-Trademark-Battle-Before-Chinas-Supreme-Court.aspx.

Innovation, Science and Economic Development Canada, "About Copyright," (last update November 2013), https://www.ic.gc.ca/eic/site/icgc.nsf/eng/07415.html#p3.

____. "Choosing a name ..." (last update June 2011), https://www.ic.gc.ca/eic/site/cd-dgc.nsf/eng/cs01191.html.

International Trademark Association, "Nontraditional Trademarks," *International Trademark Association,* (last update 2016), http://www.inta.org/TrademarkBasics/FactSheets/Pages/Non-traditionalTrademarksFactSheet.aspx.

____. "Trademark Dilution*," International Trademark Association,* (last update April 2015), http://www.inta.org/TrademarkBasics/FactSheets/Pages/TrademarkDilution.aspx.

Katul, Ziad and Zimmerman, Colleen, "Canada: Patent Ownership in Canada," *Borden Ladner Gervais LLP,* (last updated April 2006) http://www.mondaq.com/canada/x/39282/Patent/Patent+Ownership+in+Canada.

Kimble et al. v. Marvel Entertainment, LLC 576 U.S., 135 S. Ct. 2401 (2015), October 2015, http://www.supremecourt.gov/opinions/14pdf/13-720_jiel.pdf.

Kozlowski and Company, "Patents Frequently Asked Questions (FAQS)," *Kozlowski $ Company,* (2015), http://www.kozlowskiandcompany.com/patent-faqs.html#7.

MaRs, "Trademark infringement and the Trade-marks Act in Canada," (last update July 2011), https://www.marsdd.com/mars-library/trademark-infringement/.

McKeown, John,"What is a Distinguishing Guise?" *GSNH LLP,* (August 2013), http://www.gsnh.com/what-is-a-distinguishing-guise/.

Moseley v. V Secret Catalogue, Inc., (01-1015) 537 U.S. 418, (2003), 259 F. 3d 464, 2003, *Cornell Law School,* (last update March 4, 2003), https://www.law.cornell.edu/supct/html/01-1015.ZO.html.

National Paralegal College, "Remedies for Patent Infringement," *National Paralegal College,* (2016), http://nationalparalegal.edu/public_documents/courseware_asp_files/patents/Patents2/Remedies.asp.

Nelligan, O'Brien, Payne, "Trade Secrets" *Nelligan LLP*, (last update May 2012), http://www.nelligan.ca/e/tradesecretswhataretheyandhowcanyouprotectthemfromunauthorizeddisclosure-anduse.cfm.

Nissan, Uzi, "We've Been Sued," *Nissan Computer*, (last update 2009), http://www.nissan.com/Lawsuit/The_Story.php.

Nolo Law Firm, "Who owns Patent Rights? Employer or Inventor?" *Nolo Law Firm*, (2015), http://www.nolo.com/legal-encyclopedia/who-owns-patent-rights-employer-inventor.html.

Oyen Wiggs Green & Mutala LPP, "Domain Names," *Oyen Wiggs Green & Mutala LPP*, (2016), http://www.patentable.com/what-we-do/domain-names/.

____. "The Copyright Modernization Act: Big Changes to Copyright Law in Canada," *Oyen, Wiggs, Green and Mutala LLP*, (last update March 2013), http://www.patentable.com/the-copyright-modernization-act-big-changes-to-copyright-law-in-canada/.

Parliament of Canada, "Chapter 20," *Government of Canada*, (2016), http://www.parl.gc.ca/HousePublications/Publication.aspx?DocId=5697419&File=45#7.

Peterson, Gwen, "Patent Licensing Considerations", *Association of Corporate Counsel*, last update August 2013, http://www.acc.com/legalresources/quickcounsel/qcplc.cfm.

Philip Kerr, *"Computer software Law in Canada,"* (2015), http://users.trytel.com/~pbkerr/computer.html.

____."Copyright Law in Canada," (2016), http://users.trytel.com/~pbkerr/copyright.html.

Pranata, Anthony, *"Posting Videos on YouTube – Copyright Infringement or Not? The "Mash-Up" Provision,"* *Mondaq*, (last update June 2014), http://www.mondaq.com/canada/x/320054/Copyright/Posting+Videos+On+Youtube+Copyright+Infringement+Or+Not.

Queensland Government, "What are some examples of copyright works?" *Queensland Government*, (last update 2015), https://www.business.qld.gov.au/business/support-tools-grants/tools/intellectual-property-info-kit/browse/copyright/examples.

Ridout & Maybee LLP, "Trade-marks," *Ridout & Maybee LLP*, (2016), http://www.ridoutmaybee.com/Page.asp?PageID=924&ContentID=685.

Ryerson University, "Copyright Basics," *Ryerson University*, (2016), http://library.ryerson.ca/copyright/resources/general-copyright-information/copyright-basics/.

Sim, Rich, "The First Sale Doctrine," *Nolo Law Firm*, (2015), http://www.nolo.com/legal-encyclopedia/the-first-sale-doctrine.html.

Smart & Biggar, "First-to-File comes to America: What innovative Canadian companies should know," *Smart & Biggar Law Firm*, (Toronto: March 2013), http://www.smart-biggar.ca/en/articles_detail.cfm?news_id=729.

Stanford University, "Copyright Registration and Enforcement," *Stanford University*, (2015), http://fairuse.stanford.edu/overview/faqs/registration-and-enforcement/.

Supreme Court Judgments, "Monsanto Canada Inc. v. Schmeiser, [2004] 1 S.C.R. 902, 2004 SCC 34", *Supreme Court*, (Ottawa, last update May 2004), paragraph 133, http://scc-csc.lexum.com/scc-csc/scc-csc/en/item/2147/index.do.

Techform Products Ltd. V. Wolda, [2001] CanLII 8604, October 1, 2001. http://www.canlii.org/en/on/onca/doc/2001/2001canlii8604/2001canlii8604.html.

Teva Canada Ltd. v. Pfizer Canada Inc., 2012 SCC 60, [2012] 3 S.C.R. 625, November 2012. https://scc-csc.lexum.com/scc-csc/scc-csc/en/item/12679/index.do.

Theriault, Mario, "Have an Invention? We can help", *Theriault & Company,* (New Brunswick: accessed Jan 2016) http://www.patentway.com/faqs.

Tomkins, Don, "A Brief Introduction to Patents and Related Intellectual Property Rights" (presentation, University of Alberta School of Business, Edmonton, AB, November 14, 2008).

Tysver, Daniel, *Obtaining Copyright Protection, Bitlaw,* (2015), http://www.bitlaw.com/copyright/obtaining.html.

____."Rights Granted under Copyright Law," *Bitlaw,* (2015), http://www.bitlaw.com/copyright/scope.html.

UBC, "Creative Commons Guide," *UBC,* (2016), http://copyright.ubc.ca/guidelines-and-resources/support-guides/creative-commons/.

____."Bill C-11: The Copyright Modernization Act," *UBC,* (2016), http://copyright.ubc.ca/guidelines-and-resources/support-guides/bill-c-11-the-copyright-modernization-act/#pufde.

UNESCO, "Universal Copyright Convention", *United Nations Educational, Scientific, and Cultural Organization,* 2016, http://www.unesco.org/new/en/culture/themes/creativity/creative-industries/copyright/universal-copyright-convention/.

United States Copyright Office, "Duration of Copyright," *Government of the U.S.* (last update August 2011), http://www.copyright.gov/circs/circ15a.pdf.

United States Patent and Trademark Office, "Allowance and Term of Design Patent," *Government of the U.S.* (last update November 2015), http://www.uspto.gov/web/offices/pac/mpep/s1505.html.

____. "About Patent Infringement?" *Government of the U.S.* (January 2015), http://www.uspto.gov/patents-maintaining-patent/patent-litigation/about-patent-infringement.

____."Definition of a Design," *Government of the U.S.* (last update November, 2015), http://www.uspto.gov/web/offices/pac/mpep/s1502.html.

____."General Information Concerning Patents", *Government of the U.S.* (Virginia: last update Oct 2014) http://www.uspto.gov/patents-getting-started/general-information-concerning-patents.

____."General FAQs," *Government of the U.S.* (last update December 2014), http://www.uspto.gov/learning-and-resources/general-faqs.

____."How do I register a U.S. trademark?" *Government of the U.S.* (2016), http://www.stopfakes.gov/learn-about-ip/trademarks/how-do-i-register.

____."Interim Guidance for Determining Subject Matter Eligibility for Process Claims in View of Bilski v. Kappos,"*Government of the U.S.,* (June 2010) http://www.uspto.gov/sites/default/files/patents/law/exam/bilski_guidance_27jul2010.pdf.

____."Protecting Intellectual Property Rights (IPR) Overseas", *United States Government,* last update October 2015.

____."Provisional Application for Patent," *Government of the U.S.* (last update January 2015), http://www.uspto.gov/patents-getting-started/patent-basics/types-patent-applications/provisional-application-patent.

World Health Organization, "TRIPS", *WHO,* 2016, http://www.who.int/trade/glossary/story091/en/.

World Intellectual Property Organization, "Frequently Asked Questions: Internet Domain Names," (last update 2016), http://www.wipo.int/amc/en/center/faq/domains.html#7.

____, "Patenting Software", *WIPO,* (Switzerland: Accessed Jan 2016), http://www.wipo.int/sme/en/documents/software_patents_fulltext.html.

____. "PCT FAQS", *WIPO,* last update April 2015, http://www.wipo.int/pct/en/faqs/faqs.html.

____. "Summary of the Berne Convention for the Protection of Literary and Artistic Works (1886)", *WIPO,* 2016, http://www.wipo.int/treaties/en/ip/berne/summary_berne.html.

____. "Summary of the Paris Convention for the Protection of Industrial Property (1883)", *WIPO,* last update 2016, http://www.wipo.int/treaties/en/ip/paris/summary_paris.html.

____. "Summary of the Patent Cooperation Treaty (PCT) (1970), *WIPO,* (last update 2016), http://www.wipo.int/treaties/en/registration/pct/summary_pct.html.

____. "Summary of the Rome Convention for the Protection of performers, Producers of Phonograms and Broadcasting Organizations (1961)", *WIPO,* 2016, http://www.wipo.int/treaties/en/ip/rome/summary_rome.html.

____. "The Global Impact of the America Invents Act", *WIPO,* (December 2011), http://www.wipo.int/wipo_magazine/en/2011/06/article_0002.html.

____. "What is WIPO?", *WIPO,* last update 2016, http://www.wipo.int/about-wipo/en/.

Zvulony & Co, "What are Moral Rights?" *Zyulong & Co.* (last update December 2010), http://zvulony.ca/2010/articles/intellectual-property-law/copyright-law/moral-rights-author-rights/.

Zvulony, Gil, "Who Owns Copyright at Work?" *Zvulony & Co.* (last update December 2010), http://zvulony.ca/2010/articles/intellectual-property-law/copyright-law/copyright-at-work/.

CHAPTER 8

Tax

Learning Objectives

After reading this chapter, you will have an understanding of:

1. The various purposes of taxation
2. How taxation differs across various streams of income
3. How the application of tax can differ based on the choices of jurisdictions around the world
4. How different jurisdictions determine residence in regards to taxation
5. Why international tax treaties are a key aspect of international business
6. How taxes can be avoided or reduced using various strategies
7. Why electronic commerce presents a unique and important issue for taxation

Introduction

Why do states tax? Often, the concept of tax law is viewed purely as a form of revenue generation for a governing body. This is an important aspect of tax law as governments require funding for various projects. But it is important to recognize that tax policy can be used to have an impact on the behavior of those that are subject to it. Consider how a *sin tax*, for example an additional taxation on alcohol, impacts the behavior of a group of people. These groups are more likely to spend their money elsewhere because of the increased

Figure 8.1

cost, which limits the negative activities that can occur due to alcohol consumption. Tax breaks can also be used to invoke specific behaviors, such as promoting a particular investment.[1] Therefore, tax law can be used as a tool by governments to implement specific social policies. Additionally, tax law is used by governments for the redistribution of income[2] by selecting where tax revenue is spent based on the needs of society. It will be important to keep in mind how tax law is a tool to balance various needs as we continue through this chapter.

Taxable Entities

Around the world, the entities that are taxable are broken up into four major categories: individuals, corporations, partnerships, and trusts. Each of these categories have their own guidelines for taxation and can be unique to a specific country based on legislation and regulations that may have been developed over time.

Taxation

Globally, taxation generally is accomplished by two separate methods: "Direct Taxation" such as customs duties and sales type taxes which are usually calculated as a percentage of the value of a good or service. "Indirect Taxation" such as income taxes which are usually calculated on the income earned during a given period by a taxpayer. Some jurisdictions, for example the Cayman Islands only levy direct taxes whereas most developed countries levy both direct and indirect taxes.

CaseyMartin/Shutterstock.com

Figure 8.2

Taxation and Income Levels

Taxes usually are based on the amount of money that a person earns or receives over the course of an entire year. There are two major systems that are employed worldwide: a progressive tax or a flat tax. Many countries use a combination of the two systems, but we will focus on the basics of each.

A **progressive tax** is usually based on *tax brackets*, which are levels of income defined by government. Each bracket has its own tax rate and these rates increase as the income level increases.[3] Progressive systems rely on the understanding that higher-earning persons have to ability to pay more taxes. For example, Australia's government used the following rates in 2015–2016.[4]

Another important feature of a progressive system is the industry created by the system itself. A progressive system creates jobs for lawyers, accountants and governments dedicate entire departments

[1] Canada Revenue Agency,. 2016. "Line 208 – RRSP And PRPP Deduction". *cra-arc.gc.ca*. http://www.cra-arc.gc.ca/tx/ndvdls/tpcs/ncm-tx/rtrn/cmpltng/ddctns/lns206-236/208/menu-eng.html.

[2] Vern, Krishna. 2006. *The Fundamentals of Canadian Income Tax*. 9th ed. Toronto: Thomson Carswell. 4.

[3] Ibid., 1686.

[4] Australian Government. 2016. "Individual Income Tax Rates | Australian Taxation Office". *ato.gov.au*. https://www.ato.gov.au/rates/individual-income-tax-rates/.

Income Bracket	Rate
0-$18,200	No Taxation
$18,201-$37,000	19 cents for each dollar earned over $18,200
$37,001-$80,000	$3,572 plus 32.5 cents for each dollar earned over $37,000
$80,001-$180,000	$17,547 plus 37 cents for each dollar earned over $80,000
$180,001+	$53,547 plus 45 cents for each dollar earned over $180,000

Source: Courtesy Doug Peterson

Figure 8.3

to tax collection. For example, in Canada the *Canada Revenue Agency* is responsible for tax laws on behalf of the Government of Canada and also is in charge of social programs related to Canada's tax system.[5] The complex nature of progressive systems requires experts in the field. It has been posited that without a progressive system there would be less work involved in training staff, collection of the tax and the government would be able to simplify the entire process, likely resulting in the loss of jobs of many employees otherwise required.

A true **flat tax** system is defined by a single tax rate that is applied to all persons with minimal deductions, regardless of their level of income.[6] It holds an advantage in that it is less complex and easier to implement compared to a progressive system. A flat tax system encourages initiative or taking economic risk as higher earning persons are not penalized for the reward of their high risk-taking, their hard work, their initiative, and their potential higher income. A flat tax system also discourages evasion, as there is less incentive to evade tax. Lastly, it is considered a fairer system when incomes fluctuate from year to year, and to single income families as the major income earner is not exposed to the same challenges of a progressive system.[7] There are variations of the flat tax system that have been applied internationally, but they all are based on the same general principle that all persons should pay, proportionately, the same amount of tax.

Progressive Tax	Flat Tax
Key Advantages	Key Advantages
• Based on an individual's ability to pay • Creates an industry	• Simple and easy to implement • Does not kill initiative • Fairer if income fluctuates • Fairer to single-income families

Source: Courtesy Doug Peterson

Figure 8.4

[5] Canada Revenue Agency. 2014. "About The Canada Revenue Agency (CRA)". *cra-arc.gc.ca*. http://www.cra-arc.gc.ca/gncy/menu-eng.html.

[6] Krishna, 1590.

[7] Meehan, Colette. 2016. "Pros & Cons of A Flat Tax". *smallbusiness.chron.com*. http://smallbusiness.chron.com/pros-cons-flat-tax-4210.html.

Basic Charging Provision

All persons are considered legal entities and therefore are designated as "taxpayers". In law, the term person means both an individual and various types of entities, that can include corporations, partnerships, cities, counties, countries, trusts, foundations and associations. An **individual** may be a resident, non-resident, or a part-time resident of a country and different tax laws apply for these types of individuals depending on the jurisdiction.[8] A **corporation** is also a legal entity and must pay tax.[9] A corporation can also be identified as a resident or non-resident depending on how it was established and operates. Finally, trusts are also a taxable entity. A **trust** is created when the legal title to property is contractually administered to or for the benefit of a person or persons. A trust itself is not a legal entity but some countries require it to be taxed as a separate person.[10]

A *tax year* is defined as an annual accounting period during which time a person is required to record and report their income and expenses.[11] However, the term "annual" has a different meaning for different persons. Individuals may have to file their government tax returns based on their employment income on a different date than a corporation must file their tax return.

Taxable income is a measurement of the taxable base of a person. It can be described as the gross income of a person minus deductions, exemptions or other adjustments to which that person is eligible for in a given tax year.[12]

Income Tax Bases

There are many instances where more than one country can tax a corporation, an individual or a transaction. To determine which country has priority, countries enter into **tax treaties**. Tax treaties are designed to prevent double taxation as well as preventing instances of tax evasion.[13] In international law, a tax treaty usually trumps local tax laws.

Income tax relies on three main qualities of a person. These three bases are source, nationality, and residency.

Source principle is based on the fact that a government can only tax a person's income from sources within their territorial jurisdiction.[14] For example, if a Canadian gives up Canadian residence and moves to Australia and begins working for an Australian company, the Canadian government does not have the jurisdiction to tax that person's employment income. Income accrued or derived from local sources commonly includes:

1. Income derived from property located within the country
2. Income derived from any trade or profession carried on through any agency or branch within the country
3. Income derived from local employment

---

[8] Krishna, 100.

[9] Ibid., 110.

[10] Canadian Bankers Association. 2015. "FATCA And The Canada-U.S. Intergovernmental Agreement (IGA): Information For Clients". *cba.ca*. http://www.cba.ca/en/consumer-information/40-banking-basics/597-fatca-and-the-canada-us-intergovernmental-agreement-iga-information-for-clients-.

[11] Internal Revenue Service,. 2016. "Tax Years". *irs.gov*. https://www.irs.gov/Businesses/Small-Businesses-&-Self-Employed/Tax-Years.

[12] Investopedia. 2003. "Taxable Income Definition | Investopedia". *Investopedia*. http://www.investopedia.com/terms/t/taxableincome.asp

[13] Canada Revenue Agency. 2013. "Tax Treaties". *cra-arc.gc.ca*. http://www.cra-arc.gc.ca/treaties/.

[14] Money Control. 2016. "Source Principle Of Taxation". *moneycontrol.com*. http://www.moneycontrol.com/glossary/taxes/source-principletaxation_3099.html.

Under the **nationality principle,** governments have the right to tax any *worldwide income* that is earned by its "nationals", regardless of where they reside.[15] For individuals, this means the country in which they are a citizen determines their nationality. Where a corporation, or other legal entity, is incorporated or formed determines the nationality of that company. For example, if a company is incorporated in the United States, but operates mainly in India, this company is deemed a U.S. national, and is subject to taxation by the United States government. Currently, the United States uses nationality as its guiding principle for taxation, as well as Eretria.

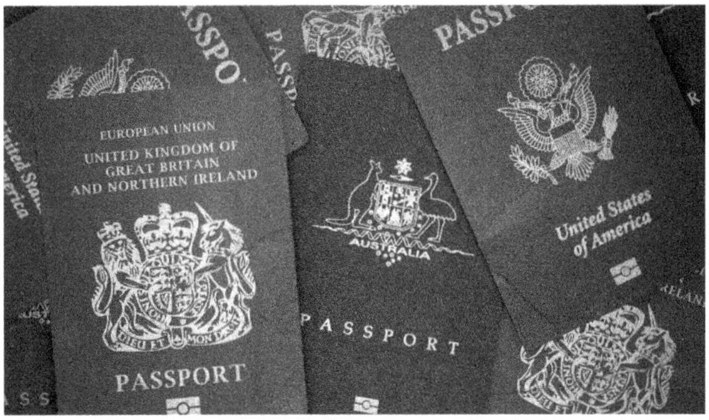

Figure 8.5

Residency principle outlines that governments tax the worldwide income of persons who are legally residing within the territories of that government.[16] **Residents** are those who have been recognized by the respective government of a country based on that country's definition of income tax residence. The definition of what constitutes income tax residence varies greatly from country to country. Income Tax residency for an individual is normally determined based on one or more of the following tests:

1. *Objective Test*: Looks at the length of time an individual resides within a state's borders. The time frame for calculation and the period used for calculation varies with each State. Most states use the 6 month, or 183 day rule.

2. *Subjective Test*: Considers the intent of the individual to make a place their permanent docile or household.

3. *Declarative Test*: Measures whether or not an individual meets the admission criteria.

4. *Closer Connection Test*: Measures the place at which an individual's economic and social ties are the greatest.

Figure 8.6

Like an individual, the residency of a corporation is determined by different tests. The United States, for example, almost uniquely looks to the country where the company was *incorporated* to determine its residency. However, for most **common law and civil law** countries, where the company is *managed* determines its residency. See the case brief for *De Beers Consolidated Mines Ltd. v. Howe (1906)*[17] as an example. This distinction has set the precedent for cases for common law jurisdictions all around the world.

---

[15] US Legal. 2016. "Nationality Principle Law & Legal Definition". *definitions.uslegal.com*. http://definitions.uslegal.com/n/nationality-principle/.

[16] Money Control. 2016. "Residence Principle Of Taxation". *moneycontrol.com*. http://www.moneycontrol.com/glossary/taxes/residence-principletaxation_3065.html.

[17] De Beers Consolidated Mines Ltd v. Howe (Surveyor of Taxes). 1906. AC 455.

De Beers Consolidated Mines Ltd v. Howe (1906)[x]

Facts:

In the case of *De Beers Consolidated Mines Ltd. V. Howe (1906)*, the court was tasked with ruling on the residence of the corporation for tax purposes. The head office of De Beers Consolidated Mines Ltd. was in Kimberly, South Africa and general meetings were held there. Some of De Beers' directors and governors lived in Kimberly and some of the director's meetings were also held in Kimberly. The majority of the directors and governors lived in England. Decisions made in London controlled the negotiations of contracts with diamond syndicates and set company policy. As well, matters that needed to be determined by the majority of directors were made in the London offices. The directors in the Kimberley office were responsible for the wages and materials of the mines in South Africa, while the London office was responsible for all other matters of expenditure.

Issue:

Whether or not De Beers should have been considered a resident of South Africa or the United Kingdom for income tax purposes.

Decision:

The court concluded that De Beers Consolidated Mines Ltd. was a resident of England for the purposes of taxation.

Reasons:

The court ruled that the test of residence for a corporation is not where it is registered as a corporation, but where central management and control of the company actually abides. Chief operations of the company were controlled, directed, and managed from the office in London. Therefore, the company is a resident of the United Kingdom.

Figure 8.7

Certain persons are exempted from taxation based on international tax treaties. This includes foreign governments as well as their associated diplomats but usually not business owned by foreign governments or their diplomats. As an example, a French diplomat may be working in South Africa on a 1-year project for their government, but the diplomat will not be subject to income taxation by South Africa because of their role. International organizations and their respective personnel generally are exempted from taxation. However, different host states may have different tax policies regarding international organizations.

These three principles can be used in conjunction to impose taxation. Source principle is usually regarded as the priority rule when a government is deciding on whether to impose taxation on a person, therefore, if an income stream does fit into one of the categories outlined by this principle, it will usually be deemed taxable, regardless of where it fits into the other two principles.

---

[x] De Beers Consolidated Mines Ltd v. Howe (Surveyor of Taxes). 1906. AC 455.

Income Categories

Income is broken up into various categories and each of these categories can be taxed in its own way.

Personal or **business income** is the earnings or profits made by an individual or by a business. For an individual, this would be the amount of money that they earn as an an employee or as a contractor. For a business this would be the net profit that they earn from sales or services or other forms of revenue usually adjusted for their costs of operations.

Capital gains income is the increase in value of an underlying asset owned or invested by a person.[18] For example, if an individual bought one stock for $50, and

Figure 8.8

then sold it when the stock price rose to $55 dollars, the $5 increase is considered a capital gain and would be subject to taxation. In a majority of countries, capital gains income is taxed at the same rate as all other types of income, but some countries choose to use a unique rate often referred to as a *Capital Gains Tax* (CGT).[19]

Dividends are payments received from companies by shareholders in respect of their shareholding in that company. The taxation of dividends can be very specific and we will be covering this topic later in this chapter.

Residence of Individuals

Different countries around the world have different ways to determine the residency of an individual. For example, the average Canadian individual whose job, family, dwelling place and other personal property are all in Canada, would clearly be considered a Canadian resident and would be liable for Canadian taxation on their worldwide income. These factors are considered on a case by case basis.[20]

As mentioned earlier, the United States uses nationality as its guiding principle for taxation. Therefore, a U.S. national is still liable for U.S. taxation even if they do not have

Figure 8.9

---

18 Krishna, 1507.
19 Ibid.
20 Canada Revenue Agency. 2016. "Determining Your Residency Status". *cra-arc.gc.ca*. http://www.cra-arc.gc.ca/tx/nnrs-dnts/cmmn/rsdncy-eng.html.

Figure 8.10

any substantial ties to the United States. Additionally, the U.S. considers someone a resident, whether or not they are a citizen, if they pass the *green card test*.[21] The green card test simply means that the individual has been given legal permission by the U.S. government to be a permanent resident.

Temporary Absences

Taxation laws are required to outline the requirements for individuals who will be travelling between countries over the course of the tax year. That is why governments use residential ties as a way to measure whether an individual should be considered a true resident. As an example, the Canadian government considers if an individual has any *basic residential ties*: a dwelling, a spouse or common-law partner, or a dependent.[22] The Canadian government may additionally consider *secondary residential ties*: personal property such as a car, social ties, economic ties such as Canadian bank accounts, government issued identification, vehicle registration, a Canadian passport, or membership to a Canadian union or professional association.[23] Most countries look at similar factors when facing a temporary absence.

If some residential ties are retained during a temporary absence, the Canadian government will consider other factors. The *intent* of the absent individual, the *frequency* of their visits back to Canada, and their residential ties *outside* of Canada are all considered as additional factors.[24]

Part year residence occurs when a person becomes a resident or gives up their residency during a tax year.[25] Someone may choose to immigrate to Canada halfway through the tax year and therefore they are not liable for a full year of income tax. In these cases, the worldwide income of the individual is pro-rated for the amount of time out of the year they are a resident. If someone becomes a resident on September 1st, only their worldwide income earned from September 1st to December 31st is liable. The initial date of residency is usually based on standard immigration rules such as when significant ties are established.[26] The departure date of residency often includes a few requirements. For Canada, the departure date for an individual is the latest of: their own departure date, the departure date of their spouse and dependents, and the establishment of a new residence.[27] For example, if a Canadian leaves on September 1st and moves into his new home in England on September 2nd, but his wife and children do not leave Canada until October 1st, depending on the particular facts it could be the earlier date of September 2nd or the later date of October 1st.

21 Internal Revenue Service. 2015. "Alien Residency - Green Card Test". *irs.gov*. https://www.irs.gov/Individuals/International-Taxpayers/Alien-Residency---Green-Card-Test.

22 Canada Revenue Agency. 2016. "Determining Your Residency Status". *cra-arc.gc.ca*. http://www.cra-arc.gc.ca/tx/nnrs-dnts/cmmn/rsdncy-eng.html.

23 Canada Revenue Agency,. 2016. "Determining Your Residency Status". *cra-arc.gc.ca*. http://www.cra-arc.gc.ca/tx/nnrs-dnts/cmmn/rsdncy-eng.html.

24 Ibid.

25 Canada Revenue Agency. 2016. "Leaving Canada (Emigrants)". *cra-arc.gc.ca*. http://www.cra-arc.gc.ca/tx/nnrsdnts/ndvdls/lvng-eng.html.

26 Canada Revenue Agency. 2016. "Determining Your Residency Status". *cra-arc.gc.ca*. http://www.cra-arc.gc.ca/tx/nnrs-dnts/cmmn/rsdncy-eng.html

27 Canada Revenue Agency. 2016. "Leaving Canada (Emigrants)". *cra-arc.gc.ca*. http://www.cra-arc.gc.ca/tx/nnrsdnts/ndvdls/lvng-eng.html.

Deemed Residents

Most countries have identified situations that regularly arise for individuals that are deemed residents in order to try and simplify the system. Continuing with Canada as an example, there are various categories that the Canadian government has created, including:

Figure 8.11

1. A temporary stay in Canada for 183 days or more.[28]

2. Members of the Canadian Armed Forces stationed outside of Canada.[29]

3. Ambassadors, ministers, officers, and other similar roles *provided* they were residents immediately prior to appointment.[30]

4. Individuals performing services under prescribed international development assistance program of the Government of Canada, *provided* they were residents for 3 months prior to beginning this service.[31]

183 Day Rule

The *183 Day Rule* is an important tool used by a majority of countries around the world for taxation purposes. If an individual stays in a country for an aggregate total of at least 183 days, they will be deemed to have been resident in that country for more than half of the year in question and face additional tax liabilities.[32] Days that should be considered when making the calculation include:

1. Days of arrival or departure

2. Partial days

3. Weekends

4. National and regular holidays

5. Short breaks

6. Days of sickness (unless the sickness prevents the individual from leaving and he or she otherwise would have qualified for an exemption)

*Note, however, the day count method of calculation varies country by country

Where the 183 Day Rule differs, however, is how the additional tax liabilities are calculated. In Canada, if an individual takes up Canadian residency for 183 days or more, they are liable for Canadian tax

---

[28] Canada Revenue Agency. 2016. "Deemed Residents". *cra-arc.gc.ca*. http://www.cra-arc.gc.ca/tx/nnrsdnts/ndvdls/dmd-eng.html.

[29] Canada Revenue Agency. 2016. "Government Employees Outside Canada". *cra-arc.gc.ca*. http://www.cra-arc.gc.ca/tx/nnrsdnts/ndvdls/gvt_mpl-eng.html.

[30] Ibid.

[31] Canada Revenue Agency. 2016. "Government Employees Outside Canada". *cra-arc.gc.ca*. http://www.cra-arc.gc.ca/tx/nnrsdnts/ndvdls/gvt_mpl-eng.html.

[32] Canada Revenue Agency. 2016. "Deemed Residents". *cra-arc.gc.ca*. http://www.cra-arc.gc.ca/tx/nnrsdnts/ndvdls/dmd-eng.html.

on their worldwide income for the *entire* year. Romania on the other hand looks specifically at the 12-month period ending in the fiscal year of concern.[33] While in Germany, an individual can either be present for more than 183 days or an average of 90 days per year over a four-year period to qualify as a resident.[34] Many of these differences are based on countries having different determinants of a fiscal or calendar year. Additionally, revisions to the *Organization of Economic Co-operation and Development* (OECD) taxation model create confusion for countries using different fiscal years.

Some countries use additional rules such as the United States, such as the 31-day *substantial presence* rule. Under this rule, an individual is considered to have substantial presence in the United States if they have been in the country for 31 days in the current year AND 183 days over the last three years with the given calculations:

1. All of the days present in the current calendar year
2. 1/3 of the days present in the previous calendar year
3. 1/6 of the days present in the second previous calendar year[35]

It is important to understand how this rule can differ around the world and to conduct specific research prior to engaging in any international contracts or extensive travel. Also, recall that an international tax treaty between countries is usually considered to trump the domestic tax laws of a single country.

Michael C. Gray/Shutterstock.com

Figure 8.12

Dual Residency

An individual may simultaneously reside in more than one country; therefore, governments have designed tax laws to accommodate such situations. As it is not considered reasonable for an individual to be fully liable for income tax in two separate countries, most governments have a system to determine which country will have priority to tax dual residents. The priority rule is the source rule as described above. Countries use different methods to reduce dual residents double taxation.

We Will Examine the Canada/U.S. Tax Treaty Dual Residency Scenario

The Canada/US Tax Treaty has "tie breaker" rules in place to determine in which country an individual will be considered as a resident.[36] The following factors are listed in order of consideration:

[33] KPMG. 2016. "Romania - Income Tax | KPMG | GLOBAL". *home.kpmg.com.* https://home.kpmg.com/xx/en/home/insights/2011/12/romania-income-tax.html.

[34] SJD Accountancy. 2015. "Tax Rates In Germany". *sjdaccountancy.com.* http://www.sjdaccountancy.com/about/ourservices/tax_rates_germany.html.

[35] Internal Revenue Service,. 2015. "Substantial Presence Test". *Irs.Gov.* https://www.irs.gov/Individuals/International-Taxpayers/Substantial-Presence-Test.

[36] Serbinski Accounting Firms. 2015. "Eliminating Double Taxation | International Tax Accountant | Serbinski Accounting Firms". *serbinski.com.* http://www.serbinski.com/taxation-in-usa/double-taxation.shtml.

1. The location of an individual's permanent home.
2. Should they have a home available in both countries the place where their economic and social interests are greatest; i.e., the center of vital interests for that individual.
3. The individual's habitual abode.
4. The individual's citizenship.
5. If the individual is a citizen of neither or both then the revenue agencies of both countries will make a joint determination.

Residence of Corporations

The topic of corporate residency has gone through some major developments around the world and various countries now use different requirements or a combination of, to determine if a corporation is considered a resident for the purpose of taxation. Some countries consider any corporations that were incorporated in that country to be a resident (figuratively where the corporation was born). Others consider where the *mind and management* of the corporation operates to be that company's place of residency. Also, corporations can be deemed a resident based on where the majority of their directors reside. For example, if a company was incorporated in Australia, or carries on business in Australia and the majority of its directors or in certain cases the majority of the shares owned by its shareholders who themselves reside in Australia, that company will be deemed a resident of Australia for income tax purposes.[37] The United Kingdom and Canada use similar models to determine the residency of corporations.

Figure 8.13

Mike Brake/Shutterstock.com

Residence of Trusts

Trusts traditionally were considered to reside where the trustee, executor, administrator, heir, and other legal representatives reside. However, refer to the case briefs of *Garron Family Trust (Trustee of) v. R. (2012)*[38] and *Thibodeau Family Trust (Trustee of) v. R. (1978)*[39] for examples of how the act of *carrying on business* and *mind and management* of a trust may significantly change the traditional method for determining the residence of trusts at least in common law jurisdictions.

---

[37] Australian Government | Australian Taxation Office. 2013. "Residency Requirements For Companies, Corporate Limited Partnerships And Trusts | Australian Taxation Office". *ato.gov. au*. https://www.ato.gov.au/Business/Starting-your-own-business/In-detail/Getting-started/Residency-requirements-for-companies,-corporate-limited-partnerships-and-trusts/?page=2#Companies.

[38] Garron Family Trust (Trustee of) v. R.2012 SCC 14, 2012 CarswellNat 953, 2012 CarswellNat 954, [2012] 1 S.C.R. 520, [2012] 3 C.T.C. 265, 2012 D.T.C. 5063 (Eng.), 2012 D.T.C. 5064 (Fr.), 212 A.C.W.S. (3d) 881, 343 D.L.R. (4th) 670, 428 N.R. 202, 75 E.T.R. (3d) 1, J.E. 2012-784.

[39] Thibodeau Family Trust (Trustee of) v. R.1978. CarswellNat 223, [1978] C.T.C. 539, [1978] F.C.J. No. 607, 3 E.T.R. 168, 78 D.T.C. 6376

Garron Family Trust (Trustee of) v. R (2012)[40][vi]

Facts:

In the case of *Garron Family Trust (Trustee of) v. R (2012)*, St Michael Trust Corp. was a corporation resident in Barbados and the trustee of two different trusts. The trusts were settled by an individual resident in Saint Vincent and the Grenadines. The beneficiaries of the trusts were residents of Canada. When the trusts disposed of shares they owned in two Ontario corporations, about $152 million was remitted to the Minister of National Revenue as withholding tax from capital gains earned by the trusts on the sale of the shares. The trustee (*St Michael*) claimed that they were exempt from the Canada capital gains tax and that amount should be returned. Under the *Canada-Barbados Income Tax Agreement*, tax is only payable in the country where the seller is resident.[vii] Since St. Michael was resident in Barbados, it claimed that the trusts were also resident in Barbados and therefore there was no basis to withhold tax in Canada. The Minister of National Revenue argued that the trusts were resident in Canada and therefore the amount was properly withheld. This case ultimately went up to the Supreme Court of Canada, which upheld the rulings of both the Tax Court of Canada and the Federal Court of Appeal.

Issue:

Whether the two trusts were to be considered resident in Canada or Barbados. Additionally, determine what should be the appropriate test for residency of a trust.

Decision:

Both the Tax Court of Canada[viii] and the Federal Court of Appeal[ix] ruled that the trusts were resident in Canada. The Supreme Court of Canada also ruled that the trusts were resident in Canada.

Reasons:

Lower Courts: The tax court judge found that the correct test for determining residency was the same as the test for corporations: the *central management and control* test. The Federal Court of Appeal agreed and found that the location of the trustee was not how you determine residence. Even though a trust is not considered a person at common law (unlike a corporation), under s. 104(2) of the *Income Tax Act* a trust is a deemed person.

Supreme Court of Canada: The main beneficiaries were the ones who exercised the central management and control of the trusts and they were residents of Canada. St. Michael had little or no responsibilities beyond providing administrative services, and therefore on the central management and control test the trusts must be resident of Canada. However, the residence of a trustee can be the residence of the trust where the trustee actually carries out the central management and control of the trust. The Supreme Court also agreed with the tax court judge that adopting a similar test for corporations and trusts promoted the "important principles of consistency, predictability and fairness in the application of tax law" (para 160 of Tax Court judgement).

---

[40] Garron Family Trust (Trustee of) v. R.2012 SCC 14, 2012 CarswellNat 953, 2012 CarswellNat 954, [2012] 1 S.C.R. 520, [2012] 3 C.T.C. 265, 2012 D.T.C. 5063 (Eng.), 2012 D.T.C. 5064 (Fr.), 212 A.C.W.S. (3d) 881, 343 D.L.R. (4th) 670, 428 N.R. 202, 75 E.T.R. (3d) 1, J.E. 2012-784.

[vi] Garron Family Trust (Trustee of) v. R.2012 SCC 14, 2012 CarswellNat 953, 2012 CarswellNat 954, [2012] 1 S.C.R. 520, [2012] 3 C.T.C. 265, 2012 D.T.C. 5063 (Eng.), 2012 D.T.C. 5064 (Fr.), 212 A.C.W.S. (3d) 881, 343 D.L.R. (4th) 670, 428 N.R. 202, 75 E.T.R. (3d) 1, J.E. 2012-784.

[vii] Canada Revenue Agency,. 2014. "View Treaty". treaty-accord.gc.ca. http://www.treaty-accord.gc.ca/text-texte.aspx?id=102234.

[viii] Carron Family Trust (Trustee of) v. R. 2009 TCC 450, 2009 CCI 450, 2009 CarswellNat 5415, 2009 CarswellNat 2600, [2010] 2 C.T.C. 2346, 181 A.C.W.S. (3d) 819, 2009 D.T.C. 1287 (Eng.), 50 E.T.R. (3d) 241.

[ix] Garron Family Trust (Trustee of) v. R. 2010. CAF 309, 2010 FCA 309, 2010 CarswellNat 4259, 2010 CarswellNat 5521, [2011] 2 C.T.C. 7, [2012] 2 F.C.R. 374, 195 A.C.W.S. (3d) 881, 2010 D.T.C. 5189 (Eng.), 411 N.R. 125, 61 E.T.R. (3d) 168.

230   **International Business**

Thibodeau Family Trust (Trustee of) v. R (1978)[i]

Facts:

In the taxation year of 1972 there were three trustees of the Thibodeau Family Trust; two Bermuda trustees (Dill and Pearman) and one Canadian trustee (Thibodeau). In the statement of defense[ii], the Minister of National Revenue admitted that the Thibodeau Family Trust had never carried on business in Canada during any of the relevant times.

Issue:

Whether the Thibodeau Family Trust was resident in Canada for the taxation year of 1972.

Decision:

The ruling was that the Thibodeau Family Trust was deemed to be a resident of Bermuda at the time in question.

Reasons:

There are no statutory rules or judicial decisions that establish a formula for how to determine residency of a trust, unlike for individuals or corporations. The *Income Tax Act* allows for there to be trusts that are resident[iii] and non-resident[iv] in Canada but does not address how this it to be determined.

The trial judge found that the judicial formula for determining residence of a corporation was not an appropriate analogy. It is not possible for a trust to have a dual residence for income tax purposes because trustees cannot delegate any of their authority to co-trustees. The judge found it impossible based on the facts of the case for the trustee to delegate their powers to someone else. Therefore, the trustee had to exercise central management and control of the trust.

The case stands for the rule that residence of a trust was determined by residence of the trustee who was assumed to manage and control the trust and trust assets. Arguably, the implicit assumption was left out in later readings of the case and the test was simply looking to the residence of the trustee to determine residence of the trust. It was not until *Garron*[v] that this was reexamined.

It should be noted that the concept of a Trust is a creature of the common law and until recently not considered in civil law jurisdictions. The difference arose from the fact that under common law persons could own both the legal interests in property while under civil law the state had a beneficial interest in all property and persons only had the "use" of it. Because of this difference most common law jurisdictions, such as, the United States, the United Kingdom, and Canada have developed guidelines for the determination where a civil law entity is a trust, a partnership or a corporation.

The *belt and suspenders approach* suggests that meetings regarding a trust should be held in the jurisdiction where the trustees reside.[41] For example, if the trustees reside in Barbados, meetings of the

---

[41] Investopedia. 2008. "Belt And Suspenders Definition | Investopedia". Investopedia. http://www.investopedia.com/terms/b/belt-and-suspenders.asp?layout=infini&v=4C&adtest=4C.

[i] Thibodeau Family Trust (Trustee of) v. R.1978. CarswellNat 223, [1978] C.T.C. 539, [1978] F.C.J. No. 607, 3 E.T.R. 168, 78 D.T.C. 6376

[ii]

[iii] Canada Revenue Agency. 2016. "Types Of Trusts". cra-arc.gc.ca. http://www.cra-arc.gc.ca/tx/trsts/typs-eng.html.

[iv] Canada Revenue Agency. 2008. "Non-Resident Trusts And Foreign Investment Entities". cra-arc.gc.ca. http://www.craarc.gc.ca/whtsnw/tms/nrt-eng.html.

[v] Garron Family Trust (Trustee of) v. R.2012 SCC 14, 2012 CarswellNat 953, 2012 CarswellNat 954, [2012] 1 S.C.R. 520, [2012] 3 C.T.C. 265, 2012 D.T.C. 5063 (Eng.), 2012 D.T.C. 5064 (Fr.), 212 A.C.W.S. (3d) 881, 343 D.L.R. (4th) 670, 428 N.R. 202, 75 E.T.R. (3d) 1, J.E. 2012-784

trustees concerning that trust should be held in Barbados. This is considered the most conservative approach and ensures that a trust is taxed in the intended state should Barbados be that state.

Taxation of Non-Residents

Most countries have similar principles governing the taxation of non-residents. Firstly, a non-resident is generally identified as an individual who does not have significant ties to a country, but does participate economically in some capacity within that country.[42] This economic participation could include employment income, carrying on business, or the disposition of taxable properties situated therein.

The definition of what constitutes *Taxable Income* varies around the world but most countries follow a model similar to that of Canada. Canada includes the following as items of taxable income[43]:

1. Income from duties of offices and employment performed by a non-resident in Canada or performed outside of Canada *if* the non-resident was a resident in Canada at the time the duties were performed.

2. Income from businesses carried on in Canada.

3. Capital gains from the disposition of "taxable Canadian property" (basically Canadian sited real estate or natural resources or certain interests therein).

4. Income from resource properties.

5. Recaptured capital cost allowance (tax deprecation) previously claimed on assets employed in a business carried on in Canada.

6. Income earned on a beneficial interest in a trust resident in Canada.

7. Income of a partnership carried on in Canada.

8. Certain research grants, scholarships, bursaries and other forms of income awards.

kenary820/Shutterstock.com

Figure 8.14

Carrying on a business can include producing, growing, mining, creating, manufacturing, fabricating, improving, packing, preserving, or the construction of products. As we have discussed, the *mind and management* of carrying on business is just as important as the physical actions of the business. Therefore, soliciting orders or offering anything else for sale in Canada also is considered the carrying on of business. The disposition of certain property (real property, business assets, shares, or the interest in partnerships or trusts) can also qualify as carrying on business depending on the jurisdiction.

Treaty protection can play a big role in determining whether an act is considered carrying on a business. Some of the factors that are considered include:

---

[42] Canada Revenue Agency. 2016. "Non-Residents Of Canada". *cra-arc.gc.ca*. http://www.cra-arc.gc.ca/tx/nnrsdnts/ndvdls/nnrs-eng.html.

[43] Ibid.

1. The location of the contracts.

2. The location of where the goods are delivered and payment is made.

3. The location of the business assets.

4. Whether an individual involved is considered an *agent* or an *independent contractor*.

5. The nature of the activities.

6. The location of the accounts.

Permanent establishment (**"PE"**) is a principle set out in domestic tax acts, however most states are consistent with the Organization for Economic Cooperation and Development's ("OECD") Model Tax Convention on Income and on Capital ("OECD Model Treaty") and its commentary ("OECD Commentary").[44] Article 5 establishes a rule known as the General PE Rule. The General PE Rule establishes three key conditions for finding a PE.

1. There must be a place of business;

2. The place of business must be fixed; and

3. The non-resident must be carrying on business wholly or partly through this fixed place of business.

This concept creates a higher standard for the act of carrying on business for non-resident corporations. It is best illustrated through an example. Based on the bi-lateral tax treaty between the United States and Canada, if Company XYZ is considered a resident of the United States, but operates part of its business in Canada, it is only liable for Canadian income taxation if it has a permanent establishment in which it operates in Canada. A permanent establishment could be an office or plant that XYZ regularly uses for its business.[45] A location is deemed not to be a permanent establishment when it is storing, displaying or delivering goods, merely used for processing or purchasing, or another aspect of preparation that is auxiliary or not part of the core process.[46]

When a foreign entity establishes a subsidiary in Canada, the first step of the General PE Rule is looked at: is there a place of business. If there is not a fixed place of business, part 3 of the General PE Rule is reviewed. This is known as the dependent PE rule under the OECD Model Treaty. There is a distinct difference between trading *IN* a country versus trading *WITH* a country. This distinction is what separates a permanent establishment from another location. As we identified, a permanent establishment is a fixed place of business with a geographic location. That is, it is a distinct location that the company identifies with

Figure 8.15

and others would identify that location with the company as well. Trading in a country would include a *dependent agent* or employee who has the authority to contract on behalf of the company itself. The key factors in the Dependent Agent PE Rule are:

1. An agent's authority to conclude contracts in Canada; these contracts must relate to operations that constitute the business of the non-resident;

2. The agent habitually exercises such authority to conclude contracts;

[44] See Income Tax Regulations, CRC, c945, Regulation 400; I.R.C. § 871, 872.

[45] Krishna, 114-115.

[46] Ibid.

3. Whether the agent is of dependent status, both legally and economically (as opposed to independent status); and

4. Whether the dependent agent is acting in the ordinary course of their business.[47]

Space at Disposal

A non-resident does not need to own or lease space to have a fixed place of business. If space is made available to a non-resident, at say its client's or wholly-owned subsidiary's facilities in Canada, this may constitute "space at the disposal." The OECD Commentary, followed by Canada, is determined by whether or not employees of the parent corporation have a significant presence in Canada (e.g., they spend significant time in Canada) at the premises of its Canadian subsidiary.

Agency

Additionally, there are some pertinent facts to establish that are useful for determining the existence of a permanent establishment. The facts examined are as follows: whether there is an agency relationship between a non-resident entity and any resident entity; whether the non-resident owns or leases a place of business in the country in question; whether or not the non-resident's personnel (employees) are present in the country for a significant period of time; whether or not the personnel have the right to execute contracts in the country. These facts generally establish whether there is a physical presence in the country. This will answer the question of whether or not there is a permanent establishment. If a non-resident corporation does not have a physical place of business, and does not have space at its disposal, and it has been determined that there is no dependent agent in Canada, or that the dependent agent does not habitually conclude contracts, Canada relies on a combination of Canadian agency law and an interpretation of paragraph 10 of the OECD Commentary to Article 5 to argue there is a PE.

Place of Management

CRA has raised PE assessments on non-resident corporations on the basis that the Canadian subsidiary constitutes a "place of management" of the parent corporation. This argument is often used in conjunction with the agency argument. Nevertheless, the OECD Commentary states that those places listed in paragraph 2 of Article 5 of the OECD Model Treaty "constitute a PE only if they meet the requirements of paragraph 1." It is questionable whether or not CRA could support a PE determination on this basis. In the case of the Canada-United States Income Tax Convention ("**Canada-US Treaty**"), once CRA determines that a US parent corporation does not have a PE in Canada under the General PE Rule or Dependent Agent PE Rule, it will generally then review the service PE rule in Article 5(9) of the Canada-US Treaty to determine if a deemed PE exists.[48]

Severing Residential Ties

Firstly, it is important to note that giving up residency is not an easy task, and requires a lot of effort from the individual, corporation, partnership, or trust in order to be no longer viewed as a resident in the eyes of the government.[49] For example, should an individual choose to severe their residential ties with a country, there are significant consequences that might arise. The individual will be deemed to have disposed of all their property for its fair market value immediately before leaving the country, also known as the *deemed disposition rule,* which is followed in Canada, and to

---

[47] *American Income Life Insurance Co. v. Canada*, 2008 TCC 306 at para. 35 [*American Income Life Insurance Co.*].

[48] *Knights of Columbus v. The Queen, 2008 TCC 307* [*Knights of Columbus*]. *American Income Life Insurance Co.*, supra note 46. Both cases dealt with a fixed place of business PE determination and the key issue was whether or not the place of business was "at the disposal" of the enterprise.

[49] Krishna, 109.

a degree in the United States (considering the US taxes based on citizenship). Any accrued capital gains on certain of the taxpayer's property (not "taxable Canadian property") are triggered upon leaving the country and becomes subject to taxation.[50] The adoption of a **departure tax** is not universal, but other countries also share models at least conceptually, similar to that of Canada. Some items that qualify for Canadian departure tax (as may be modified by a tax treaty) include foreign sited assets, such as[51]:

Figure 8.16

1. Capital properties and real estate outside of Canada

2. Unincorporated businesses outside of Canada

3. Private or public company shares in Canada or outside of Canada

4. Mutual funds

5. Partnership interests

6. Interests in non-resident *inter vivos* trusts and in unit or commercial trusts (inside or outside of the country)

7. Portfolio investments such as government or corporate bonds

8. Personal use property

9. Listed personal property such as works of art, stamps, coins, rare manuscripts, etc.

There is an option for a taxpayer to cover their departure liability by *posting security*. The security posted must meet jurisdictional standards. The departure tax is usually not due until death or a sale. Additionally, the taxpayer may be taxed a second time in the foreign jurisdiction when the property subject to deemed disposition rules in Canada is actually sold in the foreign jurisdiction, although certain tax treaties take the implications of the Canadian departure tax into consideration. Some items that can be used for security in Canada include:[52]

1. Bank letters of guarantee

2. Letters of credit

3. Government of Canada bonds

4. Shares in private or public corporations

5. Certificates in precious metals

6. Various marketable securities

7. Charge on mortgage or real property

8. Valuable personal property

Lastly, interest does not accrue on departure tax owing; the payment of which has been secured until it becomes unsecured and the tax is paid.

---

[50] Canada Revenue Agency,. 2016. "Deemed Disposition Of Property". *cra-arc.gc.ca*. http://www.cra-arc.gc.ca/tx/ndvdls/lf-vnts/dth/dmd/menu-eng.html. Deemed disposition rules apply to all capital property unless specifically excluded.

[51] Canada Revenue Agency. 2016. "Dispositions Of Property". *cra-arc.gc.ca*. http://www.cra-arc.gc.ca/tx/nnrsdnts/ndvdls/dspstn-eng.html.

[52] Canada Revenue Agency. 2002. "Security Requirements For Non-Residents". cra-arc.gc.ca. http://www.cra-arc.gc.ca/E/pub/gm/2-6/2-6-e.html.

Short-term Residents & Departure Tax

Short-term residents do not face the same requirements or consequences for severing their residential ties as do long-term residents. The definition of a short-term resident varies around the world. The deemed disposition rule does not apply to any property owned immediately before the taxpayer last became a resident in this situation. Deemed disposition does not apply to property that an individual inherited.

Double Taxation

Double taxation occurs when an individual has their income taxed twice in two different jurisdictions.[53] This topic was earlier discussed in the *dual residency* section. Various systems have been developed around the world for relief from the issue of double taxation. We will examine three major systems: the exemption system, the credit system, and the deduction system.

1. The **exemption system** is currently employed in Canada and determines a single state in which the income of a corporation is taxable. Usually the "host" state is the one in which the taxation occurs, while the individual's income is tax-exempt in the "home" state. Active business income under certain circumstances of subsidiaries of Canadian corporations is exempt earnings and becomes exempt from taxation in the home state of Canada, as the tax was already paid in the host state.

pikcha/Shutterstock.com

Figure 8.17

2. The **credit system** where the taxes imposed in one state may be used as a credit against a taxpayer's liability in another state.[54] The taxpayer who paid foreign taxes would get a credit against the taxes payable in their home state.

3. The **deduction system** allows a taxpayer to reduce its income by deducting the amount of foreign taxes paid, thereby reducing its income and consequently reducing the amount of taxable income subject to tax, compared to a foreign tax credit which reduces the payable amount of tax, but not the actual income.[55]

Tax Treaties

Tax treaties have been designed to remedy the issues surrounding double taxation between countries. Additionally, treaties have developed over time to address the issues of tax incentives, tax avoidance, and tax evasion. Some important treaties to be aware of are the Organization for Economic Co-operation and Development (OECD) Model Treaty which includes 34 countries and works with many

---

[53] Investopedia. 2007. "Double Taxation Definition | Investopedia". *Investopedia*. http://www.investopedia.com/terms/d/double_taxation.asp.

[54] Krishna, 658.

[55] Ibid. 151.

more[56] and the United Nations (UN) Model Treaty. Most tax treaties cover income taxes, capital gains taxes, and taxes on net wealth, and most tax treaties also cover both natural persons and companies.[57]

The creation of tax treaties has been useful in the elimination of double taxation.[58] The factors that are used to determine tax liability include residency, personality, and the source of the income. As a general rule of thumb, tax treaties say that states may only tax residents, but as we have seen this is not always the case. Exceptions to the general rule are:

1. Non-residents providing independent or professional services may be taxed by a tax treaty state if the person maintains a fixed base, or *habitual abode,* within that state.[59]

2. Non-resident employees may be taxed in a tax treaty state to the extent of the earnings the employee receives in that state.[60]

3. Non-resident companies may be taxed by a tax treaty state if they maintain a permanent establishment within that state.[61]

Some exceptions are also based on the sources of income. These exceptions include:

1. Immovable property is taxable only in the state where the property is located.[62]

2. Dividends remitted by a subsidiary are subject to limited withholding taxes by the host state.[63]

3. A withholding tax is paid at a beneficial rate on interest and royalties paid to a non-resident.

Tax Avoidance

Tax avoidance occurs when a person takes advantage of differences in tax laws as between states or when there is doubt around the interpretation of a tax law and a person is able to benefit from this doubt.[64]

Some of the largest companies in the world have used different strategies for tax avoidance. We will explore some of the most common examples of tax avoidance, but it is important to know that just as tax laws constantly are evolving we must be aware of the evolution of tax avoidance. Additionally, the distinction should be made

Figure 8.18

---

[56] Organisation for Economic Co-operation and Development. 2016. "Members And Partners - OECD". *oecd.org.* http://www.oecd.org/about/membersandpartners/.

[57] Internal Revenue Service. 2016. "Tax Treaties". *irs.gov.* https://www.irs.gov/Individuals/International-Taxpayers/Tax-Treaties.

[58] Krishna, 106.

[59] Ibid., 108

[60] Ibid., 107.

[61] Ibid.

[62] Ibid., 120.

[63] Cassels Brock. 2014. "Cassels Brock : Canadian Tax Fundamentals: Withholding Tax On Cross-Border Interest Payments1". *casselsbrock.com.* http://www.casselsbrock.com/CBNewsletter/Canadian_Tax_Fundamentals__Withholding_Tax_on_Cross_Border_Interest_Payments.

[64] Krishna, 1002.

that tax avoidance is not illegal, as persons can order their affairs in order to pay lower taxes as long as it is in compliance with local tax laws.[65]

Ethical Considerations 8.1

Tax

PremierOffshore.com, "U.S. Approved Offshore Corporate Inversion for your Small Business," *LowTax: Global Tax and Business Portal*, December 11, 2015.

http://www.lowtax.net/blogs/US_Approved_Offshore_Corporate_Inversion_for_Your_Small_Business-573228.html

In December 2015, Pfizer, a leading biopharmaceutical company, completed history's largest inversion case by investing $160 billion to take their tax home from the United States to Ireland. The move cut their tax rate down from 35% (in the United States) to 12.5% (in Ireland) and will lower their total tax rate, after interest expenses and deductions, to 15% by 2017. Pfizer will save approximately $2.1 billion in 2017 alone. Tax avoidance and offshore corporate inversions are not new concepts to the international market, however what is unexpected is that the US government is supporting a form of offshore inversion that will cut a company's corporate tax rate to 4%. Puerto Rico (a US territory) is offering a 10-year tax contract that has been backed by the IRS and federal government, which provides a 4% tax rate while the individuals continue to live in the United States.

Puerto Rico can offer such a deal because tax laws of a US territory overpower federal tax code meaning that you don't need to live where you incorporate. Also, Puerto Rico's government owes $72 billion to investors and they have no way of paying off their debts without defaulting (that started January 1, 2016). Inversion is not illegal, but it has been considered unethical by politicians and patriots alike. What kind of message does this move by the US government send to companies that were previously attacked for their tax evasion methods? Does an immoral business strategy become ethical when it is meant to aid the host country's economy and government? Lastly, will this open the door for allowing other tax avoidance techniques that could hurt home countries such as the United States who hold on to one of the highest corporate tax rates in the industrialized world?

Tax Haven

There is no universal agreement as to what defines a tax haven. Some believe it is a state with no tax, others include states with low tax. Obviously, definitions are subjectively influenced by political, moral, and social views. One could argue there is a legal definition and a financial definition, the latter being a state with a moderate level of taxation and liberal tax incentives for undertaking specific activities such as investing or exporting. A separate definition is a state that provides refuge for one of the following: the taxpayer themselves as the taxpayer travels there to avoid paying taxes in another country; taxpayer's income by depositing employment income into bank accounts in a foreign country; or a taxpayer's capital and other assets.[66] The OECD and other governing bodies have attempted to eliminate tax havens through various means and the OECD has gone as far as flagging certain countries as uncooperative tax havens.[67] Some methods for countering a tax haven strategy

---

[65] Stubart Investments Ltd. v. R.1984. CarswellNat 222, 1984 CarswellNat 690, [1984] 1 S.C.R. 536, [1984] C.T.C. 294, [1984] S.C.J. No. 25, 10 D.L.R. (4th) 1, 15 A.T.R. 942, 26 A.C.W.S. (2d) 53, 53 N.R. 241, 84 D.T.C. 6305, J.E. 84-479

[66] Krishna, 1422-1424.

[67] Organisation for Economic Co-operation and Development. 2016. "List Of Unco-Operative Tax Havens - OECD". *oecd.org*. http://www.oecd.org/countries/monaco/listofunco-operativetaxhavens.htm.

could include taxing income that is earned in a tax haven state, structuring state tax law to limit the usefulness of tax havens to local residents, imposing special taxes on certain types of income and transactions that commonly involve the use of tax havens.[68]

Transfer pricing is the practice of charging prices for goods or services provided by one affiliate company to another affiliated company so as to lower the tax burden of the overall enterprise.[69] The purpose of transfer pricing is to allow smaller profits to be made on the books of affiliates in countries with high taxes and the larger profits are assigned to affiliates in countries with low taxes. The main method for countering transfer pricing is to require affiliated companies to deal with each other under the *arm's length* principal. This method would attribute the profits that an affiliated establishment would earn if it were a completely independent entity dealing with another independent enterprise under ordinary market conditions. This general method has been refined and developed into several different methods around the world:

1. The *unitary business rule* states that multinational enterprises are taxed on a percentage of their worldwide income, regardless of where it was earned or by whom.[70]

2. The *comparable uncontrolled price method* (*CUP*) is designed to limit transfer pricing by considering the price that a third party would charge for the same goods, services, or property under identical conditions. It then compares these third party prices to the actual transactions and taxes it accordingly to create a balance between the two.[71] Essentially, the CUP method attaches a premium amount to the actual transaction price. The CUP method can be very effective, but it does have its drawbacks as it can't be used in every situation. Consider a transaction between two affiliated companies who produce entirely unique products. It would be impossible to find a third party who would charge for the exact same products.

3. The *resale price method* compares the gross profit when an entity re-sells goods to the gross profits realized by entities in comparable transactions.[72] The comparable profitability is determined by calculating the ratio of the initial price and the re-sell price. This method is typically used when the seller has not added substantial value to the tangible goods, such as packaging, labeling, or minor assembly. The seller is acting strictly as a *middleman* in this scenario.

4. The *cost plus method* looks at the costs incurred by the supplier in a controlled transaction and applies an appropriate *cost plus markup* to make a realistic profit.[73] This is a useful method when applied to manufacturing or assembling activities as the related manufacturing company is the tested party. This method could also be used for services offered from one affiliated company to another at a discounted price.

5. Lastly, the *profit split method* divides profits between affiliated companies. By simulating a joint venture, this method evaluates the relative value of each company's contribution to the overall project. The profit split method is typically applied when both sides own significant intangible property—patents, copyrights, trademarks – and there are existing licensing relationships between both companies. The evaluation of each company's contribution usually is based on external market data.

---

[68]

[69] Sheppard, Lee. 2010. "Transfer Pricing As Tax Avoidance". *forbes.com*. http://www.forbes.com/2010/06/24/tax-finance-multinational-economics-opinions-columnists-lee-sheppard.html.

[70] Senft, Daniel. 2013. *International Sourcing: A Method To Create Corporate Success.* Bucher: Springer Science & Business Media. 49.

[71] Ibid.

[72] Senft, Daniel. 2013. *International Sourcing: A Method To Create Corporate Success.* Bucher: Springer Science & Business Media. 49.

[73] Ibid.

Treaty shopping is a common strategy in which a company *shops* between different countries with tax treaty provisions that would provide them the most benefit. Once a country is selected that has these favorable provisions, a company, for example, may set up subsidiary enterprise in that country(s) to take advantage of that/those treaty(s). Those subsidiary companies have been termed as *conduit companies.*[74] A general method that is used to counter treaty shopping is to suspend the treaty benefits for non-residents who are seeking to abuse the relevant tax treaty(s). For example, if favorable conditions existed in the bilateral tax treaty between the United States and Barbados, a body such as OECD could pressure government to suspend these benefits.

Tax Avoidance			
Tax Haven	**Transfer Pricing**	**Treaty Shopping**	**Thin Capitalization**
Jurisdictions which provide refuge for taxpayers, their income, or capital and other assets.	Lowering the tax burden of the larger company by creating tax breaks through the prices charged between subsidaiary companies.	Selecting a jurisdiction which provides additional tax benefits specific to a company's operations.	Intentionally financing a company through debt in order to write-off interest payments as a business expense.

Figure 8.19

While most of the previous strategies are based on the actual business actions of companies, **thin capitalization** is based on how a company is financed. Using this method, where a company is purposely financed by loans instead of equity capital so that it may deduct interest paid on its loans as a business expense resulting in lower tax payments because some or all of the interest is disallowed. For example, in Canada, the existing thin capitalization rule denies a resident corporation a deduction for interest paid to a *specific non-resident shareholder* if the debt to equity ratio exceeds two to one.[75] In other words, only two-thirds of Canadian capitalization can be in the form of debt. Also, a specific non-resident shareholder is a foreign person that owns 25% or more of the voting rights of a Canadian corporation.

Tax Evasion

Tax evasion is the willful and conscious misrepresentation or concealment of a person's tax obligations *or* the sudden departure of a taxpayer to another country.[76] All governments view tax evasion as illegal and co-operate in varying degrees to prosecute international tax evaders. The OECD 1988 Draft Convention on Mutual Administrative Assistance in Tax Matters[77] provides a platform for information exchanges between member countries attempting to reduce tax evasion. Additionally, *tax amnesty* allows delinquent taxpayers to pay all or part of their overdue taxes and thereby avoid possible prosecution.[78]

---

[74] US Legal. 2016. "Conduit Company Law & Legal Definition". *definitions.uslegal.com*. http://definitions.uslegal.com/c/conduit-company/.

[75] Canada Revenue Agency. 1995. "ARCHIVED - Interest On Debts Owing To Specified Non-Residents (Thin Capitalization)". *cra-arc.gc.ca*. http://www.cra-arc.gc.ca/E/pub/tp/it59r3/it59r3-e.html.

[76] TurboTax. 2015. "Penalty For Tax Evasion In Canada: Get The Facts About What Happens When Business And Individuals Evade Taxes And The Legal Consequences For Such Actions | Turbotax Canada". *turbotax.intuit.ca*. https://turbotax.intuit.ca/tax-resources/tax-compliance/penalty-for-tax-evasion-in-canada.jsp.

[77] Organisation for Economic Co-operation and Development. 2016. "Convention On Mutual Administrative Assistance In Tax Matters - OECD". *oecd.org*. http://www.oecd.org/ctp/exchange-of-tax-information/conventiononmutualadministrativeassistanceintaxmatters.htm.

[78] Canadian Tax Amnesty. 2016. "Canadian Tax Amnesty | Tax Lawyers Toronto | Tax Help". *canadiantaxamnesty.ca*. https://www.canadiantaxamnesty.ca/.

Tax Planning

Simply put, **tax planning** is the legitimate arranging of one's financial activities in order to reduce or defer some of the related tax costs. There are three forms of tax planning: *tax avoidance*, which we have previously discussed, *tax deferral* or the delaying of paying taxes to some future time, and *income splitting* between spouses or others to balance the tax implications of income.

There are also specific restrictions on tax planning depending on the jurisdiction. For example, Canada's *Income Tax Act* specifically prohibits certain activities which are outlined in the *General Anti-Avoidance Rules (GAAR).*[79] One of the major distinctions is the difference between arm's length and non-arm's length transactions.

1. *Arm's length transactions* occur when the transacting parties *do not* have a close relationship and the goods/services/properties are not sold for fair market value.

2. *Non-arm's length transactions* occur when the parties *do* have a close relationship. Examples include family relationships such as a parent and child or two companies owned by members of the same family. Less obvious examples include directing an expected taxable receipt to be paid directly to another such as having one's salary paid to a creditor, or transferring a right to income to a related party. An example is an individual who earns consulting income but tries to transfer the right to that income to their own corporation having a more beneficial tax rate. The transferring of property to a spouse without transferring the future income from that property is also considered to be a non-arm's length transaction.

The GAAR's goal is to create a standard which defines unacceptable tax behavior. There is a lot of gray area as it can be difficult to determine if someone has done legitimate tax planning to create a benefit or if they are using an unacceptable tax avoidance strategy. A good example of how the GAAR can be problematic if interpreted too precisely is *Canada Trustco Mortgage Co. v. Canada (2005).*[80] It is important to recognize that any system must be designed with a certain amount of flexibility and the courts rulings concerning GAAR is a good example of this recognition.

Canada Trustco Mortgage Co. v. Canada (2005))[xi]

Facts:

In the case of *Canada Trustco Mortgage Co. v. Canada (2005)* the taxpayer carried on business as a mortgage lender. In the ordinary course of the taxpayer's business, it earned income from leased assets. The taxpayer purchased several trailers and then had them leased back to their vendors. The taxpayer then claimed *capital cost allowance (CCA)* on the trailers, which CCA would be subject to recapture upon the eventual disposition of the trailers. The taxpayer's intention in executing the purchase and lease-back agreements was to defer the payment of taxes and thereby realize a tax advantage. The Minister assessed the taxpayer, disallowing the CCA deductions as barred by application of the *General Anti-Avoidance Rules (GAAR).*

Issue:

Whether or not the CCA deductions should have been allowed under GAAR.

Decision:

The court concluded that the CCA deductions should have been allowed under GAAR.

---

[79] Canada Revenue Agency. 2002. "General Anti-Avoidance Rule - Section 245 Of The Income Tax Act". *cra-arc.gc.ca.* http://www.cra-arc.gc.ca/E/pub/tp/ic88-2/ic88-2-e.html.
[80] Canada Trustco Mortgage Co. v. Canada. 2005. SCC 54.

[xi] Canada Trustco Mortgage Co. v. Canada. 2005. SCC 54.

Reasons:

The taxpayer was not required to disprove that they had violated the object, spirit or purpose of the provision, but the minister was required to demonstrate that the transaction was an abuse of the Income Tax Act. The benefit of the doubt was given to the taxpayer if the Minister could not prove the transaction was an abuse. The Minister was in a better position than the taxpayer to make submissions as to the legislative intent behind particular taxation provisions and therefore they had the obligation to identify the purpose of the provisions and show how that purpose was frustrated or defeated by the taxpayer's arrangements. The fact that the transactions could have occurred in an alternative way which would have resulted in more tax *does not necessarily* make the taxpayer's particular plan illegal, even though the taxpayer's arrangement had a better tax result transaction and was primarily designed to obtain a tax benefit and hence an *avoidance transaction.*

Even though there was an alternative way the taxpayer could have structured the transaction to accomplish the same objective that would have resulted in a greater amount of tax, it does not by inference mean that this action would be considered an *avoidance transaction.*

The Double Irish & Dutch Sandwich

Although Ireland no longer allows this strategy to be used, after facing pressure from various governing bodies[81], it is still a good example of a tax avoidance technique employed by large corporations. The arrangement combines several methods in tax avoidance, including direct sales, contract production, treaty shopping, hybrid mismatch, and transfer pricing rules. The simple rule of high tax—low profit; low tax—high profit drives this concept.

This is done through the use of a combination of Irish and Dutch subsidiary companies to shift profits to lower tax jurisdictions. In simplistic terms the US parent company transfers intellectual

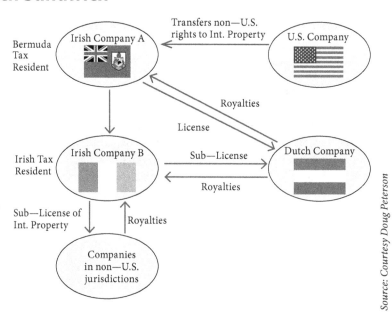

Source: Courtesy Doug Peterson

Figure 8.20

property rights to an Irish company. Profits are sent through one Irish company, then to a Dutch company, and then to second Irish company headquartered in a tax haven. It is called a double Irish because two Irish companies are required for the structure. One Irish company is located in a tax haven and is resident in that tax haven because the mind and management is located there, even though the corporation is incorporated in Ireland. The second Irish company is incorporated in Ireland as an operating company. The term Dutch Sandwich is used as a Dutch company is sandwiched in between the two Irish companies to eliminate withholding taxes. The process begins with a US parent company transferring or licensing the intellectual property (IP) to an Irish subsidiary whose *mind and management* is in a *tax haven*, in this case Bermuda (BCo). BCo is incorporated

---

81 BloombergBusiness.com. 2015. "Noonan Plans 6.25% Patent-Box Tax As 'Double Irish' Ends". bloomberg.com. http:// www.bloomberg.com/news/articles/2015-10-13/noonan-plans-6-25-patent-box-tax-as-double-irish-ends.

in Ireland but tax resident in Bermuda because the management and control is in Bermuda.[82] BCo incorporates a subsidiary in Ireland (Irish OPCo) and another subsidiary is incorporated in Holland (Dutch Co). The BCo sublicenses the IP to DutchCo in return for royalties. The addition of the *Dutch sandwich* provides further reduction to a company's tax liability.[83] In this scenario, BCo first sub-licenses the IP to a Dutch Co, who would then sub-license the IP to the Irish holding company. Irish tax law exempts certain royalties from member European Union countries and the Netherlands doesn't impose any *withholding tax*.[84] This allows royalty payments to be transferred to the first Irish subsidiary, BCo with minimal taxation on that revenue.[85] Figure 8.20 illustrates this entire arrangement.

Electronic Commerce

Electronic commerce is the means by which a company or individual is able to provide its products and services on an online platform.[86] Those products, which when supplied in person are considered tangible personal property, are no longer considered tangible through electronic commerce. This consideration also extends to telecommunication services.[87] It is difficult with e-commerce to determine the residency of the seller of goods and services and to determine the source of the income.

Figure 8.21

Permanent Establishment

Permanent establishment is an important topic within electronic commerce because of the global implications of doing business online. There is an opportunity to make sales all around the world, but that raises the question of where that revenue should be taxed. It is difficult to determine where the good or services are offered for sale and where the contract is concluded. Canada subjects non-residents to tax if the non-resident is employed in Canada or carries on business "in Canada." The United States uses similar rules. The difficult issue is to determine when an electronic commerce transaction is carried on "in Canada."

In theory, a computer server is unlikely to be considered grounds for permanent establishment, so if a company's server was located in Canada, Canada would not be entitled to taxation on any revenue as a result of the server being used for business.[88] Likewise, a website, by itself, is unlikely to be considered permanent establishment because there is nothing "permanent" in place, such as machinery or

[82] TaxTV.com. 2012. "The Double Irish Dutch Sandwich - Video". caxtv.com. http://taxtv.com/editorial/the-double-irish-and-dutch-sandwich/.

[83] Ibid.

[84] Ibid.

[85] Ibid.

[86] Canada Revenue Agency. 2015. "About E-Commerce". *cra-arc.gc.ca*. http://www.cra-arc.gc.ca/tx/bsnss/tpcs/cmm/bt-eng.html.

[87] Ibid.

[88] Ewens, Doug. 1999. "Taxation Aspects Of Electronic Commerce". *Mccarthy Tetrault LLP, 2.*

equipment.[89] Mere use of a web server by itself is not considered a permanent establishment. However, a web server that is owned or rented by the company that is using the server in that country to host its website would likely result in a deemed permanent establishment. The OECD has concluded that a web site cannot, in itself, constitute a permanent establishment, nor does a web site hosting arrangement, and finally that a business that owns or leases a server will not necessarily have a PE where the server is located.

Cloud-Based Infrastructure

Cloud-based infrastructure refers to a centralized intangible "hard-drive" without a specific geographical location. At this point in time there is no consensus on how to tax cloud based transactions. However, history shows us that governments will move towards establishing policies to tax the cloud. Governments may follow the residence analysis used for servers. In addition, a nexus argument would be central to taxing the cloud. Although cloud based providers lack a physical platform linked to a particular state, governments will try and show a nexus to the sale of the goods and services, a "minimal contacts" test. The lack of physical presence for remote cloud-based companies forces states to expand their definition of nexus through concepts like "affiliate nexus" and "economic nexus." Neither of those definitions necessarily requires an element of physicality. The result has been a flurry of affiliate or click-through nexus state laws, commonly referred to as the "Amazon laws." Several states have passed such laws which compels the seller, i.e., Amazon, to collect the sales tax from the end customer in the location the customer is resident.

Trusts

A **trust** splits the ownership of property between two components, *legal ownership* and *beneficiary ownership*.[90] This is illustrated in Figure 8.22, as the settlor (initial owner of property splits the ownership between the *trustee* (legal owner) and the *beneficiary* (equitable owner). It is important to note that more than one person can make up any of the THREE components. The objectives of a trust may be to:

1. Obtain specific personal and/or business financial goals
2. Preserve and enhance capital
3. Secure assets
4. Minimize taxation

Offshore Trusts

Trusts are often taxed as individuals. In order to capitalize on certain taxation advantages, many trusts are established in Tax Havens as a so-called **offshore trust** usually with a local *trustee*.[91] This strategy allows the trust to take advantage of the different tax laws regarding the income generated by a trust located in that jurisdiction. Consider, non-resident discretionary trusts that can be structured so as not

Figure 8.22

Source: Courtesy Doug Peterson

[89] Ibid.

[90] Thefreedictionary.com. 2016. "Trust". *thefreedictionary.com*. http://legal-dictionary.thefreedictionary.com/trust.

[91] Businessdictionary.com. 2016. "What Is Offshore Trust? Definition And Meaning". *businessdictionary.com*. http://www.businessdictionary.com/definition/offshore-trust.html.

to attract any immediate tax liability if: all of its property is acquired from a non-resident; it does not receive financial assistance from a resident of Canada; and the majority of the trustees are non-residents of Canada, and exercise the mind and management of the trust within the tax haven country.

Offshore trusts have been used in the past to accomplish a variety of business and personal goals. Some examples include:

1. Replacing or improving professional liability insurance for directors and officers
2. Reducing domestic insurance coverage, particularly where large insurance coverage attracts litigation
3. Protect against risks un-associated with professional practice
4. Remove assets from jurisdictions with high probability of litigation
5. Avoid forced heirship provisions in country of domicile
6. Reduce a financial profile and increase financial privacy
7. Avoid or supplement pre-nuptial agreements
8. Protect retirement benefits plan
9. Protect business assets

There are also a number of considerations to be made on the location of an offshore trust. Some jurisdictions may provide *specific protection* within their legislation for trusts and trustees. There may be *local tax exemption* on income or capital gains, which can provide a major advantage compared to other jurisdictions. There may be *limited foreign exchange control,* which would allow income to be transferred both in and out of the country easily in different currencies. There also may be more general considerations, such as the *financial infrastructure* of the jurisdiction, which would provide benefit in terms of investment and management. The *political stability, technology, time-zone,* and *dominant language* of a country can also play a role in a person's ability to access their income.

Dividends

Dividends are used by companies in order to redistribute some portion of the company's earnings to shareholders.[92] They usually come in the form of cash payments, but shares and other forms of property are also used as dividends.[93] For a corporation, dividend income creates an interesting opportunity to avoid taxation depending on the jurisdiction. For example, a Canadian corporation can receive dividend income *tax-free* from a foreign affiliate *if* the foreign affiliate satisfies these requirements:

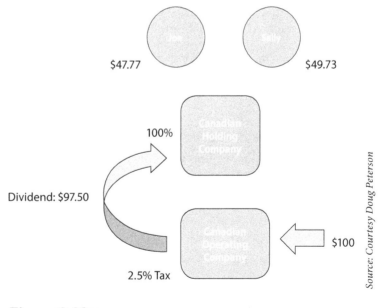

Figure 8.23

---

[92] Hayes, Adam. 2003. "Dividend Definition | Investopedia". Investopedia. http://www.investopedia.com/terms/d/dividend.asp?layout=infini&v=4C&adtest=4C.
[93] Ibid.

1. Carries on an *active business*. Any business agreed upon by the affiliate other than certain prescribed businesses.
2. Is a resident of a country with which Canada has an Income Tax Treaty or exchange of Information Treaty in place.

A *foreign affiliate* is defined as a non-resident corporation in which a Canadian corporation holds at least 10% of the shares.[94]

This exemption is an important consideration for international business. Consider a Canadian company which has a particular active business interest in a non-resident country and displays it by owning >10% of the equity of the foreign affiliate. The additional earnings, or surplus, of a foreign affiliate are classified as *exempt surplus*[95] which can be paid out as dividends to its Canadian counterpart, free of Canadian income tax. Figure 8.23 illustrates this arrangement.

Chapter Summary

The ultimate goal of taxation is to create a source of funding for government programs, but it is also used to deter or encourage particular behaviors, promote social policies, and to redistribute income.

International tax law is a complex topic that includes specific rules and regulations regarding the taxation of any legal person. Each of these entities is subject to the tax law of their resident country as well as the international treaties that have been created in order to regulate our global economy. The tax law of a particular country can differ greatly from another based on what types of income are included, the timing a country's tax year, and how a country determines a person to be a resident. Additionally, these laws may be altered over time to provide various economic incentives, such as tax exclusions or credits for various economic activities.

There are numerous strategies and methods that have been developed over time for the purpose of avoiding taxation. Depending on the jurisdiction, some of these strategies have been ruled to be unacceptable or in some cases illegal, while in others they are common practice. Understanding which methods are allowed is an important consideration for any business.

Due to the constant growth and interconnected nature of business, as well as the development of new technology, a good understanding of international tax law is a necessity.

Glossary

Business Income: The earnings or profits of a corporation or other business.

Capital Gains Income: The profit derived on the sale or exchange of capital property based on the increase in its value over its cost.

Double Taxation: Occurs when a person has its income taxed twice: being taxable in two different jurisdictions.

Electronic Commerce: The means by which a person is able to provide a service or supply a product on an online platform.

---

[94] Vern, Krishna. 2006. The Fundamentals Of Canadian Income Tax. 9th ed. Toronto: Thomson Carswell.

[95] Natural Resources Canada. 2015. "Canadian International Income Tax Rules | Natural Resources Canada". nrcan.gc.ca. http://www.nrcan.gc.ca/mining-materials/taxation/8880.

Flat Tax: An income tax system in which all persons pay a single fixed percentage of tax, regardless of their income level.

Individual: A single natural being.

Nationality Principle: States that a government has the right to tax any income of any person who is deemed to be a national of that country.

Part Year Residence: Any person who becomes a resident or gives up their residency part way through the tax year.

Permanent Establishment: A fixed place of business or base within a geographic location.

Personal Income: The earnings or profits of an individual.

Progressive Tax: An income tax system in which income in higher amounts results in paying a higher percentage in the form of taxes.

Residency Principle: The concept that governments may tax any income of persons who are legally residing or are deemed to reside within that government's jurisdiction.

Source Principle: States that a government can only tax a person's income derived within the government's territorial jurisdiction.

Tax Avoidance: Occurs when a person takes advantage of acceptable methods, or ambiguous interpretations of tax law in order to reduce or avoid for their own benefit.

Tax Evasion: The willful, conscious misrepresentation or concealment of a person's tax obligations or sudden departure from its taxing jurisdiction.

Tax Haven: A state that provides an opportunity for residents of other countries to enjoy the tax advantages such as lower tax rates and/or large credits or deductibles.

Tax Planning: The legitimate arranging of one's financial activities in order to reduce or defer tax costs.

Tax Treaties: Agreements between countries which provide a specific arrangement to avoid double taxation and other issues related to international tax law.

Thin Capitalization: A method in which a company finances itself primarily with debt in order to deduct loan interest payments as a business expense.

Transfer Pricing: The practice of charging prices between affiliated companies to lower the overall tax burden.

Treaty Shopping: The practice of evaluating the differing tax treaty provisions of countries and selecting the most favorable outcomes.

Trust: A contract under which the legal ownership of property is vested in a party, known as a trustee (s), who administers that property pursuant to the provisions of that contract to or for the benefit of disclosed or undisclosed person(s) known as the beneficiaries.

Index

G

H

I

Y

YouTube, 199

Z

Zero-sum dispute resolution alternative, 68
Z.K. Marine, 140–141

CPSIA information can be obtained
at www.ICGtesting.com
Printed in the USA
LVHW031104140819
627549LV00005B/7/P